D0606376

AFTER THE CRASH

AFTER THE CRASH

PSYCHOLOGICAL ASSESSMENT AND TREATMENT OF SURVIVORS OF MOTOR VEHICLE ACCIDENTS

SECOND EDITION

EDWARD B. BLANCHARD, PhD
EDWARD J. HICKLING, PsyD

■

AMERICAN PSYCHOLOGICAL ASSOCIATION
WASHINGTON, DC

Copyright © 2004 by the American Psychological Association. All rights reserved. Except as permitted under the United States Copyright Act of 1976, no part of this publication may be reproduced or distributed in any form or by any means, or stored in a database or retrieval system, without the prior written permission of the publisher.

Published by
American Psychological Association
750 First Street, NE
Washington, DC 20002
www.apa.org

To order
APA Order Department
P.O. Box 92984
Washington, DC 20090-2984
Tel: (800) 374-2721
Direct: (202) 336-5510
Fax: (202) 336-5502
TDD/TTY: (202) 336-6123
Online: www.apa.org/books/
E-mail: order@apa.org

In the U.K., Europe, Africa, and the Middle East, copies may be ordered from
American Psychological Association
3 Henrietta Street
Covent Garden, London
WC2E 8LU England

Typeset in Goudy by World Composition Services, Inc., Sterling, VA

Printer: Data Reproductions, Auburn Hills, MI
Cover Designer: Minker Design, Bethesda, MD
Project Manager: Debbie Hardin, Carlsbad, CA

The opinions and statements published are the responsibility of the authors, and such opinions and statements do not necessarily represent the policies of the American Psychological Association.

Library of Congress Cataloging-in-Publication Data

Blanchard, Edward B.
     After the crash : psychological assessment and treatment of survivors of motor vehicle accidents / by Edward B. Blanchard and Edward J. Hickling.—2nd ed.
          p. cm.
     Includes bibliographical references and index.
     ISBN 1-59147-070-6 (alk. paper)
     1. Traffic accident victims. 2. Traffic accidents—Psychological aspects. 3. Post-traumatic stress disorder.   I. Hickling, Edward J. II. Title.

RC1045.P78B56   2003
616.85'21—dc21   2003052466

British Library Cataloguing-in-Publication Data
A CIP record is available from the British Library.

Printed in the United States of America
Second Edition

To John, my favorite MVA survivor.

—Edward B. Blanchard

To Linda, Matthew, and Michael and all my family and friends.

—Edward J. Hickling

CONTENTS

ACKNOWLEDGMENTS

There are many people who have helped make this book a reality. We first acknowledge grants from the National Institute of Mental Health (NIMH) MH-48476 and MH-55478, the funds from which underwrote most of this research. In addition, we acknowledge the assistance and support of four of the staff of the Violence and Traumatic Stress Branch of the NIMH: for the first edition of this book, Drs. Ellen Gerrity, Susan Solomon, and Phyllis Gordon; and for the second edition, Dr. Farris Tuma.

We thank the various University at Albany graduate students who worked on this project for the first edition: Alisa Vollmer, Shannon Turner, Catherine Forneris, Kristine Barton, Jackie Jones-Alexander, and Janine Walsh; our special thanks go to Ann Taylor and to Todd Buckley for running many additional analyses. For the second edition, we thank Todd Buckley, Elizabeth Mundy, Tara Galovski, Connie Veazey, Trishul Devineni, Kristin Tatrow, Loretta Malta, Mark Canna, Brian Freidenberg, Laurie Keefer, Eric Kuhn, and Mark Sykes. Special thanks go to Loretta Malta for running seemingly endless additional analyses.

We also thank Dr. Warren Loos and Dr. Claudette Ozoa for serving as therapists for the participants in the treatment project. Finally, we acknowledge and thank Ms. Sandy Agosto, who typed numerous drafts of chapters and who served a central coordinating role throughout the project.

INTRODUCTION TO THE
SECOND EDITION

Since *After the Crash* was first published in 1997, there has been an explosion of research in the fields of psychological assessment and treatment of motor vehicle accident (MVA) survivors. Psychology and psychiatry have awakened to the size of the mental health problem MVAs create, a point first raised by Norris in 1992 in her pioneering epidemiological work on posttraumatic stress disorder (PTSD) and echoed by Kessler and colleagues in 1996 in their National Co-Morbidity Survey. We felt obligated to update the coverage of the field.

We have continued our work with MVA survivors since the publication of the first edition, especially focusing on the treatment of chronic PTSD in MVA survivors, and have recently completed a randomized controlled trial of our cognitive–behavioral therapy protocol. This has given us fresh insights into the treatment of MVA-related PTSD, which we want to share with our readers.

The overall format of the book remains the same: We summarize what is known on various topics from the world's English language literature and then present our own data on the topic. Since the first edition, we have assessed a second cohort of MVA survivors, all of whom were seeking treatment 6 to 24 months after their MVAs. The first cohort included research assessment volunteers initially seen 1 to 4 months post-MVA.

The book has grown, primarily because of much expanded coverage of treatment. We present our empirically validated treatment with commentary and clinical hints gleaned from our experience. We also cover research done by a growing group of investigators in this field.

PROLOGUE:

THE CASE OF MARY J.

Mary signaled for a left turn and moved into the left lane. She pressed her foot on the brake, waiting for oncoming traffic to clear, and was pleased to see very few cars in the parking lot. "I should be in and out in 10 minutes," she said to herself.

Suddenly, Mary saw headlights in her rearview mirror just before the crash. The next thing she felt was a tremendous blow to the rear of her car. She felt her neck snap back and then flew forward against the shoulder belt. She also saw out of the corner of her eye a large oncoming car bearing down on her.

"No!" she remembers screaming just before the other car struck her right front fender. At that moment she was afraid she would be killed. She also saw the look of surprise and horror on the face of the other driver just before they hit.

Another crash followed with the sound of crunching metal, along with violent jerking from side to side; then she heard the tinkling of glass as it fell to the pavement. Mary was thrown against the seatbelt and then against the post supporting the roof of the vehicle.

She immediately became aware of pain in her neck and shoulders and on the side of her head. Next she realized that her right ankle hurt and that she could not get her right foot loose.

All case examples in this book have been modified to prevent ready identification of the participant; however, important facts are accurate. At times the case material represents a composite of cases to illustrate a point in the text.

She began to think, "My beautiful car is smashed—it's ruined." Mary had loved the car. Her parents had made the down payment as a graduation present, and she had paid it off in three years. She had been pleased to have no monthly car payment.

Only a few minutes earlier, at 4:30 p.m. on Friday, Mary closed up her desk, shut off her computer, and put on her boots and heavy coat. As she was leaving, she saw her supervisor and said, "Remember that I am taking the day off on Monday and won't be in."

"Oh yes, have a good trip. It looks like you'll have fresh snow on the mountain."

"Thanks."

Mary walked across the employee's parking lot to her car, unlocked the driver's door to her white Escort, and got in. It started on the first try. "Good car," she thought. She picked up the snow brush and got out to clear her windows. She brushed the two inches of new snow off her front and back windows, and then cleared the side windows.

"There," she said to herself, "At least I can see." It was snowing fairly heavily and was already dark. She gave the driver's window one more brush, got in, and buckled her seatbelt.

She left the parking lot and headed up Manning Boulevard to cut over to Washington Avenue. Traffic was moving steadily as she made the left turn onto Washington Avenue. She noticed a little skidding as she made the turn.

Traffic was moving at a moderate pace on Washington Avenue; the cars seemed to be turning the snow to slush. She thought again how much she liked her car: the heater worked well, the windshield wipers were doing their job, and the radio station came in clear on the stereo speakers.

After passing the university, traffic began to thin out and speed up. Mary thought, "This isn't as bad as I thought it would be."

On impulse she decided to stop for Chinese take-out. That would save time when she got home. Besides, there was not much in the refrigerator.

Just as the weather forecast had predicted, it had started to snow in the middle of the afternoon on Friday. Mary J. heard about the snow from a coworker who had been in another part of the building and was passing by her door. Although she had spent 27 winters in Albany, and did not look forward to driving home in the snow, she considered herself a good winter-weather driver.

"It will take me an hour to get home," she thought, "And then I'll be behind." She was reviewing her plans for leaving town Saturday morning for a long weekend of skiing at Sugarbush. "I have to get home, do my laundry and my grocery shopping tonight, and then pack for the trip."

"Oh, well, I'll just stay up until midnight so everything will be ready when Tim, Bob, and Judy come by at 6:00 a.m. to get me."

Then in her usual optimistic way she said to herself, "At least there will be fresh powder on the slopes."

As Mary was fighting through the pain, she noticed someone at her car window. She rolled down the window part way. "Are you all right? Are you all right?" The man yelled. As she struggled to gain composure she grew more aware of her ankle pain and neck and shoulder pain.

Through the partially opened window she said, "I can't get my foot loose and my ankle hurts." Then she added, "And my neck hurts too."

The stranger told her, "See if you can open your door and I'll help you get out."

Mary tried the door handle but nothing happened. The door was jammed. She felt panicky and trapped.

The stranger said, "Just try to sit still. We've called the police and an ambulance." Mary then noticed the large blue Buick that had hit her on the right side and could see people around that vehicle.

The stranger said, "My name's Ed; just try to stay still and help will be here in a minute. Can I call anyone for you?"

Mary's thoughts were racing: "I'm still alive"; "How can I reach Tim and get him to help?"; "Oh no, my vacation is ruined"; "Oh no, my beautiful car"; "God, my ankle and neck are really hurting."

Finally, the stranger's questions penetrated. "Can I call anyone?" she heard.

She stammered, "Call Tim B. at 555-2407," and then she said, "Call my mother, Ellen J., at 555-6189," and she began to tear up and cry.

Ed asked, "Are you all right?"

Mary replied, "Nooo! My ankle hurts and my car is ruined." And then the tears came.

Ed was replaced by another stranger, a woman. She said, "Don't cry, honey. Help is on the way."

Next, Mary heard a siren in the distance. The rescue squad arrived first, followed by the police.

The woman in the firefighter's suit and hat came to the window. She said, "My name is Betty. What is your name?"

"Mary J."

"How are you, Mary? Are you hurt?"

"Yes, my foot is trapped and my right ankle hurts and so does my neck and shoulders—and my head hurts."

Betty said, "I want you to sit very still. I'm going to reach in and roll the window down. Then I'm going to put this collar around your neck to stabilize your head. Okay? Then we are going to get you out of the car, okay? Things will be all right, but I want to stabilize your head and neck first."

Mary felt reassured by Betty's calm manner and mumbled "Okay."

Then Betty reached in through the window and put the collar carefully in place, all the time reassuring Mary.

Next, Betty tried to open the car door by reaching inside. It was stuck.

Betty called to another firefighter. "Fred, we're going to need the Jaws-of-Life to get this door open. It's stuck."

"Okay," yelled Fred.

Betty began to take down information, name: Mary J.; age 27; address; 12 Pinedale Court-West. "Who should we call?"

"My mother Ellen J. I asked the other fellow to call her."

Betty reassured Mary, "I'm going to stay here with you until we can get you out and into the ambulance."

Fred and another firefighter brought over a large tool. Betty explained, "We are going to have to pry the door loose from the frame. It will sound awful but it won't hurt you."

The door was forced open with a terrible screech of metal. Betty reached in to check on Mary's foot and freed it.

Then Betty and Fred carefully removed Mary from the wrecked car and put Mary on a backboard. Her head was stabilized and the strap tightened around her forehead. The lower part of her right leg was also stabilized in an air cast.

Out of the corner of her eye Mary saw the mangled wreck that had been her car and she sobbed again.

Her mother arrived, looking fearful. "Are you all right?" she exclaimed.

"No," Mary said, "My ankle and neck hurt," and with a sob, "My car is ruined."

At 6:35 p.m., Mary J. was at St. Peter's Hospital, arriving by ambulance at the emergency room.

X-rays revealed a broken right ankle, which was put in a cast, but there was no structural damage to her neck and upper back. She was given a set of crutches, a soft collar, a three-day prescription for Tylenol with codeine, and a follow-up appointment with the orthopedist. She was told to rest in bed as much as she could.

After a brief debate, she agreed to go home with her mother rather than to her own apartment.

With this accident, Mary J. joined the three million-plus Americans who in 1993 were involved in a personal injury motor vehicle accident (MVA). She joined our study two months later and was found to meet the criteria for posttraumatic stress disorder (PTSD). Her symptoms, which were consistent with PTSD, included the following: She was positive for intrusive memories of the accident and had frequent and severe distress at reminders of the accident, some mild flashbacks, and frequent distressing dreams about the accident that woke her in the night. She also was exerting moderate effort to avoid thoughts about the accident. She avoided riding in a car except as absolutely necessary and not at all if the weather was threatening, had diminished interest in activities she had previously enjoyed, felt estranged from her friends and family to some degree, and had a restricted range of affect in that she no longer felt the warmth and affection she had previously had for most people. In addition, she was having almost nightly sleep disturbance and noticeable irritability and hypervigilance on a daily basis; she had difficulty concentrating and had become easily startled and jumpy. Finally, she reported feeling her heart pound and her palms become sweaty when in a car that was in close traffic. She had a Clinician Administered PTSD Scale (CAPS)[1] score of 86. She still wore an elastic brace on her ankle for support. Her whiplash injury was extremely bothersome and prevented her from returning to work (she had tried for two weeks and two days before calling us and could not last the day because of the pain).

She had not returned to driving because she had no vehicle and found herself anxious when riding with others.

At the six-month follow-up she still met the full criteria for PTSD with a CAPS score of 65. She had not been able to return to work and was becoming desperate financially. She was driving an older, used car her parents had helped her buy. She was fearful of losing her apartment because her savings were almost depleted. At this point she also met the criteria for a major depressive episode.

At the 12-month follow-up she was noticeably improved in appearance and overall manner of presentation; the depression had lifted. She was back at work. Her CAPS score was 14, and she no longer met the criteria for PTSD despite being positive for distress when exposed to events that reminded her of the accident, avoidance of thoughts related to the accident, some sleep difficulty, and some continued exaggerated startle response.

This case typifies the MVA survivors we have seen. The chapters that follow flesh out the psychological assessment and treatment work on this large, understudied population.

---

[1]CAPS is a structured interview for assessing PTSD. It is described in detail in chapter 4.

I

QUANTIFYING THE PROBLEM

1

OVERVIEW OF THE VOLUME

Involvement in motor vehicle accidents (MVAs) is a widespread American experience. As chapter 2 will detail, more than 1% of the American population is involved in a serious (personal injury) MVA each year. Moreover, as a large-scale survey has shown (Kessler, Sonnega, Bromet, Hughes, & Nelson, 1995), MVAs are the most frequent, directly experienced trauma for males (25.0% lifetime) and second most frequent for females (13.8%). Moreover, Norris (1992), in another large-scale survey, found that MVAs were the single leading cause of posttraumatic stress disorder (PTSD) in the general population.

Despite the large scope, in trauma prevalence, of the problem, the psychological assessment and treatment of the road-crash survivor had been little studied in this country. In the early and mid-1990s when the first edition of *After the Crash* was written there had been fairly widespread study of the MVA survivor in other countries over the 10 years leading up to 1996. There were active research groups in Norway, the Netherlands, United Kingdom (at least three different groups), Australia (two groups), and Canada (two groups).

Now, several years later, there are other research groups in the United States studying the MVA survivor as well as in many other countries. In addition to the countries described above, there are now active research groups in Israel (two groups), Switzerland, Germany (two groups), Sweden and Denmark as well as additional research teams in the United Kingdom and Australia.

This book describes the details of two different five-year studies of MVA survivors in the Albany, New York, area. As noted earlier, our initial efforts were on the recruitment, assessment, and prospective follow-up of a cohort of MVA survivors who sought medical attention because of the accident (Cohort 1). More recently, we recruited a second cohort of injured MVA survivors who were 6 to 24 months post-MVA and who were seeking treatment for psychological distress arising from that MVA (Cohort 2). Moreover, we have tried to summarize and integrate the results from this worldwide array of research groups with our own findings to present the reader with a comprehensive view of what is known about the survivors of serious MVAs.

PTSD AND MVA SURVIVORS

PTSD has been much studied since it was introduced as a distinct diagnosis by *DSM–III* (American Psychiatric Association, 1980), with numerous books appearing on the broad topic and on special segments of the PTSD population. There are four primary groups of trauma victims who have been studied: combat veterans, especially veterans of the Vietnam War (these individuals are mostly male and are typically 10 to 25 years posttrauma when studied); sexual assault victims (these are almost all female and have been studied either within days or weeks of the trauma or five plus years posttrauma [for treatment]); survivors of natural disasters who are of both genders and have been studied acutely and over long-term follow-up; and adult survivors of child sexual and physical abuse who are studied as adults.

MVA survivors present a different population in many ways: (a) Males are typically as frequently represented as females so that potential gender differences in response to trauma and response to treatment for PTSD can be studied. Historically, there are few data on the treatment of males with PTSD of relatively short (months) duration. (b) Frequently there are lingering physical injuries in this population that thus offers an opportunity to see what role (potentially negative) physical injury plays in treatment and recovery. (c) The MVA survivor with PTSD is frequently involved in litigation so that studying this population can enable us to learn, in part, what role litigation plays (see chapter 10) in recovery. (d) Finally, as Norris (1992) documents, the MVA survivors with PTSD constitute a large population by themselves, and their similarities and differences with other PTSD populations needs to be elucidated.

SCOPE OF THE BOOK AND ITS ORGANIZATION

There are four broad conceptual themes covered in this book. First, we identify the scope of the problem in chapters 2, 3, and 4 to try to arrive at an answer to the question, "What proportion of motor vehicle accident survivors develop PTSD?" In this section, as in all sections, we present two answers to the rhetorical questions: (a) the best answer we can find in the worldwide English language literature and (b) the answer we find from our own research data. We then try to reconcile these two if they are markedly different. In this first part we also present a description of the populations we studied and our methodology (chapter 4).

The second broad conceptual theme is a description of the short-term psychosocial consequences of having been in a serious MVA. This is covered in chapters 5, 6, and 11 (devoted to acute stress disorder). Again, we summarize our results and those from the world's literature.

The third conceptual theme is the short-term natural history of MVA-related PTSD (chapter 7) and factors that could influence this natural history such as physical injury (chapter 9), litigation (chapter 10), and delayed-onset PTSD (chapter 8).

In the third section of the book we turn from assessment to treatment. Thus, our fourth conceptual theme is psychological treatment of the MVA survivor with PTSD. The conceptual underpinning of our cognitive–behavioral approach to treatment is given in chapter 16. Again, we try to review the English language literature on treatment (chapter 14).

Chapter 15 presents a detailed description of preliminary uncontrolled evaluations of our two treatment conditions, cognitive–behavior therapy (CBT) and supportive psychotherapy (SUPPORT). These two preliminary studies set the stage for our randomized, controlled comparison of CBT and SUPPORT. Chapter 17 describes the methodology and results of that trial along with one- and two-year follow-up information.

Chapter 18 is a detailed, step-by-step description of the CBT treatment along with many clinical hints and observations. Chapter 19 is a similar detailed description of the SUPPORT Condition. Because it was clearly psychologically active and yielded results comparable to those found in some other reports of CBT treatment, and because it is similar to some of the counseling and therapy currently being provided to MVA survivors, this treatment was highlighted for potential application.

CLINICAL HINTS

This book is an accurate description of what we did, what we found, and how it fits into what is known from other sources. Thus, we have tried to make conclusions empirically based. However, scattered throughout the book are *clinical hints*, clearly labeled as such. These are clinical impressions that cannot be backed up firmly with data or suggestions of what to do when available data give no guidance. We hope they are useful. We have added them because we are often asked at meetings and workshops what is best or what we would do based on our experience, and thus these hints are in answer to such questions.

As will be obvious to the reader from the citations and references, we have published much of our data from the Albany MVA Project in piecemeal fashion over the years. In this volume we attempt to pull all of the data together in an integrated fashion. At the same time, we tried to summarize fairly the rest of the English language literature on this topic and to integrate these two sources.

AUDIENCE FOR THE BOOK

We foresee four broad audiences for this book. First, we expect that those psychologists, psychiatrists, and other mental health professionals who are called on to assess and to treat the survivors of serious motor vehicle accidents will find much value in this book. We have tried to describe our procedures fully so that others can incorporate them. Moreover, we described our population carefully so that the clinician can see if his or her patient is similar. We provide two sets of MVA survivor norms on the psychological tests we used in chapter 5, one set from those we recruited for assessment and the second from a treatment-seeking population.

Second, we believe this book will help attorneys who handle MVA survivor cases. Again, we describe what we expect to find acutely and over at least a year follow-up for MVA survivors in terms of psychosocial status. We also address the issue of the effects of litigation on the clinical course (chapter 10) of PTSD and the possible role of dissimulation and malingering (chapter 11).

Third, we believe the physicians who treat the MVA survivor, the orthopedists, the physiatrists, and the primary care physicians will value this book because 3 million Americans per year are likely to present to them, collectively, because of involvement in a serious MVA. We also believe the psyche and the soma interact in the long-term healing process (see chapter 9) and that physicians can optimize their care of the MVA survivor by being aware of the psychological issues likely to present among MVA survivors.

Fourth, we hope that this book sparks interest among researchers, both those who are established and their students. We provide some answers but realize we raise many questions. The survivors of serious MVAs continue to represent a large population who should be studied more.

2

THE MAGNITUDE OF THE PROBLEM

Motor vehicle accidents (MVAs) are a widespread experience both in the United States and in the rest of the industrialized world. In fact, they are so ubiquitous that one could guess that a majority of the adult males in the United States will have experienced at least a minor MVA by the age of 30. Many of the women in the country will have joined the men in this experience. Precise data are not available on the total number of MVAs occurring in the United States each year, however.

EPIDEMIOLOGY OF MOTOR VEHICLE ACCIDENTS

If we move from the minor MVA in which there is only some property damage (those we colloquially call "fender benders"), to those more serious MVAs in which one or more individuals are injured enough to seek medical attention, then reasonable estimates are available from the U.S. Department of Transportation (DOT). Furthermore, the DOT has precise data on the number of MVAs that resulted in fatalities and the number of individuals killed. In Table 2.1 are summarized data from the DOT on the estimated number of personal injury MVAs, number of persons injured, number of fatal MVAs, and number of fatalities for the years 1996 through 2000.

The average number of persons over the five years in Table 2.1 is 3,290,000 per year. This compares to 3,179,000 for the five years (1991–

TABLE 2.1
U.S. Department of Transportation Nationwide Summaries of Personal
Injury Accidents and Fatal Accidents: 1996–2000

Year	Estimated number of personal injury MVAs	Estimated number of persons injured	Number of fatal MVAs	Number of fatalities
1996	2,238,000	3,483,000	37,494	42,065
1997	2,149,000	3,348,000	37,324	42,013
1998	2,029,000	3,192,000	37,107	41,501
1999	2,054,000	3,236,000	37,140	41,611
2000	2,070,000	3,189,000	37,526	41,821
2001	2,003,000	3,033,000	37,795	42,116

Note. Data taken from: *Traffic Safety Facts 2000: A Compilation of Motor Vehicle Crash Data from the Fatal Accident Reporting System and General Estimates Systems,* December. National Highway Traffic Safety Administration, U.S. Department of Transportation.

1995) immediately proceeding. It is clear that there is a large population who have been injured and may be suffering psychologically as well as physically.

We have focused our own research on individuals who were injured in MVAs (driver, passenger, or pedestrian when the motorized vehicle was automobile, truck, bus, or motorcycle) and who sought medical attention for those injuries within 48 hours of the accident. Thus, for us a *serious* motor vehicle accident is one in which one or more participants was injured sufficiently to seek medical care.[1] In this way we have excluded participants

---

[1] As we have sought to present our own research on MVA victims, a frequently raised issue has been on the "seriousness of the accident." To the best of our knowledge there are no validated scales of accident seriousness or severity. One could try to scale severity in terms of property damage: the greater the property damage, in all likelihood, the higher the speed of impact. However, degree of property damage is confounded by value of the vehicle and by number of vehicles involved and thus does not seem useful. One could try to scale severity by the total number of vehicles involved or total number of individuals involved or total number of individuals injured. The last two of these are probably related.

If by seriousness one means the extent of physical injuries to the victim (which can be scaled) or the extent of psychological distress suffered by the victim, one could use these constructs. However, it becomes tautological then to study if serious MVAs lead to PTSD because that would mean that MVAs that lead to great psychological distress cause PTSD.

One could also restrict "serious" to MVAs in which there is a fatality. This seems too restrictive because the number of MVAs involving fatalities are thankfully rare in comparison to personal injury MVAs, about 1 to 55 (see Table 2.1).

Our solution has been to label an accident as serious if one of those involved sought medical attention and to restrict our study sample to individuals who themselves sought medical attention.

It came to our attention that Bryant and colleagues, working in Australia, have published a 5-point scale of MVA severity: 1 = no injury; 2 = mild injury not requiring hospitalization; 3 = injury requiring hospitalization for less than 2 weeks; 4 = injury requiring hospitalization for more than 2 weeks; 5 = the MVA involved a fatality (Bryant & Harvey, 1995c). This scale is thus tied to physical injury severity (in part) and to recuperation rate. There are better ways to scale injury severity, for example, the Abbreviated Injury Scale (AIS; American Association for Automotive Medicine, 1985) that is described at length in chapter 4, which do not confound it with

from the minor MVAs (although we know of instances in which even this kind of accident has had noticeable psychological effects).

EPIDEMIOLOGY OF POSTTRAUMATIC STRESS DISORDER

One of the major potential consequences of serious MVAs is posttraumatic stress disorder (PTSD). Although psychological morbidity resulting from traumatic events has long been recognized, it was only with the publication of the *DSM–III* (American Psychiatric Association, 1980) that major professional attention began to be paid to this condition. (We might also note that "serious MVAs" were one of the stressors of "traumatic events outside the range of normal human experience," listed in the *DSM–III*.)

Estimates of the incidence and prevalence of PTSD in the general U.S. population have varied widely. The largest American epidemiological study devoted to mental disorders (Regier et al., 1984), the Environmental Catchment Area (ECA) study, assessed approximately 21,000 individuals, spread across five geographic sites (New Haven, CT; Baltimore, MD; Durham, NC; St. Louis, MO; and Los Angeles, CA) with individual face-to-face interviews using trained lay interviewers and the DIS (Diagnostic Interview Schedule; Robins, Helzer, Croughan, & Ratcliff, 1981; Robins, Helzer, Croughan, Williams, & Spitzer, 1981). The original DIS did not include questions specifically designed to detect PTSD. However, Helzer, Robins, and McEvoy (1987) added some questions to the DIS as administered at the St. Louis site on the third interview related to the respondent's having experienced an event that frightened him or her and that led to one or more PTSD symptoms (as defined in the *DSM–III*; American Psychiatric Association, 1980). The rapidity with which the symptoms began after the event, their duration, and their frequency were assessed in the 2,493 face-to-face interviews.

The authors found prevalence of PTSD of 5 in 1,000 for males and 13 in 1,000 in females, for a population lifetime prevalence of about 1%. Only 0.5 in 1,000 were a result of serious accidents, indicating that PTSD lifetime from MVAs is infrequent.

This low estimation of lifetime prevalence of PTSD from all causes has been criticized because of the assessment methodology; research has shown that the original DIS was relatively insensitive to PTSD in a Vietnam War veteran population (Kulka et al., 1990).

---

recuperation. Moreover, hospital admission and length of stay may be determined by third-party payer parameters rather than injury parameters. No data are yet available on this scale regarding reliability (which should be very high) or validity.

Norris (1992) surveyed 1,000 adults in four southern cities by telephone. Her response rate was 71%. Half of the sample was male, half female; moreover, half was White and half was Black. They were evenly balanced among young (18–39), middle-aged (40–59), and older (60+). Lifetime occurrence of nine traumatic events was determined; this was followed by a series of questions (the Traumatic Stress Schedule) to determine if the individual met the *DSM–III–R* (American Psychiatric Association, 1987) criteria for PTSD following the trauma. Norris found a lifetime prevalence of 7.4 in 100 for PTSD from all causes. Most relevant to us, for MVAs, 23.4% had experienced this trauma during their lifetime and 2.6% in the past year. Overall, 69% experienced some qualifying traumatic event in their lifetime and 21% in the past year.

Of those who experienced a serious MVA over their lifetime, 11.5% met the criteria for PTSD; for those who had been in an MVA within the past year, the value was 9.5%, meeting criteria for PTSD. Norris commented specifically on the relative high rate of PTSD possible from MVAs that she calculated to be 2.7 in 100 over a lifetime.

Breslau, Davis, Andreski, and Peterson (1991) assessed by telephone interview 1,007 young adults (ages 21 to 30) who were enrolled in a health maintenance organization (HMO) in Detroit. The assessors were trained lay interviewers using the DIS. Attention was paid to the possible occurrence of eight specific stressors, including "serious MVAs"; diagnoses were based on the *DSM–III–R* (American Psychiatric Association, 1987) criteria. They found that 39.1% had suffered at least one traumatic event and 3.6% at least three or more traumatic events. They found that 9.2% of the total population had developed PTSD (23.6% of those suffering any traumatic event). Of these, 9.4% were involved in serious MVAs, with 11.6% of those developing PTSD in approximate equal proportions for males and females. This leads to a lifetime prevalence (for this young population) of 1.09 in 100 for PTSD secondary to serious MVA with injury.

THE NATIONAL CO-MORBIDITY SURVEY

A major American psychiatric epidemiology study, the so-called National Co-Morbidity Survey (NCS), has been described (Kessler et al., 1994). Lifetime and 12-month prevalence estimates of 14 *DSM–III–R* (American Psychiatric Association, 1987) psychiatric disorders were obtained by trained lay interviewers using the Composite International Diagnostic Interview (CIDI; Peters et al., 1996) with a sample of 8,098 individuals between the ages of 15 to 54. The survey was conducted during the period 1990 to 1992 by trained interviewers who were closely supervised; the sample demographics were designed to mirror the U.S. population.

A report especially relevant to this book's topic was detailed assessment of the lifetime prevalence of specific traumatic events suffered by the sample (and an open-ended "other traumatic event question") and subsequent assessment for possible PTSD using *DSM–III–R* criteria (Kessler et al., 1995). Respondents were asked to select the single most upsetting traumatic event and assessed for the development of PTSD secondary to this event. Finally for this event they were asked for how long (weeks, months, years) the symptoms of an index episode persisted. Thus the duration data are retrospective. Assessment for a large number of possible comorbid conditions was also carried out. As is readily acknowledged in Kessler et al.'s (1995) report, the possibility of developing PTSD from other experienced traumatic events, other than the one identified as most traumatic, was not assessed.

Relevant to our concerns are the number of individuals who acknowledged being involved in a life-threatening accident (it is not clear if all accidents were MVAs). Twenty-five percent of the males ($n = 703$) and 13.8% of females ($n = 422$) admitted to being in life-threatening accidents. (The gender difference in prevalence is significant.) For men in life-threatening accidents, 44.6% nominated it as the most traumatic event; for women the value was comparable at 44.5%. Lastly, 6.3% of males in life-threatening accidents developed PTSD ($n = 314$), whereas for women the comparable value was 6.8% ($n = 188$). These rates do not differ statistically. These values are probably an underestimate because the possibility of developing PTSD from the serious MVA was *not* assessed if the subject identified some other trauma as more serious. Moreover, despite careful attention to assessing the experience of various trauma, in many instances the trauma occurred many years ago, so that the assessment for subsequent PTSD was retrospective by many years. Nevertheless, these data seem to indicate that, at a minimum, 1.6% of males and 1.2% of females will meet the criteria for PTSD secondary to a serious MVA over their lifetime.

The overall survey found women who were exposed to any extreme trauma were more than twice as likely as men to develop PTSD (20.4% for women compared to 8.2% of men, $p = .001$). Of all of the male cases of PTSD ($n = 139$) identified in the NCS, 12.1% were a result of accidents; for the 320 women with PTSD, 5.1% were a result of accidents. Of the males with a lifetime history of PTSD, 88.3% met the criteria for at least one other disorder; for women, the comorbidity rate was 79%.

Finally, in the retrospective examination of remission of PTSD from all causes, there was a significant advantage for having received mental health treatment (but not necessarily for PTSD) out to about six years posttrauma. Beyond that point, about 40% of the sample continued to have PTSD as long as 10 years posttrauma. At one year about 30% have remitted, whereas at two years it is close to 40%. Remission rates specific to accident victims with PTSD were not available.

We believe the lifetime prevalence values, multiplied by the population of the United States from the last three studies (1 to 3%) give some indication of the size of the potential problem, 2.5 to 7 million cases in the United States alone. Thus, we have a sizable mental health problem in this country that has been all but ignored by American researchers and perhaps by the mental health treatment community. We hope this book will begin to reverse that neglect.

3

WHAT PROPORTION
OF MVA SURVIVORS
DEVELOP PTSD?

In this chapter we seek to provide an answer to this question. As with most of the topics addressed in this book, we provide three answers to the question: (a) what does the published literature say on the topic; (b) what do our data say on the topic; and (c) what is our best estimate of truth and how do we reconcile any differences among other studies and our own results.

THE PRE-*DSM–III* LITERATURE

Because the term posttraumatic stress disorder (PTSD) was introduced as a term to American mental health in 1980 with the publication of *DSM–III* (American Psychiatric Association, 1980), its publication makes a useful demarcation point in reviewing the literature. Much of the psychological and psychiatric literature before 1980 did not have great precision in its diagnostic labels. Nevertheless, there was descriptive literature on motor vehicle accident (MVA) survivors. It is summarized in Table 3.1.

One finds little solid information based on current diagnostic standards in Table 3.1. Modlin's (1967) report is probably the most useful, because

TABLE 3.1
Rates of PTSD in MVA Samples Evaluated Before *DSM–III*

Study and country of origin	Description of sample	% MVA	Male/ female	Age	How assessed	Results
Thompson (1965) United States	500 cases of postaccident neurosis evaluated for litigation	N/R	N/R	N/R	Clinical interview, *DSM–I*	406 cases of anxiety state 25 cases of phobic neurosis 156 cases superimposed depressive neurosis (52% improved with no treatment)
Modlin (1967) United States	40 cases of postaccident syndrome out of 150 referred for evaluation for litigation	N/R	27/13	17–62	Clinical interview	Good, stable premorbid functioning; symptom: Anxiety, tension, irritability, impaired concentration repetitive nightmares, anhedonia, withdrawal, startle, hypervigilant (probably PTSD 27%)
Allodi (1974) Canada	50 cases referred for evaluation for accident litigation	30%	N/R	N/R	Clinical interview	98% had accident neurosis
Parker (1977) Australia	750 cases referred for evaluation of accident litigation, 296 with neurosis	N/R (about half)	170/126 57.4%	N/R	Clinical interview	12% had "traumatic neurosis" for MVAs; For MVA survivors; 35% anxiety 35% phobia 34% irritability 18% anhedonia 15% insomnia
Mendolson (1981) Australia	101 accident victims referred for evaluation or treatment	42/101 42%	N/R	N/R	Clinical interview	25/42 MVA victims returned to work before litigation

Note. N/R = not reported.

in the 40 cases (out of 150) he highlighted, all appear to meet current criteria for PTSD. Otherwise, we are left with the author's diagnostic impression in the absence of symptomatic criteria. We find estimates of "accident neurosis" or "traumatic neurosis" ranging from 98% (Allodi, 1974) to 12% (Parker, 1977) of accident survivors who were evaluated because of litigation. (However, about a third of Parker's MVA survivors had symptoms consistent with PTSD.) One other point stands out in terms of possible preaccident psychopathology. Although Modlin (1967) identified a group with good, stable premorbid functioning, Parker (1977) reported that 20% of his sample had preaccident neurotic symptoms, whereas Allodi (1974) found evidence of preaccident "neurotic proneness" in 24% of his sample.

Almost all of the accident survivors reported in Table 3.1 were involved in compensation litigation. We will return to this topic in chapter 10.

THE POST-*DSM–III* LITERATURE

In Tables 3.2 and 3.3 are listed the studies that address the central problem in this chapter. In Table 3.2 all of the samples were either treatment-seeking individuals or individuals referred to mental health professionals for medico–legal evaluation.

Examining Table 3.2, one can see that samples referred for mental health evaluation or treatment tend to yield a fairly high percentage of cases with PTSD, from a low of 14.5% (Goldberg & Gara, 1990) to 100% in two treatment samples (Burstein, 1986b, 1989; Kuch, Swinson, & Kirby, 1985). The average across nine samples is 59.9%. Almost all of the diagnoses were ascertained by clinical interview; almost all used objective criteria from *DSM–III* ($n = 5$) or *DSM–III–R* ($n = 2$). One ambiguous result is that of Brom, Kleber, and Hofman (1993), who assessed a Dutch sample solely by a Dutch version of the Impact of Event Scale (IES; Horowitz, Wilmer, & Alvarez, 1979). We have taken their 22% who had severe symptoms (total scores greater than 30) to indicate PTSD. Unfortunately, the IES does not assess the hyperarousal symptoms, so that a precise estimate is hard to determine.

In Table 3.3 all of the other nontreatment seeking samples are described. Examining Table 3.3, a somewhat different picture of prevalence of PTSD following an MVA is presented. Values range from about 1% (Malt, 1988; actually 0.9%) to 100% (Kuch, Cox, Evans, & Shulan, 1994). This latter study might belong in Table 3.2, because all participants were suffering from chronic pain. Across the eight studies, the average value is 29.5%. If we eliminate the very low values from Malt's studies and the very high value from Kuch et al. (1994), from the remaining five studies we find an average of 26.4%.

TABLE 3.2

Rates of PTSD Found in Treatment- and Evaluation-Seeking MVA Survivors

Study and country of origin	Description of sample	% MVA	Male/female	Mean age, range	Time since MVA	How assessed	Diagnostic criterion	% PTSD
Kuch et al. (1985) Canada	30 MVA victims referred for evaluation (18) or treatment (12)	100%	8/22	N/R	N/R	Clinical interview and questionnaire	DSM–III	100%
Tarsh & Royston (1985) United Kingdom	35 cases of accident neurosis assessed for insurance claims; gross somatization	25%	18/17	42 28–58	5 years	Clinical interview	N/R	N/R
Burstein (1986b) United States	19 MVA victims referred for treatment	100%	4/15	37.5 range: N/R	29 weeks	Clinical interview	DSM–III	100%
Platt & Husband (1986) United States	31 MVA victims, referred for evaluation re: legal suits	100%	9/22	37 18–63	7.4 months	Clinical interview	DSM–III	77.4% 24/31
Hoffman (1986) Canada	98 accident victims referred for evaluation by lawyers	Some	N/R	N/R	N/R	Clinical interview	DSM–III	10.2% 10/98
Jones & Riley (1987) Australia	327 accident victims referred for evaluation by lawyers (180 MVA)	55.7%	58.6% male	N/R	N/R	Semistructured clinical interview	DSM–III	12 clear cases of PTSD from MVA 6.7%
Burstein (1989) United States	70 MVA victims referred for treatment	100%	N/R	N/R	N/R	Clinical Interview	DSM–III	100%
Goldberg & Gara (1990) United States	55 MVA victims referred for evaluation/ 31 had lawsuits pending	100%	14/41	37 range: N/R	15 months (2–60 months)	Clinical interview	N/R	14.5%

Study / Country	Sample	%		Age	Time since	Assessment	Criteria	Prevalence
Horne (1993) Australia	7 MVA victims seeking treatment	100%	2/5	31.3 26–37	23 months (7–45 months)	Clinical interview	*DSM–III–R*	43%
Dalal & Harrison (1993) United Kingdom	56 MVA victims referred for evaluation by lawyers	100%	N/R	N/R	2.7 years (1.3–7.0)	Interview	*DSM–III–R*	32.1%
Brom et al. (1993) Netherlands	151 victims of serious MVA out of 738 solicited by letter to participate in treatment research	100%	89/62	37.5 range: N/R	N/R probably weeks	Dutch IES	N/R	22% had severe symptoms

Note. IES = Impact of Event Scale; N/R = not reported.

TABLE 3.3
Rates of PTSD Found in Unselected Samples of MVA Victims

Study and country of origin	Description of sample	% MVA	Male/ female (% male)	Mean age, range	Time since MVA	How assessed	Diagnostic criterion	% PTSD
Malt (1988) Norway	113 hospitalized accident victims	46%	85/28 75.7% male	36.2 15–69	Within days of injury	Clinical interview/ IES, STAI, GHQ–20	DSM–III/ ICD–9	1% (3 cases with PTS symptoms)
Malt et al. (1989) Norway	551 adults with accidental injuries who were hospitalized (out of 683—83.5%)	43.6%	N/R	N/R 15–69	3 years	Questionnaire	? 26.7% had some DSM–III diagnosis	N/R
Feinstein & Dolan (1991) United Kingdom	48 hospitalized patients with leg fractures; reassessed at 6 weeks and 6 months	56.3	34/14 (70.8%)	30.5 16–60	1 week	Clinical Interviews Questionnaire for PTSD syptoms at follow-up	DSM–III–R	25% at 6 weeks 14.6% at 6 months
Green et al. (1993) Australia	24 of 69 hospitalized MVA victims reassessed at 1 month and 18 months	100%	19/5 (79.2%)	N/R	1 week	DIS, GHQ	DSM–III–R	2/24 PTSD (8.3%) 7 sub-PTSD at 1 month 6/18 PTSD (33%) at 6 months
Mayou et al. (1993) United Kingdom	188 of 200 consecutive MVA victims admitted to hospital (includes 63 whiplash only) reassessed at 3 months and 12 months	100%	128/60 (68%)	30.1 18–70	9 days	Present State Exam	DSM–III–R	14/174 8% at 3 months 19/171 11.1% within 1 year

Study	Sample		Gender (M/F)	Age	Time	Assessment	Criteria	Findings
Malt et al. (1993) Norway	192 MVA victims who were hospitalized	100%	N/R	N/R 15–69	3 years	Clinical interview GHQ–20	N/R	Less than 5%
Epstein (1993) United States	15 patients hospitalized in trauma center; reassessed every 10 weeks for 9 months	N/R (most)	10/5 (66.7% male)	34.4 20–82	Few days	Structured interview	DSM–III–R	40% (6 total cases within follow-up)
Kuch et al. (1994) Canada	55 MVA victims with minimal injury and chronic pain	100%	19/36 (34.5%)	38.0 N/R	2 years or longer	SCID for PTSD & Phobia	DSM–III–R	100%
Bryant & Harvey (1995b) Australia	56 hospitalized MVA victims (of 131)	100%	45/11 (80.4%)	34.4 15–79	1 year	IES and GHQ	None GHQ > 3 high IES score	41% GHQ > 3 46.4% IES > 30
Bryant & Harvey (1996) Australia	114 successive hospitalized MVA victims (posttraumatic amnesia of < 1 day)	100%	82/32 (79.1%)	29.3 16–60	1–15 days	Questionnaires IES, STAI, & interview	none (high IES scores)	31% had high IES (> 30)

Note. DIS = Diagnostic Interview Schedule; GHQ = General Health Questionnaire; IES = Impact of Event Scale; N/R = not reported; SCID = Structured Clinical Interview for *DSM*; STAI = State–Trait Anxiety Inventory.

All of the studies but two (Bryant & Harvey, 1995b, 1996) used *DSM–III* or *DSM–III–R* criteria, and many used structured clinical interviews of demonstrated reliability and validity. Bryant and Harvey (1996) identified 31% of their hospitalized MVA survivor sample as scoring in the high IES (> 30) range. In an earlier study Bryant and Harvey (1995b), surveying formerly hospitalized MVA survivors one year after the MVA, found 41% were still "cases" (noticeably distressed and disturbed) based on a General Health Questionnaire (GHQ; Goldberg, 1972) score of < 3. Using their IES score of > 30, 46.4% still had notable posttraumatic symptoms. (We address the issue of the possible diagnosis of PTSD with the IES in chapter 5.)

An interesting feature of the studies summarized in Table 3.3 is that almost all (eight of nine) were hospitalized patients. Patients, who were hospitalized, even for a brief one- to two-day period, tend to be more seriously injured. It is probably the case that not all of the 62 whiplash injury cases included in Mayou, Bryant, and Duthie's (1993) 188 cases had been admitted to a hospital.

An examination of the low-rate outliers (studies by Malt in Norway and by Mayou in the United Kingdom) reveals that part of the explanation for the low rate of case finding could lie in the diagnostic instruments used. Malt and colleagues (Malt, 1988; Malt, Blikra, & Hivik, 1989, 1993) all used clinical interviews or questionnaires. Mayou et al. (1993) used the Present State Examination (Wing, Cooper, & Sartorious, 1974), a well-known structured psychiatric interview. It could be that it is not especially sensitive to PTSD. Samples clustering around the average mostly used structured psychiatric interviews. They came from the United Kingdom, Australia, and the United States.

POST-1996 STUDIES

As we mentioned in chapter 1, there has been rapid growth in literature on the psychosocial consequences of MVAs. Using the same dimensions as in Table 3.3, in Table 3.4 we summarize the literature that has appeared since 1996.

Examining the information from the 20 studies in Table 3.4, several important points emerge: (a) there are a number of duplications, especially among reports from Shalev's study of emergency room attendees in Israel, from Ursano's (Ursano et al., 1999a) report on hospitalized patients in the United States, and the reports of Harvey and Bryant (1982, 1999b) on hospitalized MVA patients from Australia. From the latter research group, part of the duplication is reports of longer-term follow-ups on initial samples. (b) Except for the longer-term follow-up studies (Harvey & Bryant, 1999b; Koren,

TABLE 3.4
Rates of PTSD Found in Unselected Samples of MVA Survivors After 1996

Study and country of origin	Population	Male/ female (% male)	Mean and age range	Time since MVA	How assessed	Diagnostic criteria	% PTSD
Shalev et al. (1996) Israel	61 hospitalized for injury (53% MVA); 51 (83.6%) completed; reassessed at 6 months	31/20 (60.8%)	35.2 18–60	2–6 days	SCID PTSD Module	DSM–III–R	25.3% n = 13 at 6 months
Shalev et al. (1998) Israel	211/270 ER attendees (85.8% MVA), part admitted; Reassessed at 1 mo., 4 mo.	103/108 (48.8%)	— 16–65	1 week	CAPS	DSM–III–R	29.9% n = 63 at 1 month n = 37 at 4 months
Shalev et al. (1997) Israel	207 from above	98/109 (47.3%)	29.0 16–65	1 week	CAPS	DSM–III–R	30.4% n = 58 at 1 month 16.9% n = 35 at 4 months
Freedman et al. (1999) (from Shalev, 1997) Israel	62 from ER study (75% MVA) 23/41 PTSD; 39/194 non-PTSD; reassessed at 4 months and 1 year	28/33 (46.7%)	28.2 —	1 week	CAPS	DSM–III–R	25 PTSD at 4 months 12 PTSD at 1 year 5 sub-PTSD at 1 year
Shalev et al. (1998) Israel	86 of 191 ER study completers, seen in ER only (83% MVA) reassessed at 1 month and 4 months	52/34 (60.5%)	27.3 —	1 week	CAPS	DSM–III–R	23.3% n = 20 at 4 months

(continued)

TABLE 3.4 (Continued)

Study and country of origin	Population	Male/ female (% male)	Mean and age range	Time since MVA	How assessed	Diagnostic criteria	% PTSD
Delahanty et al. (1997) United States (part of Ursano et al., 1999a)	130 hospitalized MVA survivors (10 days or less; 25% of police referrals agree); reassessed 80 at 3 months, 6 months, 1 year	N/R (53.2%)	35.7 18–65	14–21 days	SCID PTSD Module	DSM–III–R	23.8% n = 19/80 acute 28.8% sub-PTSD 16.1% n = 10/62 at 6 months 11.8% n = 6/51 at 12 months
Ursano et al. (1999a) United States	122 hospitalized MVA survivors (same as Delahanty et al.); reassessed at 6 months 99 (81.1%) reassessed at 12 months 86 (70.5%)	64/58 (53.9%)	35.6 18–65	1 month	SCID PTSD Module	DSM–III–R	34.4% at 1 month 18.2% at 6 months 14.0% at 12 months 2 delayed-onset
Mayou et al. (1997) United Kingdom	ER attendees from Mayou et al. (1993; some admitted) 188 initially, 171 at 1 year, 111 at 5 years	N/R 66%	31 17–69	5 years	Foa's PSS Questionnaire	?	8% at 5 years 9 cases, only 1 case for whole 5 years, 8/9 delayed-onset

Study	Sample	Gender	Age	Time of assessment	Measure	Criteria	Results
Ehlers, Mayou, et al. (1998) United Kingdom	967 ER attendees from MVAs, 26% admitted to hospital, reassessed at 3 months and 1 year	54%	33.4 17–69	75% within 8 days	Foa's PSS Questionnaire	*DSM–IV*	23.1% (of 888) at 3 months; 16.5% (of 781) at 1 year; 6.2% delayed-onset
Mayou et al. (2001) United Kingdom	689 cases from Ehlers et al. (1998) all MVA ER attendees 24.2% admitted Reassessed at 3 months and 1 year	N/R 55%	32.5 17–69	75% within 8 days	Foa's PSS PTSD Scale	*DSM–IV*	23% at 3 months; 17% at 1 year; 5% delayed-onset PTSD
Frommberger et al. (1998) Germany	179 hospitalized MVA survivors 152 followed up at 6 months	93/59 (61%)	36.0 17–?	1–30 days; mean = 8.6	ADIS–R	*DSM–III–R*	18.4% n = 28 at 6 months; sub-PTSD n = 43 (28.3%)
Harvey & Bryant (1998a) Australia	92 hospitalized MVA survivors (of 222) excluded 98 with traumatic brain injury, 71 reassessed at 6 months	61/31 (66%)	33.3 17–63	1–30 days; mean = 6.8; 13% ASD; 20.7% sub-ASD	CIDI PTSD module	*DSM–III–R*	25.4% n = 18/71 at 6 months; sub-PTSD n = 7 (9.9%)
Harvey & Bryant (1999a) Australia	56 of 92 from Harvey & Bryant 1998a Reassessed at 2 years	29/27 (52%)	34.4	2 years	CIDI PTSD module	*DSM–III–R*	30.4% 17/56 at 2 years; 4 delayed-onset

(continued)

TABLE 3.4 (Continued)

Study and country of origin	Population	Male/female (% male)	Mean and age range	Time since MVA	How assessed	Diagnostic criteria	% PTSD
Koren et al. (1999) Israel	99 hospitalized MVA survivors; 74 reassessed at 1 year	66/33 (66.7%)	27.5 18–65	Within 1 week	SCID	DSM–III–R	32% 24/74 at 1 year
Jeavons (2000) Australia	72 ER attendees from MVAs (of 96) (33% admitted); reassessed at 3 months, 6 months, & 12 months	38/34 (52.3%)	32 18–72	Within 2 weeks	PTSD interview	DSM–III–R	9.7% 6/62 at 3 months, 8.1% at 6 months, 8.6% at 1 year
Bryant et al. (2000) Australia	146 hospitalized MVA survivors, reassessed at 6 months	93/53 (63.7%)	16–65	2–26 days mean = 6.9 days	CIDI PTSD module	DSM–III–R	21% at 6 months
Smith (1998) United Kingdom	80 (of 165) ER attendees from MVAs; 37.5% admitted; reassessed at 6 weeks (69), 6 months, 1 year (52)	42/38 53%	34.5	Within 1 week	PCL as interview	DSM–III–R	24.6% 17/69 at 6 weeks 6/69 (8.7%) at 6 months 4/52 (7.6%) at 1 year
Schnyder et al. (2001) Switzerland	121 admitted to ICU 64% MVA; reassessed at 1 year (106)	79/27 (74.5%)	37.9 18–70	3–29 days; mean = 13.4 days	CAPS	DSM–III–R	4.7% 5/106 at 2 weeks 22/106 sub-PTSD 2/106 at 1 year (1.9%)

Study	Sample	N	Age	Time	Measure	DSM	Results
Koren et al. (2001)	58 hospitalized MVA survivors from Koren et al. (1999); reassessed at 3 years	38/20 (65.5%)	27.9	3 years	SCID module	*DSM–IV*	19/58 32.7% at 1 year 12/58 20.7% at 3 years 2 delayed-onset
Murray Ehlers, & Mayou (2002) United Kingdom	27 hospitalized and 176 (of 439) ER attendees from MVA; reassessed at 4 weeks and 6 months	118/85 (58.1%)	33.3 17–76	Within 48 hours	Foa's PTSD Questionnaire	*DSM–IV*	31.6% inpatient 28.3% outpatient at 4 weeks 19.0% inpatient 24.3% outpatient at 6 months

Note. ADIS–R = Anxiety Disorders Interview Schedule–Revised; CAPS = Clinical Administered PTSD Scale; CIDI = Composite International Diagnostic Interview; N/R = not reported; PCL = PTSD Checklist; PSS = Posttraumatic Stress Scale; SCID = Structured Clinical Interview for *DSM.*

Arnon, & Klein, 2001; Mayou et al., 1997), all of these efforts initially assessed the MVA survivors within the first four weeks after the MVA and many within the first week after the MVA. (c) The rate of PTSD at the first reassessment (when sufficient time has elapsed to make a diagnosis of PTSD) is highly variable, ranging from 4.7% in Schnyder, Moergeli, Klaghofer, and Buddeberg (2001) to 34.4% in Ursano et al. (1999a). The range in these newer studies is somewhat attenuated from that described for the earlier studies in Table 3.3. (d) The vast majority of the studies have used *DSM–III–R* criteria for the diagnosis of PTSD, with a few studies published since 2000 using *DSM–IV* (American Psychiatric Association, 1994). They have also used various structured interviews. (One might hope an energetic researcher might compare the case finding ability of these various instruments.)

In an attempt to understand the variability across studies to determine the proportion of motor vehicle accident survivors developing PTSD, we have performed a meta-analysis of the studies in Tables 3.3 and 3.4 by calculating correlation coefficients between certain study parameters, as possible predictors, and the rate of PTSD found in a particular study (as the criterion). We then sought to learn if a multivariate combination of possible predictors yielded a higher overall correlation.

The variables we considered were (a) the percentage of the study population who were male, because Kessler et al. (1995) have shown that, across all types of trauma, women are twice as likely (10.4%) to develop PTSD over their lifetimes as men (5.0%); (b) age, in the form of the mean age of the sample; (c) extent of injury as a predictor of MVA-related PTSD at the individual patient level. (We have tried to characterize the average extent of injury in a study's population by determining if they were all outpatients (assigned a "1"), a mixture of outpatients and those admitted to the hospital (assigned a "2"), all inpatients admitted to the hospital (assigned a "3"), or all inpatients on a critical care or intensive care unit (ICU; assigned a "4"). We have reasoned that those with more serious injuries were more likely to be admitted to the hospital and that those admitted to an ICU were even more severely injured); (d) Lastly, as we document in chapter 7, injured MVA survivors with PTSD do show some degree of remission of symptoms over time. Thus, our last variable is the time since the MVA when the diagnosis of PTSD was made.

Our correlational analyses yielded the following zero-order (simple) correlations between percentage of the population with PTSD at the earliest assessment point (the criterion) and the predictors of (a) percentage of sample who were male ($r = -.670$, $p < .001$); (b) injury severity [whether all, some, or none]—in other words, if patients were admitted to the hospital ($r = -.284$, $p = .152$); (c) average age of the sample ($r = .252$, $p = .22$; and time since MVA when diagnosis of PTSD was made ($r = .09$, ns). A multiple regression using the first three predictors yields a multiple R of .627 ($R^2 = .394$, sig. = .021).

Thus, we can account for almost 40% of the variance in rate of PTSD found in a study from these variables. However, only a percentage of the sample who were male loaded significantly, accounting for almost 38% of variance, with injury severity adding only 1% of variances.

CLINICAL AND RESEARCH HINT

The finding that the greater the fraction of males in a sample of MVA survivors, the lower the rate of PTSD for the sample is consistent with the epidemiology of PTSD described in chapter 2. Women are more likely to develop PTSD from MVAs (and other trauma). This is the first risk factor the clinician should consider (more on this in chapter 6).

For the researcher, these findings carry the obvious implication that one should consider the gender mix of a sample of MVA survivors, because it can bias the rate of PTSD found in the sample.

EPIDEMIOLOGIC SURVEYS

Four American epidemiological surveys, which focused on PTSD, were reviewed in detail in chapter 2. Their results are summarized in Table 3.5.

Again, we find a range of values with Breslau et al.'s (1991) survey of young urban adults yielding the lowest lifetime prevalence of involvement in serious MVAs. This is understandable given the attenuated age range.

The two more representative epidemiological studies reveal that being involved in a serious MVA over one's lifetime is a fairly common occurrence for Americans, 19.4% from Kessler et al. (1995) and 23.4% from Norris (1992). We also find a fairly sizable proportion of individuals—who were in MVAs and who found them traumatic—developed PTSD: 6.5% of MVA victims in Kessler et al. (1995) compared to 11.5% in Norris (1992). The lower value from Kessler et al. (1995) could result from a failure to assess for PTSD from the MVA if the respondent nominated another event as more traumatic. There is no way to know from these epidemiological studies the extent of injury of the MVA survivors who were studied and whether they were hospitalized.

The average value from the two studies, about 9% of MVA survivors developing PTSD, is certainly within the range of values seen in Table 3.3.

THE ALBANY MVA PROJECT

We will present our data on this topic in detail in chapter 4. To jump ahead, among the 158 MVA survivors we assessed, 62 (39.2%) meet the

TABLE 3.5
Summary of MVA-Related PTSD From American Epidemiological Surveys

| Authors | Sample | | Age range | Diagnostic instrument | Rate of MVAs | Rate of PTSD from MVAs | Overall rate of PTSD |
	Size	How selected					
Helzer et al. (1987)	2,493	ECA sample in St. Louis; face-to-face interview		DIS + extra quest. *DSM–III*		0.5/1,000 overall	5/1,000 male 13/1,000 female
Breslau et al. (1991)	1,007	HMO member in Detroit; telephone interview	21-30	DIS *DSM–III–R*	9.4/100	11.6/100 1.09/100 overall	9.2/100
Norris (1992)	1,000	Adults in 4 southern cities 50% male 50% Black telephone interview	18–60+	Traumatic Stress Schedule *DSM–III–R*	23.4/100	11.5/100 3% overall	
Kessler et al. (1995)	5,877	National probability sample; telephone interview	15–55	Composite International Diagnostic Interview *DSM–III–R*	25/100 males 13.3/100 female	6.3/100 male 8.8/100 female 1.6% males 1.2% females overall	5.0/100 males 10.4/100 females

Note. DIS = diagnostic instrument; ECA = Environmental Catchment Area.

criteria for PTSD one to four months post-MVA, based on the Clinical Administered PTSD Scale (CAPS; Blake et al., 1990a) interview (see chapter 4 for a detailed description) and another 45 (28.5%) met the criteria for subsyndromal PTSD. Moreover, eight of those with initial subsyndromal PTSD developed full PTSD during the follow-up, giving us a total of 70 (44.3%) cases of PTSD in the sample. (Delayed-onset PTSD is discussed in chapter 8.) Ours was not a treatment-seeking sample or a sample referred for specific medico–legal evaluation. About half were referred from various practitioners, and the other half were self-referred based on advertisements, media coverage, and so forth.

The values given earlier were based on *DSM–III–R* (American Psychiatric Association, 1987) criteria using a "rule of 3" on CAPS items to decide if a symptom was present to a sufficient degree to be counted. These are the criteria used throughout chapters 1 to 13 of this book.

One can see that the fraction of the sample with PTSD changes somewhat with differing diagnostic criteria. *DSM–IV* added the requirement (A-2) that the subjective reaction to the traumatic event be one of "intense fear, helplessness or horror." One can see that this change leads to a 10% change in who meets the full diagnostic criteria. Likewise, changing the scoring rule on the CAPS leads to a 15% change.

If we can compare our Albany results (39.2%) for rate of developing PTSD initially from an MVA, we are on the high side for earlier non-treatment-seeking samples (Table 3.3; average 29.5%) and more recent samples (Table 3.4; average 21.8%). Moreover, although all of our sample had sought medical attention as a result of the MVA, only 24 (15.2%) were actually admitted to the hospital; another 94 (59.5%) were seen in the emergency room and released. It could be that our relatively high level of case finding is a result of the diagnostic instrument we used, the CAPS (Blake et al., 1990a). Perhaps it is more sensitive to cases of PTSD.

Most of the non-treatment-seeking samples were seen initially within a few days of the MVA, and many were followed up on one or more occasions. The follow-up is, of course, necessary to establish the diagnosis of PTSD because the diagnosis requires at least one month of symptoms. In our Albany study we delayed initial assessment at least one-month post-MVA to be certain the individual could meet the temporal requirement.

It appears that 15 to 45 percent of survivors of serious MVAs, defined as an accident in which someone is injured sufficiently to require medical attention, may develop PTSD either acutely or within a year of the MVA. This wide range of percentages highlights the large degree of mental and emotional suffering resulting from the MVAs in this country.

II

PSYCHOLOGICAL EFFECTS
OF MVAs

4

ALBANY MVA PROJECT

As mentioned in chapter 1, we have studied two separate samples of MVA survivors over the past 10 years. They differed in how and why they were recruited. For convenience we refer to them as Albany Cohort 1 and Albany Cohort 2.

ALBANY COHORT 1

Over a five-year period we initially studied a cohort of survivors of serious MVAs for up to two years each. Under the auspices of a grant from the National Institute of Mental Health (NIMH), during the period from September 1991 through May 1996, we recruited and assessed 158 survivors of recent motor vehicle accidents (MVAs) and followed them up for one year or longer. We also assessed 93 individuals who matched our MVA sample demographically who had had no MVAs, even a minor "fender bender," for the previous year. These two groups comprised Cohort 1. In the first part of this chapter we present basic descriptive information on our Cohort 1 MVA sample and the controls and we describe the assessment procedures in detail. Similar information on Cohort 2, a treatment-seeking sample, is provided in a second part of this chapter.

Entry Criteria

To be included in Cohort 1 the individual had to have been in an MVA one to four months before the assessment, had to seek medical attention within 48 hours of the MVA, and had to be at least 17 years of age. We chose the interval of one to four months post-MVA for two reasons: first, an individual must be symptomatic for at least one month to meet the criteria for posttraumatic stress disorder (PTSD; *DSM–III–R*, American Psychiatric Association, 1987). Thus, our research participants could be legitimately diagnosed, whereas other prospective studies of traumatized populations (e.g., Rothbaum, Foa, Riggs, Murdock, & Walsh, 1992) cannot make a diagnosis when seeing assault survivors one to two weeks postassault. Likewise, studies that accrue samples of MVA survivors in emergency rooms (e.g., Mayou, Bryant, & Duthie, 1993) or while the patients are acutely hospitalized (e.g., Bryant & Harvey, 1996; Epstein, 1993) cannot make the diagnosis of PTSD at that point. Some investigators (e.g., Delahanty et al., 1997; Schnyder et al., 2001) have made what Keane, Kaufman, and Kimble (2000) have recently termed diagnoses of "provisional PTSD." (See chapter 11 for a discussion of this idea.)

Although ideally we would have seen everyone at the one-month anniversary of the MVA, this was not possible in a community volunteer sample. We set an arbitrary window of one to four months to see participants close in time to the MVA.

Second, we were interested in learning how the participants evaluated themselves before the accident. Many studies of individuals with PTSD have made attempts to assess, retrospectively, the participant's pretrauma status. We feared that living with PTSD for many months or even years could color the participant's pre-MVA recollections. We have compromised by allowing a maximum of four months to elapse between the MVA and initial assessment. In assessing pre-MVA psychopathology, we have the advantage that our instrument, the SCID (Structured Clinical Interview for *DSM–III–R*; Spitzer, Williams, Gibbon, & First, 1990a) was designed to assess lifetime psychopathology and seems to do so adequately.

The MVA Survivor and Control Samples

Table 4.1 presents the demographic characteristics of our samples. We have subdivided the MVA sample into three subgroups that seem helpful, as will be apparent in coming chapters: those with full PTSD, those with what we termed subsyndromal PTSD (positive for Criterion B [reexperiencing] and either Criterion C [avoidance and psychic numbing] or Criterion D [hyperarousal] but not both, and non-PTSD (positive for only one criterion or none of the criteria).

Examining the data in Table 4.1, one can see that the non-MVA controls match the overall MVA sample well on basic demographic variables of age, gender, and ethnic status. The controls were somewhat better educated. The percentage of the sample who were non-Caucasian matches the 1990 U.S. Census value (about 10% of adults) for non-Caucasian in the four-county area surrounding Albany.

Two other points show up in these basic demographics: there are significantly more women in the MVA–PTSD subgroup (79%) than in the other two subgroups combined (61.5%; $p = .020$). Minorities are disproportionately represented in the MVA–PTSD subgroup (19.4%) compared to the other two subgroups combined (6.3%; $p = .011$).

The gender finding is consistent with data from the National Co-Morbidity Survey (NCS; Kessler et al., 1995), which also found women disproportionately represented among trauma survivors who developed PTSD over their lifetime: 5.0% of males versus 10.4% of females.

Two other basic characteristics of our sample should be noted: 149 (94.3%) were either drivers or passengers in the automobile or truck involved in the accident; 6 were pedestrians, 2 had been riding bicycles and were struck by motorized vehicles, and 1 participant was on a motorcycle. Among the 149, 120 were drivers and only 29 were passengers. One-hundred-eighteen (74.7%) of our sample were initially treated in an emergency room, and the others ($n = 40$, 25.3%) saw a variety of health care providers within two days after their MVA. Of the 118, 24 (15.2% of total MVA sample) were admitted to the hospital.

In comparison to most of the other samples described in chapter 3, our sample had a very wide range of injuries, with many on the milder side. Most other samples were either all hospitalized or at least all seen in the emergency department.

More than half of the sample were referred to our project by local health care practitioners, and the rest were self-referred based on advertising or local media coverage. Referral sources were asked to bring the project to the attention of all MVA survivors (readily identified in New York because of no-fault insurance as the third-party payer) not just those in obvious distress. We do not know what proportion of those informed and referred to the project followed up on the referral.

All participants (MVA survivors and controls) were paid for their participation: $50 for the first interview and first follow-up and $75 for the second (12-month) follow-up. We do not know what bias the payment may have introduced. We do believe the honorarium was an important incentive for a portion of the population, especially those with low family

TABLE 4.1
Demographic Characteristics of Subsamples of MVA Survivors and Controls: Cohort 1

| | Subsample | | | | |
| | MVA survivors | | | | |
Characteristic	PTSD	Subsyndromal PTSD	Non-PTSD	All MVA survivors	Non-MVA controls
Gender (m/f)	13/49	14/31	23/28	50/108	28/65
(% male in subsample)	(21.0)	(31.1)	(45.1)	(31.6)	(30.1)
Age, mean (SD)	34.8	35.4	36.2	35.4	37.7
	(11.2)	(11.7)	(14.7)	(12.5)	(14.0)
Range	18–73	17–65	17–71	17–73	20–78
Ethnic Status:					
(Caucasian/minority)	50/12	42/3	48/3	140/18	84/9
(% minority in subsample)	(19.4)	(6.7)	(5.9)	(11.4)	(9.7)
Education level:					
high school or less	14	13	14	41	11
Some College through BA	29	19	27	75	41
Graduate Training	19	13	10	42	41
CAPS Score (SD)	59.4	29.9	9.6	—	—
	(21.4)	(11.2)	(7.8)		

Note. CAPS = Clinical Administered PTSD Scale.

income. In fact, we might not have been able to attract the latter without the incentive. (It works out to about $6 to $7 per hour counting travel time.)

The Assessment Procedures

The bulk of our assessments were conducted by means of structured interview schedules administered by trained and experienced doctoral-level interviewers. All four assessors were doctoral-level psychologists, each of whom had more than five years experience assessing Vietnam War veterans for possible PTSD.

We describe the assessments in the order in which participants experienced them.

The MVA Interview

We developed a structured interview to assess details of the MVA, immediate physical and medical consequences and treatments, subjective reactions to the accident, and effects of the MVA on subsequent travel behavior. A copy of the MVA Interview is contained in Appendix A.

The interview begins by having the participant tell his or her account of the accident, including the circumstances leading up to the accident. We paid special attention to thoughts and sensory experiences the MVA victim described to have the raw material for the idiosyncratic audiotapes used in the psychophysiological assessment described in chapter 12.

For our sample, 35 (22.2%) were single-vehicle accidents, 98 (62%) involved two vehicles, and 25 (15.8%) involved three or more vehicles.

Clinical Hint

We believed it was very important for the participant to tell his or her story first and in great detail (after all, the accident is what brought them to the study).

We made no attempt to check on the veracity of the participants' reports but found no obvious reasons to doubt them. We also had promised the participants confidentiality and that we would send a copy of our full report to any professionals of their choosing, free of charge, with their written permission. MVA survivors typically had the opportunity to review the full written report before it was committed to our files.

In assessing the impact of the MVA on travel behavior, we paid special attention to two points: travel behavior post-MVA foregone or endured with great distress and whether the avoidance was a result of physical limitations (e.g., unable to drive because of a broken leg or no vehicle yet available to replace the damaged one) or to psychological limitations. These results are in presented in chapter 5.

The Role of Alcohol and Drugs

Our sample was probably atypical of all injured MVA survivors in that only eight (5.1%) admitted to using alcohol or drugs at the time of the accident. In 16 instances, our participants were fairly certain that the other driver had been using alcohol or drugs, based on police reports or observations at the time of the accident.

Clinician-Administered PTSD Scale (CAPS)

We next administered the CAPS, a structured interview for assessing the symptoms of PTSD, developed by personnel at the Boston branch of the National Center for PTSD (Blake et al., 1990a).[1] Psychometric evaluations show test–retest reliabilities among three independent clinician assessors of 0.90 to 0.98; the internal consistency alpha was 0.94. Validation of the CAPS versus the Mississippi Scale for PTSD (Keane, Caddell, & Taylor, 1988) was 0.91 and the SCID PTSD module was 0.89 (Weathers et al., 1992; Weathers & Litz, 1994). One of the psychologists (RJG) who participated in the development of the CAPS trained the other three assessors in its use.

For each of the 17 symptoms of PTSD the CAPS assesses both a frequency of occurrence (or percentage of time or of relevant activities for which the symptom is present) over the last month and the severity of symptoms at its worst over the previous month. Both frequency and severity are rated on 0 to 4 scales; this means that an individual symptom can have a score of 0 to 8, and a total CAPS score (sum of all 17 symptom scores) of 0 to 136. (Our MVA-PTSD subgroup had a mean CAPS score of 59.4; see Table 4.1.)

In addition to ratings on symptoms and a diagnosis, the CAPS also obtains ratings of overall impairment in vocational and social spheres and overall severity.

We adopted the scoring rule (rule of 3) that the total CAPS score for a symptom had to equal 3 (either a 2 on frequency and 1 on severity or a 1 on frequency and 2 on severity) or greater for the symptom to count toward the presence of PTSD. Thus, items that had a score of 1-1 (for a total of 2) were not counted as clinically meaningful. (An internal analysis of data from 100 cases showed slight differences in verifiers (role impairment, etc.) if one used a rule of 3 rather than rule of 2. Moving to a rule of 4

---

[1] Information on the availability of the CAPS and of the newer version, adapted to the *DSM–IV*, can be obtained from the National Center for PTSD, Behavioral Science Division (Boston), 150 South Huntington Avenue, Boston, MA 02130.

TABLE 4.2
Rates of PTSD Among Albany MVA Project Participants as a Function of
Diagnostic Criteria

Diagnostic criteria	Diagnosis					
	PTSD		Subsyndromal PTSD		Non-PTSD	
	Frequency	%	Frequency	%	Frequency	%
DSM–III–R CAPS rule of 3	62	39.2%	45	28.5%	51	32.3%
DSM–III–R CAPS rule of 4	53	33.5%	34	21.5%	71	45.0%
DSM–IV CAPS rule of 3 (ignore Criterion A-2)	61	38.6%	44	27.8%	53	33.5%
DSM–IV CAPS rule of 3 (+ Criterion A-2)	55	34.8%	50	31.6%	53	33.5%

Note. CAPS = Clinical Administered PTSD Scale.

(scores of 1-3, 2-2, or 3-1 on an individual symptom) for a symptom to count for the diagnosis does identify a significantly more impaired and distressed group (Blanchard, Hickling, Taylor, et al., 1995). For additional discussion, consult Weathers, Keane, and Davidson (2001), who have published an extensive look at various CAPS scoring rules.

All statements about PTSD were based on *DSM–III–R* criteria using a "rule of 3" on CAPS items to decide if a symptom was present to a sufficient degree to be counted. These are the criteria used throughout chapters 1 to 12 of this book. Table 4.2 shows the results for Cohort 1 of using modified scoring rules for the CAPS (rule of 4 rather than rule of 3) or modified diagnostic criteria (*DSM–IV*).

One can see that the fraction of the sample with PTSD changes somewhat with differing diagnostic criteria. *DSM–IV* added the requirement (A-2) for PTSD that the subjective reaction to the traumatic event be one of "intense fear, helplessness or horror." One can see that this change leads to an 11% decrease change in who in our study meets the full diagnostic criteria. Likewise, changing the scoring rule on the CAPS from a rule of 3 to a rule of 4 leads to a 15% change.

To give one a clearer sense of what our MVA subgroups were like in terms of PTSD symptoms, Table 4.3 presents the percentages of each MVA subgroup that were positive for each of the 17 symptoms.

We compared the three subsamples by nonorthogonal X^2s: one compared those with full PTSD to the subsyndromal PTSDs; the other compared

TABLE 4.3

Percentages of MVA Survivors Who Were Positive for Each of the 17 Symptoms of PTSD at Initial Assessment: Cohort 1

| | MVA Subgroups | | | Comparisons | | | |
| | | | | PTSD vs. Sub-PTSD | | Sub-PTSD vs. Non-PTSD | |
Symptom	PTSD ($n = 62$)	Subsyndromal PTSD ($n = 45$)	Non-PTSD ($n = 51$)	χ^2	p	χ^2	p
Reexperiencing symptoms							
1. Intrusive recollection	67.7	35.6	7.8	10.88	.0010	11.13	.0009
2. Distress at reminders	96.8	84.4	13.7	5.15	.0233	48.01	.00000
3. Flashbacks	43.5	42.2	3.9	0.02	.8912	20.52	.00001
4. Recurrent distressing dreams	51.6	31.1	5.9	4.47	.0345	10.44	.0012
Avoidance & numbing symptoms							
5. Avoid thoughts/feelings	83.9	26.7	9.8	35.50	.00000	4.66	.0308
6. Behavioral avoidance	75.8	35.6	9.8	17.45	.00003	9.28	.0023
7. Event amnesia	38.7	4.4	11.8	16.64	.00005	1.68	.1953
8. Loss of interest/anhedonia	74.2	11.1	9.8	41.60	.00000	0.04	.8343
9. Estrangement	72.6	0	7.8	56.37	.00000	3.68	.0550
10. Emotional numbing	62.9	6.7	5.9	34.58	.00000	0.03	.8741
11. Foreshortened future	37.1	2.2	0	18.23	.00002	1.15	.2845
Hyperarousal							
12. Sleep disturbance	69.4	60.0	23.5	1.01	.3152	13.18	.0003
13. Irritability/anger	79.0	62.2	17.6	3.65	.0560	20.05	.00001
14. Difficulty concentrating	74.2	31.1	13.7	19.65	.00001	4.23	.0398
15. Hypervigilance	53.2	68.9	15.7	2.66	.1028	28.05	.00000
16. Exaggerated startle	66.1	60.0	13.7	0.42	.5155	22.38	.00000
17. Physical reaction to reminders	75.8	62.2	13.7	2.30	.1298	24.27	.00000

Note. From Table 3, "Psychiatric Morbidity Associated With Motor Vehicle Accidents," by E. B. Blanchard et al., 1995, *Journal of Nervous and Mental Disease, 183*(8), pp. 495–504. Copyright 1995 by Williams & Wilkins. Adapted with permission.

the subsyndromal PTSDs to the non-PTSDs. The probabilities for those comparisons are also tabulated in Table 4.3.

Examining the table one can see five things: (a) The major difference between the survivors with full PTSD and those with the subsyndromal form of PTSD lies in the Criterion C symptoms of avoidance and psychic numbing. The two groups of survivors are markedly different on all seven symptoms. (b) These two survivor groups are not different on five of six hyperarousal symptoms, they differ significantly only on impairment of concentration. (c) The full PTSDs and subsyndromal PTSDs differ on three of the four reexperiencing symptoms (at < .05), with flashbacks being the symptom that does not discriminate. (d) Turning to the comparisons of those with subsyndromal PTSD and those classified as non-PTSD, we find significant differences on all four reexperiencing symptoms and on all of the hyperarousal symptoms. (e) Those with subsyndromal PTSD endorse more avoidance, both of thoughts and feelings and of situations, than those with non-PTSD. In essence, individuals with subsyndromal PTSD tend to have reexperiencing symptoms and hyperarousal symptoms. They have markedly less avoidance than those with full PTSD and little psychic numbing symptoms.

Examining Table 4.3, one can see that, for 3 of the 17 possible symptoms of PTSD, less than half of the sample with PTSD acknowledge these symptoms. These three include flashbacks (43.5%), event amnesia (38.7%), and sense of foreshortened future (37.1%).

Table 4.4 presents the distribution of total CAPS scores for all three MVA survivor subgroups. This information can serve as norms on total CAPS scores for others working with MVA survivors. It is apparent from Table 4.4 that a few of our survivors who met the full criteria for PTSD were not very symptomatic. Also, one notices a substantial overlap of total CAPS scores between the upper third of those with subsyndromal PTSD and those who meet the full criteria. As will be discussed at length in chapter 8, some of these individuals with subsyndromal PTSD were found to develop delayed onset PTSD during the follow-up.

CAPS Reliability Check

We sought to establish interrater reliability on the CAPS by tape-recording all interviews. A set of 15 audiotapes (five from each of the three primary interviewers) were randomly selected and rescored by an advanced graduate student in clinical psychology who was unaware of diagnosis. Kappa for agreement on diagnosis was 0.810, $p < .0005$. Pearson correlation coefficients for scores on individual symptoms ranged from 0.82 to 0.99 with a mean (using Fisher's r to Z transformation) of 0.975, $p < .001$. Thus, this crucial variable was satisfactorily reliable, both for symptom scores and diagnosis.

TABLE 4.4
Total CAPS Scores of MVA Survivor Subgroups: Cohort 1

| | Cumulative percentage of subgroups | | |
| | PTSD | Subsyndromal PTSD | Non-PTSD |
Score	*n* = 62	*n* = 45	*n* = 51
0–5	—	—	41.2
6–10	—	2.2	51.0
11–15	—	8.9	76.5
16–20	—	24.4	90.2
21–25	1.6	40.0	98.0
26–30	6.5	53.3	100.0
31–35	12.9	66.7	—
36–40	21.0	82.2	—
41–45	30.6	91.1	—
46–50	38.7	97.8	—
51–55	46.8	97.8	—
56–60	56.5	100.0	—
61–65	64.5	—	—
66–70	69.4	—	—
71–75	80.6	—	—
76–80	83.9	—	—
81–85	85.5	—	—
86–90	87.1	—	—
91–95	91.9	—	—
96–100	95.2	—	—
100–105	98.4	—	—
105+	100.0	—	—
Mean	59.4	29.9	9.6
SD	21.4	11.2	7.8

Previous Trauma and PTSD

We next assessed for previous trauma and PTSD. Participants were asked about any previous MVAs. For any MVA in which either the participant or someone else sought medical attention, we assessed for possible PTSD from that accident.

Then we inquired about other previous trauma, using the questions developed by Breslau et al. (1991). Particular attention was paid to other accidents or injuries, destruction of property as a result of fire or natural causes, assaults or other injuries to the participant or a close family member. When there was a noticeable trauma, we assessed for possible PTSD.

Table 4.5 summarizes the results of this assessment for the three MVA subgroups and the controls. (Two of the controls had been involved in previous MVAs for which there was a fatality.) The table shows that a large proportion of our population (at least half of each subgroup), MVA survivors

TABLE 4.5
Previous Trauma (Including Previous Serious MVAs) and Previous PTSD for all MVA Survivor Groups and Controls: Cohort 1

Measure	MVA Subgroups			Non-MVA controls	Comparisons			
	PTSD	Subsyndromal PTSD	Non-PTSD		MVA vs. Controls		PTSD vs. Sub and Non	
					χ^2	p	χ^2	p
Previous serious MVA	38 (61.3)	34 (75.6)	36 (70.6)	48 (51.6)	6.98	.0083	2.35	.125
Previous PTSD from MVA	6 (9.7)	7 (15.6)	0 (0)	6 (6.5)	0.26	.607	0.28	.594
Other previous trauma	46 (74.2)	31 (68.9)	30 (58.8)	33 (35.5)	24.67	.00000	1.96	.162
Any previous trauma including MVA	55 (88.7)	41 (91.1)	45 (88.2)	64 (68.8)	16.31	.0001	0.03	.862
Any previous PTSD	11 (17.7)	13 (28.9)	2 (3.9)	7 (7.5)	5.59	.018	2.32	.127

Note. Values in parentheses represent the percentage of the subsample represented by the tabulated frequencies. From Table 7 "Psychiatric Morbidity Associated With Motor Vehicle Accidents," by E. B. Blanchard et al., 1995, Journal of Nervous and Mental Disease, 183, pp. 495–504. Copyright 1995 by Williams & Wilkins. Adapted with permission.

and controls, had been involved in previous serious MVAs. Also, a large proportion had experienced at least one previous traumatic event, including earlier serious MVAs, by our criteria; however, as a group the MVA survivors were significantly more likely to have experienced an earlier serious MVA or any earlier trauma than the non-MVA controls. Earlier PTSD was disproportionately present in the history of the MVA survivors who had the more severe reactions (PTSD or subsyndromal PTSD) to the current MVA. These results that show that previous PTSD sensitizes an individual to develop PTSD with a new trauma (the current MVA) are consistent with the work of Breslau et al. (1991), who initially reported this finding.

Psychosocial History

This portion of the assessment was not conducted with a structured interview. Instead, we gathered a brief psychosocial history with emphasis on developmental milestones such as schools attended, moves from location to location, divorces or deaths of parents, marriage and childbirths, and work history. Relationships with extended family were explored.

As part of this we also assessed for previous medical problems and research participants' rating of their physical health before and after the MVA and previous psychological–psychiatric treatment for themselves and family members.

LIFE–Base

The LIFE–Base is a semistructured interview developed by Keller et al. (1987) to assess current psychosocial status in their longitudinal follow-up studies. It was modified for our purposes to assess status for the month before the accident and for current (post-MVA) status. Performance at work, school (for part-time or full-time students), and at household activities were assessed on 5-point scales (1 = high level of performance with no impairment; 2 = satisfactory level of performance with no impairment; 3 = mild impairment; 4 = moderate impairment—person misses a lot of work or has considerable difficulty carrying out duties; 5 = very poor performance with severe impairment). Quality of social relations before and after the accident with all relevant first-degree relatives (parents, siblings, children, and spouse or partner) was assessed. Again, ratings were made on 5-point scales (1 = very good, close emotional relationship; 5 = very poor relationship; feels no emotional closeness, avoids family member or almost always has hostile contact). We averaged the ratings across all first-degree relatives to derive a measure of perceived social support.

We also assessed quality of relationships with friends and level of participation in recreational activities again on similar 1 to 5 scales. Finally, a Global Assessment Scale (GAS; Endicott, Spitzer, Fleiss, & Cohen, 1977) rating (0 to 100 in 10-point increments) was made.

The assessors were trained by personnel at Brown University under Dr. Keller's supervision,[2] in use of the LIFE–Base and the LIFE. The latter was adapted to use to follow-up the MVA survivors and assess PTSD symptoms on a week-by-week basis as well as psychosocial status variables on a month-by-month basis.

Structured Clinical Interview for *DSM–III–R* (SCID)

We used the SCID–NP (Version 1.0; Spitzer et al., 1990a) to assess for current and lifetime *DSM–III–R* disorders. Two of the assessors were trained in its use by personnel from New York State Psychiatric Institute. The first two assessors trained the other two, who had also reviewed the training videotapes ("SCID–101").

SCID–II

Finally, we assessed for possible personality disorders (Axis II disorders) by use of the SCID–II (Version 1.0; Spitzer et al., 1990b). A screening questionnaire was mailed to the participants before the initial appointment. From it (a series of 113 yes–no questions, grouped by *DSM–III–R* personality disorder) we determined if the participant had answered affirmatively to enough items so that he or she might be positive for the disorder. Thus, we formally assessed only for personality disorders that were likely to be present. Symptoms were scored: absent, subthreshold, or present based on the interview.

We also adopted a convention of labeling a participant as subthreshold for a personality disorder (a) if he or she was positive for one less than the required minimum number of symptoms to make the diagnosis or (b) if he or she was positive for the minimum number of symptoms needed for the diagnosis if both fully present and subthreshold ratings are counted.

This concluded the interview. It took from two hours to five hours. The participant was given an appointment for the psychophysiological assessment and a feedback appointment with the assessor. (The psychophysiological assessment procedures and results are contained in chapter 12.)

A long narrative of all of the interview material was created and diagnoses made. Any participant with any positive Axis I diagnosis, including PTSD, was given an explicit referral for treatment.

---

[2] We wish to acknowledge the assistance of Dr. Martin Keller and Dr. Tracie Shea in providing our training and assistance in adapting the LIFE to our use.

The research participant returned in about one week and was asked to read the narrative. Corrections were made in the final version at that point. In this way, participants had full knowledge of what would be said about them if a report was sent to any third party.

Psychological Tests

A second part of our overall assessment battery were several standardized psychological tests. They included:

- *Beck Depression Inventory* (BDI; Beck, Ward, Mendelson, Mock, & Erbaugh, 1961), a 21-item self-report measure with well-established reliability and validity (Beck, Steer, & Garbin, 1988).
- *State–Trait Anxiety Inventory* (STAI; Spielberger, Gorsuch, & Lushene, 1970), a 40-item self-report measure that yields values measuring both one's current state anxiety level and one's overriding trait anxiety level.
- *Impact of Event Scale* (IES; Horowitz, Wilmer, & Alvarez, 1979), a 15-item scale widely used in PTSD research, which yields a score on *intrusion* or reexperiencing symptoms and a score on *avoidance* symptoms. The two sums together for a total score.
- *Keane's PTSD Scale* (P–K Scale; Keane, Malloy & Fairbank, 1984) is a 49-item scale for which the items have been shown empirically to differentiate Vietnam War veterans with PTSD from similar Vietnam War veterans who do not have PTSD.
- *Reaction Index* (Frederick, 1985) is a 20-item scale used to detect possible cases of PTSD.

To make our results maximally useful to others, we present norms for each of our MVA subgroups and for the controls on each test, as well as the means and standard deviations in chapter 5.

Assessment of Non-MVA Controls

The non-MVA controls underwent many of the same structured interviews. For this group we began with the psychosocial history, followed by the assessment of previous traumatic events and possible PTSD, then the SCID, SCID–II, and finally the LIFE–Base. They also participated in the psychophysiological assessment during which they heard a randomly selected audiotape developed for an MVA victim.

Follow-Up Assessments

The primary purpose of this research project was to examine the short-term natural history of PTSD and other disorders that were caused by an injury-producing MVA. Thus, the project was designed to reassess all MVA survivors, both those who initially met the criteria for PTSD and the others, at six-month intervals over one year. The six-month intervals were chosen for several reasons: (a) to minimize the burden on the participants (and [1a] thus also reduce the costs of the research because each reassessment costs more than $200 out of pocket) and (b) to take advantage of a follow-up methodology used successfully in the mood disorders, the LIFE (Longitudinal Interval Follow-up Evaluation) of Keller et al. (1987). Keller's research had shown that with his structured form of interviewing, six-month intervals were a viable strategy. Thus, although shorter intervals, such as used by Epstein (1993) in his small sample, might yield more sensitive data, six months was demonstrably viable for this kind of work.

Participants were given an explicit appointment for a reassessment six months from the date of the initial assessment. About one week before the appointment, a set of questionnaires (repeats of the ones described earlier) were mailed to the participant along with a reminder of the appointment. This was followed with a phone call reminder.

We had taken the precaution of obtaining the name, address and phone number of someone the MVA victim said would know their whereabouts. These were used to track individuals. Despite our best efforts (including completing some follow-up interviews by telephone for individuals who had moved), we lost 13 individuals for the six-month follow-up and an additional 13 individuals for the 12-month follow-up. At the 12-month follow-up, one participant had died, 13 refused to participate, and 12 had moved, left no forwarding address, and were unreachable through family contacts. (Part of this stemmed from the failure of one assessor to continue in the research and to actively pursue his research participants.)

The demographic characteristics of the samples assessed at each of the follow-up points are described in Table 4.6. Although there are no significant differences in most of the demographic variables between dropouts and completers at 6 months or 12 months, there was a trend, especially at 12 months, for disproportionate loss among those initially diagnosed with full PTSD (p = .09). There was significantly greater loss of minority MVA survivors (p = .0005). Thus, dropouts were more likely to be single, female, younger, a minority group member, and to have initially been diagnosed with PTSD.

TABLE 4.6

Demographic and Diagnostic Information on Completers and Dropouts at Each Assessment: Cohort 1

Variable	Sample				
	Initial	6-month completers	6-month dropouts	12-month completers	12-month dropouts
Initial diagnosis	62	55	7	48	14
PTSD	(39.2%)[a]	(37.9%)	(11.3%)[b]	(36.4%)[a]	(22.6%)[b]
Subsyndromal	45	43	2	42	3
	(28.5%)	(29.7%)	(4.4%)	(31.8%)	(6.6%)
Non-PTSD	51	47	4	42	9
	(32.3%)	(32.4%)	(7.8%)	(31.8%)	(17.6%)
TOTAL	158	145	13	132	26
			(8.2%)		(16.4%)
Gender (m/f)	50/108	48/97	2/1	44/88	6/20
(% female)	(68.4%)	(66.9%)	(84.6%)	(66.7%)	(76.9%)
Age X (SD)	35.4	36.0	29.3	36.2	31.7
	(12.5)	(12.7%)	(7.7%)	(12.6)	(11.8)
Ethnicity					
Caucasian/minority	140/18	131/14	9/4	123/9	17/9
(% minority)	(11.4%)	(9.7%)	(30.8%)	(6.8%)	(34.6%)
Education					
Some college/ high school or less	117/41	38/106	10/3	100/32	17/9
(% college)	(74.1%)	(73.8%)	(76.9%)	(75.8%)	(65.4%)
Marital Status					
Married/not married	65/93	62/83	3/10	57/75	8/18
(% married)	(41.1%)	(42.8%)	(23.1%)	(43.2%)	(30.8%)

[a] Percentages of the total sample at that assessment. For follow-ups, the frequencies are of those available based on initial diagnosis. [b] Percentages for dropouts are percentage of initial diagnostic subsample who dropped out.

LIFE Interviewing

As noted earlier, all four assessors were trained in the LIFE Interviewing by personnel at Brown University under the guidance of Dr. Martin Keller.

The essence of the LIFE is to use personal event anchors to assist participants in recalling when symptomatic changes occurred. Thus, major holidays (e.g., Thanksgiving, Christmas, Fourth of July) as well as birthdays of the participant and close family members, anniversaries, and so forth, are used as anchors.

The research participant is assessed for his or her current status on the variable of interest (say, the intrusive recollection symptom of PTSD). If it is different than the status at the previous assessment, the participant is then helped to identify when (on a week-by-week basis) the change occurred. He or she is also asked for any other worsening or lessening of the symptom. If the symptom is not changed, he or she is also asked if it has been better or worse over the interval and the time of the changes pinpointed.

We used the LIFE Interview directly for tracking Axis I comorbidity, treatment(s) received (psychological and drugs), and psychosocial variables. The latter were assessed on a monthly basis.

We adopted the LIFE interviewing format to examine each of the 17 symptoms of PTSD as well as the physical injuries and travel behaviors. Weekly grid sheets were created for each variable of interest. On these weekly grids we also noted when any legal events related to the MVA occurred (visits to lawyers, depositions, etc.) and when any new MVAs or other stressful events (so defined by the participant) occurred to the participant or close family members. The locally designed follow-up interview and the grid sheets used for the tracking of PTSD symptoms and other variables are contained in Appendix B.

We also assessed the patient for PTSD in a formal manner using the CAPS–2 (Blake et al., 1990b), a version of the CAPS designed for follow-up studies and detecting change. We used CAPS-based diagnoses for all of the follow-up analyses (see chapter 7), not "follow-up grid-based" diagnoses.

Through tracking all 17 symptoms of PTSD, it was possible to determine with some precision when a participant who had initially met criteria for PTSD no longer met the full criteria (and also when someone deteriorated from subsyndromal PTSD to the point that he or she met the full PTSD criteria; see chapter 8 on delayed-onset PTSD). Although Keller's procedures were designed to track full diagnostic disorders, the procedures lend themselves well to this symptom-by-symptom approach.

Psychological Tests

The participants completed the BDI, STAI, and IES at each follow-up. The psychophysiological assessment was repeated at the 12-month follow-up only.

18-Month Follow-Up

We made an attempt to follow-up all of those participants with an initial diagnosis of PTSD for one additional six-month interval, out to 18 months. We had the inevitable additional loss of research participants, but gathered data on 35 with initial PTSD using the same procedures.

Longer Term Questionnaire Follow-Up

The development of a standardized and validated questionnaire for assessing PTSD, the PTSD Checklist (PCL; Weathers, Litz, Herman, Huska, & Keane, 1993; Weathers, Litz, Huska, & Keane, 1994) of the National

Center for PTSD (Boston Branch) led to a decision to try to gather one last round of follow-up data.

Blanchard, Jones-Alexander, Buckley, and Forneris (1996) restandardized the PCL on a new cohort of MVA survivors (and sexual assault survivors; $N = 30$) who were also assessed with the CAPS. We found high intercorrelations of total PCL score with total CAPS score ($r = 0.929$, $p < .0001$). We found that a cut-off score of 44 had the greatest predictive power, rather than the 50 recommended by Weathers et al. (1993) based on their standardization with Vietnam War veterans. Using a total score of 44 yielded a sensitivity of 0.944, a specificity of 0.864, and a diagnostic efficiency of 0.900.

We mailed a small packet of questionnaires including the PCL, BDI, STAI, IES and questions about additional treatment and new MVAs to all original participants. They were offered $5 to complete the questionnaires and return them to us. These data thus represented a follow-up of 16 to 24 months.

We were able to collect 100 of 157, for a 64% return, based on two mailings when the first packet was not returned by the Post Office as undeliverable because the addressee was no longer at the address and no forwarding address was available.

Clinical Hint

It is obvious that our overall assessment procedures were long and detailed, testing the stamina and endurance of both assessor and MVA survivor. Because this was a research project, we tried to err on the side of thoroughness, sacrificing some degree of patient convenience. As the following chapters will show, we believe there is potential value in each set of information gathered. However, for the practicing clinician, we could see omitting the psychological tests and possibly the psychophysiological assessment as well as the SCID–II. We believe the remainder of the information is needed to adequately characterize and understand the MVA survivor.

ALBANY COHORT 2

Our second cohort of MVA survivors was recruited between September 1996 and July 2000. Research participants were all seeking treatment for MVA-related psychological distress and were assessed to see if they would be eligible for a controlled treatment trial. We have collected full or partial information on 161 individuals.

Many of the assessment procedures were identical or very similar to those described for Cohort 1. There were a number of important differences, however:

1. The participant was seeking treatment for psychological distress secondary to the MVA.

2. Potential participants were initially screened over the telephone to determine potential eligibility in terms of receiving medical care, the interval since the MVA, and previous or current psychological treatment for their MVA-related problems. The latter was an exclusion. We also administered the PCL as a structured interview to assess the patient's status in the month right after the MVA and the previous month (current). Those with questionably low current PCL scores were eliminated.

3. The participant was 5 to 24 months post-MVA. We were recruiting a sample that met criteria for chronic PTSD (greater than three months). Because our Cohort 1 results showed that about half of those who met criteria for full PTSD initially would remit fully or in part by a six-month follow-up (see chapter 7 and Blanchard, Hickling, Forneris, et al., 1997), we wanted a population who were less likely to show spontaneous remission. Hence, we selected the six-month minimum duration. We selected the 24-month maximum duration to have a relatively homogeneous sample.

4. We used the CAPS–DX (Blake et al., 1995), a new version of CAPS from the National Center for PTSD designed to be consistent with the *DSM–IV*. We continued to use the rule of 3 to count a CAPS symptom as present.

5. We used the new version of the SCID–I, Version 2.0 (First, Spitzer, Gibbon, & Williams, 1996), also revised to be consistent with the *DSM–IV* and the new version of the SCID–II, Version 2 (First, Spitzer, Gibbon, Williams, & Benjamin, 1996) for Axis II disorders, also designed to be consistent with *DSM–IV*.

6. We switched to the use of advanced doctoral students in clinical psychology for all of the assessments. These students were trained by the two authors in all of the structured interviews. Their initial interviews were reviewed in detail. Training also included sitting in on interviews and scoring the instruments in parallel with an experienced assessor. Later, the new assessor conducted the interview while the experienced assessor scored it in parallel. By using these assessors, we were able to have assessors who were blind to treatment condition for posttreatment and follow-up interviews.

A reliability check on the CAPS for 49 interviews yielded a kappa of 0.789, $p < .001$, for agreement on diagnosis and a correlation of $r(N = 49) = .94$, $p < .001$, for total CAPS scores based on someone rescoring from the audiotape of the interview. Interrater agreement (kappa) on SCIDs for major depression (.800, $p < .001$) and generalized anxiety disorder (GAD; .857, $p < .001$) were determined for 20 cases.

7. The project director (the first author) reviewed all initial and follow-up interview reports generated by the student assessors for internal consistency and overall quality.

Assessments that remained the same were the MVA interview, the psychosocial history, and the LIFE–Base. The psychophysiological assessments remained essentially the same (see chapter 12). Participants were paid for completing each assessment $50 for initial, posttreatment, three-month follow-up and $75 for the one-year follow-up. These honoraria were paid regardless of eventual eligibility. The psychological tests remained essentially the same except we eliminated the Reaction Index and Keane et al.'s (1984) P–K scale and added the PCL and the Brief Symptom Inventory (Derogatis, 1993), scored only for the Global Severity Index as a measure of overall psychological distress.

We gathered initial interview data, including CAPS diagnoses, on a total of 161 individuals. A portion of these 132 (82%) completed the initial psychophysiological assessment.

Of the 161, 32 were ineligible because of too few PTSD symptoms, 11 because of exclusionary diagnoses (schizophrenia or other psychotic disorders including one with delusional disorder, bipolar I or II [1 exclusion], current alcohol or drug dependence [5 exclusions], and 2 suspected of malingering). Two with noticeable cognitive impairment secondary to the MVA were excluded. Eleven had participated in a pilot study described in chapter 16.

This left 107 who were eligible for treatment. Nine of these declined or failed to keep an initial appointment with a treating therapist despite several scheduled appointments.

As noted in chapter 17, 98 attended at least one treatment session and pre- and postdata on them were analyzed. Seventy-eight completed treatment or the wait-list condition; their data constitute the essence of chapter 17.

The demographic characteristics of the whole Cohort 2, those who were eligible for treatment and those who actually began treatment, are presented in Table 4.7. To provide the reader with the maximum amount of information, we have summarized the psychological test data, psychiatric diagnosis data, and LIFE–Base data for the entire treatment-seeking sample (Cohort 2) at the appropriate places in chapters 4 and 5. Thus, the data will be presented on the Cohort 1 sample first and then the Cohort 2 treatment seeking sample in the same fashion.

TABLE 4.7
Demographic Data on All of Cohort 2, for Those Eligible for Treatment and
for Those Who Started Treatment

| | Sample | | |
Variable	All Cohort 2	Cohort 2 who were eligible for treatment	Cohort 2 who began treatment
Current diagnosis			
PTSD	110	89	81
Subsyndromal	33	18	17
Non-PTSD	18	0	0
TOTAL	161	107	98
Gender (m/f)	47/114	29/78	26/72
(% female)	(70.8)	(72.9)	(73.5)
Age X (*SD*)	40.4 (12.0)	40.4 (12.2)	39.8 (11.9)
Ethnicity			
Caucasian/minority	141/20	96/11	88/10
(% minority)	(12.4)	(10.3)	(10.2)
Education			
Some college/high school or less	111/50	68/37	63.55
(% college)	(68.9)	(63.6)	(65.6)
Marital status			
married/not married	67/94	46/61	45/53
(% married)	(41.6)	(43.0)	(45.9)

Clinical Hint

We suspect the Cohort 2 norms may be of more interest and value to
the clinician because he or she is most likely to be dealing with a treatment-
seeking individual.

CAPS Data on Cohort 2

In line with providing as much information as possible on this
treatment-seeking Cohort, in Table 4.8 we replicate the data from Table
4.3 by providing the percentages of each diagnostic subgroup of MVA
survivors who were positive for each of the 17 symptoms of PTSD.

With this treatment-seeking sample, those with full PTSD differed
significantly from those with subsyndromal PTSD, on all 17 symptoms
including flashbacks and the hyperarousal symptoms on which the same
groups from Cohort 1 did not differ. The subsyndromal PTSD group did
not differ from the non-PTSD group on any reexperiencing symptom (unlike
Cohort 1, for which all reexperiencing symptoms were different). The

TABLE 4.8

Percentages of MVA Survivors Who Were Positive for Each of the 17 Symptoms of PTSD at Initial Assessment: Cohort 2

Symptom	MVA Subgroups			Comparisons			
	PTSD $n = 110$	Subsyndromal PTSD $n = 33$	Non-PTSD $n = 18$	PTSD vs. Sub-PTSD		Sub-PTSD vs. Non-PTSD	
				χ^2	p	χ^2	p
Reexperiencing symptoms							
1. Intrusive recollection	78.2	39.4	38.9	17.93	.000	.001	1.000
2. Recurrent distressing dreams	48.2	15.2	0	11.49	.001	3.02	.148
3. Flashbacks	45.5	24.2	22.2	4.74	.042	.026	1.000
4. Distress at reminders	94.5	57.6	55.6	28.84	.000	.019	1.000
5. Physical reaction to reminders	85.5	42.4	44.4	25.43	.000	.019	1.000
Avoidance & numbing symptoms							
6. Avoid thoughts/feelings	77.3	45.5	11.1	12.22	.001	6.18	.015
7. Behavioral avoidance	86.4	30.3	38.9	40.89	.000	.386	.551
8. Event amnesia	54.5	27.3	22.2	7.56	.009	.156	.750
9. Loss of interest/anhedonia	79.1	30.3	16.7	27.69	.000	1.14	.336
10. Estrangement	86.4	24.2	0	48.62	.000	5.18	.039
11. Emotional numbing	75.5	33.3	5.6	20.00	.000	5.00	.037
12. Foreshortened future	68.2	18.2	22.2	25.84	.000	.121	.727
Hyperarousal							
13. Sleep disturbance	89.1	60.6	11.1	14.28	.000	11.63	.001
14. Irritability/anger	85.5	54.5	11.1	14.28	.000	9.22	.003
15. Difficulty concentrating	88.2	39.4	0	34.04	.000	9.52	.002
16. Hypervigilance	69.1	45.5	5.6	6.13	.022	8.61	.004
17. Exaggerated startle	78.2	45.5	11.1	13.11	.001	6.18	.015

TABLE 4.9
Total CAPS Scores of MVA Survivor Subgroups: Cohort 2

| | Cumulative percentage of subgroups | | |
| | PTSD | Subsyndromal PTSD | Non-PTSD |
Score	$n = 110$	$n = 33$	$n = 18$
0–5	0	0	5.6
6–10	0	0	11.1
11–15	0	6.1	38.9
16–20	0	12.1	61.1
21–25	0	21.2	88.9
26–30	0	42.4	100.0
31–35	1.8	63.6	—
36–40	4.5	78.8	—
41–45	7.3	84.8	—
46–50	19.1	93.9	—
51–55	23.6	97.0	—
56–60	33.6	97.0	—
61–65	39.1	97.0	—
66–70	49.1	100.0	—
71–75	58.2	—	—
76–80	69.1	—	—
81–85	78.2	—	—
86–90	80.0	—	—
91–95	89.1	—	—
96–100	90.9	—	—
100–105	92.7	—	—
105+	100.0	—	—
Mean	71.7	33.6	18.3
SD	20.3	11.3	6.4

Note. CAPS = Clinical Administered PTSD Scale.

subsyndromal PTSDs were more likely to endorse all of the hyperarousal symptoms, than the non-PTSD, replicating Cohort 1 results. Finally, those with subsyndromal PTSD were more likely to endorse the numbing symptoms of estrangement and emotional numbing as well as the avoidance of thoughts and feelings related to the trauma.

Table 4.9 presents the norms for CAPS scores for each diagnostic subgroup assessed for Cohort 2. Comparing the results from Table 4.9 (Cohort 2) and Table 4.3 (Cohort 1) one sees that those with PTSD in the treatment-seeking sample had a higher average CAPS score than those in Cohort 1 (71.7 versus 59.4) and that the median score was higher (about 70 for Cohort 2 versus about 57 for Cohort 1). Likewise, the Cohort 2 participants with subsyndromal PTSD show higher mean and median CAPS scores, as did those with non-PTSD. It should be remembered that those with non-PTSD had acknowledged some level of symptoms on the initial telephone screen.

TABLE 4.10
Previous Trauma (Including Previous Serious MVAs) and Previous PTSD:
Cohort 2

Measure	PTSD (N = 107) N (%)	Subsyndromal & non-PTSD (N = 49) N (%)
Previous serious MVA	44 (41.1%)[a]	22 (44.9%)[a]
Previous PTSD from MVA	7 (6.5%)[a]	2 (4.3%)[a]
Other previous trauma	91 (85.0)[a]	37 (75.5%)[a]
Previous PTSD from other trauma*	49 (45.8%)[a]	13 (27.1%)[b]
Any previous trauma (including MVA)	98 (91.6%)[a]	42 (85.7%)[a]
Any previous PTSD* (including MVA)	52 (48.6%)[a]	14 (29.2%)[b]

Note. Values with the same superscript are not significantly different at an alpha level of .05 (chi-square).
*N = 155.

Trauma History of Cohort 2

We took our history of previous trauma somewhat differently. We first asked about the history of any previous serious (someone was injured and had medical attention) MVA and then assessed for possible PTSD secondary to that accident using the PCL. Participants had also completed the Life Events Checklist (Gray, Wang, Litz, & Lombardo, 2001), another measure from the National Center for PTSD, that asks whether respondents have ever experienced 16 different specific traumas, and an "other" category. We then checked for subsequent PTSD for any of these.

We especially noted the history of previous serious MVAs and other trauma, as well as past diagnoses of PTSD.

Table 4.10 presents the Cohort 2 data comparable to those from Cohort 1 shown in Table 4.5. Comparing the two groups, one finds a lower percentage of Cohort 2 had prior serious MVAs, about 43% in Cohort 2. There were comparable levels of any prior trauma, about 90%, in the two cohorts. However, Cohort 2 had much higher levels of prior PTSD, 42% overall more than found in Cohort 1 (about 16%). For those in Cohort 2 with current PTSD, 48.6% had also previously met criteria for PTSD secondary to a different trauma.

Clinical Speculation

It may be that the previous PTSD leads to the persistence of PTSD in the treatment-seeking sample (because they were on average 13 months post-MVA). The data on Cohort 2 from the psychological tests, LIFE–Base, SCID, and SCID–II are presented in chapter 5.

5

WHAT ARE THE PSYCHOSOCIAL EFFECTS OF MVAs ON SURVIVORS?

In chapter 3 we described the primary effect of undergoing a traumatic event, the development of posttraumatic stress disorder (PTSD), or a subsyndromal form of it, among those exposed to the trauma. In that chapter we also found the rate with which motor vehicle accident (MVA) survivors develop PTSD is highly variable. In this chapter we examine the other psychosocial consequences that may befall a MVA survivor, including the development of disorders in addition to PTSD, or comorbid psychiatric disorders, effects on driving and travel, and other psychosocial effects such as performance of major role functions.

We begin the chapter with a discussion of the largest, and most soundly conducted, study of comorbidity associated with PTSD from various causes, the National Co-Morbidity Study (NCS; Kessler et al., 1995). Next, we focus more closely on the MVA literature and the comorbidity found as a consequence of MVAs. Then, following the pattern of chapter 3, we describe our own data, which speak to this topic.

THE NATIONAL CO-MORBIDITY STUDY

The NCS (Kessler et al., 1995) provides a good overview of the psychiatric comorbidity among those with PTSD from a wide array of traumatic events, including MVAs. The interviews for the NCS were conducted in such a way that it was possible to obtain good estimates of whether PTSD or the various comorbid disorders assessed was primary—that is, if the MVA survivor had PTSD and major depression over the lifetime, did the major depression precede or follow the onset of the PTSD?

In the NCS study, both males and females with PTSD were more likely to have mood disorders (major depressive episode, dysthymia, or mania) than those participants who did not have PTSD. In fact, about 48% of those with PTSD of either gender had comorbid major depression and 22% had comorbid dysthymia. It was estimated, statistically, that from 53% to 78% of the mood disorders were secondary to the PTSD.

For anxiety disorders, the rate of comorbidity for those with PTSD ranged from 7% (for males with panic disorders) to 31.4% (for females with simple phobia). The authors estimated that from 30% to 56% of the anxiety disorders were secondary to the PTSD. Finally for substance use disorders, the rate of comorbidity ranged from 27% (women with drug abuse or dependence) to 52% (men with alcohol abuse or dependence). The substance use disorders were estimated to be secondary to the PTSD from 52% to 84% of the instances, on a par with the mood disorders. Separate data on MVA survivors were not available in the NCS report.

COMORBIDITY AMONG MVA SURVIVORS

Comorbid psychiatric conditions were not routinely reported in the studies of MVA survivors described in chapter 3 in Tables 3.2 and 3.3. A summary of the available information is provided in Table 5.1 for studies of MVA survivors who were seeking evaluation or treatment and in Table 5.2 for the other basic descriptive studies of MVA survivors published through 1996. The basic descriptions of the samples and rate of PTSD are repeated in Tables 5.1 and 5.2.

Among the treatment–evaluation-seeking samples in Table 5.1, mood disorders are the major comorbid condition, with 3% to 51% having notable depressive disorders. Like the NCS sample, the MVA survivors described in Table 5.1 also have notable anxiety disorders. Unlike the NCS sample, there is a large degree of comorbid somatoform disorders, 9 to 29%, and many patients have pain problems (not necessarily somatoform pain disorders).

Among the earlier unselected samples represented in Table 5.2, mood disorders are much less prevalent, ranging from 4 to 7%. There was much

TABLE 5.1

Comorbidity Found in Treatment- and Evaluation-Seeking MVA Survivors

Study and country of origin	Description of sample	% PTSD	Comorbidity	% driving phobia
Kuch et al. (1985) Canada	30 MVA victims referred for evaluation (18) or treatment (12)	100%	Depressed mood, muscle pain	77%
Tarsh & Royston (1985) United Kingdom	35 cases of accident neurosis assessed for insurance claims; gross somatization	N/R	severe depression = 1 (3%) paranoid psychosis = 1 (3%) hypochondriasis = 10 (29%) widespread mild depression	N/R
Platt & Husband (1986) United States	31 MVA victims for evaluation relegal suits	77.4%	7 females (of 22) met criteria for major depression (32%)	N/R
Jones & Riley (1987) Australia	327 accident victims referred for evaluation by lawyers	N/R	13.5% mood disorders 6% anxiety disorders 9% somatoform disorders depressive symptoms = 67% Sleep disturbance = 73% Headache = 72% Irritability = 75%	N/R
Goldberg & Gara (1990) United States	55 MVA victims referred for evaluation/31 had lawsuits pending	14.5%	Depression 28/55 (51%) Limb pain 11/55 (20%) Postconcussive syndrome 12/55 (22%)	N/R
Horne (1993) Australia	7 MVA victims seeking treatment	43%	3 with phobic anxiety	N/R
Dalal & Harrison (1993) United Kingdom	56 MVA victims referred for evaluation by lawyers	32.1%	7.1% mood disorder 17.9% anxiety disorder 26.8% somatoform pain disorder 5.4% adjustment disorder	10.7% (6/56) with phobic travel anxiety
Hickling & Blanchard (1992) United States	20 MVA victims referred for treatment of headache or other pain	50% (15% sub-PTSD)	45% major depression 20% dysthymia 20% panic disorder 10% alcoholism 25% organic brain syndrome	60%

Note. N/R = not reported.

TABLE 5.2
Comorbidity Found in Unselected Samples of MVA Victims Through 1996

Study and country of origin	Description of sample	% PTSD	Comorbidity	% driving phobia
Malt (1988) Norway	113 hospitalized accident victims	1%	Major depression 1% Atypical anxiety 3% Dysthymia 3% Adjustment disorder (Depressed) 5% Atypical organic brain syndrome 9%	N/R
Malt et al. (1989) Norway	551 adults with accidental injuries who were hospitalized (out of 683—83.5%)	N/R	Psychiatric case 33.7% Some *DSM–III* symptoms 26.7%	N/R
Feinstein & Dolan (1991) United Kingdom	48 hospitalized MVA patients with leg fractures; reassessed at 6 weeks and 6 months	25% at 6 weeks 14.6% at 6 months	62.5% were "cases" CIS > 14 25% cases at 6 weeks 10/48 (21%) "cases" at 6 months 12.5% had depressive symptoms at 6 weeks	N/R
Green et al. (1993) Australia	24 of 69 hospitalized MVA victims; reassessed at 1 month and 18 months	8% at 1 month 25% at 18 months	33% had clinically significant symptoms	N/R
Mayou et al. (1991) United Kingdom	418 MVA victims admitted to hospital (of 864) assessed 4–6 years post-MVA by questionnaire	N/R	N/R	2% stopped driving 8% showed much avoidance
Mayou et al. (1993) United Kingdom	188 of 200 consecutive MVA victims admitted to hospital (includes 63 whiplash only) Reassessed at 3 months and 12 months	8% at 3 months 11.1% at 12 months	6.9% had mood or anxiety disorders 25/188 (13.3%) were psychiatric cases	18.4% travel anxiety at 1 year

Study	Sample			
Malt et al. (1993) Norway	192 MVA victims who were hospitalized	< 5%	68/183 (37%) were psychiatric cases by GHQ 48/183 (26%) had "nervousness"	N/R
Kuch et al. (1994) Canada	55 MVA victims with minimal injury and chronic pain	100%	only assessed for accident phobia	38.2% accident phobia
Bryant & Harvey (1995c) Australia	56 hospitalized MVA victims (of 131) 1 year after MVA	41% had high GHQ > 3	31% substance abuse	N/R
Bryant & Harvey (1996) Australia	114 consecutive hospitalized MVA victims	31% had high IES > 30	37% high state anxiety (50+) 25% high trait anxiety (50+)	N/R

Note. CIS = Clinical Interview Schedule (Goldberg et al., 1970); GHQ = General Health Questionnaire; IES = Impact of Event Scale.

more emphasis in these studies on identifying the fraction of the sample that represented a "psychiatric case" by one measure or the other. These individuals manifest sufficient symptoms of subjective distress or role impairment to be detected and thus noted as a "psychiatric case"; however, the specific disorder may not necessarily be specified. The term "caseness" is sometimes used to describe this construct. On this dimension the rate of caseness ranges from 13.3% (Mayou et al., 1993) to 62.5% (Feinstein & Dolan, 1991), with an average across the studies of 33.4%.

Post-1996 Psychiatric Comorbidity in Unselected Samples of Injured MVA Survivors

As we mentioned earlier, there has been a great deal of new research on MVA survivors published since 1996. Results, similar to the ones presented in Table 5.2, are presented for these more recent studies in Table 5.3.

The seven prospective follow-up studies summarized in Table 5.3 provide some information on comorbidity. Two (Mayou, Bryant, & Ehlers, 2001; Vingilis et al., 1996) used only questionnaires to assess for comorbidity, whereas the other five used structured psychiatric diagnostic interviews.

Mood disorders, especially depression, across the entire MVA sample were noted in six of eight studies with highly variable rates: from 6% at one year (Mayou et al., 2001) to 23% with a major depressive episode at one year (Koren et al., 1999). Frommberger et al. (1998) found 12.5% had major depression overall at six months, whereas Smith (1998) at six weeks found 27% of those admitted to the hospital for injuries met criteria for a major depressive episode at six weeks. There is clearly a great deal of variability.

Of those who met criteria for PTSD at the follow-up point, the rate of comorbid major depression is noticeably higher than is found for the whole sample, with rates of 46% of PTSDs at one year (Koren et al., 1999), and 39% of PTSDs at six months (Frommberger et al., 1998). Clearly the rate of depression among those survivors with PTSD is very noticeable.

Some form of anxiety-based problem was noted in seven of eight studies. Travel anxiety (or travel fear [Malt] or fear of driving [Vingilis]) was noted in four studies with rates ranging from 28% at five years (Mayou, Tyndel, & Bryant, 1997) to 29.5% with "travel fear" at three years (Malt, Hoivik, & Blikra, 1993) to 16% at one year (Mayou et al., 2001) and 33% with "fear of driving" only weeks after the MVA (Vingilis et al., 1996). Koren et al. found 11% met criteria for an anxiety disorder at one year. Mayou et al. (2001) noted 19% with GAD at one-year post-MVA whereas Smith found 21% met criteria for a phobia at six weeks post-MVA.

Finally, substance use problems were noted in one study: Frommberger et al. (1998) found 17% with alcohol abuse six months post-MVA.

TABLE 5.3
Comorbidity Found in Unselected Samples of MVA Victims After 1996

Study and country of origin	Population	Time since MVA	% Population with PTSD	Comorbidity
Vingilis et al. (1996) Canada	149 MVA survivors admitted to regional trauma center fewer blood alcohol positive cases in sample; mean stay in hospital 26 days (excluding those who seemed to have emotional stress)	Few days after admitted	N/R 30+% with some symptoms	Some ratings of depression 39.6% more than one third had fear of driving
Mayou et al. (1997) United Kingdom	ER attendees 188/200 from Mayou et al. (1993) 171 at 1 year 111 at 5 years	5 years	9 (8%) at 5 years; only 1 case over whole 5 years; 8/9 were delayed onset after 1 year	Travel anxiety = 31 (28%) 10% continuing major physical problems
Smith (1998) United Kingdom	165 ER attendees after MVA 30 admitted 50 not admitted 36 referred 49 not seen	6 weeks 6 months 1 year	6 weeks 30% of admits 14% of nonadmits *p = ns* at any time admit 37% nonadmit 12% *p < .02*	Depression admissions 27% nonadmits 14% phobia in admits 40% nonadmits 10%; any psychiatric disorder admits 43% nonadmits 30% 47% of PTSD cases were mildly depressed
Frommberger et al. (1998) Germany	231 patients admitted to hospital after MVA, 179 included (85%) exclude head injury, 152 at follow-up	Mean 8.6 days 1–30 6 months	28 (18.4%) at 6 months subsyndromal PTSD *n = 43* (28.2%) 1	N = 30 (19.7%) without PTSD 11/28 PTSD had MDD (43%) 3 of 11 also anxiety disorder 8/43 had MDD or 17% alcohol abuse

(continued)

TABLE 5.3 (Continued)

Study and country of origin	Population	Time since MVA	% Population with PTSD	Comorbidity
Koren, Arnon, & Klein (1999) Israel	99 hospitalized MVA survivors + 21 hospitalized controls at least 2 days, exclude head injury, coma, active psychiatric treatment	12 months	24 at 12 months (32%)	67% among PTSDs 16/24 (11 mood disorder, 5 anxiety disorder at 1 year) Non-PTSD 9/50 18% 6 mood disorder, 3 anxiety disorder
Mayou, Bryant, & Ehlers (2001) United Kingdom	1,148 ER attendees for MVAs exclude head trauma 24.2% admitted to hospital	3 months 1 year	23% at 3 months 17% at 1 year 5% delayed onset	3-month depression 5% travel anxiety 22% GAD 17% 1-year depression 6% travel anxiety 16% GAD 19% 27% with no comorbidity

Note. GAD = generalized anxiety disorder; MDD = major depressive disorder.

In summary, whereas there is a lack of consensus on the rate of specific comorbidity among MVA survivors, there is good agreement that the most likely problems to be found are major depression, especially among those survivors with PTSD, anxiety disorders, especially travel anxiety or GAD, and substance use problems. Thus, the results for MVA survivors mirror to a reasonable degree the picture for all cases of PTSD reported in the NCS by Kessler et al. (1995).

Clinical Hint

The varying lengths of follow-up post-MVA at which these comorbid conditions are found lends emphasis to their overall importance in the clinical picture with which the MVA survivor will present. Although one should certainly assess the MVA survivor for PTSD, one should also be on the lookout for mood disorders, travel anxiety, and GAD. As chapter 17 will make clear, we have found that these comorbid conditions may have an effect on treatment outcome.

COMORBIDITY IN THE ALBANY MVA STUDY

As mentioned earlier, in the Albany MVA Study, we devoted much effort to examining our Cohort 1 study samples (MVA survivors and controls) for both comorbid psychiatric conditions and the general psychosocial impact of the MVA on the individual. This work was previously summarized in Blanchard, Hickling, Taylor, and Loos (1995).

Comorbid Mood Disorders: Cohort 1

In Table 5.4 are tabulated our findings on comorbid mood disorders for our Cohort 1 MVA sample and the controls, based on Structured Clinical Interview for *DSM–III–R* (SCID; Spitzer et al., 1990a) interviews. In all cases we have compared by X^2 the frequencies with two orthogonal contrasts: a comparison of all MVA survivors to controls and then a comparison of those MVA survivors with PTSD to those with subsyndromal PTSD or non-PTSD. Statistics are listed only for significant comparisons.

In Table 5.4 three findings stand out: first, the MVA survivors showed more current major depression than the controls. This finding was primarily a result of the high percentage of major depression among those MVA survivors with PTSD (53.2%), which was significantly greater ($p < .0001$) than found in the other two MVA survivor groups (4.1%). Second, this high percentage of current major depression among MVA-PTSDs was a result of two factors: first, more of those MVA survivors who developed

TABLE 5.4
Comorbid Mood Disorders Among MVA Survivors and Controls: Cohort 1

| | MVA victims | | | | Comparisons | | | |
| | | | | | MVA vs. Control | | PTSD vs. Subsyndromal and non-PTSD | |
Disorder	PTSD	Subsyndromal PTSD	Non-PTSD	Non-MVA Controls	χ^2	p	χ^2	p
Current major depression	33 (53.2)	3 (6.7)	1 (2.0)	4 (4.3)	15.65	< .0001	50.60	< .0001
Onset before MVA	6 (9.7)	2 (4.4)	0	—	—	—	4.52	.034
Onset after MVA	27 (43.5)	1 (2.2)	1 (2.0)	—	—	—	47.8	< .0001
Current dysthymia	3 (4.8)	3 (6.7)	3 (5.9)	2 (2.2)		ns		ns
Current bipolar disorder	0	1 (2.2)	0	1 (1.1)		ns		ns
Any current mood disorder	35 (56.5)	7 (15.6)	4 (7.8)	6 (6.5)	18.30	< .0001	34.80	< .0001
Lifetime major depression	31 (50.0)	16 (35.6)	6 (11.8)	25 (26.9)		ns	12.40	.0004
Lifetime dysthymia	3 (4.8)	3 (6.7)	3 (5.9)	2 (2.2)		ns		ns
Lifetime bipolar disorder	4 (6.5)	2 (4.4)	0	3 (3.2)		ns		ns
Any pre-MVA mood disorder	32 (51.6)	20 (44.4)	7 (13.7)	29 (31.2)		ns		ns

Note. Values in parentheses represent the percentage of the subsample the tabulated frequency represents. n.s. = not significant. From Table 6, in "Psychiatric Morbidity Associated With Motor Vehicle Accidents," by E. B. Blanchard et al., 1995, *Journal of Nervous and Mental Disease, 183,* pp. 495–504. Copyright 1995 by Williams & Wilkins. Adapted with permission.

PTSD were clinically depressed at the time of the MVA (9.7%) than among the other two MVA survivor groups (2.1%). Second, and of greater importance, 43.5% of those MVA survivors with PTSD developed a major depression after the MVA. We feel fairly confident in these figures because great care was taken with individuals who were currently depressed to determine when the depressive episode started. Third, the MVA survivors who developed PTSD had a greater history of major depression than found in the other two survivor groups, 50% versus 23% (p = .0004).

Thus, our first finding is not surprising; the MVA-PTSD group is clearly more vulnerable to developing a major depression with the traumatic event, given their history. It appears that previous major depression is a clear risk factor for developing PTSD from an injury-producing MVA. We address this issue in detail in the next chapter (chapter 6). The finding that pretrauma major depression is a risk factor for PTSD has been previously noted in Breslau et al.'s (1991) report on a young urban sample assessed retrospectively.

The high level of comorbid major depression with PTSD has also been noted in two epidemiological studies of PTSD: Breslau et al. (1991) reported that 36.6% of her sample with PTSD also met the criteria for major depression; Kessler et al. (1995) in the NCS found that 47.9% of men and 48.5% of women with PTSD also had a comorbid major depression. These values are similar to ours and to reports in Table 5.1 (e.g., Goldberg & Gara, 1990, 51%; Hickling & Blanchard, 1992, 45%) but not to those in Table 5.2. They are also similar to the values noted in Table 5.3 and the subsequent discussion. We should note that Kessler et al. (1995) calculated that the PTSD was primary to the current comorbid mood disorders in 53 to 78% of instances, echoing our finding.

Comorbid Mood Disorders: Cohort 2

As noted earlier, because Cohort 2 was a treatment-seeking sample that were on average 13 months post-MVA, we have presented their data separately. The data from these individuals may be of more interest and have more value to the practicing clinician.

Table 5.5 presents the data on comorbid mood disorders for those seeking treatment. Again, we used the SCID (*DSM–IV* version) and very careful questioning to determine the timing of onset of the mood episode relevant to the MVA and the onset of PTSD. In this case we subjected our three groups to pairwise comparisons. In no instance were those with current subsyndromal PTSD different from those with non-PTSD; in only one instance, lifetime major depressive disorder (MDD), were the results of the comparisons of PTSD to subsyndromal PTSD (p = .045) and PTSD to non-PTSD (*ns*) different.

TABLE 5.5
Comorbid Mood Disorders Among Treatment-Seeking MVA Survivors: Cohort 2

Disorder	PTSD (N = 107) N (%)	Sub (N = 32) N (%)	Non (N = 18) N (%)	PTSD vs. non p*	PTSD vs. sub p*	Sub vs. non p*
Current MDD	62 (57.9%)	6 (18.8%)	1 (5.6%)	.000	.000	ns
MDE at time of MVA	14 (13.1%)	8 (25%)	2 (11.1%)	ns	ns	ns
MDE 1 month post-MVA	47 (43.9%)	7 (21.9%)	3 (16.7%)	.029	.025	ns
MDE between MVA & initial assessment	67 (62.6%)	11 (34.4%)	3 (16.7%)	.000	.005	ns
Current dysthymic disorder	6 (5.6%)	1 (3.1%)	1 (5.6%)	ns	ns	ns
Any mood disorder current	72 (67.3%)	7 (21.9%)	2 (11.1%)	.000	.000	ns
Lifetime MDD	80 (74.8%)	21 (65.6%)	8 (44.4%)	.009	ns	ns
Lifetime bipolar I	3 (2.8%)	0	0	ns	ns	—
Lifetime bipolar II	4 (3.7%)	0	1 (5.6%)	ns	ns	ns
Any mood disorder lifetime	88 (82.2%)	21 (65.6%)	8 (44.4%)	.001	.045	ns

Note. MDD = Major depressive disorder; MDE = major depressive episode; ns = not significant.
* Fisher's exact or chi-square tests.

The major findings for this treatment-seeking cohort are that those who met criteria for PTSD at the time of the assessment were more likely ($p < .001$) to also meet criteria for current major depression (57.9%), to have been more likely ($p < .025$) to become depressed in the month after the MVA (43.9%), to have suffered from a major depressive episode between the accident and the assessment for treatment (62.6%), and to be more likely to have a history of mood disorder (82.2%).

In fact, comparing the Cohort 1 participants with PTSD to those with PTSD from Cohort 2, we find many more similarities than differences. More than half of each sample met criteria for major depression at the time of the assessment despite the noticeable difference in time since accident (Cohort 1, 2 months; Cohort 2, 13 months). Most of these major depressive episodes were a consequence of the MVA. There were similar relatively low rates of dysthymia and bipolar disorders. There were, however, significant ($p = .014$) differences in rates of lifetime major depressive disorder (Cohort 1, 50%; Cohort 2, 74.8%).

The major differences between the samples were in the level of mood disturbance between those with subsyndromal PTSD in the two cohorts. Whereas those from Cohort 1 showed little current major depression (6.7%), it was higher ($p = .10$) in Cohort 2 (18.8%). Moreover, those in Cohort 2 were significantly ($p < .001$) more likely to develop a major depressive disorder (MDD) after the MVA (34.4%) than those in Cohort 1, (2.2%). And finally, those from Cohort 2 were significantly ($p < .009$) more likely to have suffered from major depressive disorder at some time in their lives (65.6%) than those from Cohort 1 (35.6%).

Comorbid Anxiety Disorders: Cohort 1

Similar information on comorbid anxiety disorders is presented in Table 5.6, again for the three MVA survivor groups and the controls of Cohort 1.

Two things stand out in Table 5.6: First, there are no differences between the MVA survivors as a group and the controls on anxiety disorders. There are, however, a number of low-level significant differences between the MVA survivors with PTSD and the other two MVA survivor groups. Those with PTSD show a higher rate of current panic disorder (6.5% vs. 1%), with most of that panic having started after the MVA (three out of four cases). There was also more current simple phobia (21.0% versus 7.3%). These combine to lead to more current and more lifetime anxiety disorders among those with PTSD than among the other MVA survivors.

Breslau et al. (1991) found more panic disorder, obsessive–compulsive disorder (OCD), and generalized anxiety disorder (GAD) among their young urban adults with PTSD than among the comparison group. Likewise, Kessler

TABLE 5.6
Comorbid Anxiety Disorders Among MVA Survivors and Controls: Cohort 1

| | MVA survivors | | | Non-MVA Controls | Comparisons | | | |
| | | | | | MVA vs. Control | | PTSD vs. Subsyndromal and non-PTSD | |
Disorder	PTSD	Subsyndromal PTSD	Non-PTSD		χ^2	p	χ^2	p
Current panic disorder	4 (6.5)	1 (2.2)	0	0		ns	3.60	.058
Onset after MVA	3 (4.8)	0	0	0		ns	4.76	.024
Lifetime panic disorder	7 (11.3)	3 (6.7)	0	6 (6.5)		ns	4.24	.040
Current agoraphobia with panic	0	0	0	0	—	—	—	—
Current social phobia	5 (8.1)	3 (6.7)	1 (2.0)	3 (3.2)		ns		ns
Current simple phobia	13 (21.0)	6 (13.3)	1 (2.0)	6 (6.5)		ns	6.37	.012
Current OCD	2 (3.2)	0	0	1 (1.1)		ns		ns
Current GAD	2 (3.2)	1 (2.2)	2 (3.9)	5 (5.4)		ns		ns
Any current anxiety disorder	17 (27.4)	10 (22.2)	4 (7.8)	13 (14.0)		ns	3.93	.047
Any lifetime anxiety disorder	18 (29.0)	11 (24.4)	3 (5.9)	15 (16.1)		ns	4.87	.027

Note. Values in parentheses represent the percentage of the sub-sample the tabulated frequency represents. GAD = generalized anxiety disorder; ns = not significant. From Table 6, "Psychiatric Morbidity Associated With Motor Vehicle Accidents," by E. B. Blanchard et al., 1995, *Journal of Nervous and Mental Disease, 183*, pp. 495–504. Copyright 1995 by Williams & Wilkins. Adapted with permission.

et al. (1995) in the NCS found higher levels of comorbid anxiety disorders (panic disorder, GAD, simple phobia, social phobia, and agoraphobia) among those with PTSD versus those without it. Their levels of comorbid anxiety disorders were generally 1.5 (panic disorder) to 5 (GAD) times greater than we found.

Comorbid Anxiety Disorders: Cohort 2

Table 5.3 and the subsequent discussion noted that anxiety disorders, especially GAD, were a second common comorbid condition among MVA survivors. Our Cohort 1 data support this to some degree. Table 5.7 presents the data on current anxiety disorders in Cohort 2, similar to what is tabulated in Table 5.6, as well as lifetime rates of DSM–IV panic disorder and any anxiety disorder.

Similar to the results from Cohort 1 in Table 5.6, there are very few significant differences in Table 5.7. In fact, only the comparison of lifetime panic disorder of full PTSD (18.7%) and subsyndromal PTSD (3.1%) is significant ($p = .045$).

Comparing the results of Cohort 1 to Cohort 2, the only noticeable differences are in rates of GAD. Those with PTSD from the treatment-seeking sample (Cohort 2) (26.2%) are significantly ($p < .001$) more likely to meet criteria for GAD than those from Cohort 1 (3.2%). Similarly, among those with subsyndromal PTSD, those from Cohort 2 (18.8%) were significantly ($p = .018$) more likely to meet criteria for GAD than those in Cohort 1 (2.2%). These findings could be because of the timing of the assessment (Cohort 1, two months post-MVA, versus Cohort 2, 13 months post-MVA) and thus having enough time to develop GAD, or because of the change in diagnostic criteria for GAD from DSM–III–R to DSM–IV.

There was also a significantly ($p = .025$) higher overall level of current anxiety disorders among those with PTSD in Cohort 2 (44.9%) than in Cohort 1 (27.4%). The relatively high levels of comorbid anxiety disorders, and GAD in particular for Cohort 2, are consistent with the recent reports summarized in Table 5.3.

Comorbid Alcohol and Drug Abuse–Dependence in Cohort 1

Table 5.8 presents the data on alcohol and drug abuse–dependence comorbidity. The only significant finding was a higher lifetime level of drug dependence among our MVA survivors (13.9%) than among our controls (2.2%; $p = .002$). There were no differences among the MVA survivor subgroups. There was also remarkably little current alcohol or drug abuse–

TABLE 5.7
Comorbid Anxiety Disorders Among Treatment-Seeking MVA Survivors: Cohort 2

Disorder	PTSD (N = 107) N (%)	Sub (N = 32) N (%)	Non (N = 18) N (%)	PTSD vs. non p*	PSTD vs. sub p*	Sub vs. non p*
Current panic	17 (15.9%)	1 (3.1%)	0	ns	.073	ns
Lifetime panic	20 (18.7%)	1 (3.1%)	0	.075	.045	ns
Current social phobia	8 (7.5%)	2 (6.3%)	1 (5.6%)	ns	ns	ns
Current specific phobia	18 (16.8%)	2 (6.3%)	2 (11.1%)	ns	ns	ns
Current OCD	6 (5.6%)	0	0	ns	ns	—
Current GAD	28 (26.2%)	6 (18.8%)	0	.070	ns	ns
Current anxiety NOS	3 (2.8%)	0	0	ns	ns	—
Any anxiety disorder current	48 (44.9%)	9 (28.1%)	4 (22.2%)	.071	ns	ns
Any anxiety disorder lifetime	52 (48.6%)	11 (34.4%)	6 (33.3%)	ns	.091	ns

Note. OCD = obsessive–compulsive disorder; GAD = generalized anxiety disorder; NOS = not otherwise specified; ns = not significant.
* Fisher's exact or chi-square tests.

TABLE 5.8

Comorbid Substance Abuse/Dependence Among MVA Survivors and Controls: Cohort 1

| | MVA survivors | | | Non-MVA Controls | Comparisons | | | |
| | | | | | MVA vs. Control | | PTSD vs. Subsyndromal and non-PTSD | |
Disorder	PTSD	Subsyndromal PTSD	Non-PTSD		χ^2	p	χ^2	p
Current alcohol abuse or dependence	1 (1.6)	1 (2.2)	2 (3.9)	0		ns		ns
Current drug abuse or dependence	0	1 (2.2)	0	0		ns		ns
Lifetime alcohol abuse	1 (1.6)	0	0	2 (2.2)		ns		ns
Lifetime alcohol dependence	9 (14.5)	8 (17.8)	1 (2.0)	6 (6.5)		ns		ns
Lifetime drug abuse	2 (3.2)	0	1 (2.0)	0		ns		ns
Lifetime drug dependence	9 (14.5)	4 (8.9)	9 (17.6)	2 (2.2)	9.38	.002		ns

Note. Values in parentheses represent the percentage of the subsample the tabulated frequency represent. From Table 6, "Psychiatric Morbidity Associated With Motor Vehicle Accidents," by E. B. Blanchard et al., 1995, *Journal of Nervous and Mental Disease, 183,* pp. 495–504. Copyright 1995 by Williams & Wilkins. Adapted with permission.

TABLE 5.9
Comorbid Substance Abuse/Dependence: Cohort 2

Disorder	PTSD (N = 107) N (%)	Sub N = 32) N (%)	Non (N = 18) N (%)
Current alcohol abuse or dependence	2 (1.9%)	2 (6.3%)	0
Current drug abuse or dependence	3 (2.8%)	1 (3.1%)	0
Lifetime alcohol abuse	13 (12.1%)	3 (9.4%)	3 (16.7%)
Lifetime alcohol dependence	15 (14.0%)	9 (28.1%)	1 (5.6%)
Lifetime drug abuse	8 (7.5%)	0	1 (5.6%)
Lifetime drug dependence	15 (14.0%)	5 (15.6%)	0

Note. No group differences were significant.

dependence (3.2%). This may well represent an unavoidable recruiting bias: individuals who were heavily involved in misusing substances at the time of their MVA may be unlikely to volunteer for research. In fact, only eight (5.1%) individuals admitted to having alcohol or other drugs in their system at the time of the MVA, and only two were cited by the police for driving under the influence.

Breslau et al. (1991) found more substance abuse–dependence among her research participants with PTSD (43.0%) than those without it (24.7%). Kessler et al. (1995) made similar observations in the NCS. Bryant and Panasetis (2001) and Frommberger et al. (1998) reported relatively high levels of alcohol or substance diagnoses among their MVA survivor cohorts.

Table 5.9 presents the results for Cohort 2 on alcohol and drug abuse or dependence. As with the Cohort 1 data, these results are relatively unremarkable, with no significant differences for Cohort 2 among the MVA survivor groups.

The only between-cohort differences were for lifetime history of alcohol abuse. For Cohort 1, there was only 1 case in 158 participants as compared to 19 cases in 157 participants for Cohort 2 (12.1%). This difference was highly significant ($p < .001$). This could be a result of the change in diagnostic criteria for alcohol abuse from *DSM–III–R* to *DSM–IV*.

The overall low rates for Cohort 2 may again reflect a recruiting bias—those who are currently significantly involved in alcohol or drugs (3.2%) probably do not volunteer for research. It may be the case, however, that those MVA survivors with substance problems are not as reticent to seek treatment in general.

Other Axis I comorbidity data are presented in Table 5.10 for Cohort 1 and Table 5.11 for Cohort 2. They are unremarkable for Cohort 1 and are equally unremarkable except that we did find a few cases of current somatoform disorder among those in Cohort 2.

TABLE 5.10
Other Comorbidity Comparisons Among MVA Survivors and Controls: Cohort 1

| | MVA Victims | | | | Comparisons | | | |
| | | Subsyndromal | | Non-MVA | MVA vs. Control | | PTSD vs. Subsyndromal and non-PTSD | |
Disorder	PTSD	PTSD	Non-PTSD	Controls	χ^2	p	χ^2	p
Lifetime somatoform disorder	0	0	0	0	—	—	—	—
Current/lifetime eating disorder	5 (8.1)	2 (4.4)	2 (3.9)	2 (2.2)	—	ns	—	ns
Current/lifetime psychotic disorder	0	0	0	0	—	—	—	—

Note. Values in parentheses represent the percentage of the subsample the tabulated frequency represent. ns = not significant. From Table 6, "Psychiatric Morbidity Associated With Motor Vehicle Accidents," by E. B. Blanchard, 1995, *Journal of Nervous and Mental Disease, 183,* 495–504. Copyright 1995 by Williams & Wilkins. Adapted with permission.

TABLE 5.11
Other Comorbidity: Cohort 2

Disorder	PTSD (N = 107) N (%)	Subsyndromal (N = 32) N (%)	Non (N = 18) N (%)
Current somatoform disorder	5 (4.7%)	0	0
Current eating disorder	8 (7.5%)	0	0
Lifetime eating disorder	16 (15.0%)	1 (3.1%)	0
Current psychotic disorder	1 (0.9%)	1 (3.1%)	0
Lifetime psychotic disorder	2 (1.9%)	1 (3.1%)	0

Note. No group differences were significant (Fisher's Exact Test).

COMORBID PERSONALITY DISORDERS

Table 5.12 presents the tabulated results of the SCID–II interviews on comorbid personality disorders or Axis II disorders for Cohort 1. Examining the material in Table 5.12, one finds relatively low levels of Axis II disorders among the various subgroups and no significant differences on any of the comparisons. Overall, 13.3% of the MVA survivors met the criteria for one or more personality disorders. Among those who were diagnosed with PTSD, obsessive–compulsive personality disorder was the most common (9.7%).

We also assessed for possible personality disorders in Cohort 2. The results for this treatment seeking population are presented in Table 5.13. We again find a relatively low rate of personality disorders in this sample, with 22.2% of the treatment-seeking sample meeting the criteria for one or more personality disorders. As with Cohort 1, in Cohort 2 the most commonly occurring personality disorder was obsessive–compulsive personality disorder, with 11.5% of the total sample meeting these criteria, including 14% of those with PTSD.

The only other study to address the Axis II disorders (Ursano et al., 1999a) unfortunately relied on clinical assessment for personality disorders. These authors used the SCID to diagnose PTSD and Axis I disorders. They identified 17 of 122 (13.9%) MVA survivors who had been hospitalized as having some Axis II disorder. They found that the presence of an Axis II disorder was not a significant predictor of who met criteria for PTSD at one-month post-MVA but was a significant predictor ($p = .03$ or better) of who continued to meet PTSD criteria at three months and six months post-MVA.

In a reanalysis of our Cohort 1 data, Malta, Blanchard, Taylor, Hickling, and Freidenberg (2002) examined the role of an Axis II diagnosis, made using the SCID–II, in remission of posttraumatic stress symptoms over a year-long prospective follow-up. We found those with a personality disorder

TABLE 5.12
Comorbid Personality Disorders Among MVA Survivors and Controls: Cohort 1

| | MVA survivors | | | | Comparisons | | | |
| | | | | | MVA vs. Control | | PTSD vs. Subsyndromal and non-PTSD | |
Disorder	PTSD	Subsyndromal PTSD	Non-PTSD	Non-MVA Controls	χ^2	p	χ^2	p
Borderline personality disorder	2 (3.2)	1 (2.2)	0	1 (1.1)		ns		ns
Antisocial personality disorder	2 (3.2)	0	1 (2.0)	0		ns		ns
Obsessive–compulsive personality disorder	6 (9.7)	3 (6.7)	2 (3.9)	5 (5.4)		ns		ns
Paranoid personality disorder	2 (3.2)	2 (4.4)	0	1 (1.1)		ns		ns
Avoidant personality disorder	3 (4.8)	3 (6.7)	2 (3.9)	1 (1.1)		ns		ns
Dependent personality disorder	2 (3.2)	0	0	2 (2.2)		ns		ns
Any Axis II personality disorder	11 (17.7)	5 (11.1)	5 (9.8)	8 (8.6)		ns		ns

Note. Values in parentheses represent the percentage of the subsample the tabulated frequency represent. ns = not significant. From Table 6, "Psychiatric Morbidity Associated With Motor Vehicle Accidents," by E. B. Blanchard et al., 1995, *Journal of Nervous and Mental Disease, 183,* pp. 495–504. Copyright 1995 by Williams & Wilkins. Adapted with permission.

TABLE 5.13
Comorbid Personality Disorders Among Cohort 2

Disorder	PTSD (*N* = 107) *N* (%)	Subsyndromal (*N* = 32) *N* (%)	Non (*N* = 18) *N* (%)
Avoidant personality disorder	7 (6.5%)	2 (6.3%)	0
Dependent personality disorder	2 (1.9%)	0	0
Obsessive–compulsive personality disorder	15 (14.0%)	2 (6.3%)	1 (5.6%)
Paranoid personality disorder	9 (8.4%)	0	0
Schizotypal personality disorder	0	0	0
Schizoid personality disorder	0	1 (3.1%)	0
Histrionic personality disorder	0	0	0
Narcissistic personality disorder	3 (2.8%)	0	0
Borderline personality disorder	10 (9.3%)	1 (3.1%)	0
Antisocial personality disorder	3 (2.8%)	1 (3.1%)	0
Any personality disorder*	27 (25.2%)*	7 (21.9%)*	1 (5.6%)*

Note. PTSD vs. subsyndromal was not significant. No other group differences were significant.
* PTSD vs. non: *p* < .072 (Fisher's exact).

were more likely ($p < .05$) to have a history of anxiety disorders and to have a lower ($p < .01$) Axis V score pre-MVA (74.2 versus 81.7 for those with no personality disorder). At a six-month follow-up, those with personality disorders had higher ($p < .05$) Clinical Administered PTSD Scale (CAPS) scores (34.4 versus 16.7), were more likely to meet criteria for PTSD (7/18 [38.9%] versus 20/127 [15.8%] and to meet criteria for major depression [38.9% versus 11.5%]).

At the one-year follow-up, those with personality disorders and PTSD were less likely ($p < .05$) to have remitted (3/9 [33.3%] versus 29/39 [74.4%]) and more likely ($p < .05$) to continue to meet criteria for full PTSD (6/18 [33.3%] versus 13/114 [11.4%]). Not surprisingly, the mean CAPS score at one year was higher for those with an Axis II disorder than for those who did not meet criteria (26.6 versus 13.0).

Clinical Hint

It seems clear that the presence of a personality disorder is a risk factor for delayed spontaneous remission of acute PTSD from MVAs. It thus may pay to invest the time at initial assessment to examine patients for possible Axis II disorders because their presence is a factor that predicts remission.

A noteworthy absence in our Axis II findings is any noticeable frequency of antisocial personality disorder (1.9% of all MVA survivors) from both cohorts. This may again represent a recruiting bias: those with antisocial personality disorder may not readily volunteer for a research project. Breslau et al. (1991) did find a high percentage of their young adults with PTSD had a family history of antisocial behavior (41.3%). Kessler et al. (1995) in the NCS found 43.3% of their males with PTSD and 15.4% of their females with PTSD met the *DSM–III–R* criteria for conduct disorder, and its presence was a clear significant risk factor for PTSD among both sexes.

PSYCHOMETRIC MEASURES OF PSYCHOLOGICAL DISTRESS

As Tables 5.1, 5.2, and 5.3 show, there is a sizable literature on psychiatric comorbidity among MVA survivors who developed PTSD. The material in this section departs from that literature, and its notion of categorical diagnoses, to examine psychological distress from the dimensional perspective of the psychological test. Only one such measure has found widespread use in the MVA–PTSD literature: Horowitz et al.'s (1979) Impact of Event Scale (IES). Table 5.14 summarizes data from other studies of MVA survivors on the IES.

Despite fairly widespread use (seven separate studies) of the IES, it is a bit difficult to determine what score one might expect of an MVA survivor with PTSD. Of the three studies that speak to this (Burstein, 1986a; Epstein, 1993; Green et al., 1993) the total IES scores of MVA–PTSDs range from 34 to 49, with a mean of 41.1. The highest score comes from a psychological treatment-seeking sample (Burstein, 1986a) that might be expected to be highly distressed.

As chapter 15 will reveal, the IES has been used as an outcome measure in most controlled treatment trials of MVA survivors. Table 5.15 presents the mean pretreatment IES scores for these treatment trials and our own study (summarized in chapter 17).

One can see that the range of pretreatment IES scores is also highly variable, with most treatment samples having average scores above 30, and usually at 40 or higher.

The Albany MVA Project

To make our psychometric data maximally useful, we present the distribution of scores on each of the psychological tests administered to our MVA survivors by diagnostic subgroup, and on controls (when appropriate). The values for the IES are presented in Table 5.16a for Cohort 1 and Table 5.16b for the treatment-seeking Cohort 2.

In Table 5.16a we find a mean IES score for our PTSD subgroup of 35.4, which is within the range reported in Table 5.8 for comparable populations. We found 59% of our PTSD group with total IES scores of greater than 30 or greater, the level used by Bryant and Harvey (1996).

TABLE 5.14

Summary of Findings with Impact of Event Scale Among MVA Survivors

| Study and country of origin | Population | % MVA | % PTSD | Impact of Events Scale | | Total survivor sample |
| | | | | PTSD vs. other | | |
				Mean (SD)	Mean (SD)	Mean (SD)
Burstein (1986a) United States	19 MVA survivors with PTSD referred for treatment vs. 11 with sudden loss and PTSD	100	100	MVA–PTSD 49.3	Loss PTSD 48.0	— —
Malt (1988) Norway	113 hospitalized; accident victims 46 from MVA	40.7	1		21% 9+ on intrustion 44% 9+ on avoidance	intrusion: 5.5 (6.0) avoidance: 9.3 (8.5)
Feinstein & Dolan (1991) United Kingdom	48 MVA survivors with leg fractures	100	25% at 6 weeks	Initial IES predicts PTSD at 6 weeks		intrusion: 24.4 avoidance: 14.9
Green et al. (1993) Australia	24 hospitalized MVA survivors	100	8% at 1 month 29% sub-PTSD	PTSD 34.4 (15.7) vs. 18.3 (9.5) vs. 16.1 (9.0) vs.	Non-PTSD 7.0 (5.8)* total 6.3 (5.8)* intrusion 2.5 (3.3)* avoidance	— — —
Brom et al. (1993) Netherlands	151 (of 738) survivors of serious MVAs	100	N/R			Dutch Version of IES intrusion: 10.7 avoidance: 7.8 TOTAL 19.5
Epstein (1993) United States	15 accident survivors hospitalized on trauma unit	100	40	PTSD 21.5 (10.5) vs. 18.7 (7.1) vs.	Non-PTSD 10.2 (6.9)* intrusion 7.5 (3.6)* avoidance	
Bryant & Harvey (1996) Australia	114 hospitalized MVA survivors	100	N/R			31% had high (total IES scores): 30+ 25% had high (intrusion): 20+ 18% had high (avoidance): 20+

Note. N/R = Not reported.
* Significant difference.

TABLE 5.15
Pretreatment Impact of Event Scale Scores From Treatment Trials of
MVA Survivors

Study and country of origin	Population	Time since MVA	Pretreatment IES score
Brom et al. (1993) Netherlands	154 survivors of moderate to severe MVAs	1 month	19.4 (Dutch version)
Hobbs et al. (1996) United Kingdom	106 hospitalized MVA survivors	1–2 days	15.2
Conlon et al. (1999) United Kingdom	40 ER attendees, no admits	7 days	31.4
Bryant et al. (1998) Australia	24 hospitalized: 14 MVA, 10 industrial accidents	10 days	53.6
Bryant et al. (1999) Australia	45 MVA + nonsexual assault, some hospitalized	2 weeks	52.6
Fecteau & Nicki (1999) Canada	20 MVA survivors	19 months (3–95)	48.2
Blanchard et al. (2003) United States	78 MVA survivors	13 months (6–24)	39.8

We can see the effects of dealing with a treatment-seeking sample in a comparison of the scores for those with PTSD in Table 5.16a and 5.16b. The mean for those in Cohort 2 with PTSD is about 7 points higher than those with PTSD in Cohort 1. Those with subsyndromal PTSD show a similar difference. The difference is even greater, almost 15 points, for those who are classified as non-PTSD.

Use of IES to Diagnose PTSD

Some authors have used scores above a certain level on the IES to infer that a subject met criteria for PTSD or not (e.g., Brom et al., 1993; Bryant & Harvey, 1996). We examined our Cohort 1 data to see how well certain scores on the IES discriminated among MVA survivors with diagnoses based on the CAPS interview of PTSD, subsyndromal PTSD, and non-PTSD. The results are presented in Table 5.17.

One can see from Table 5.17 that 58% of our PTSDs were correctly identified with an IES total score of greater than 30. Unfortunately, 28%

TABLE 5.16a
Impact of Event Scale Scores of Albany MVA Survivor Victim Subgroups: Cohort 1

	Cumulative percentage of subgroup		
Score	PTSD	Subsyndromal PTSD	Non-PTSD
n	61	44	50
0–5	4.9	20.0	64.0
6–10	11.5	37.8	78.0
11–15	14.8	55.6	82.0
16–20	23.0	60.0	86.0
21–25	27.9	75.6	90.0
26–30	41.0	80.0	90.0
31–35	52.5	88.9	92.0
36–40	63.9	91.1	98.0
41–45	70.5	97.8	100.0
46–50	78.7	100.0	—
51–55	82.0	—	—
56–60	91.8	—	—
61–65	96.7	—	—
66–70	98.4	—	—
71+	100.0	—	—
Mean	35.4	17.8	8.2
SD	17.7	13.0	11.4

TABLE 5.16b
Impact of Event Scale Scores of Treatment-Seeking Albany MVA Survivor Victim Subgroups: Cohort 2

	Cumulative percentage of subgroup		
Score	PTSD	Subsyndromal PTSD	Non-PTSD
n	109	30	18
0–5	0	16.7	11.1
6–10	.9	30.0	22.2
11–15	4.6	40.0	33.3
16–20	9.2	46.7	44.4
21–25	14.7	56.7	55.6
26–30	22.0	60.0	66.7
31–35	30.3	66.7	72.2
36–40	41.3	76.7	83.3
41–45	55.0	86.7	94.4
46–50	68.8	86.7	100.0
51–55	79.8	90.0	—
56–60	88.1	96.7	—
61–65	95.4	100.0	—
66–70	98.2	—	—
71+	100.0	—	—
Mean	42.7	25.4	23.8
SD	14.8	18.4	14.5

TABLE 5.17

Comparison of Impact of Event Scale Scores to CAPS Diagnoses Among MVA Survivors

IES score	Diagnosis based on CAPS		
	PTSD	Sub	Non
20 or less	14 (23%)*	27 (60%)	43 (86%)
21–30	11 (18%)	9 (20%)	2 (4%)
31 or more	36 (58%)	9 (20%)	5 (10%)

*Percentages refer to column values.

of those with IES scores of 31 or higher do not meet the full criteria for PTSD, including 10% who are non-PTSD. Similarly, at the other end of the scale, we found 23% of our PTSDs had IES scores of 20 or less. Although those with PTSD amount to only 12% of all the participants with IES scores of 20 or lower, the false negative rate seems high.

Clinical Hint

We believe the IES is a useful psychometric measure but do not believe it can be used as a substitute for a structured clinical interview in making a definitive diagnosis. In fact, if one wants to use a questionnaire for making tentative diagnoses, we would recommend the PCL (PTSD Checklist; Weathers et al., 1993). As mentioned in chapter 4, we used it in this fashion in our longer term (two-year) follow-ups with Cohort 1. Moreover, Smith (1998) used it as a diagnostic instrument.

We recommend using joint criteria of the appropriate distribution of Criteria B, C, and D symptoms with individual item scores of 3 or greater *and* a total score of 44. This cut-off score yields a diagnostic efficiency of .900. In Tables 5.18 through 5.24 we present the data on our other psychological test measures for both Cohort 1 and Cohort 2. Norms for the PCL for Cohort 2 are contained in Table 5.21.

Clinical Hint

These data are presented in the forms of norms for each test so that the clinician can compare his or her individual case to norms from a set of MVA survivors. The Cohort 1 data are from a set of MVA survivors who volunteered to be assessed. The Cohort 2 data are from the treatment-seeking sample and thus are more relevant to a client who is seeking treatment.

*   *   *

TABLE 5.18a
Beck Depression Inventory Scores of Albany MVA Survivor Subgroups and Controls: Cohort 1

	Cumulative percentage of subgroup			
Score	PTSD	Subsyndromal PTSD	Non-PTSD	Non-MVA Controls
n	61	44	50	95
0–3	3.3	25.0	50.0	50.5
4–6	18.0	56.8	74.0	77.9
7–9	23.0	68.2	82.0	87.4
10–12	36.1	75.0	86.0	93.7
13–15	54.1	86.4	94.0	100.0
16–18	75.4	97.7	96.0	—
19–21	85.2	97.7	100.0	—
22–26	91.8	97.7	—	—
27–30	91.8	97.7	—	—
31–33	95.1	100.0	—	—
34–36	95.1	—	—	—
37–39	98.4	—	—	—
40+	100.0	—	—	—
Mean	15.5	7.6	5.0	4.4
SD	9.0	6.4	5.6	4.2

TABLE 5.18b
Beck Depression Inventory Scores of Albany Treatment-Seeking MVA Survivor Subgroups: Cohort 2

Score	PTSD	Subsyndromal PTSD	Non-PTSD
n	109	31	18
0–3	.9	6.5	16.7
4–6	.9	22.6	38.9
7–9	1.8	38.7	66.7
10–12	7.3	38.7	72.2
13–15	10.1	61.3	88.9
16–18	18.3	64.5	88.9
19–21	28.4	71.0	94.4
22–24	45.9	83.9	100.0
25–27	56.0	90.3	—
28–30	67.0	93.5	—
31–33	72.5	96.8	—
34–36	78.9	96.8	—
37–39	86.2	96.8	—
40–42	90.8	100.0	—
43–45	93.6		
46–48	98.2		
49+	100.0		
Mean	27.3	15.2	8.8
SD	10.2	9.8	6.3

TABLE 5.19a
STAI–State Anxiety Scores on Albany MVA Survivor Subgroups and Controls: Cohort 1

Score	Cumulative percentage of subgroup			
	PTSD	Subsyndromal PTSD	Non-PTSD	Non-MVA Controls
n	61	44	50	95
20–30	1.6	0	8.0	10.5
31–35	1.6	6.8	38.0	26.3
36–40	9.8	25.0	58.0	40.0
41–45	14.8	40.9	74.0	55.8
46–50	21.3	50.0	82.0	69.5
51–55	34.4	63.6	86.0	75.8
56–60	47.5	72.7	88.0	83.2
61–65	57.4	79.5	90.0	91.6
66–70	65.6	86.4	90.0	96.8
71–75	77.0	90.9	94.0	97.9
76–80	80.3	95.5	96.0	97.4
81–85	85.2	97.7	98.0	100.0
86–90	90.2	100.0	100.0	—
91–95	91.8	—	—	—
96–100	96.7	—	—	—
101+	100.0	—	—	—
Mean	64.4	52.5	42.7	45.8
SD	17.9	14.4	14.5	13.1

TABLE 5.19b
STAI–State Anxiety Scores on Albany Treatment-Seeking MVA Survivor Subgroups and Controls: Cohort 2

Score	PTSD	Subsyndromal PTSD	Non-PTSD
n	109	31	18
20–30	.9	22.6	27.8
31–35	1.8	25.8	44.4
36–40	4.6	32.3	66.7
41–45	11.0	45.2	88.9
46–50	18.3	64.5	94.4
51–55	31.2	87.1	94.4
56–60	44.0	90.3	94.4
61–65	61.5	100.0	100.0
66–70	65.6		
71–75	89.9		
76–80	100.0		
Mean	60.8	44.0	36.4
SD	11.1	12.7	10.5

TABLE 5.20a
STAI–Trait Anxiety Scores on Albany MVA Survivor Subscales and Controls: Cohort 1

	Cumulative percentage of subgroup			
Score	PTSD	Subsyndromal PTSD	Non-PTSD	Non-MVA Controls
n	61	44	50	95
20–30	1.6	2.3	8.0	7.4
31–35	4.9	9.1	38.0	24.2
36–40	6.6	20.5	50.0	37.9
41–45	16.4	29.5	60.0	48.4
46–50	21.3	52.3	76.0	64.2
51–55	37.7	63.6	88.0	78.9
56–60	47.5	72.7	88.0	88.4
61–65	55.7	81.8	92.0	92.6
66–70	80.3	88.6	96.0	92.6
71–75	93.4	90.9	100.0	96.8
76–80	96.7	95.5	—	97.9
81–85	98.4	95.5	—	100.0
86–90	98.4	97.7	—	—
91–95	98.4	97.7	—	—
96–100	98.4	100.0	—	—
100+	100.0	—	—	—
Mean	60.2	53.2	43.3	46.6
SD	13.6	14.7	12.3	12.8

TABLE 5.20b
STAI–Trait Anxiety Scores on Treatment-Seeking Albany MVA Survivor Subscales: Cohort 2

Score	PTSD	Subsyndromal PTSD	Non-PTSD
n	109	31	18
20–30	0	12.9	27.8
31–35	2.8	25.8	33.3
36–40	4.6	41.9	38.9
41–45	8.3	58.1	72.2
46–50	18.3	64.5	88.9
51–55	33.9	83.9	94.4
56–60	56.0	87.1	100.0
61–65	71.6	100.0	—
66–70	86.2	—	—
71–75	94.5	—	—
76–80	100.0	—	—
81–85	—	—	—
86–90	—	—	—
91–95	—	—	—
96–100	—	—	—
100+	—	—	—
Mean	59.1	44.4	39.2
SD	10.3	11.9	11.3

TABLE 5.21
PTSD Checklist Scores on Albany MVA Survivor Subgroups: Cohort 2

Score	Cumulative percentage of subgroup		
	PTSD	Subsyndromal PTSD	Non-PTSD
n	109	30	18
21–25	.9	0	11.1
26–30	.9	23.2	38.9
31–35	3.7	43.3	55.6
36–40	5.5	50.0	66.7
41–45	11.0	63.3	83.3
46–50	20.2	80.0	88.9
51–55	37.6	90.0	100.0
56–60	49.5	100.0	—
61–65	66.1	—	—
66–70	83.5	—	—
71–75	90.8	—	—
76–80	100.0	—	—
Mean	59.4	40.9	35.8
SD	11.6	10.8	9.8

TABLE 5.22
Global Severity Index of BSI: Cohort 2

Score	Cumulative percentage of subgroup		
	PTSD	Subsyndromal PTSD	Non-PTSD
n	109	30	18
31–35	1.0	0	6.7
36–40	1.0	0	13.3
41–45	1.0	3.7	20.0
46–50	1.0	11.1	33.3
51–55	1.0	14.8	60.0
56–60	3.0	25.9	73.3
61–65	8.0	51.9	86.7
66–70	25.0	63.0	93.3
71–75	55.0	77.8	100.0
76–80	100.0	100.0	—
Mean	73.5	65.7	53.8
SD	7.0	10.4	11.1

It is interesting to note the differences in mean scores for those with PTSD on the Beck Depression Inventory (BDI; Beck et al., 1961) for Cohort 1 and Cohort 2 (15.5 versus 27.3). There is similar difference for those with subsyndromal PTSD (7.6 versus 15.2). These differences probably reflect two things: (a) that Cohort 2 members were treatment-seeking and thus more noticeably psychologically distressed and (b) that Cohort 2 members,

TABLE 5.23
Keane's MMPI PTSD Scale Scores of Treatment-Seeking Albany MVA Survivor Subgroup: Cohort 1

Score	Cumulative percentage of subgroup		
	PTSD	Subsyndromal PTSD	Non-PTSD
n	62	45	50
0–5	17.7	46.7	66.0
6–10	40.3	64.4	88.0
11–15	58.1	77.8	92.0
16–20	72.6	91.1	94.0
21–25	88.7	95.6	98.0
26–30	91.9	97.8	100.0
31–35	96.8	97.8	—
36–40	98.4	100.0	—
41–49	100.0	—	—
Mean	14.7	9.0	5.2
SD	10.4	8.3	6.0

TABLE 5.24
Reaction Index Scores on Albany MVA Survivor Subgroups: Cohort 1

Score	Cumulative percentage of subgroup		
	PTSD	Subsyndromal PTSD	Non-PTSD
n	61	44	50
1–5	1.8	7.1	29.2
6–10	1.8	16.7	47.9
11–15	3.6	31.0	77.1
16–20	10.7	52.4	85.4
21–25	16.1	59.5	93.8
26–30	39.3	73.8	97.9
31–35	48.2	85.7	100.0
36–40	58.9	97.6	—
41–45	60.7	100.0	—
46–50	69.6	—	—
51–55	87.5	—	—
56–60	94.6	—	—
61–65	96.4	—	—
66–70	100.0	—	—
Mean	38.5	21.5	11.2
SD	14.9	10.8	7.8

on average, had been symptomatic for more than a year as opposed to Cohort 1 who were, on average, two months post-MVA. These cohort differences were not present on State-Anxiety or Trait-Anxiety scores of the State Trait Anxiety Inventory (STAI; Spielberger et al., 1970).

Table 5.25 presents the comparisons of the group means in Cohort 1 for each of the psychometric measures. In each instance the one-way ANOVA across the groups was significant at $p < .01$ or better. Follow-up

TABLE 5.25
Psychological Test Measures of Subjective Distress for All MVA Survivor
Subgroups and Controls: Cohort 1

	MVA Subgroups			Non-MVA controls
Measure	PTSD	Subsyndromal PTSD	Non-PTSD	
Beck Depression Inventory	15.5[a] (9.0)	7.6[b] (6.4)	5.0[c] (5.6)	4.4[c] (4.2)
Trait–Anxiety	60.2[a] (13.6)	53.2[b] (14.7)	43.3[c] (12.3)	46.7[c] (12.8)
State–Anxiety	64.4[a] (17.9)	52.5[b] (14.4)	42.7[c] (14.5)	46.0[c] (13.1)
Impact of Events				
Total score	35.4[a] (17.7)	17.8[b] (13.0)	8.2[c] (11.4)	—
Avoidance	18.3[a] (9.0)	9.2[b] (7.0)	4.1[c] (5.9)	—
Intrusion	17.1[a] (9.0)	8.6[b] (6.5)	4.1[c] (6.0)	—
Keane's MMPI				
PTSD Scale	15.0[a] (10.3)	9.0[b] (8.3)	5.2[c] (6.0)	6.4[b,c] (6.1)
Reaction Index	38.5[a] (14.9)	21.5[b] (10.8)	11.2[c] (7.8)	—

Note. Values that share the same superscript are not significantly different at the .05 level by Duncan's Test. From Table 4, "Psychiatric Morbidity Associated With Motor Vehicle Accidents," by E. B. Blanchard et al., 1995, *Journal of Nervous and Mental Disease, 183*, pp. 495–504. Copyright 1995 by Williams & Wilkins. Adapted with permission.

comparisons reveal that in each instance those MVA survivors with PTSD have higher scores (more distress) than those with subsyndromal PTSD who are higher than those with non-PTSD. The latter do not differ from the nonaccident controls in any comparison. In one instance (Keane's PTSD Scale; Keane et al., 1984) the subsyndromals do not differ from the controls.

The average score for those with PTSD on the Keane PTSD scale is certainly at variance with the standardization data for this scale based on Vietnam veterans. For that sample, a score above 35 correctly identified 85% with PTSD. The difference might be explained by the duration of the diagnoses: Our sample was approximately two months posttrauma (and predominantly female), whereas Keane et al.'s (1984) sample was exclusively male and on average 15 years posttrauma.

Other Psychosocial Effects of MVAs and the Concept of "Caseness"

One of the important aspects of all diagnoses in the newer *DSMs* has been that, in addition to meeting symptomatic and temporal criteria, an individual must also experience subjective distress or major role performance impairment (impaired functioning at work or school, impaired relationships with family or friends, impaired use of leisure time or recreational activities) to warrant a diagnosis. As mentioned earlier, these two latter factors, subjective distress and role impairment, define the concept of "caseness"—that is, the symptoms interfere in the latter two spheres of an individual's life enough to warrant being called a "psychiatric case."

There has been some information on caseness in MVA survivors; most of it has come from use of questionnaires or interview schedules such as Mayou et al.'s (1993) use of the Present State Examination (Wing et al., 1974) to determine caseness or Malt et al.'s (1993) use of the GHQ–20 (General Health Questionnaire; Goldberg, 1972) to determine caseness (also used by Green et al., 1993, and by Bryant & Harvey, 1995b, in their Australian studies).

For example, Mayou et al. (1993) identified 25 "cases" (out of 188 MVA survivors seen in the emergency room) for a caseness rate of 13.9% initially. Green et al. (1993) found 9 cases out of 24 assessed (37.5%), and Malt et al. (1993) found 37.2% of his sample had GHQ scores indicating caseness. Bryant and Harvey (1995b) found 41% of their sample met criteria for caseness one year after the MVA.

In the Albany MVA project we approached the concept of caseness and psychosocial impact using the LIFE–Base interview (Keller et al., 1987) at the initial assessment (see chapter 4 for description of items). We derived ratings on four psychosocial variables: (a) performance in major role function (either work, school if full-time or part-time student, or homemaking if the individual did not work out of the home and was not a student); (b) average relationship with all first-degree relatives plus spouse or partner (if living in a long-term relationship); (c) relationships with friends; (d) participation in recreational activity.

The values for these ratings for each of the MVA survivor subgroups and the controls from Cohort 1 are contained in Table 5.26.

We find in Table 5.26 that the PTSD group was more impaired than the other two MVA subgroups and the controls on all four measures. For major role performance the difference between the PTSDs and subsyndromal PTSDs is a full-scale unit (the difference between a satisfactory level of performance with no impairment [value of 2.0] and mild impairment [value 3.0; worked less than expected or had mild difficulties carrying out duties]). Likewise, the difference is almost a full scale unit on participation in recreational activities (the difference between *good* (participates in several activities; 2.0) versus *fair* (value 3.0; occasional participation in recreational activities with limited enjoyment). The other two MVA survivor groups do not differ. They are functioning at a significantly poorer level than the controls on major role performance and participation in recreation.

Table 5.27 presents similar results from Cohort 2. Examining these data, one sees that those with PTSD are more impaired than those with subsyndromal PTSD or non-PTSD on Major Role Function (by a whole scale unit) and Participation in Recreation (by a whole scale unit). There are lesser differences in primary relationships with family. We calculated interrater reliability on these ratings by having 42 tape-recorded interviews rescored by someone else. The average correlation for the two ratings was 0.94.

TABLE 5.26

LIFE–Base Ratings of Role Performance for All MVA Survivor Subgroups
and Controls: Cohort 1

| Measure | MVA Subgroups | | | Non-MVA Controls |
	PTSD	Subsyndromal PTSD	Non-PTSD	
Work, school, homemaking performance	3.1[a] (1.4)	2.1[b] (1.2)	1.9[b] (1.2)	1.4[c] (0.7)
Relations with family (average across all first-degree relatives and mate)	2.3[a] (1.0)	2.1[b] (0.8)	1.9[b,c] (0.7)	1.8[c] (0.6)
Relations with friends	2.4[a] (1.2)	1.8[b] (1.0)	1.9[b] (1.1)	1.6[b] (0.8)
Recreational participation	3.3[a] (1.4)	2.4[b] (1.1)	2.2[b] (1.4)	1.8[c] (1.1)
Global Assessment Scale rating	53.6[a] (14.7)	65.3[b] (15.7)	76.7[c] (16.1)	81.2[c] (14.0)

Note. All measures except Global Assessment Scale ratings are on 1 (very good) to 5 (very poor) scales. Values that share the same superscript are not significantly different at the 0.05 level by Duncan's Test. From Table 5, "Psychiatric Morbidity Associated With Motor Vehicle Accidents," by E. B. Blanchard, 1995, *Journal of Nervous and Mental Disease, 183*, pp. 495–504. Copyright 1995 by Williams & Wilkins. Adapted with permission.

TABLE 5.27

LIFE–Base Ratings of Role Performance for All Treatment-Seeking MVA
Survivor Subgroups and Controls: Cohort 2

| Measure | MVA Subgroups | | |
	PTSD	Subsyndromal PTSD	Non-PTSD
Work, school, homemaking performance	3.1[a] (1.4)	2.0[b] (1.2)	2.0[b] (1.3)
Relations with family (average across all first-degree relatives and mate)	2.4[a] (0.8)	2.1[a,b] (1.0)	1.8[b] (0.9)
Relations with friends	2.8[a] (1.2)	1.9[b] (1.0)	1.6[b] (0.7)
Recreational participation	3.5[a] (1.1)	2.6[b] (1.2)	2.1[b] (0.9)
Global Assessment Scale rating	55.5[a] (9.8)	68.9[b] (12.1)	74.9[b] (11.3)

Note. All measures except Global Assessment Scale rating are on 1 (very good) to 5 (very poor) scales. Values that share the same superscript are not significantly different at the 0.01 level.

Comparing the values in Table 5.27 (Cohort 2) to those in Table 5.26 (Cohort 1), we see very few differences for any of the subgroups for any of the measures. For the most part the mean values are within one or two tenths of scale unit.

The only other study to examine similar factors was the prospective follow-up by Mayou et al. (1993) in the United Kingdom. When they examined all individuals who met the criteria for PTSD during the year-long follow-up ($n = 19$) and compared them to the other MVA survivors ($n = 150$), they found significantly ($p < .01$ or better) greater levels of impairment among the PTSDs for: effects on leisure (74%) and effects on work (67%) (percentages are of those with PTSD who acknowledged moderate to great impairment effects).

Taking the results of our two studies together with those of Mayou and Bryant (1994), it is clear that meeting the criteria for PTSD subsequent to an MVA usually implies major impact on the individual's life. (Rereading the last few pages of the case of Mary J. in the prologue gives one a flavor of this impact.)

EFFECTS ON MVAs ON TRAVEL BEHAVIOR

A consequence one might logically expect of serious MVAs is altered travel behavior, especially varying degrees of phobic avoidance. Given the American dependence on the private automobile, this problem assumes possibly greater importance in the United States than other Western nations. In Tables 5.1, 5.2, and 5.3 we presented the rates of driving phobia and related travel behavior alterations found in the various studies of MVA survivors. Two of the reports on treatment-seeking MVA survivors (Hickling & Blanchard, 1992; Kuch et al., 1985) reported very high levels of driving phobia (77% and 60%, respectively). It could well be that the interference in every day life and the distress experienced by those who do not avoid driving were some of the primary reasons for seeking treatment.

In the most detailed examination of this topic, Mayou and Bryant (1994) presented data from their one-year prospective follow-up of MVA survivors (Mayou et al., 1993). At the one-year follow-up, 65% of those who had been drivers in their MVAs and 44% of those who had been passengers claimed there were still effects on their driving behavior. Moreover, 18.7% of the one-year sample was showing either phobic avoidance of certain travel behavior (avoiding certain routes or travel conditions [e.g., driving at night or on high-speed highways] or extreme distress if those conditions had to be endured). Finally, 42% of motorcyclists (who were 37.4% of the total follow-up sample) had given up riding motorcycles. Two individuals who were "learner car drivers" had not returned to driving because of fear. Individuals who had been passengers in the MVAs experienced greater level of effects on travel (84% had noticeable difficulty as a passenger at the one-year follow-up). Mayou and Bryant (1994) found that experiencing phobic travel anxiety was associated with having other diagnosable disorders over the course of the year, with being female, and with having "initial 'horrific' memories" of the MVA.

In another report, Kuch et al. (1994) reported on 55 MVA survivors who had minimal injury and chronic pain. They found 21 (38.2%) met *DSM–III–R* criteria for simple phobia. They provided a definition of "accident phobia": (a) intensification of symptoms associated with exposure to driving; (b) fear-related substantial reduction of miles normally traveled; (c) when driving, restrictions to certain roads or weather conditions; and (d) excessive cautioning of the driver when the patient was a passenger and possibly restriction of seats taken in the vehicle. Eight of their 21 accident phobics also met the criteria for PTSD.

The Albany MVA Study

The effects of the MVA on the travel behavior of our Cohort 1 sample of MVA survivors are presented in Table 15.28 as a function of subgroup. We defined *driving phobia* as either complete elimination of all driving or severe restriction of all driving (e.g., only drove from home to work and home to grocery store, both of which were close by). We also described a category we termed *driving reluctant*, which included avoidance of the MVA site; avoidance of MVA-related weather conditions (e.g., snowing, heavy rain); avoidance of certain road and traffic conditions (e.g., high-speed highways or similar roads at heavy traffic times); and avoidance of all travel (driving or passenger role) for pleasure. As an example, one young man avoided the intersection at which his accident happened. This necessitated his driving an extra eight miles to enter the major north–south thruway every day he went to work.

Thus, our definition of driving phobia is more restrictive than Kuch et al.'s (1994) "accident phobia." Our driving reluctance would more closely approximate Kuch et al.'s (1994) accident phobia.

One can see from Table 5.28 that driving phobia, as we have termed it, is found only among MVA survivors with PTSD (15.3% of PTSDs). We do find some driving reluctance among the subsyndromal PTSD and even the non-PTSD groups, but it is significantly higher among the subgroup with full PTSD. One can also see that almost all (93.2%) of the subsample with MVA-related PTSD acknowledges noticeable effects of the MVA on their travel behavior. We do find some of this in the other two subgroups of MVA survivors (79.5% in sub-PTSD, 17.8% in non-PTSD).

Our results are similar to Kuch et al.'s (1994) results if one defines accident phobia as they did. However, we find 93% (55/59) of the accident phobics (driving reluctant) meet the criteria for PTSD as compared to Kuch's 38.2%. We also found four individuals (6.5% of total PTSDs) who met the criteria for PTSD but not for accident phobia.

Without question, one of the serious, interfering effects of MVAs is the effect on travel behavior. In an area such as ours, with limited public

TABLE 5.28
Effects of Accident on Driving Behavior of Cohort 1 MVA Groups

| | MVA subgroups | | | Comparisons | | |
| | | | | | PTSD vs. Sub and Non | |
Measure	PTSD	Subsyndromal PTSD	Non-PTSD	PTSD χ^2	Sub and Non p
Does not drive (no license, injuries)	3 (4.8)	1 (2.2)	6 (11.8)		ns
Driving phobia	9 (15.3)	0 (0)	0 (0)	14.46	.00014
Driving-reluctant					
Avoids MVA site	20 (33.9)	9 (20.4)	4 (8.9)	8.11	.0044
Avoids highways, etc.	14 (23.7)	6 (13.6)	2 (4.4)	6.47	.011
Avoids driving/riding for pleasure	26 (44.1)	6 (13.6)	1 (2.3)	17.02	.00004
Any noticeable driving reluctance	55 (93.2)	35 (79.5)	8 (17.8)	12.23	.00047

Note. Values in parentheses represent the percentage of the subsample of possible drivers (eliminating those in first row) that the tabulated frequencies represent. From Table 8, "Psychiatric Morbidity Associated With Motor Vehicle Accidents," by E. B. Blanchard, 1995, *Journal of Nervous and Mental Disease, 183,* pp. 495–504. Copyright 1995 by Williams & Wilkins. Adapted with permission.

EXHIBIT 5.1
Travel Anxiety Questionnaire

Please rate how you handled the following travel conditions in the *month after* your *most distressing MVA* by circling yes *or* no after each condition.

Avoided driving at nighttime	YES	NO
Experienced great anxiety driving at nighttime	YES	NO
Avoided driving in snow	YES	NO
Experienced great anxiety driving in snow	YES	NO
Avoided driving in the rain	YES	NO
Experienced great anxiety driving in rain	YES	NO
Avoided highway driving	YES	NO
Experienced great anxiety driving on the highway	YES	NO
Avoided heavy traffic	YES	NO
Experienced great anxiety driving in heavy traffic	YES	NO
Avoided location of this MVA only	YES	NO
Experienced great anxiety driving by the location of this MVA	YES	NO
Avoided pleasure trips	YES	NO
Experienced great anxiety driving during pleasure trips	YES	NO
Avoided being the passenger	YES	NO
Experienced great anxiety being the passenger	YES	NO

Did you do any of the following in the month after this MVA? (Please circle yes *or* no after each condition.)

Restrict your driving speed	YES	NO
Drive to work *only*	YES	NO

transportation, and widely spread out communities, daily travel by a motor vehicle is almost a necessity. As an example, one woman gave up driving entirely after her MVA. Later, during the follow-up, she had returned to driving of necessity because her husband became ill and could not drive. Most of our participants engage in "exposure therapy" of sorts, forcing themselves to travel while enduring the distress or finding alternative routes.

Cohort 2 Travel Anxiety

Influenced both by the work of Mayou and Bryant (1994) and our own Cohort 1 data, we approached the topic of the effects of an MVA on travel behavior somewhat differently for Cohort 2. For a series of travel situations, we asked questions both about avoiding the travel situations and about enduring these travel situations with noticeable anxiety. We developed a Travel Anxiety Questionnaire that was administered as a semistructured interview, a copy of which is reproduced in Exhibit 5.1. It is administered as part of the MVA Interview (see Appendix A).

In addition to the norms on the items on the Travel Anxiety Questionnaire presented in Table 5.29, we have examined its internal consistency

TABLE 5.29
Travel Anxiety Questionnaire Responses for All Three Diagnostic Groups: Cohort 2

Situation	Generally or always avoids situation				Endures situation with noticeable to great anxiety			
	% positive			p for PTSD vs. others	% positive			p for PTSD vs. others
	PTSD	Sub	Non		PTSD	Sub	Non	
MVA site	57.8	27.6	44.4	.007	77.4	58.3	75.0	.145
Nighttime driving	47.1	23.3	23.5	.006	64.6	27.6	50.0	.001
Driving in snow	64.8	31.8	60.0	.032	65.0	20.0	71.4	.025
Driving in rain	50.0	26.7	29.4	.010	65.3	28.6	62.5	.007
Highway driving	50.0	25.8	22.2	.003	69.1	31.0	43.8	.000
Heavy traffic	67.6	43.3	27.8	.000	81.6	62.1	52.9	.003
Being a passenger	51.9	31.3	11.1	.001	82.1	38.7	41.2	.000
Driving for pleasure	65.4	29.0	16.7	.000	53.6	32.1	25.0	.010
Restrict own driving speed	77.5	48.4	50.0	.000				
Only drive to work	25.0	7.7	13.3	.049				
Some avoidance	93.6	66.7	83.3	.000				
or								
some endurance with anxiety					93.6	81.8	88.9	.058

(or concurrent reliability) by calculating Cronbach's alpha. We find the value to be 0.922; thus it is highly internally consistent.

The results of this systematic inquiry into travel behavior for each of the diagnostic groups in Cohort 2 are presented in Table 5.29.

As this chapter has documented, among survivors of serious MVAs, there are noticeable psychosocial effects of the accident in addition to developing PTSD. The two of these that are most prevalent are also primary reasons why MVA survivors seek mental health services: the subjective distress that accompanies the comorbid mood disorders and the role interference and subjective distress one finds among driving reluctant and driving phobic individuals.

Examining the results in Table 5.29, one can see that half or more of those with PTSD avoid each individual situation listed in the Travel Anxiety Questionnaire and that 93.6% of those with PTSD avoid at least one situation. This percentage corresponds well to the results in Table 5.28 for Cohort 1 participants with PTSD. For each situation, a significantly ($p <$ .05 or better) greater proportion of those with PTSD avoid than do those with subsyndromal PTSD or non-PTSD. Interestingly, however, more than two thirds of the latter two groups acknowledge some avoidance.

Turning to the situation in which the participant endures travel situations with noticeable or great anxiety, we again find more than half of those with full PTSD acknowledging this for each situation and 93.6% acknowledging at least one situation that arouses noticeable anxiety. A greater percentage ($p <$ .05 or better) of those with PTSD acknowledge anxiety for each situation in the questionnaire except visiting the MVA site. For that particular item, those who are classified as non-PTSD are at the same level as those with full PTSD. There was a trend ($p =$ .058) for those with PTSD to be more likely to experience anxiety in at least one situation than the other two groups.

It is probably the case that those from Cohort 2 with subsyndromal PTSD or non-PTSD acknowledge more avoidance or anxiety than those from Cohort 1 because they were a treatment-seeking sample.

As this chapter has documented, among survivors of serious MVAs, there are noticeable psychosocial effects of the accident in addition to developing PTSD. The two of these that are most prevalent are also primary reasons why MVA survivors seek mental health services: the subjective distress that accompanies the comorbid mood disorders and the role interference and subjective distress one finds among driving reluctant and driving phobic individuals.

6

DETERMINING WHO DEVELOPS
PTSD FROM MVAs

Determining who develops posttraumatic stress disorder (PTSD) from motor vehicle accidents (MVAs) is important if there are limited treatment resources available for MVA survivors. We know from chapter 3 that a sizable proportion of MVA survivors who seek medical attention (from 5 to 45%) will develop PTSD in the year following the accident and that another 15 to 30% will develop a subsyndromal form of PTSD (Green et al., 1993; Hickling & Blanchard, 1992) and consequently experience notable subjective distress and role impairment.

Given this potential degree of morbidity and limited treatment resources, one must consider a triage effort of referring those most likely to develop diagnosable conditions to treatment promptly while withholding such a referral from those we expect to do well. Under these circumstances, it becomes important to know who, among MVA survivors, is at relatively greater risk, and who is at lesser risk, to develop PTSD. (A related issue to be dealt with in chapter 7 is predicting who remits relatively quickly [with or without treatment] and who continues to suffer more chronically from PTSD or subsyndromal PTSD.)

We present data from other studies of MVA survivors and from studies of victims of other kinds of trauma. Finally, we summarize our own data.

REVIEW OF MOTOR VEHICLE ACCIDENT LITERATURE

Table 6.1 summarizes the earlier studies on MVA survivors that have sought to predict who develops PTSD from a group of accident survivors. We have also included material that speaks explicitly to variables that did *not* predict.

In Table 6.1 we find only limited help. One major point emerges from these data: High scores on the factors measured by the Impact of Event Scale (IES; Horowitz et al., 1979), intrusion and avoidance, in the time shortly after the accident tend to be the most consistent predictors of later PTSD. Thus, Feinstein and Dolan (1991) and Green et al. (1993) found high IES scores at less than one week, or at one-month post-MVA, respectively, predicted later PTSD. Epstein (1993) also found high scores on IES intrusion and avoidance in his six cases who developed PTSD over his follow-up. Consistent with this, Mayou et al. (1993) found that "horrific and intrusive memories" at the initial assessment (usually in the emergency room) predicted PTSD. Finally, Kuch et al. (1994) found that accident phobia predicted PTSD; the essence of the accident phobia is *avoidance*.

Although this information is very clinically useful, it is a bit tautological: Higher scores on two of the four symptom clusters that define PTSD (intrusive recollection and avoidance) predict the later presence of PTSD. A similar finding is that of Green et al. (1993), that early presence of a subclinical form of PTSD (similar to our subsyndromal PTSD) predicts full PTSD later.

In addition to the finding that some early level of characteristic symptoms predicts later PTSD, two other factors emerge from Table 6.1: "Perceived threat of life" in the MVA (Green et al., 1993) was a predictor. Scotti et al. (1992) made a similar observation. Perceived threat to life is now part of the required criteria in the *DSM–IV* definition (American Psychiatric Association, 1994; Criterion A-2). Death of someone in the accident also seems to lead to difficulty, but was not a significant predictor in Bryant and Harvey (1996). Malt et al. (1989) identified death of one of the participants in the accident as a predictor of later difficulty. Foeckler, Garrard, Williams, Thomas, and Jones (1978) interviewed 29 drivers who were involved in fatal accidents. Although no formal diagnostic evaluations were conducted, they noted that 16 out of 29 (55%) had a "crisis" (probably noticeable psychological distress) after the fatal MVA. Ten (34%) seemed to have some clear reexperiencing symptoms, and ten (it is not clear what the degree of overlap is between these two subsets) had long-term (at least one year) depression. This is graphically depicted in numerous anecdotes in Gwendolyn Gilliam and Barbara Russell Chesser's "Fatal Moments: The Tragedy of the Accidental/Killer" (1991). On one point there is noticeable disagreement—the role played by the extent of physical injury.

TABLE 6.1
Predictors of Development of PTSD Among MVA Survivors

Study and country of origin	Population	% PTSD	What variables predict PTSD	What variables do not predict
Malt et al. (1989) Norway	551 adults (240 MVA) hospitalized for accidental injuries	N/R	Death in the accident predicts worse family relations	N/R
Feinstein & Dolan (1991) United Kingdom	48 hospitalized patients with leg fractures (27 MVA)	25%	Initial (< 1 week) IES score predicts 6 month PTSD and "caseness"	Demographics, initial injury severity, subjective rating of severity and extent of injury
Scotti et al. (1992) United States	80 college undergrads (61 had been in MVAs)	N/R	High level of PTSD symptoms predicted by accident severity (car totaled and degree of injury) and perceived threat of harm	N/R
Mayou et al. (1993) United Kingdom	188 consecutive MVA survivors (of 200) admitted to hospital or whiplash (n = 63)	8% at 3 months	Initial (< 1 week) "horrific and intrusive memories"	No memory of MVA (23.4%); neuroticism; previous psychological problems; baseline depression
Green et al. (1993) Australia	24 hospitalized MVA survivors	8% at 1 month 30% at 18 months	Subclinical PTSD at 1 month predicts PTSD at 18 months; high IES score at 1 month; perceived threat to life	Extent of injury; extent of physical impairment
Malt et al. (1993) Norway	192 MVA survivors	Less than 5%	"Nervousness" predicted by older age and severity of injury (p = .016)	N/R
Epstein (1993) United States	15 MVA survivors hospitalized on trauma unit	40%	High avoidance and intrusion scores on the IES	N/R
Kuch et al. (1994) Canada	55 MVA survivors with minimal injury and chronic pain	14.5%	Presence of accident phobia predicts PTSD	N/R
Bryant & Harvey (1996) Australia	114 successive MVA victims hospitalized	31% had high IES (> 30) scores	Trait anxiety (.41), fear of new MVA (.40), head injury (−.27) predict IES intrusion	Death of loved one in MVA; extent of injury

Note. IES = Impact of Event Scale; N/R = not reported.

Malt et al. (1993) found that severity of injury predicts the degree of "nervousness."

PREDICTION OF WHO DEVELOPS PTSD FROM STUDIES OF OTHER TRAUMA

Within the vast literature on PTSD, there are other studies involving other traumatic events, which provide some guidance on this topic. For example, Breslau et al. (1991) identified six independent predictors of the development of PTSD in a traumatized population: female sex; neuroticism; early separation from parent; preexisting anxiety–depression; a family history of anxiety; and a family history of antisocial behavior. Kessler et al. (1995) in the National Co-Morbidity Study (NCS) found female sex, and being currently married for males and previously married for females, were predictors. Likewise, comorbid anxiety disorders, mood disorders, and substance use disorders were predictors. Kilpatrick et al. (1989) found that whether a woman was injured or not during a criminal assault predicted the development of consequent PTSD.

MORE RECENT STUDIES OF PREDICTORS OF DEVELOPMENT OF PTSD AMONG MVA SURVIVORS

Reports relevant to the topic of prediction of PTSD from literature published since 1996 are summarized in Table 6.2.

We found the total amount of information in Table 6.2 a bit overwhelming. This stems in part from multiple published studies using almost the same population and from the total volume of new research on this topic.

We have taken two steps to try to make this information easier to assimilate. Table 6.3 lists predictors that have appeared in two or more studies, along with references to which study. Duplicate references (that is two or more studies using the same population that report the same predictor) are noted by citations in italics. Second, to jump ahead slightly, we have indicated when our own work replicates this predictor significantly.

Several predictors stand out in Table 6.3 for their consistency of significant prediction across studies; for other predictors, what is most noteworthy is the large number of studies of the predictor that have yielded inconsistent results.

The most consistent results are for the report of the presence of dissociative experiences during the accident, labeled as *peritraumatic dissociation*. It has been found to be a predictor of short-term (one to four months post-MVA) and longer term (6 to 12 months) PTSD in five separate studies.

TABLE 6.2.
Studies of Prediction of PTSD Found in Unselected Samples of MVA Survivors After 1996

Study and country of origin	Population	Rate of PTSD	Variables that predict PTSD	Variables that do not predict PTSD
Shalev et al. (1996) Israel	61 hospitalized for injury (53% MVA), 51 (83.6%) Reassessed at 6 months	25.3% $n = 13$ at 6 months	Lower education level; peritraumatic dissociation* (from PDEQ); higher IES intrusion score; higher state anxiety; higher major depression (CES-D);	Gender event severity IES avoidance trait anxiety
Shalev et al. (1998) Israel	211/270 ER attendees (85.8% MVA), part admitted to hospital Reassessed at 1 month, 4 months	29.9% $n = 63$ at 1 month 17.5% $n = 37$ at 4 months	Prior major depression Higher heart rate at ER Higher PDEQ score at ER Higher state anxiety at 1 week Higher IES score at 1 week Higher BDI score at 1 week	
Shalev et al. (1997) Israel	207 from above	30.4% $n = 58$ at 1 month 16.9% $n = 35$ at 4 months	Higher IES at 1 week Higher state anxiety at 1 week Higher PDEQ score at ER	Age, gender
Freedman et al. (1999) (from Shalev, 1997)	62 from ER study (75% MVA) 23/41 PTSD; 39/194 non-PTSD—reassessed at 4 months and 1 year	25 PTSD at 4 months 12 PTSD at 1 year 5 sub-PTSD at 1 year	Higher BDI at 1 week Higher IES intrusion at 1 week jointly predict PTSD at 1 month, 4 months, 1 year	

(continued)

TABLE 6.2 (Continued)

Study and country of origin	Population	Rate of PTSD	Variables that predict PTSD	Variables that do not predict PTSD
Shalev et al. (1998) Israel	86 of 191 ER study completers, seen in ER only, (83% MVA; not admitted to hospital) reassessed at 1 month and 4 months	23.3% n = 20 at 4 months	Higher event severity Higher heart rate in ER jointly predict PTSD at 4 months	
Delahanty, Ursano, et al. (1997) United States	130 hospitalized MVA survivors (10 days or less) (25% of police referrals agree) Reassessed 80 at 3 months, 62 at 6 months, 51 at 1 year	23.8% n = 19/80 at 3 months 28.8% Sub-PTSD 16.1% n = 10/62 at 6 months 11.8% n = 6/51 at 12 months	Self-responsible drivers less likely to suffer PTSD or sub-PTSD initially and at 6 and 12 months than other-responsible drivers	
Ursano et al. (1999a) United States	122 hospitalized MVA survivors (same as Delahanty et al.) Reassessed 99 (81.1%) at 6 months Reassessed 86 (70.5%) at 12 months	34.4% at 1 month 18.2% at 6 months 14.0% at 12 months 2 delayed onset PTSD at 12 mo.	1 month = female sex,* minority race, previous PTSD*, previous anxiety disorder, previous major depression, 3 month = minority race; lower education level, age, previous PTSD, Axis II disorder 6 months = minority race; lower education level, previous anxiety disorder, Axis II disorder†	3 months Female sex, previous major depression 6 months Female sex, previous PTSD, previous major depression

Dougall, Ursano et al. (2001) United States	Part of Ursano et al. (1999) 115 hospitalized MVA survivors, 108 assessed at 1 month, 86 at 6 months, 75 at 1 year	61% PTSD or sub-PTSD at 1 month 45% at 6 months; 37% at 1 year; 5 delayed-onset cases at 6 months, 3 at 1 year	1 month = gender, degree of perceived threat in MVA 6 months = presence of passengers, coping by wishful thinking 12 months = presence of passengers, coping by wishful thinking (all multivariate predictors)	Injury severity Gender, education level, perceived threat Gender, perceived threat
Ursano et al. (1999b) United States	Part of Ursano et al. (1999a) 122 hospitalized MVA survivors, 99 reassessed at 3 months	34.4% PTSD at 1 month 25.3% PTSD at 3 months	1 month = presence of peritraumatic dissociation in MVA, previous PTSD 3 months = presence, and number, of symptoms of peritraumatic dissociation	Previous PTSD
Mayou et al. (1997) United Kingdom	ER attendees from Mayou et al. (1993) (some admitted) 188 initially, 171 at 1 year, 111 at 5 years	8% at 5 years 9 cases, only 1 case for whole 5 years, 8/9 delayed	5 years = initial intrusive memories, immediate emotional distress after MVA, continuing physical problems	

(continued)

TABLE 6.2 (Continued)

Study and country of origin	Population	Rate of PTSD	Variables that predict PTSD	Variables that do not predict PTSD
Ehlers, Mayou, et al. (1998) United Kingdom	967 ER attendees from MVAs, 26% admitted to hospital, 888 reassessed at 3 months and 781 reassessed at 1 year	23.1% at 3 months 16.5% at 1 year 6.2% delayed onset	Admission to hospital 3, 12 Persistent medical problems 3,† 12,† D, financial problems 3,† 12,† D, perceived threat at time of accident 3,† 12,† peritraumatic dissociation 3,† 12,† gender 3,† 12,† previous emotional problems 3,† 12,† litigation initiated 3,† 12,† trait worry 3, rumination on MVA memories 3, 12, D, negative interpretation of intrusions 3, 12, attempted thought suppression 3, 12, angry cognitions 3, 12, D Note: 3 predicts PTSD at 3 months 12 predicts PTSD at 12 months D predicts delayed onset PTSD	Injury severity
Mayou et al. (2001) United Kingdom	689 cases from Ehlers et al. (1998) all MVA ER attendees 24.2% admitted Reassessed at 3 months, 1 year	23% at 3 months 17% at 1 year 5% delayed-onset PTSD	1 year PTSD, admitted to hospital, previous emotional problems, MVA was frightening, high post-MVA level of negative emotions, peritraumatic dissociation, 3 month variables that predict financial problems, continuing health problems, litigation, high level of rumination,† high level of anger, high level of thought suppression, high level of negative interpretation of intrusions†	Gender

Author	Sample	Rates	Findings	Predictors
Frommberger et al. (1998) Germany	179 hospitalized MVA survivors 152 followed up at 6 months	18.4% n = 28 at 6 months sub-PTSD n = 43 (28.3%)		Severity of injury, length of hospitalization, gender
Harvey & Bryant (1998b) Australia	92 hospitalized MVA survivors (of 222) excluded 98 with TBI, 71 reassessed at 6 months	25.4% n = 18/71 at 6 months sub-PTSD n = 7 (9.9%)	Those with full ASD (78%) and those with sub-ASD (60%) more likely to have PTSD at 6 months	
Harvey & Bryant (1999c) Australia	56 of 92 from Harvey & Bryant 1998 Reassessed at 2 years	30.4% 17/56 at 2 years 4 delayed-onset PTSD	Those with full ASD (62%) and those with sub-ASD (70%), more likely to have PTSD at 2 years	
Koren et al. (1999) Israel	99 hospitalized MVA survivors; 74 (75%) reassessed at 1 year	32% 24/74 at 1 year	PTSD symptoms at 1 week predict PTSD symptoms at 1 year; IES score at 1 week predicts PTSD at 1 year	Severity of injury, responsibility for MVA, litigation, gender
Koren et al. (2001) Israel	58 of Koren et al. (1999) available at 3 years	20.7% PTSD at 3 years (includes 2 delayed-onset cases)	Higher level of education predicts PTSD at 3 years	Severity of injury, gender

(continued)

TABLE 6.2 (Continued)

Study and country of origin	Population	Rate of PTSD	Variables that predict PTSD	Variables that do not predict PTSD
Jeavons (2000) Australia	72 ER attendees from MVAs (of 96) (33% admitted); reassessed at 3 months, 6 months ($n = 62$), 12 months ($n = 58$)	9.7% 6/62 at 3 months, 8.1% at 6 months, 8.6% at 1 year	3 months: life threat,† expectation of injury,† use of emotion coping,† previous psychological treatment,† thought would die,† self-rating of initial injury† 12 months: use of emotion coping,† days in hospital,† distressed by accident†	
Bryant et al. (2000) Australia	146 hospitalized MVA survivors, reassessed at 6 months	21% at 6 months	Diagnosis of ASD, higher resting heart rate at hospital discharge	Length of hospitalization, injury severity, blood pressure
Smith (1998) United Kingdom	80 (of 165) ER attendees from MVAs; 37.5% admitted Reassessed at 6 weeks (69), 6 months (69), 1 year (52)	24.6% 17/69 at 6 weeks 6/69 (8.7%) at 6 months 4/52 (7.6%) at 1 year	Admission to hospital IES score at 1 week	Previous psychiatric history, gender
Schnyder et al. (2001) Switzerland	121 admitted to Intensive Care Unit 64% MVA Reassessed at 1 year (106)	4.7% 5/106 at 2 weeks 22/106 sub-PTSD 2/106 at 1 year (1.9%)	IES intrusion score at 2 weeks PTSD symptoms at 2 weeks Sense of death threat Problem-focused coping	Injury severity, gender, social support

| Murray, Ehlers & Mayou (2002) United Kingdom | 27 hospitalized and 176 (of 439) ER attendees from MVA Reassessed at 4 weeks and 6 months | 31.6% inpatient 28.3% outpatient at 4 weeks 19.9% inpatient 24.3 outpatient at 6 months | Pre-MVA dissociative tendencies Peritraumatic dissociation (in MVA) Rumination at initial assessment Persistent dissociation (4 weeks post-MVA) Persistent rumination | Injury severity |

Note. ASD = Acute Stress Disorder; BDI = Beck Depression Inventory; ER = emergency room; IES = Impact of Event Scale; PDEQ = Peritraumatic Dissociative Experiences Questionnaire (Marmar et al., 1994); TBI = traumatic brain injury.
*Only significant variable in multivariate prediction.
†Multivariate prediction.

TABLE 6.3
Factors That Frequently Predict Onset or Maintenance of PTSD Among MVA Survivors

Peritraumatic dissociation	ASD or sub-ASD
Shalev et al. (1996): 6 months	Harvey & Bryant (1998b): 6 months
Shalev et al. (1997–1998): 1 month, 4 months	Harvey & Bryant (1999c): 2 years
Ursano et al. (1999b): 3 months, 12 months	
Ehlers et al. (1998): 3 months, 12 months	
Mayou et al. (2001): 12 months	
Murray et al. (2002): 1 month, 6 months	

Subthreshold PTSD (Early)	High IES score early or high IES intrusion score early
Green et al. (1993): 18 months	Feinstein & Dolan (1991): 6 months
Ursano et al. (1999a): 3 months	Green et al. (1993): 18 months
Koren et al. (1999): 12 months	Epstein (1993): 3 months
Schnyder et al. (2001): 12 months	Shalev (1996): 6 months (I)
	Shalev et al. (1997, 1998): 1 month, 4 months
	Koren et al. (1999): 12 months
	Smith (1998): 6 weeks
	Schnyder et al. (2001): 12 months
	Mayou et al. (1993): 3 months (horrific/intrusive memories)

Perceived threat during MVA
Blanchard & Hickling (1997): 2 months
Ehlers et al. (1998): 3 months, 12 months
Mayou et al. (2001): 12 months
Jeavons (2000): 3 months, 6 months
Dougall et al. (2001): 1 month

Injury severity YES	Injury severity NO	Admitted to hospital / Length of hospitalization	Continuing physical problems	Gender YES	Gender NO	Minority status
Malt et al. (1993)	Feinstein & Dolan (1991)[a]	**Admitted to hospital**				Blanchard & Hickling (1997): 2 months
Blanchard & Hickling (1997): 2 months	Green et al. (1993): 18 months[a]	Ehlers et al. (1998): 3 months, 12 months				Ursano et al. (1999a): 1 month, 3 months, 6 months
Frommberger et al. (1998): 6 months[a]	Bryant & Harvey (1996)[a]	Smith (1998): 6 months				
	Ehlers et al. (1998): 3 months					
	Koren et al. (1999): 12 months[a]	**Length of hospitalization**				
	Bryant et al. (2000): 6 months[a]	Frommberger et al. (1998): 12 months				
	Schnyder et al. (2001): 12 months[a]	Jeavons et al. (2000): 12 months				
	Dougall et al. (2001): 1 month[a]	Negative				
		Bryant et al. (2000): 6 months				

Continuing physical problems		Gender YES	Gender NO
Ehlers et al. (1998): 3 months		Ursano et al. (1999a)	Dougall et al. (2001): 6 months
Mayou et al. (2001): 12 months		Dougall et al. (2001): 12 months	Shalev et al. (1996)
Blanchard & Hickling, (1997): 12 months		Ehlers et al. (1998): 3 months, 12 months	Shalev et al. (1998)
		Frommberger et al. (1998): 12 months	Mayou et al. (2001): 12 months
		Blanchard & Hickling, (1997): 2 months	Koren et al. (1999): 12 months
			Smith (1998): 6 weeks, 6 months
			Schnyder et al. (2001): 12 months

(continued)

TABLE 6.3 (Continued)

Litigation initiated	Death in MVA
Blanchard & Hickling (1997): 2 months	Malt et al. (1989)
Ehlers et al. (1998): 3 months	Blanchard & Hickling (1997)
Mayou et al. (2001): 12 months	Negative
Negative	Bryant & Harvey (1996)
Koren et al. (1999): 12 months	

Other driver is responsible	Emotional problems
Delahanty et al. (1997): 6 months, 12 months	Ehlers et al. (1998): 3 months, 12 months
Hickling et al. (1998): 6 months, 12 months	Mayou et al. (2001): 12 months
Negative	Jeavons (2000): 6 months
Koren et al. (1999): 12 months	Negative
	Smith (1998): 6 weeks

Previous major depression	
Blanchard & Hickling (1997): 2 months	
Shalev et al. (1998): 1 month, 4 months	
Ursano et al. (1999a): 1 month	

[a]Entire population was hospitalized.

Related to that is the finding by Harvey and Bryant (1998b, 1999c) that the presence of acute stress disorder (ASD; which includes reports of three or more disassociative symptoms) predicts PTSD at six months and two years, respectively.

Related to the predictive value of ASD in the first month after the MVA are four studies that found that having *noticeable symptoms of PTSD* (meeting all criteria for PTSD except the one-month duration or meeting two of three symptom clusters early) *in the first few weeks after the MVA* predicts PTSD later (3 months to 18 months). Another related predictor is having high scores either on the total IES or on the intrusion subscale of the IES in the first weeks after the MVA is a significant predictor of short-term (one to four months; Shalev et al., 1997) or long-term (6 to 12 months; Freedman, Bandes, Peri, & Shalev, 1999) PTSD. This venerable test is a significant predictor in eight studies. Moreover, the report by interview of horrific or intrusive memories in the week after the MVA was found by Mayou et al. (1993) to be a predictor of three-month PTSD.

In sum, the report of symptoms associated with diagnosis of ASD (dissociation, intrusive memories, and avoidance) during the first couple of weeks after the MVA are consistent predictors of later PTSD.

One other part of the defining criteria for ASD and PTSD, Criterion A-2, the strongly negative subjective reaction to the trauma, was found in four studies (including our own work to be summarized later in this chapter) to be predictive of short-term (one to three months) PTSD. For our work, it was especially significant how fearful the person was that he or she would die in the MVA.

An area of some controversy is whether the severity of the injury in the MVA predicts later PTSD. Only three studies (including our own) find injury severity a significant predictor, whereas eight studies mention explicitly that it was not a predictor of PTSD in the short-term or longer term. One reason for the negative findings could be that these later studies (with one exception, Ehlers et al., 1998) all used hospitalized populations of MVA survivors. These studies thus have an attenuated range of injury severity scores because those with more minor injuries who were not admitted to the hospital would have been excluded. In three other studies, including Ehlers et al. (1998), surrogates for injury severity—such as whether the MVA survivor was admitted to the hospital (Ehlers et al., 1998; Smith, 1998) or length of hospitalization (Frommberger et al., 1998; Jeavons, 2000) were significant predictors of later PTSD. Related to this, the presence of continuing physical problems from the MVA is a predictor of PTSD at 12 months post-MVA (Mayou et al., 2001; see also chapter 9, this volume).

Thus, unlike the psychological symptoms mentioned earlier, there is no consensus on whether the severity of the physical injury is a significant predictor of who is likely to develop PTSD.

Another controversial potential predictor is gender. Four separate studies, including our own work (see chapter 4, this volume), find injured female MVA survivors more likely to meet criteria for PTSD both short-term and long-term. On the other side, six studies find gender is not a significant predictor. The latter negative studies contradict the epidemiological studies summarized in chapter 2. More work is obviously needed on this issue.

Being of minority ethnic background was found in two American studies (Blanchard & Hickling, 1997; Ursano et al., 1999a) to predict short-term (one to six months) PTSD. Studies from outside the United States do not tend to report this variable, perhaps because of the lack of a significant minority population.

Other variables with inconsistent findings are whether a death occurred in the MVA. Malt et al. (1989) and our work find a fatality in the MVA predicts PTSD; Bryant and Harvey (1996) found it did not. Likewise, whether the MVA survivor has initiated litigation was a significant short-term predictor in our work and for Ehlers et al. (1998). Koren et al. (1999) found it not to be a predictor, but more than 90% of his population was involved in litigation, thus possibly artificially attenuating the range of the variable. Finally, whether the MVA survivor viewed him- or herself as responsible for the MVA or someone else as responsible was a significant predictor for Delahanty et al. (1997) at 6 months and 12 months. Our data (Hickling et al., 1999) replicated this finding. Koren et al. (1999) found this variable not to be a significant predictor of PTSD at his 12-month reassessment.

The final set of potential predictors of PTSD from MVAs is previous diagnosable psychiatric problems. Three studies, including our own work, found that having previously met criteria for a major depression was a risk factor for developing PTSD in the short-term (one to four months post-MVA). Likewise, having pre-MVA "emotional problems" was a predictor of PTSD in Ehlers et al. (1998) at 3 months and 12 months and in Jeavons (2000) at 6 months. Contradicting this finding was the report by Smith (1998) who found this variable was not a predictor at six weeks post-MVA.

The answer to our rhetorical opening question of who develops PTSD in MVAs is thus a very complex one. In the next section we present our own answers to this question.

THE ALBANY MVA STUDY

Our philosophy in addressing this question of prediction of who develops PTSD was to cast a broad net with regard to potential predictors. Thus, we included as potential predictors (a) pre-MVA variables derived from the psychosocial history, psychiatric history, and LIFE–Base and (b) variables related to the MVA and its immediate consequences such as degree of physical injury. In all, we derived 36 variables.

Because our study involved assessing individuals one to four months post-MVA, by which time they could meet the criteria for PTSD, we did not believe we could use concurrently administered psychological tests (such as the IES) or specific PTSD symptoms because these variables were a part of the criterion we sought to predict.

We then calculated the simple univariate correlation of each predictor with our criterion variables, either the dichotomous variable of whether the participant met the criteria for PTSD or not or the continuous variable of total Clinical Administered PTSD Scale (CAPS) score, representing the total amount of psychological distress as a result of posttrauma stress symptom effects. The simple univariate correlations are summarized in Table 6.4. (This work was previously presented in Blanchard, Hickling, Taylor, Loos, & Forneris, 1996.)

One notes in Table 6.4 a number of significant, but low-level, correlations with one of the two criterion variables, either total CAPS score as a measure of posttraumatic stress symptoms or the dichotomous variable of diagnosis of full PTSD or not. Variables emerge from simple demographics (gender that appeared in Breslau et al., 1991, and Kessler et al., 1995) and ethnic status, which was apparent in chapter 4, but not from pre-MVA functioning. Previous (pre-MVA) psychiatric disorders (mood, anxiety, and PTSD) also emerge as significant predictors, echoing the findings of Breslau et al. (1991) and Kessler et al. (1995).

Finally, a number of variables emerged from those we labeled as "accident-related," including three of the strongest individual predictors: MVA survivors' fear of death, agreeing with the report of Mayou et al. (1993) and Scotti et al. (1992); degree of physical injury, agreeing with Malt et al. (1989) and Scotti et al. (1992) and contradicting Mayou et al. (1993) and Feinstein and Dolan (1991), and whether the survivor had initiated litigation. In fact, this latter variable (litigation initiated) has the highest single correlation coefficient ($r = .371$) with total CAPS score, accounting for 13.6% of the variance in it. (As noted earlier, there are no variables related to the intrusion or avoidance symptoms of PTSD because we believed they would be highly redundant with the criterion at the time they were measured.)

As a next step, we eliminated all potential predictors that did not individually account for at least 2% of the variance in one of the two criteria—that is, a simple correlation of 0.141 or greater. This left us with a potential predictor pool of 19 variables. Finally, in the multiple regression we required that a variable account for at least 2% of new variance in R^2 and that the change in R^2 represented by the variable be significant at

TABLE 6.4
Description of Potential Predictors and Their Simple Correlations With Criterion Variables

Variable: how measured	Simple correlation with		
	Total CAPS score	Diagnosis of PTSD	
		1 = PTSD	0 = Non-PTSD
Demographics			
Age: years at time of interview	-.102	-.038	
Gender: 1 = female 0 = male	.187*	.185*	
Marital status: 1 = married, 0 = unmarried (single, divorced, separated)	-.056	-.040	
Education level: high school diploma or less = 1; Some college or bachelor's degree = 2; Bachelor's degree & more = 3	.016	.082	
Ethnic Status: 1 = caucasian, 0 = minority (African American, Hispanic, Asian)	-.266*	-.201*	
Pre-MVA Functioning			
Pre-MVA GAS rating: 0–100	-.048	-.094	
Pre-MVA work status: 1 = full-time employment, student or volunteer; 2 = full-time with layoffs of more than 3 months; 3 = part-time employment or volunteer (30 hours/week or less); full-time homemaker; 4 = unemployed but expected to work by self or others; 5 = unemployed, not expected to work (e.g., disabled)	.100	.013	
Pre-MVA health status: 0–100 (100 = super healthy)	-.153	-.148	
Pre-MVA family relations: average rating of relationship with all first-degree relatives including spouse or partner (1 = very good, 5 = very poor)	.026	-.018	
Family size—number of relatives rated in item above	-.015	.040	
Pre-MVA relations with friends: 1 = very good 5 = very poor	.005	.045	
Pre-MVA Psychiatric Status			
Previous major depression 1 = yes, 0 = no	.237**	.254**	
Depressed at time of MVA 1 = yes, 0 = no	.161*	.169*	
Previous mood disorder 1 = yes, 0 = no	.270**	.237**	
Previous anxiety disorder 1 = yes, 0 = no	.242**	.176*	

Variable	Coding		
Previous substance abuse/dependence	1 = yes, 0 = no	.127	.045
Any previous Axis I disorder	1 = yes, 0 = no	.258**	.231**
Any previous Axis II disorder	1 = yes, 0 = no	.144	.105
Previous serious MVA	1 = yes, 0 = no	-.130	-.122
Any previous trauma	1 = yes, 0 = no	.139	.111
Previous PTSD	1 = yes, 0 = no	.211**	.121
Previous psychological/psychiatric treatment	1 = yes, 0 = no	.056	.002
Accident-related variables			
Number of vehicles involved: 1–up		.152	.112
Were others hurt or killed?	1 = yes, 0 = no	.254**	.220**
Driver or passenger/pedestrian	1 = yes, 0 = no	-.061	-.044
Were traffic citations issued?	1 = yes, 0 = no	.050	.003
Was participant cited?	1 = yes, 0 = no	.042	.049
Degree of responsibility for MVA			
Subject: 0–100		-.011	.088
Other drivers: 0–100		.172*	.049
Road conditions: 0–100		-.217**	-.151
Was participant unconscious?	1 = yes, 0 = no	.216**	.170*
Has participant begun litigation (contacted lawyer)?	1 = yes, 0 = no	.370**	.224**
Participant rating of fear of death			
0 = none, 100 = certain I would die		.275**	.310**
Subject rating of degree of control during MVA			
0 = none, 100 = complete control		-.037	.042
Degree of physical injury (AIS scores) 0–upward		.250**	.245**
Did participant experience whiplash injury?	1 = yes, 0 = no	.201*	.132

Note. AIS = Abbreviated Injury Scale; GAS = Global Assessment Scale. From Table 2, "Who Develops PTSD From Motor Vehicle Accidents?" by E. B. Blanchard et al., 1996, *Behaviour Research and Therapy, 34,* pp. 1–10. Copyright 1996 by Elsevier Science Ltd. Adapted with permission

*p < .05. ** p < .01.

$p < .05$. There was considerable overlap among the pre-MVA psychiatric status variables; this was permitted because it was not clear which ones might be important. For example, previous major depression and previous PTSD, both potential predictors based on the literature, are subsumed under previous mood disorder and previous anxiety disorder, respectively, and also both are jointly under any previous Axis I disorder.

There are two different prediction problems: (a) to predict the dichotomous criterion of whether the participant met the full *DSM–III–R* diagnostic criteria for PTSD or not and (b) to predict the degree of posttraumatic stress symptoms (PTS symptoms) as indicated by the CAPS scores at the time of the initial assessment. For the first problem the appropriate statistic is logistic regression, because the criterion is dichotomous. For the second problem the appropriate analysis is multiple regression.

Prediction of Posttraumatic Stress Symptoms (Total CAPS Score)

We used stepwise multiple regression to predict our measure of PTS symptoms across the entire sample. The final equation, containing eight variables, yielded a multiple R of 0.617 ($p < .0001$), accounting for 38.1% of the variance in total CAPS score at the initial assessment. It is summarized in Table 6.5.

If we rely on the size of the standardized regression weights and zero-order correlations as a rough indicator of the relative importance of predictor variables, we find the litigation variable (whether the MVA survivor had contacted a lawyer, and thus was contemplating litigation, by the time of the initial assessment—about two months post-MVA on average) is the strongest predictor.

This predictor is a bit problematic and points to the difficulty inherent in trying to draw causal conclusions from correlational research. The direction of causality is unclear. It could be that those seriously enough injured or distressed enough to meet the criteria for a diagnosis of PTSD (and thus to have relatively high CAPS scores) are more likely to seek the services of a lawyer and begin litigation. (The correlation between degree of injury [Abbreviated Injury Scale, or AIS, score] and CAPS score is $r = .185$, $p = .020$.) However, it is possible that those who have decided to seek litigation are subsequently inclined to portray themselves as more symptomatic, hence having higher CAPS scores, even to an independent assessor, and thus more likely to meet the criteria for PTSD.

The existence of "no fault" insurance in the state in which this study was conducted (New York) means that most of the medical care needed for recovery will be paid automatically, removing that incentive from MVA survivors to seek legal services. However, "no fault" does not compensate for pain and suffering and does not, in some cases, cover full rehabilitative (e.g., physical therapy) services. We return to this topic of effects of litigation in chapter 10.

We will save additional discussion of predictors until after the logistic regression analysis to predict the diagnosis of PTSD to combine discussion of predictors that appear in both analyses.

Logistic Regression to Predict PTSD Diagnosis

As described earlier, we have used stepwise logistic regression to predict the categorical or dichotomous variable of who develops PTSD among our MVA survivors and who does not. We could have followed the example of Kilpatrick et al. (1989) in their work with criminal assault survivors and used multiple regression with the dichotomous criterion. However, we believe logistic regression, which was developed for use with a dichotomous criterion, is more appropriate and yields an equation that optimizes correct classification of research participants as PTSD or non-PTSD. We should note that with a sample containing 39.2% PTSDs, one could be correct 60.8% of the time by calling everyone non-PTSD. Table 6.6 summarizes the results.

The variables are listed in the order they entered the equation to jointly maximize the correct classification of those with PTSD and overall correct classification. With this prediction equation, the four variables that entered (extent of injury, litigation, fear of death, and previous major depressive episode) correctly classify 69.6% of participants overall, including 56.5% of the PTSDs and 78.1% of the non-PTSDs ($p < .0001$).

Three of the four variables would be expected based on previous PTSD (and non-MVA) research: extent of injury, fear of death during the MVA, and history of earlier major depressive episode. That the litigation variable, our best single predictor, enters is no surprise statistically.

Logistic regression yields coefficients for an equation to predict the natural logarithm of an odds ratio—that is the probability of a participant's being classified as PTSD or non-PTSD divided by the probability of a participant's being non-PTSD. Again, using base rates, the odds ratio of PTSD to non-PTSD is 0.392 to 0.608, or 0.645 to 1; or conversely the odds of being non-PTSD is 1.55 to 1.0.

As an example, consider the situation in which both of the dichotomous predictors, previous major depression and initiation of litigation are positive (value of 1) and the fear of dying and extent of injury variables were at the mean for the population plus one standard deviation (67.4 and 10.05, respectively). This yields an equation:

$$\ln \text{ (odds ratio)} = -.768 + 0.014 \ (67.4) + 0.634 \ (1.0) + 0.794 \ (1.0) + 0.104 \ (10.05)$$

TABLE 6.5
Summary of Final Multiple Regression to Predict Posttraumatic Stress Symptoms in MVA Survivors

Variable	B	β	t	p	Multiple R	R²	Change in R²	Significance of F for change
Litigation	13.872	.256	3.83	.0002	.369	0.136	—	—
Previous mood disorder	9.480	.158	2.41	.0172	.459	0.210	0.074	0.0002
Fear of dying (in MVA)	0.091	.146	2.19	.0300	.502	0.252	0.042	0.0041
Ethnicity	-15.675	-.193	2.97	.0035	.534	0.285	0.033	0.0083
Road conditions								
Responsible for MVA	-0.114	-.149	2.28	.0242	.558	0.311	0.026	0.0173
Extent of injury (AIS Score)	1.005	.216	3.16	.0019	.578	0.335	0.024	0.0225
Previous PTSD	10.822	.170	2.58	.0107	.600	0.360	0.025	0.0158
Whiplash injury	8.828	-.164	2.49	.0138	.617	0.381	0.021	0.0269
constant	25.724							

Note. From Table 4, "Who Develops PTSD From Motor Vehicle Accidents?" by E. B. Blanchard, 1996, *Behaviour Research and Therapy, 34*, pp. 1–10. Copyright 1996 by Elsevier Science Ltd. Adapted with permission.

TABLE 6.6
Summary of Final Logistical Regression to Predict Posttraumatic Stress Disorder in MVA Survivors

Variable	B	Wald	Significance	R	Cumulative % correct classification		
					PTSD	Non-PTSD	Total
					0	100.0	60.8
Fear of dying (in MVA)	.014	8.67	.0032	.1775	40.3	84.4	67.1
Previous major depression	.634	10.30	.0013	.1981	45.2	85.4	69.6
Litigation	.794	4.53	.0333	.1094	50.0	83.3	70.3
Extent of injury	.104	5.34	.0209	.1256	56.5	78.1	69.6
constant	-2.768						

Note. From Table 3, "Who Develops PTSD From Motor Vehicle Accidents?" by E. B. Blanchard, 1996, *Behaviour Research and Therapy, 34*, pp. 1–10. Copyright 1996 by Elsevier Science Ltd. Adapted with permission.

or

(fear of dying)   (previous major depression)
(litigation)   (extent of injury)
    ln (odds ratio) = −0.6488;
    odds ratio = 1.913 to 1

This means that likelihood of such an MVA victim's meeting the criteria for PTSD is 1.91 to 1.0.

As a second example in the opposite direction, consider the case in which both dichotomous predictors are negative (value of zero) and the fear of dying and extent of injury variables were at one standard deviation below the population mean (−12.4 and 00.89, respectively).

This yields an equation:

ln (odds ratio) = 2.768 + 0.014 (−12.4) + 0.634 (0) +
0.794 (0) + 0.104 (−0.89)

or

(fear of dying)   (previous major depression)   (litigation)
(extent of injury)
    ln (odds ratio) = −3.03416
    odds ratio = 0.0481

This means that the likelihood of this second MVA victim's meeting the criteria for PTSD is 0.05 to 1.0, or about 1 chance in 20.

Four of the significant predictors to enter the equation to predict PTS symptoms also are predictors in the logistic regression analysis for the diagnosis of PTSD. We have already discussed the litigation variable. The three other significant predictors are not unexpected: The presence of a previous major depressive episode has been shown by others (Breslau et al., 1991; North, Smith, & Spitznagel, 1994) to predict the development of PTSD in newly traumatized individuals. For the regression analysis to predict PTS symptoms, the variable becomes previous mood disorder, a slightly broader category. The results in chapter 5 certainly point to strong association in our data between previous depression and developing PTSD after an MVA. Likewise, fear of dying in the MVA was found to be a predictor by Mayou et al. (1993) in their study of MVA survivors and is related to the idea put forth by March (1993). Although the previous evidence on the predictive value of extent of injury is mixed, as noted earlier (Malt et al., 1993, report finding an association whereas Mayou et al., 1993, and Feinstein & Dolan, 1991, do not), finding that it enters is not unexpected. In an earlier report examining that variable and fear of dying only with our first 100 MVA survivors, we found both made independent contributions to prediction (Blanchard et al., 1995).

Prediction of PTS Symptoms

When one turns to the question of predicting the extent of PTS symptoms, the results are stronger but more complicated. Because one has a continuous dependent variable, total CAPS score, and thus can use multiple regression, one might expect better results.

As noted earlier in chapter 5, presence of earlier PTSD from other, earlier trauma, is consistent with the pioneering work of Breslau et al. (1991). Thus, finding it in our analyses is not unexpected. It may be that both previous PTSD and a previous major depressive episode leave "psychic scars" with an individual and that these scars constitute vulnerabilities to new traumatic events. In both instances there is substantial past distress and symptoms, more than the everyday stress of life.

The significant correlation with ethnicity is difficult to understand. It may be a function of a small minority population (11% of the sample) and some unknown selection bias. However, Ursano et al. (1999a) also found that being of minority ethnic status was a significant predictor of meeting criteria for PTSD at one, three, and six months post-MVA in their sample of 122 hospitalized MVA survivors. Their study included 29 of minority status or 24%. Moreover, a recent report by Breslau, Davis, and Andreski (1995) found in a sample of more than 1,000 young urban-dwelling adults that Blacks were more likely to experience new trauma in a three-year prospective follow-up. The Ursano et al. (1999a) replication of our results with a somewhat larger sample of injured minority MVA survivors adds some confidence in this finding.

The attribution of responsibility for the accident to road conditions yields a low-level, negative correlation ($r = -.217$, $p < .01$) with PTS symptoms. This implies that the greater the attribution to road conditions, the less PTS symptoms. This could mean that when road conditions were substantial contributors to the MVA, such as snowy or icy road conditions, poorly banked curves or poorly marked roads, the MVA victim realized that he or she was not personally responsible and thus took on less blame and was consequently less symptomatic. Again, caution is warranted in assuming causality from correlations.

The whiplash variable does not appear in the cross-validation analyses (Blanchard et al., 1996) and thus one should be cautious in relying on it. It may enter separately, because this kind of soft tissue injury receives a very low AIS score yet can be quite debilitating.

Overall, we are pleased with the results. They represent, to the best of our knowledge, the first systematic attempt at predicting PTSD and PTS symptoms shortly after the trauma. The elegant work of Kilpatrick et al. (1989) with criminal assault survivors is comparable (and in many ways stronger because of the straightforward nature of their results); however, their time since trauma averaged 9.4 years in that study and they used multiple regression rather than logistic regression as the analytical tool. Mayou et al. (1993) studied a similar population to ours but did not examine the same range of predictors nor attempt the multivariate prediction.

There are two obvious limitations to these data and their generality. First, we had a self-selected sample of injured MVA survivors rather than a random sample. This could introduce unknown biases. Second, the recent trauma of the MVA may distort the participant's recall of his or her psychiatric and psychosocial history. To compensate we have used a psychiatric diagnostic instrument (Structured Clinical Interview for *DSM–III–R*; SCID) that seems to yield reliable historical data in psychiatric patients and a psychosocial rating instrument (LIFE–Base; see chapter 4), which also yields reliable data. Moreover, our participants have been living with the sequelae of their trauma for only weeks to a few months, not years as in the study of many other traumatized populations.

Death of an MVA Participant

In our sample of 158 MVA survivors, only two survivors had been involved in fatal accidents. Both developed PTSD. Among our controls, two had been involved in fatal MVAs earlier in their lives; one of these two developed PTSD from that accident. We strongly believe participants in fatal accidents, even when the patient is not responsible (not the driver) are at great risk for developing PTSD. Bryant and Harvey's (1996) findings are at odds with this, but they were not predicting PTSD, only IES scores. (Larger samples are probably needed to address this issue in a definitive fashion.)

Clinical Hint

For the clinician called on to evaluate newly injured MVA survivors, say within a week of the MVA, we would recommend nine variables be assessed to determine the likelihood that the new MVA survivor may have short-term (the next few months) difficulties.

1. Did the patient experience dissociative symptoms (out of body experiences, things seeming unreal, time alteration [typically things occurring in slow motion], the sensation of fuzziness) during or immediately after the accident (this is called *peritraumatic dissociation*), or is he or she continuing to have dissociative experiences? If yes, the patient may meet criteria for ASD and later for PTSD.

2. Is the patient having reexperiencing symptoms (intrusive rec-ollections, nightmares, flashbacks, or distress when reminded of the accident)?
3. Does the patient seek to avoid thoughts or behavioral remind-ers of the accident?
4. How serious were the physical injuries? The more serious (higher AIS score), the higher the likelihood of difficulty.
5. How frightened or terrified by the prospect of dying in the MVA was the patient?
6. Has the patient suffered from a previous major depression?
7. Has the patient previously been traumatized and had diagnos-able PTSD?
8. Is the patient female?
9. Was anyone killed in the accident?

Positive responses to each of these questions seem to increase the risk of later PTSD and thus might trigger early intervention.

7

WHAT IS THE SHORT-TERM NATURAL HISTORY OF MVA-RELATED PTSD AND WHAT PREDICTS REMISSION?

To this point we have been concerned with the initial impact of the motor vehicle accident (MVA) on the survivor in terms of posttrauma-specific problems such as developing posttraumatic stress disorder (PTSD) or subsyndromal PTSD and in terms of developing comorbid conditions and the overall psychosocial impact on the survivor. In this chapter we begin to examine the longer term consequences for those MVA survivors who were psychological casualties of the trauma. The primary question becomes, what happens to those individuals who initially developed PTSD or even subsyndromal PTSD over time, or what is the natural history of PTSD? Corollary questions of interest are (a) what is the impact of psychological or pharmacological treatment on that natural history and (b) what variables or factors predict relatively early remission versus prolonged periods of being symptomatic?

SHORT-TERM NATURAL HISTORY OF PTSD

We depart from our usual format of examining the specific MVA survivor literature followed by a selected review of the literature on other kinds of trauma survivors by reversing the order and describing the other literature first. Three studies are especially pertinent. First of all the National Vietnam Veterans Readjustment Study (NVVRS; Kulka et al., 1988), conducted with face-to-face interviews on 3,016 veterans, approximately 15 to 20 years after their exposure to combat in Southeast Asia, revealed that approximately 15% of those who served in Vietnam (exposed to combat) were, in 1986–1988, suffering from PTSD. Furthermore, approximately 30% of those surveyed (a carefully selected representative sample of all of the Americans who served in Southeast Asia) had met the criteria for combat-related PTSD at some point in their lives. Thus, over approximately 20 years about 50% had remitted sufficiently to no longer meet the full criteria.

Rothbaum et al. (1992) conducted a prospective study of sexual assault victims with the initial assessment an average of 12 days ($SD = 9.4$) after the assault. These victims were reassessed every week for 12 weeks for the symptoms of PTSD. Although these women could not technically meet the criteria for PTSD at the initial assessment (because of not having been symptomatic for one month [Criterion E]), if one looks only at the symptom picture (which Rothbaum et al. did), then 94% met the criteria initially. By four weeks this percentage was reduced to 64%, by three months it was down to 47%; (by six months [in Rothbaum & Foa, 1993] it was down to 42%). In a comparable report on assault victims (in Rothbaum & Foa, 1993) the initial percentage with PTSD (again relaxing the Criterion E requirement) was 65%; by three months this was down to 14.6%, and to 11.5% by six months. Obviously, assault, especially sexual assault, leads to a very high percentage of the victims developing PTSD initially; however, the recovery or remission curve seems to be fairly steep, with more than 50% of those initially meeting the full PTSD criteria remitted by three months.

McFarlane (1988) conducted a prospective follow-up of Australian fire fighters exposed to large-scale and devastating brush fires. He assessed them at three points (4 months, 11 months, and 29 months posttrauma) with the Impact of Event Scale (IES; Horowitz et al., 1979) and the General Health Questionnaire (Goldberg, 1972), which McFarlane alleged permit reasonable diagnostic approximations. Of the 315 individuals assessed at all three time points, 95 (30.2%) developed PTSD initially and another 62 (19.7%) developed it later. Of those 95 with initial PTSD, 45 (47.4%) had remitted seven months later, 18 (18.9%) others had remitted by 29 months, with 32 (33.7%) showing persistent, chronic PTSD. Sixty-two (19.7% of the total sample) developed delayed-onset PTSD. Of those 62, 17 (27.4%) remitted 18 months later and 45 continued to be symptomatic.

THE OLDER MOTOR VEHICLE ACCIDENT LITERATURE

Table 7.1 summarizes the available data from the MVA literature through 1995 on the short-term natural history and remission of PTSD. All of these studies included an initial assessment shortly after the MVA, at which the diagnosis of PTSD could be established and then a later follow-up assessment.

We find a mixed picture in Table 7.1 with regard to remission of PTSD. Three studies (Brom et al., 1993; Feinstein & Dolan, 1991; Mayou et al., 1993) find remission rates among those with PTSD of 41.7%, 38.5%, and 63.6%, respectively, over follow-ups of 6, 12, and 6 months. The average remission rate is 47.9% and the sample retention rate is 82%.

There is a clear exception to these findings: Green et al. (1993) followed up hospitalized MVA victims for 18 months in Australia. They report no remission; moreover, 5 out of 7 (71%) of those with subclinical PTSD at one month had deteriorated to full PTSD by 18 months. Mayou et al. (1993) also reported cases of delayed-onset PTSD. (We address this topic in chapter 8, this volume.)

For the most part it appears that for MVA survivors, a lower percentage develop PTSD from their accidents (see chapter 3 again) than among assault or rape victims. However, the remission curve for MVA-related PTSD appears less steep than that for assault victims: About 50% of PTSDs remit by six months to one year compared to assault-related PTSDs showing 50% remission at three months.

THE MORE RECENT MOTOR VEHICLE ACCIDENT LITERATURE

As with other topics in this book, there has been a great deal of new research on the topic of the natural history of the psychological problems of the MVA survivor. There are nine new prospective follow-up studies of MVA survivors that have been published since 1996. The studies all include an initial assessment to make the diagnosis of PTSD and then follow-up assessments to determine what has happened to those affected survivors. There was also a longer term follow-up of Mayou et al.'s (1993) initial sample. All of this work is summarized in Table 7.2.

In some of the reports determining the rate of remission of PTSD is straightforward because the same number of MVA survivors were assessed at each point in time, and the authors have made the rate of remission clear as well as clearly identifying new cases of PTSD that were not positive at the initial assessment. In other reports we have both a loss of part of the overall sample and presentation of the rate of PTSD at the follow-up point

TABLE 7.1
Summary of MVA Studies on Remission of PTSD

Study and country of origin	Population	% PTSD	Follow-up interval	Results % PTSD remitted	% sample loss	Predictors of remission
Feinstein & Dolan (1991) United Kingdom	48 patients with leg fractures (56% MVA)	25% at 6 weeks	6 months	5/12 remitted (41.7%) IES total 24.4, 6 weeks—18.5, 6 months—15.9	(7/48) 14.6	N/R
Mayou et al. (1993) United Kingdom	188 consecutive MVA victims either admitted to hospital or whiplash ($n = 63$)	8.0% at 3 months	12 months	5/13 remitted (38.5%)	14.5	N/R
Brom et al. (1993) Netherlands	151 victims of serious MVA—83 in symptom monitoring	N/R (22% with severe symptoms)	6 months	Total IES: Initial 17.4 6 months 7.4 8% had severe symptoms; remission—63.6%	24	N/R
Green et al. (1993) (Australia)	24 of 69 hospitalized MVA victims	1 month 8.3% 18 months 25%	18 months	No remission 5/7 subclinical PTSD are worse at 18 months	25	N/R

Note. N/R = not reported; IES = Impact of Event Scale.

TABLE 7.2
Summary of Recent MVA Studies on Remission of PTSD

Study and country of origin	Population	% PTSD initially	Follow-up interval(s) (from MVA)	% PTSD remitted	% sample retained	Predictors of remission
Shalev et al. (1998) Israel	211 ER attendees (85.8% MVA) Part admitted	1 month n = 63 29.9%	4 months	39/63 = 61.9% 10 new PTSD cases at 4 months	100%	Comorbid major depression predicts nonremission
Freedman et al. (1999) (from Shalev, 1998) Israel	62 from ER study (75% MVA) Part admitted	4 months n = 25	12 months	15/25 = 60% 2 new delayed-onset PTSD cases at 12 months	29.4%	BDI at 1 week predicts PTSD at 1 year
Delahanty (1997) United States	130 hospitalized MVA survivors 80 at 3 months 62 at 6 months 51 at 12 months	2–3 weeks 23.8% Sub-PTSD 23 28.8%	6 months 12 months	10/62 (16.1%) still PTSD 6/51 (11.8%) still PTSD	47.7% 39.2%	Self-responsible remit more readily
Ursano et al. (1999a) United States	122 hospitalized MVA survivors 99 at 3 months 99 at 6 months 86 at 12 months	1 month n = 42 34.4%	3 months 6 months 12 months	25/99 (25.3%) still PTSD 18/99 (18.2%) still PTSD 12/86 (14.0%) still PTSD	81.1% 81.1% 70.5%	N/R

(continued)

TABLE 7.2 (Continued)

Study and country of origin	Population	% PTSD initially	Follow-up interval(s) (from MVA)	% PTSD remitted	% sample retained	Predictors of remission
Mayou et al. (1997) United Kingdom	MVA ER attendees from Mayou et al. (1993) some admitted 188 initially 171 at 1 year 111 at 5 years	3 months 8.0%	5 years	8% PTSD at 5 years, only 1 case for whole 5 years 8/9 delayed-onset PTSD	59%	N/R
Ehlers, Mayou et al. (1998) United Kingdom	967 MVA ER attendees 26% admitted 888 at 3 months 781 at 1 year	3 months $n = 205$ 23.1%	12 months	49.7% remitted 34/549 (6.2%) delayed-onset PTSD	88%	Lower initial symptom severity
Mayou et al. (2002) United Kingdom	546 of Ehlers et al. at 3 years post-MVA	1 year	3 years	53% remitted 21/433 (5%) delayed-onset	59%	Lower initial symptom severity; predictors of nonremission, persistent medical and financial problems, female, how frightened in MVA, ongoing litigation, peritraumatic dissociation, rumination on intrusion, continued anger
Harvey & Bryant (1999c) Australia	71 (of 92) hospitalized MVA survivors	6 months $n = 18$ 25.4%	2 years	2/15 = 13.3% 4 delayed-onset PTSD cases	78.9%	Initial ASD and sub-ASD less likely to remit
Smith (1998) United Kingdom	69 MVA ER attendees (37.5% admitted) Reassessed 69 at 6 months 52 at 1 year	6 weeks $n = 14$ 20.3%	6 months 1 year	8/14 = 57.1% 2/6 = 33.3% 1 delayed-onset case	100% 75.4%	Those not admitted remit more quickly, lower IES score at 1 week remits

Study	Sample					Predictors/Findings
Jeavons (2000) Australia	72 MVA ER attendees (24% admitted) Reassessed 62 at 3 months 62 at 6 months 58 at 1 year	3 months $n = 6$ 9.7%	6 months 1 year	1/6 = 16.7% 0/5 = 0%	100% 93.5%	Thought they would die in MVA and previous psychological treatment predict not remitting at 6 months
Koren et al. (2001) Israel	74 hospitalized MVA survivors Reassessed 58 at 3 years	1 year $n = 24$ 32.4%	3 years	9/19 = 47.4% 2 delayed-onset cases	78.4%	Days in hospital predicts not remitting at 12 months, lower education level predicts remission
Schnyder et al. (2001) Switzerland	121 admitted to Intensive Care Unit (60.4% MVA) 106 reassessed at 1 year	2 weeks $n = 5$ 4.7%	1 year	5/5 = 100% 15/22 sub-PTSD = 68% 2 sub-PTSD became PTSD	87.6%	Subjective death threat and IES intrusion predict more symptoms
Murray et al. (2002) United Kingdom	27 inpatients & 176 outpatients seen in ER from MVAs 21 inpatient & 146 outpatient at 1 month 21 inpatient & 140 outpatient at 6 months	1 month $n = 7$ inpatient 33% $n = 41$ outpatient 28.3%	6 months	3/7 inpatient = 42.8% 7/41 outpatient = 17.1%	77.8% inpatient 79.5% outpatient	ASD predicts 6-month PTSD, peritraumatic dissociation predicts PTSD symptom severity

Note. ASD = Acute Stress Disorder; BDI = Beck Depression Inventory; ER = emergency room; IES = Impact of Event Scale.

with no distinctions made in the latter value as to whether they are continuing cases of PTSD or new delayed-onset cases. A prime example is Ursano et al. (1999a), for which the rate of PTSD decreases from 34.4% at one-month post-MVA to 14.0% at 12 months. However, the sample size has slipped from 122 to 86 (29.5% loss) and no mention is made of delayed-onset cases available at 12 months. This could represent a 59.5% remission rate, but one cannot be certain. By way of contrast is the five-year follow-up by Mayou et al. (1997), who were able to reassess 59% of their initial 188. Their rate of PTSD was 8.0% at three months post-MVA and *again* at five years post-MVA. They also noted that of the nine cases of PTSD found at five years, only one case had had PTSD for the entire five years; the other eight cases were all delayed-onset after the first year.

With these caveats in place, we find remission rates ranging from 0% (Jeavons, 2000) to 100% (Schnyder et al., 2001). The average value across the 10 different studies was 45.9% at six months to one year. For the follow-ups of more than 12 months, the average value is 38% across three studies. In two of the studies these relatively lower values make sense (Koren et al., 2001; Mayou, Ehlers, & Bryant, 2002) because the follow-up is from one-year post-MVA to three years post-MVA. As our own work on this topic, to be presented later in this chapter, has shown, the rate of improvement markedly decreases after the first six months, and especially after the first year. The reason for the low remission rate (13.3%) in the third study (Harvey & Bryant, 1999c) is not apparent.

PREDICTORS OF REMISSION

All but two of the studies in Table 7.2 provide some information from which one could predict either remission—or its opposite, maintenance of PTSD. The predictor variables are similar to those in chapter 6 that predicted who would initially develop PTSD.

Looking first at what explicitly predicts remission, we find (a) being a driver who was responsible for the MVA (Delahanty et al., 1997; Hickling et al., 1999); (b) relatively lower level of posttraumatic stress symptoms (Ehlers et al., 1998; Mayou et al., 2002); (c) relatively less severely injured (and thus not admitted to hospital [Smith, 1998]); and (d) lower education level (Koren et al., 2001). Related variables that predict persistence of PTSD are (e) days in hospital (Koren et al., 2001) and/or persistent medical and financial problems (Mayou et al., 2002).

Variables that predict *persistence* of PTSD diagnoses or symptoms at follow-up include: (f) comorbid major depression (Shalev et al., 1998) or prior (to MVA) psychological treatment (Jeavons, 2000); (g) peritraumatic dissociation (Mayou et al., 2002; Murray et al., 2002; Ursano et al., 1999b) and meeting initial criteria for ASD or sub-ASD (Harvey & Bryant, 1999c; Murray et al., 2002); (h) being relatively more frightened and fearful of death during the accident (Jeavons, 2000; Schnyder et al., 2001); (i) higher levels of intrusion on the IES (Schnyder et al., 2001); higher overall IES score (Smith, 1998) and rumination on intrusions (Mayou et al., 2002). Other predictor variables appearing a single time that predicted persistence of PTSD were female gender, ongoing litigation, and continued anger. A cross-check with Table 6.3 will reveal highly overlapping lists of variables.

We use two terms in this chapter, which warrant definition: *remission* and *recovery*. We mean by remission that the individual no longer meets the full diagnostic criteria for PTSD or subsyndromal PTSD. Given the categorical nature of that change, and of the diagnostic criteria for PTSD, one could have remission accompanied by a dramatic reduction in overall level of symptoms or one could have remission resulting from a slight change in one symptom. This is awkward clinically because in the former instance almost everyone would agree that meaningful improvement has occurred whereas in the latter one might not agree about improvement, even though the patient had technically changed diagnostic categories.

We use the term *recovery* to indicate that an individual falls in our non-PTSD category. Some symptoms may still be present but not enough to warrant a diagnosis.

THE ALBANY MVA STUDY

As noted in chapter 4, we conducted two extensive follow-up assessments, at 6 months after the initial assessment and again at 12 months (there was a more limited assessment of initial PTSDs only at 18 months). As noted in Table 4.5, we retained 91.8% of the sample at six months and 84.6% at one year. Thus, our retention rates are comparable, or better, than most of the studies in Table 7.1. We did have a noticeable loss among our MVA survivors initially diagnosed with PTSD: We lost 22% of the initial PTSDs by the 12-month follow-up. Because there are two somewhat different samples for each follow-up point, we will present the data for the 6-month follow-up and for the 12-month follow-up separately. It then follows that the information on the prediction of remission will also be presented separately for the 6-month and 12-month follow-up samples.

Six-Month Follow-Up

Figure 7.1 illustrates the remission curve for those individuals initially diagnosed with PTSD. Using Guilford's X^2 for correlated proportions (Guilford, 1965, p. 242, formula 11.13), we tested each month's proportion against

Six-Month Follow-Up of
Initial PTSD Individuals

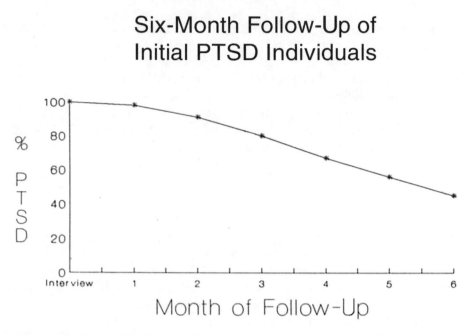

Figure 7.1. Six-month follow-up: Remission curve for individuals initially diagnosed with PTSD.

the initial diagnostic data. We found a significant ($p < .05$) drop by month 2 (5 of 55 had remitted). By month 3, 20% had remitted fully ($n = 5$) or in part ($n = 6$); by month 6, 54.5% had remitted (17 [30.9%] fully and 13 [23.9%] partially to subsyndromal PTSD).

Thus, our six-month data show a slightly greater percentage of our initial PTSDs have remitted than the average for other MVA follow-up studies (47.9%). It is also the case that our MVA survivors with PTSD do not remit as rapidly, as a group, as sexual or other assault victims.

The six-month follow-up data for those initially diagnosed with subsyndromal PTSD are displayed in Figure 7.2. This group shows more rapid remission of symptoms than those with full PTSD. By the first month of the follow-up, the proportion that remitted (9.3%) is significant at the $p < .05$ level. At three months 46.5% have remitted; by six months the value is 67.4% (but two participants had worsened and met the criteria for delayed onset PTSD).

Prediction of Short-Term Remission

There are four separate prediction problems to be covered in this section: for the initial PTSDs and initial subsyndromal PTSDs, we wish to predict the dichotomous variable of remitted or not (for the PTSDs we thus

Six-Month Follow-Up of
Initial Subsyndromal Individuals

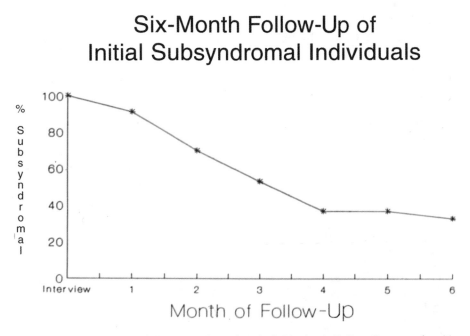

Figure 7.2. Six-month follow-up data for Individuals initially diagnosed with subsyndromal PTSD.

combined those who at six months were either non-PTSD or subsyndromal PTSD; for the initial subsyndromals, we combined the unremitted subsyndromals with the deteriorated [to full PTSD] patients). We also sought to predict six-month CAPS (Clinical Administered PTSD Scale) score.

As in chapter 6, we used logistical regression to predict the dichotomous outcome variable and stepwise multiple regression to predict CAPS score, our measure of posttraumatic stress symptoms. Also, as in chapter 6, we have cast a wide net for potential predictors relying on: (a) demographic variables; (b) accident related variables; (c) variables related to the physical effects of the MVA, including the degree of recovery from physical injury (measured by the Physical Injury Quotient—see chapter 9 for details of how this value is calculated)—at each month; (d) subjective reactions to the MVA; (e) pre-MVA psychopathology; (f) psychopathology diagnosed at the initial assessment; (g) psychosocial factors; and (h) new MVA-related and other psychosocial stresses since the MVA. The simple correlations of each of the 45 predictors with the two criteria for each subgroup (PTSD and subsyndromal PTSD) are presented in Table 7.3.

As before, we eliminated any potential predictor that did not account for at least 4% of variance in the criterion ($r = .20$ or higher). This reduced the potential predictor pool to 35 variables. (This work is summarized in Blanchard et al., 1997).

TABLE 7.3
Values of Individual Predictors of Remission of MVA-Related PTSD and Subsyndromal PTSD at Six Months

Predictor	PTSD		Subsyndromal	
	Diagnosis 1 = PTSD 0 = sub/non-PTSD	CAPS 6 months	Diagnosis 1 = sub or PTSD 0 = non-PTSD	CAPS 6 months
Demographics				
Age	.042	−.001	.095	.113
Sex				
1 = female	.040	.165	.271*	.097
0 = male				
Education level				
1 = high school	−.190	−.220*	.109	.109
2 = bachelors or less				
3 = graduate				
Marital status				
1 = married	.040	−.039	.049	−.086
0 = unmarried				
Race				
1 = caucasian	−.188	−.163	−.082	.030
0 = other				
Accident related variables				
Number of vehicles involved	.009	.071	.309*	.377*
Role in MVA				
1 = driver	.078	−.012	.077	.291*
0 = other				
Physical effects of MVA				
Abbreviated Injury Scale	.306*	.162	.116	.088
Whiplash injury				
1 = yes	.052	.127	.236	.319*
0 = no				
Loss of consciousness				
1 = yes	.389**	.163	−.097	−.131
0 = no				

Physical injury Quotient			
Month 1	.144	.080	.449**
Month 2	.251*	.237*	.489***
Month 3	.234*	.291*	.425**
Month 4	.288*	.321*	.452**
Month 5	.250*	.288*	.484***
Month 6	.300*	.301*	.474***
Subjective reactions to MVA			
Degree of responsibility, %	−.322*	.413**	.078
Fear of death at time of MVA, %	.061	.053	−.252*
Degree of control participant had, %	−.057	−.151	.011
Subjective reactions to MVA (at time of assessment)			
Current vulnerability in vehicle %	.322*	.342*	−.020
Present total functioning as % of pre-MVA functioning (participant estimate)	−.178	−.198	−.522**
Post-MVA GAS/Pre-MVA GAS	−.269*	−.306*	.018
Psychopathology—(pre-MVA)			
Pre-MVA depression	−.184	−.225*	.112
1 = yes			
0 = no			
Pre-MVA PTSD	−.078	−.070	−.125
1 = yes			
0 = no			
Any pre-MVA Axis I disorder	−.101	−.070	.030
1 = yes			
0 = no			
Any pre-MVA Axis II disorder	.188	.171	.269*
1 = yes			
0 = no			
Pre-MVA mental health treatment	.069	.050	.300*
1 = yes			
0 = no			

(continued)

TABLE 7.3 (Continued)

Predictor	PTSD		Subsyndromal	
	Diagnosis 1 = PTSD 0 = sub/non-PTSD	CAPS 6 months	Diagnosis 1 = sub or PTSD 0 = non-PTSD	CAPS 6 months
Psychopathology (at time of assessment)				
Initial CAPS	.415**	.603***	.319*	.515***
Current major depression				
1 = yes	.256*	.433**	.318*	.146
0 = no				
Major depression at time of MVA				
1 = yes	−.035	.038	.222	.230
0 = No				
Current alcohol abuse/dependence				
1 = yes	.149	.244*	−.107	−.143
0 = no				
Current substance abuse/dependence				
1 = yes	—	—	−.107	−.143
0 = no				
Current anxiety disorder (except PTSD)				
1 = yes	−.022	.008	−.332*	−.192
0 = no				
Psychosocial effects of MVA				
Post-MVA role functioning work/school/home (1–5)	.240*	.382**	.250	.191
Pre-MVA family relations (1–5)	.171	.148	.092	.334*
Post-MVA family relations (1–5)	.252*	.396*	.068	.293*
Pre-MVA friend relations (1–5)	.033	−.016	.109	.145
Post-MVA friend relations (1–5)	.227*	.207	.068	.108

Post-MVA factors

Received psychological and/or drug treatment post-MVA				
1 = yes	.000	.066	.433**	.455**
0 = no				
Settled legal suit				
1 = yes	–.124	–.138	.222	.027
0 = no				
Settled traffic charges or insurance issues				
1 = yes	.219	.070	.145	–.096
0 = no				
New MVA (participant)				
1 = yes	–.035	.040	.212	–.111
0 = no				
New MVA family member				
1 = yes	–.009	–.083	.007	–.225
0 = no				
New other trauma (participant)				
1 = yes	.232*	.102	.087	.044
0 = no				
New other trauma (family member)				
1 = yes	.305*	.121	–.100	–.055
0 = no				

Note. GAS = Global Assessment Scale.
*$p < .10$. **$p < .05$. ***$p < .01$. ****$p < .001$.

Logistical Regression to Predict Remission of Initial PTSDs

The results of this analysis are summarized in Table 7.4 and show that with four variables one can correctly characterize 83.6% of the initial PTSDs, including 80% of those who do not remit and 86.7% of those who remitted in part or altogether. This compares favorably to a base rate of 54.6% correctly classified if everyone were classified as a remitter.

As shown in Table 7.4, the four variables are CAPS score at the initial assessment, the initial Abbreviated Injury Scale score, the degree of physical injury remission (Physical Injury Quotient [PIQ]) at four months, and whether a close family member had suffered some traumatic experience over the six-month follow-up.

These data suggest that the physical status and psychological status interact (the topic of chapter 9) but have independent effects on remission. They also suggest that initial degree of injury, both physical and psychological, are powerful predictors of short-term status.

One can apply the detailed description of how to use logistical regression beta weights, presented in chapter 6, to the data in Table 7.4.

Multiple Regression to Predict Six-Month CAPS Score

The next set of analyses were designed to predict the continuing level of PTS symptoms, or CAPS score at six months for those survivors initially diagnosed with PTSD. The results of the stepwise multiple regression are in Table 7.5.

The dominant variable is the initial CAPS score with a simple correlation of 0.603, $p < .001$. Degree of physical injury remission by the fourth month also enters to produce a final multiple R of 0.647, accounting for 42% of variance.

As an exploratory step, we recalculated the regression with the initial CAPS score deleted. Those results are in Table 7.6.

Interestingly, with initial CAPS removed we find a larger final multiple R (0.709) accounting for 50.3% of variance. Noticeably different variables enter, including whether the survivor met criteria for major depression at the time of the initial assessment and whether he or she had experienced a pre-MVA major depression or alcohol abuse. Reaction to being in a vehicle (perceived vulnerability) at the time of the initial assessment and family relationship after the MVA also enter.

Logistical Regression to Predict Remission of
Those With Initial Subsyndromal PTSD

The results of this prediction problem are summarized in Table 7.7. With three variables, two related to comorbid disorders present at the initial

TABLE 7.4

Summary of Logistical Regression to Predict Remission of PTSD Among MVA Survivors Over Initial Six-Month Follow-Up

Variable	B	Wald	Significance	R	Cumulative % correct classification		
					PTSD	Sub-PTSD or non-PTSD	Total
					0	100.0	54.6
Initial CAPS score	.0520	6.976	.0083	.2562	60.0	80.0	70.9
New trauma to family	2.4868	6.708	.0096	.2492	64.0	83.3	74.6
Abbreviated injury scale score	.1252	2.5772	.1084	.0873	72.0	86.7	80.0
Physical injury quotient Month 4	2.7914	4.1073	.0427	.1667	80.0	86.7	83.6
Constant	−6.2987	12.2139	.0005	—			
Total correct classification: 83.6%							

Note. From Table 3, "Prediction of Remission of Acute Post-Traumatic Stress Disorder in Motor Vehicle Accident Victims," by E. B. Blanchard, 1997, *Journal of Traumatic Stress, 10*, pp. 215–234. Copyright 1997 by Plenum Publishing Corp. Adapted with permission.

TABLE 7.5

Multiple Regression Analysis to Predict Six-Month Follow-Up CAPS Score Among MVA Survivors With Initial PTSD Diagnosis

Variable	B	β	t	p	Multiple R	R^2	Change in R^2	Significance of F for change
Initial CAPS	.7642	.5681	5.32	<.0001	.603	.346	—	—
Physical injury quotient (Month 4)	24.5288	.2377	2.23	.0305	.647	.419	.055	.0305
Constant	−22.0673							

Note. From Table 4, "Prediction of Remission of Acute Post-Traumatic Stress Disorder in Motor Vehicle Accident Victims," by E. B. Blanchard, 1997, *Journal of Traumatic Stress, 10*, pp. 215–234. Copyright 1997 by Plenum Publishing Corp. Adapted with permission.

TABLE 7.6
Multiple Regression Analysis to Predict Six-Month Follow-Up CAPS Score Among MVA Survivors With Initial PTSD Diagnosis (Omitting Initial CAPS Score)

Variable	B	β	t	p	Multiple R	R²	Change in R²	Significance of F for change
Major depression at initial assessment	10.7757	.3546	3.24	.0022	.433	.188	—	—
Perceived vulnerability in vehicle at initial assessment	0.3494	.2859	2.80	.0073	.538	.290	.102	.0085
Pre-MVA major depression	−10.4822	−.3511	−3.40	.0014	.623	.388	.098	.0061
Post-MVA family relations	9.3342	.3038	2.82	.0069	.678	.459	.071	.0132
Alcohol abuse	47.6363	.2152	2.07	.0434	.709	.503	.044	.0434
Constant	−12.1297							

Note. CAPS = Clinical Administered PTSD Scale. From Table 4, "Prediction of Remission of Acute Post-Traumatic Stress Disorder in Motor Vehicle Accident Victims," by E. B. Blanchard et al., 1997, *Journal of Traumatic Stress, 10,* pp. 215–234. Copyright 1997 by Plenum Publishing Corp. Adapted with permission.

TABLE 7.7
Logistical Regression to Predict Remission of Subsyndromal PTSD Among MVA Survivors Over Initial Six-Month Follow-Up

						Cumulative % correct classification		
Variable	B	Wald	Significance	R		Sub-PTSD or PTSD	Non-PTSD	Total
Physical injury quotient Month 2	4.579	8.1828	.0042	.3375		64.3	89.7	81.4
Major depression at initial assessment	6.193	.0161	.899	.0000		71.4	89.7	83.7
Anxiety disorder at initial assessment	−9.821	.0355	.8506	.0000		71.4	93.1	86.1
Constant	−9.409	.0372	.8470					
						0.0	100.0	67.4

Total correct classification: 86.1%

assessment and the third, the PIQ at two months, one can correctly classify 86.1% of the sample. This compares to a baseline level of correct classification of 67.4% if everyone is called a remitter.

Multiple Regression to Predict CAPS Score of Those With Initial Subsyndromal PTSD

The final prediction effort for this section is found in Table 7.8. With five variables we find a final multiple R of 0.776, accounting for 60.1% of the variance in CAPS score. Again, initial CAPS score enters as does the survivor's subjective assessment of how well he or she was functioning at the time of initial assessment. Pre-MVA family relationships, the number of vehicles in the MVA, and whether the survivor received mental health treatment after the MVA also enter.

Interestingly, the latter variable has a negative beta weight. This means receiving treatment is associated with a higher follow-up CAPS score. An additional examination shows that those survivors with subsyndromal PTSD who received mental health services tended to be the more symptomatic (higher CAPS scores at initial assessment). Thus, those who were worse initially continue worse in six months.

Mental Health Treatment and Initial Remission

An interesting aspect of these short-term follow-up data is that receiving mental health treatment is essentially irrelevant, on a group basis, for the MVA survivors initially diagnosed with PTSD. As Table 7.3 shows, the phi coefficient for receiving mental treatment of any sort after the MVA and remission of PTSD is 0. Data on this point are displayed in more detail in Table 7.9.

There is the same rate of remission among survivors with initial PTSD for those who receive any treatment versus those who do not (54.5%). These results are consistent with the data on early intervention with troubled MVA survivors reported by Brom et al. (1993): These authors found no difference in reduction of IES scores for those receiving a brief treatment versus those receiving no treatment. They are at odds with the data from the National Co-morbidity Study (NCS; Kessler et al., 1995), who found an advantage in remission rates for PTSDs who received mental health treatment at some time (not necessarily for the PTSD) versus those who never received treatment: At 6 months 20% remission for treated versus 15% for never treated; at 12 months the remission values are 35% versus 26%, respectively. The data are retrospective, unfortunately, and not necessarily specific to treatment for the PTSD.

In chapter 15 we present a comprehensive review and summary of the research literature on the psychological treatment of MVA survivors,

TABLE 7.8
Multiple Regression Analyses to Predict Six-Month Follow-Up CAPS Score Among MVA Survivors With Initial Subsyndromal PTSD Diagnoses

	With functioning measure				Without functioning measure				Multiple R	R^2	Change in R^2	Significance of F for change
	B	β	t	p	B	β	t	p				
Participant's assessment of functioning at time of initial assessment	-0.0320	-1.0434	-0.29	.7706					.522	.272		
Pre-MVA family relations	5.6556	.3071	2.91	.0060	5.6399	.3063	2.94	.0055	.612	.375	.103	.0142
Participant received mental health treatment after MVA	12.8075	.3438	2.98	.0051	13.2811	.3566	3.37	.0017	.663	.439	.064	.0412
Number of vehicles in MVA	9.3836	.3821	3.29	.0022	9.7514	.3970	3.84	.0004	.725	.526	.087	.0119
Initial CAPS score	0.4513	.3434	2.67	.0113	0.4783	.3639	3.41	.0016	.776	.602	.076	.0113
Constant	-30.3311				34.2559				.776	.601	.001	.7706

Note. CAPS = Clinical Administered PTSD Scale. From Table 6, "Prediction of Remission of Acute Post-Traumatic Stress Disorder in Motor Vehicle Accident Victims," by E. B. Blanchard et al., *Journal of Traumatic Stress, 10,* pp. 215–234. Copyright 1997 by Plenum Publishing Corp. Adapted with permission.

TABLE 7.9
Results of Uncontrolled Evaluation of Mental Health Treatments of MVA Survivors Initially Diagnosed With PTSD

	Treatment status			
Variable	Treated		Not treated	
Initial diagnostic status				
PTSD	22		33	
6-month follow-up diagnostic status				
PTSD	10		15	
Sub-PTSD	4		4	
Non-PTSD	8		14	
Initial CAPS score	63.0	(22.6)	57.5	(22.0)
6-month follow-up CAPS score	39.3	(29.8)	35.3	(30.3)

Note. From Table 7, "Prediction of Remission of Acute Post-Traumatic Stress Disorder in Motor Vehicle Accident Victims," by E. B. Blanchard et al., *Journal of Traumatic Stress, 10*, pp. 215–234. Copyright 1997 by Plenum Publishing Corp. Adapted with permission.

including information on remission and recovery. The picture on the response to treatment is complex and consistent with the contradictory statements listed earlier.

One-Year Follow-Up

The last major topic in this chapter is the results from the one-year follow-up. As Table 3.5 shows, we collected data on 83.5% of our initial sample of 158 MVA survivors. Unfortunately, there was some differential attrition: We lost a significantly larger proportion of our minority participants than we did those of Caucasian background. There was also a trend ($p = .09$) for differential loss among those initially diagnosed with PTSD: We lost 22% of those participants. Of those for whom we were unable to obtain 12-month data: 12 had moved and left no forwarding address and were unreachable through family contacts; 13 refused or had dropped out, and 1 had died. Details of this part of the project can be found in Blanchard et al. (1996).

Month-by-Month Remission Results

Figure 7.3 plots the month-by-month diagnostic status data for the 48 MVA survivors who were initially diagnosed with PTSD.

The figure shows that by six months the degree of remission had essentially plateaued, with the fraction of the sample still meeting the criteria for full PTSD ranging from 41.7% (months 10, 11, and 12) to 50% (month 7). The diagnostic breakdown based on the 12 months CAPS interview

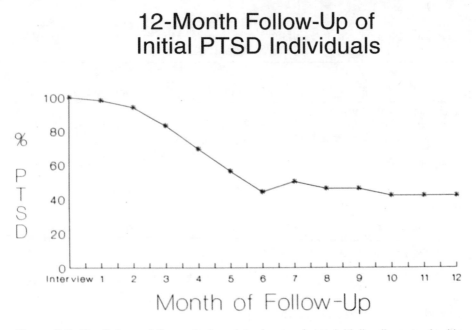

12-Month Follow-Up of Initial PTSD Individuals

Figure 7.3. Month-by-month remission data for survivors initially diagnosed with PTSD.

was 16 (33.3%) with full PTSD, 7 (14.6%) with subsyndromal PTSD, and 25 (52.1%) non-PTSD.

Effect of Initial Diagnostic Criteria on 12-Month Remission Rate

In chapter 4 we outlined how the rate of initial diagnosis of PTSD from an MVA could vary by as much as 15% depending on whether one used *DSM–III–R* or *DSM–IV* criteria and whether one used in scoring CAPS symptoms a rule of 3 or a rule of 4. If one used *DSM–IV* criteria instead of the *DSM–III–R* we have used throughout, the rate of remission at 12 months is 67.3% rather than 66.7%. If one used the rule of 4 to make the initial diagnosis, then the remission rate is 64.3% rather than 66.7%. Thus, one obtains essentially the same rate of remission regardless of the initial diagnostic criteria applied.

Figure 7.4 plots the similar month-by-month results for those 42 survivors initially diagnosed with subsyndromal PTSD. We changed the format of the graph to show the percentage of the subsample who had deteriorated enough to meet the full PTSD criteria. (These individuals with delayed-onset PTSD are discussed in detail in chapter 8.)

We again see from Figure 7.4 an essential plateau of the remission curve with the fraction who have not remitted (or who have worsened), ranging from 33.3% (month 6) to 23.8% (month 10). The diagnostic break-

12-Month Follow-Up of
Initial Subsyndromal Individuals

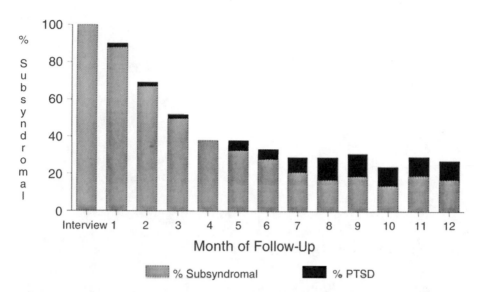

Figure 7.4. Month-by-month remission data for survivors initially diagnosed with subsyndromal PTSD.

down from the 12-month CAPS interview was 3 (7.1%) with full PTSD, 9 (21.4%) still with subsyndromal PTSD, and 30 (71.4%) non-PTSD.

18-Month Follow-Up on Initial PTSDs

As noted earlier, we followed up 35 of those with initial PTSD (73% of those available at 12 months, but only 56.5% of the initial sample) with interviews at 18 months. The results for this longer follow-up are shown in Figure 7.5. We continue to see in the figure our plateau effect: From the 12-month point to the 18-month CAPS, the proportion of the sample who remain with full PTSD ranges from 34.3% (months 17 and 18) to 40% (months 14 and 15).

Altogether it is apparent that a majority of MVA survivors who initially develop PTSD remit over the first six to eight months (our assessment took place at approximately two months post-MVA) following the trauma. Thereafter there continues to be a gradual remission rate, with a 12-month remission rate of about 60%. Kessler et al. (1995) noted continued gradual improvement as far as six years posttrauma in their retrospective study of a large sample of mixed trauma victims with PTSD.

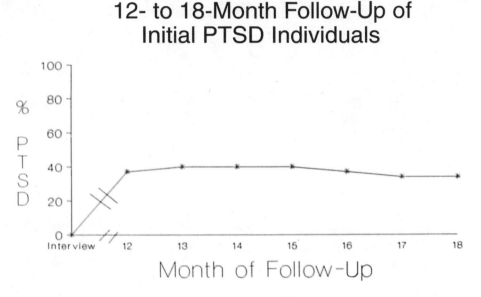

12- to 18-Month Follow-Up of Initial PTSD Individuals

Figure 7.5. Long-term follow-up data for initial PTSDs.

The relatively high rate of remission over the first six months, combined with the data in Table 7.8 showing no appreciable beneficial effect of early treatment, have led us to focus our treatment efforts on individuals who remain distressed six months or longer after the MVA (see chapter 17 for details).

We interpret, with considerable caution, the finding that, on a group basis, receiving mental health treatment over the first six months after an MVA is not beneficial or perhaps irrelevant in comparison to no treatment. The high remission rate would necessitate an extremely large treatment effect to show a statistically significant effect. There may have been a treatment effect in the first six months that we could not detect in our data.

As the rate of spontaneous remission appears to slow after the first six months (as the next section demonstrates), it may be easier to show a treatment effect in periods after the first six months.

Prediction of Remission by 12 Months

We repeated our analysis of variables that might predict remission by 12 months. We restrict this discussion to the prediction of remission of initial PTSDs only, again focusing on logistical regression to predict the dichotomous outcome of meeting criteria for PTSD or not and on multiple regression to predict the continuous variable of 12 months CAPS score.

We cast an even wider net for potential predictors, examining the simple correlation of 101 potential predictors. To control for random relations, we restricted the final potential predictor battery to variables that accounted for 4% or more of the variance in one of the two criteria ($r = 0.20$). In addition, for the multiple regression analysis, we specified that each new variable entered must account for at least 3% of new variance. The final predictor battery is presented in Table 7.10.

As is obvious, a wide array of variables have significant bivariate relations, with one of the two criteria; in fact, 45 variables met the initial screening criteria. There is clear redundancy among the variables; this was planned in an effort to find the best overall prediction equations.

Logistical Regression to Predict 12-Month Diagnostic States

Table 7.11 presents the results of the logistical regression. One can see that base rates would correctly classify 66.7% of the sample if one said everyone had remitted. Using three variables, the overall accuracy improves to 79.2% and the correct classification of those who still meet criteria for full PTSD improves from 0% with base rates to 62.5% correctly classified. Interestingly, all three variables came from the initial assessment: the foreshortened future symptom from Criterion C for PTSD, the irritability symptom from Criterion D for PTSD, and the degree of vulnerability the participant felt when in an automobile (as driver or passenger) at the time of the initial assessment. The physical injury variables, which played a large role in the six-month predictor analysis, were absent in this analysis.

Again, the reader is referred back to the section of this chapter that explains in detail how to use the coefficients from the logistical regression.

Multiple Regression to Predict 12-Month CAPS Scores

The results of the multiple regression analysis to predict 12-month CAPS score are summarized in Table 7.12. Four variables emerged from this analysis as significant predictors. Two are related to initial CAPS score, which was a strong predictor of the six-months CAPS score: the sum of the initial CAPS scores for the hyperarousal (Criterion D) symptoms and the sum of the initial CAPS scores for the avoidance symptoms of Criterion C. Two other variables from the overall assessment enter the final equation: the presence of any Axis II disorder and the presence of an alcohol abuse diagnosis at the initial assessment. This latter variable was also a predictor of six-months CAPS score for initial PTSDs.

Thus, we continue to find that the initial level of PTSD symptom severity predicts both later symptom severity and overall remission. The alcohol abuse and Axis II diagnosis may serve as moderator variables: The presence of either of these indicates long-standing overall difficulty in functioning and thus are associated with continued symptoms.

TABLE 7.10

Predictor Battery to Predict 12-Month Follow-Up Status of MVA Survivors Initially Diagnosed as PTSD

	Initial PTSDs	
Predictor	Diagnosis at 1 year 0 = sub or non 1 = PTSD	12 month CAPS scores
Physical effects of MVA		
Abbreviated Injury Scale		.22
Loss of consciousness	.25	
Physical injury quotient		
Month 10	.24	.20
Month 12	−.23	.25
Month 11	.21	
Subjective reactions to MVA		
Degree of responsibility	−.28	−.38
Fear of death at time of MVA	.30	.21
Degree of control participant had		−.23
Estimate of how life-threatening MVA was	.36	
Subjective reactions to MVA (at time of assessment)		
Current vulnerability in vehicle	.27	.39
Present total functioning as % of pre-MVA functioning		.26
Psychopathology (pre-MVA)		
Past alcohol abuse		.26
Past major depression	−.37	−.20
Any pre-MVA Axis II disorder	.34	.33
Psychopathology (at time of initial assessment)		
Initial CAPS	.31	.56
Major depression: current		.26
Alcohol abuse: current	.21	.56
Psychosocial effects of MVA		
Post-MVA family relations		.21
Post-MVA friend relations: Month 3	−.23	
Pre-MVA friend relations	−.23	

Post-MVA factors		
Received psychological treatment and/or drug treatment over 1 year post-MVA	.24	.23
New MVA (participant)		-.23
New trauma (family member)		.29
Involved in litigation at 1 year	.30	
Initial CAPS scores		
Symptom #1		.20
Symptom #2		.29
Symptom #3		.31
Symptom #4		.25
Symptom #5		.27
Symptom #6	.22	.39
Symptom #7		.24
Symptom #10	.26	.42
Symptom #11	.40	.40
Symptom #12	.31	.40
Symptom #13	.41	.33
Symptom #14	.31	.42
Symptom #15		.22
Symptom #17		.20
Numbing cluster (*DSM–III–R*)	.24	.38
Avoidance cluster (*DSM–III–R*)	.23	.45
Avoidance/numbing (*DSM–IV*)	.30	.50
Reexperiencing (*DSM–III–R*)		.33
Reexperiencing (*DSM–IV*)		.36
Hyperarousal (*DSM–III–R*)	.38	.52
Hyperarousal (*DSM–IV*)	.39	.51

TABLE 7.11
Logistical Regression to Predict One-Year Clinical Status Among Initial PTSDs

Predictor	B	S.E.	Wald	df	Significance	% Correctly Identified		
						PTSD	Less than PTSD	Overall
Base rate	—	—	—	—	—	0	100	66.7
Initial CAPS-13, Irritability	.5251	.1944	7.294	1	.0069	50.0	78.1	68.8
Initial CAPS foreshortened future	.4723	.1889	6.254	1	.0124	56.3	90.6	79.2
Vulnerability in automobile at initial assessment	.0379	.0186	4.141	1	.0419	62.5	87.5	79.2
Constant	−6.6571	2.0234	10.824	1	.0010			

Note. From Table 4, "One-Year Prospective Follow-Up of Motor Vehicle Accident Victims," by E. B. Blanchard et al., 1996, *Behaviour Research and Therapy, 34*, pp. 775–786. Copyright 1996 by Elsevier Science Ltd. Adapted with permission.

TABLE 7.12
Summary of Final Multiple Regression to Predict Posttraumatic Stress Symptoms at One Year in Initial PTSDs

Variable	B	beta	t	p	Multiple R	R^2	Change in R^2	Significance of F for change
Alcohol abuse at time of initial assessment	85.53	.476	4.97	.000	.563	.317	—	—
Sum of initial CAPS hyperarousal symptoms	1.06	.347	3.62	.0008	.712	.506	.189	.0001
Pre-MVA Axis II disorder	18.07	.275	2.91	.0056	.770	.593	.087	.0039
Sum of initial CAPS avoidance symptoms	1.12	.223	2.29	.0268	.798	.637	.044	.0268
Constant	−11.64		−1.51	.1394				

Note. From Table 5, "One-Year Prospective Follow-Up of Motor Vehicle Accident Victims," by E. B. Blanchard et al., 1996, *Behaviour Research and Therapy, 34*, pp. 775–786. Copyright 1996 by Elsevier Science Ltd. Adapted with permission.

Clinical Hint

It seems clear that initial severity of PTSD symptoms is a major pre-dictor of short-term and longer term remission. More severely symptomatic individuals are more likely to continue to be symptomatic over time. Severity of physical injury and relative degree of healing play a role in short-term recovery but are not influential in the longer term. Finally, indications of chronic psychological problems before the MVA are associated with poorer recovery.

Another point that seems clear to us is that individuals who have not improved on their own by six to eight months after an MVA are relatively unlikely to remit spontaneously with further passage of time. Thus, although 50% of those with initial PTSD will remit within six months, only about 25% of those who still have PTSD at six to eight months post-MVA will remit over the next six months. Moreover, for those with PTSD at a year after the MVA, less than 10% will remit over the next six months.

MVA survivors who still meet the criteria for PTSD six months or more after the MVA should clearly be given focused specific treatment—a topic for the sections of this book.

Long-Term Psychosocial Effects of Motor Vehicle Accidents

In chapter 5 we documented the initial psychosocial impact MVAs can have on individuals, showing that those who met the criteria for PTSD had more subjective distress and were more role-impaired than MVA survi-vors who did not meet the full PTSD criteria. In this section we present the data on these same variables from the 12-month follow-up assessment. We have restricted this to those with initial PTSD because the others were not especially impaired. We have also subdivided the initial PTSD group into those who have remitted entirely or in part (12-month classification of non-PTSD or subsyndromal PTSD) and those who continue to meet the full criteria for PTSD at 12 months.

Table 7.13 summarizes the indicators of subjective distress, our psycho-logical test scores, whereas Table 7.14 summarizes the indicators of role impairment. All were subjected to a two-way repeated-measures MANOVA followed up with univariate ANOVAs on each variable.

From Table 7.13 one can see that on each measure those initial PTSDs who remit were less distressed than those initial PTSDs who do not remit within the 12 months (all ps .002 or better). On IES, both subgroups of initial PTSDs show a decline in IES score over the 12 months (p = .002). There is an interesting pattern of results on trait anxiety: Those who do not remit show an increase over time whereas those who do remit show a slight decrease. For the Beck Depression Inventory (BDI; Beck et al., 1961)

TABLE 7.13
Psychological Test Scores for Participants With Initial PTSD Based on 12-Month Clinical Status

Measure	12-month diagnosis	Initial assessment $\bar{x}$	SD	12 month assessment $\bar{x}$	SD	Effects Group F	p	Time F	p	Group × time F	p	Within group t	p
Beck Depression Inventory	PTSD ($n = 16$)	20.6	(11.4)	20.3	(10.5)	12.71	.001	1.34	.253	.89	ns	.10	ns
	Sub + non ($n = 32$)	13.1	(2.2)	9.9	(7.2)							2.21	.034
Impact of Event	PTSD	41.7	(14.2)	39.5	(17.4)	17.00	<.001	18.77	<.001	11.15	.002	.65	ns
	Sub + non	31.6	(16.2)	14.6	(9.7)							6.38	<.001
State–Anxiety	PTSD	75.0	(18.3)	77.1	(16.0)	19.4	<.001	0.80	ns	2.63	.112	-.44	ns
	Sub + non	59.7	(18.6)	52.5	(18.8)							2.12	.042
Trait–Anxiety	PTSD	64.4	(18.6)	76.3	(16.3)	11.41	.002	5.09	.029	12.46	.001	-3.89	.002
	Sub + non	57.7	(9.1)	55.1	(12.5)							1.06	ns
Global Assessment Scale	PTSD	57.0	(8.9)	56.8	(11.6)	4.98	.031	10.20	.003	10.81	.002	.064	ns
	Sub + non	57.2	(12.3)	70.2	(12.9)							5.31	.001

TABLE 7.14
Ratings of Role Performance Variables for Participants With Initial PTSD Based on 12-Month Clinical Status

Measure	12-month diagnosis	Initial assessment χ	SD	12 month assessment χ	SD	Effects Group F	p	Time F	p	Group × time F	p	Within group t	p
Major role function[a] (work, school, homemaking)	PTSD	3.4	(1.2)	2.8	(1.7)	2.77	.103	7.05	.011	.26	ns	1.62	ns
	Sub + non	2.9	(1.6)	2.0	(0.8)							2.65	.013
Relations with family[b] (average of all first-degree relatives plus spouse/partner)	PTSD	2.3	(.8)	2.5	(.7)	.50	ns	.14	ns	2.90	.096	-1.71	.11
	Sub + non	2.3	(1.0)	2.1	(.6)							1.07	ns
Relations with friends	PTSD	2.1	(1.3)	2.7	(1.4)	.40	ns	.24	ns	3.66	.062	1.13	ns
	Sub + non	2.4	(1.6)	2.0	(1.1)							1.51	ns
Recreation participation	PTSD	3.9	(0.8)	3.3	(1.2)	8.33	.006	10.6	.002	.06	ns	2.03	.06
	Sub + non	3.0	(1.9)	2.3	(1.3)							3.06	.005

[a]1 = no impairment, high level of performance; 3 = mild impairment; 5 = severe impairment. [b]1 = very good, very close emotional relationship; 3 = fair, believes relationship needs to be closer; 5 = very poor, no emotional closeness, avoids family member.

those who do not remit show no decrease in depressive symptoms whereas those who remit show a slight decline. In all instances, those with initial PTSD who do not remit over the year were noticeably more psychologically distressed from the initial assessment until the follow-up point.

In Table 7.14 the results show improvement over the year in performance of major role function ($p = .011$) and in participation in recreation ($p = .002$) for both subgroups. For both of these variables, the two subgroups are about one half to one whole scale unit apart (difference between satisfactory performance with no impairment [remitters] and somewhat impaired performance [nonremitters]).

Relationships with friends deteriorate for those who continue to meet the criteria for PTSD while improving slightly for the remitters. It could be that the feelings of estrangement in those with PTSD become reality as these individuals withdraw over time from friends and social activities. Relationships with close family members remain stable at a generally good level.

Total CAPS scores for these two subgroups of PTSDs are revealing: For those who do not remit the initial and 12-month CAPS scores are 69.2 and 55.6, respectively. Although the nonremitters continue to show a relatively high CAPS score, the decline is significant ($p = .008$). For the remitters, there is a dramatic and highly significant decrease in total CAPS scores, from 55.0 to 15.7 ($p < .0001$).

The subgroup who has not remitted continues to be a symptomatic, distressed, and impaired set of individuals who clearly are in need of psychological treatment.

EFFECTS ON TRAVEL BEHAVIOR

Our last point in this chapter on follow-up is to examine travel behaviors. In chapter 5 (Table 5.18) we noted a large initial effect of the MVA on travel behavior, especially for those MVA survivors who were initially diagnosed with PTSD. Table 7.15 presents a summary of these effects for those initially diagnosed with PTSD who were reassessed at 12 months.

Of the nine initial PTSDs who met our criteria for driving phobia, eight were followed up at 12 months. The two whose PTSD had not remitted were still not driving, whereas all of the remitters had returned to driving. As Table 7.15 shows, there was still some travel reluctance in a sizable minority (40.6%) of those initial PTSDs who had remitted. For those who still met full criteria for PTSD, there had been a slight, nonsignificant decrease in the frequency of those showing any travel reluctance. Again, it is clear that there is a substantial subset of MVA survivors greatly in need of psychological help, even a year after their accidents.

TABLE 7.15
Travel Behavior Effects at One-Year Follow-Up for MVA Survivors Initially Diagnosed With PTSD

12-month diagnosis	Driving phobia		Within group *p*
	Initial	12-month	
PTSD (*n* = 16)	2 (12.5%)	2 (12.5%)	ns
Remitted (*n* = 32)	6 (18.8%)	0	.0313
	Any travel reluctance		
PTSD	14 (87.5%)	11 (68.8%)	ns
Remitted	29 (90.6%)	13 (40.6%)	< .001

LONGER TERM FOLLOW-UP BY MAIL

In chapter 4 we described our final follow-up, a mail survey using the PTSD Checklist (PCL; Weathers et al., 1993). A set of questionnaires, including the PCL, IES, BDI, and STAI (State–Trait Anxiety Inventory; Spielberger et al., 1970), and a set of questions about new MVAs and other new personal traumas and about mental health treatment for symptoms related to the original MVA, were mailed to all participants, including those who had dropped out at the 6-month or 12-month follow-up point. For individuals who did not respond to the first mailing, and for whom the envelope was not returned by the postal service as "addressee unknown," a second mail request was sent. Included in the request for answers was an offer of $5 for returning the completed questionnaires in the stamped return envelope.

We received 100 replies, of which 98 were complete, for an overall return rate of 62% (of the 158 original MVA survivors). These 98 represented 75% of those available at the 12-month follow-up. Thus, any conclusions have to be tempered with knowledge that there may be a bias as a result of nonresponders. (The return rate is comparable to that which is noted in Table 7.2 for other follow-ups of greater than 12 months.) The results represent the status of these MVA survivors 18 to 30 months after their initial assessment or almost two years postaccident.

Diagnoses were made based on responses to the PCL, using both the locally derived total PCL score of 44 or greater and also an inspection of individual symptom scores to see if the required pattern of symptoms for *DSM–III–R* was met. Table 7.16 presents the overall diagnostic results.

We can see from the table that we were able to collect data on 72.5% of the initial non-PTSDs, 60.0% of the initial subsyndromal PTSDs, but only 54.8% of those originally diagnosed as PTSD. These findings mirror the results in Table 4.5 that showed relatively poorer retention among those with an initial diagnosis of PTSD, beginning at the six-month follow-up.

TABLE 7.16
Results of Mail Survey of MVA Survivors

Initial diagnosis (CAPS)	Follow-up diagnosis (PCL)	Frequency	Average interval from initial diagnosis to follow-up months	Average follow-up PCL score	Average follow-up IES score	Average follow-up BDI score
PTSD	PTSD	6	26.0 (3.1)	62.0 (15.4)	42.8 (22.4)	36.0 (13.7)
	Sub-PTSD	2	28.4 (4.6)	35.0 (5.7)	46.0 (33.9)	4.0 (0.0)
	Non-PTSD	26	27.7 (6.2)	25.2 (7.7)	7.3 (7.8)	7.2 (6.9)
Sub-PTSD	Sub-PTSD	4	24.4 (1.9)	38.3 (6.3)	24.0 (6.5)	12.3 (9.0)
	Non-PTSD	23	25.4 (7.7)	19.8 (4.3)	4.2 (7.2)	4.6 (6.2)
Non-PTSD	Sub-PTSD	2	18.9 (0.2)	39.0 (2.8)	30.0 (21.2)	7.0 (4.2)
	Non-PTSD	35	26.8 (6.0)	20.1 (5.8)	4.5 (8.6)	4.5 (5.0)

Note. BDI = Beck Depression Inventory; CAPS = Clinical Administered PTSD Scale; IES = Impact of Event Scale; PCL = PTSD Checklist.

TABLE 7.17
Other Results of Mail Survey of MVA Survivors

Initial diagnosis	Follow-up diagnosis	Frequency	Frequency of new MVAs in follow-up interval	Frequency of new family member MVA in follow-up	Frequency of new other trauma in follow-up	Frequency of receiving mental health services in follow-up
PTSD	PTSD	6	2	1	3	3
	Sub-PTSD	2	1	0	2	1
	Non-PTSD	26	4	6	11	16
Total for initial PTSD		34	7	7	16	20
Sub-PTSD	Sub-PTSD	4	0	1	0	3
	Non-PTSD	23	1	7	6	11
Total for initial sub-PTSD		27	1	8	6	14
Non-PTSD	Sub-PTSD	2	1	0	1	0
	Non-PTSD	35	7	6	18	12
Total for initial non-PTSD		37	8	6	19	12
	Total sample	98	16	21	41	46

Of those originally diagnosed with PTSD, eight (23.5%) are still notice-ably symptomatic over two years after their MVA, with an average PCL score of 55. The other psychological tests reflect the subjective distress these individuals still acknowledge. Other information from this longer term follow-up, including data on new MVAs, are summarized in Table 7.17.

Table 7.17 shows that seven individuals had had new MVAs since their last contact with us, an interval ranging from 6 to 24 months (average interval since index MVA was 26.4 months), whereas in nine other cases, a close family member had had an MVA. This finding echoes Norris's (1992) conclusion about the high rate of MVAs one finds in the American population.

Looking especially at those initially diagnosed with PTSD, we find only two have had new MVAs and 14 acknowledged other new trauma. Twelve of the 34 initial PTSDs have had some form of mental health treatment during the follow-up interval, including half ($n = 3$) of those who still meet criteria for full PTSD.

Fortunately, many of the most seriously affected MVA survivors, those initially diagnosed with PTSD, remit over the first six to eight months after the MVA, and by one year at least 60% have remitted. Beyond that point, our prospective data tend to agree with the large-scale retrospective results of Kessler et al. (1995)—there are a sizable proportion of PTSDs from MVAs who have a very chronic course.

8

DELAYED-ONSET PTSD

It is well-recognized that some individuals do not develop posttraumatic stress disorder (PTSD) immediately following the trauma; instead, for reasons that are not clear at this time, the onset of the full PTSD syndrome is delayed for some period of time. The *DSM–IV* (American Psychiatric Association, 1994) recognizes this phenomenon officially and classifies PTSD with delayed onset as a subcategory of PTSD for which there is a delay of at least six months between the trauma and the individual's meeting the full diagnostic criteria. There is a limited literature on this phenomenon among motor vehicle accident (MVA) survivors. This is in part probably because the best way to identify these cases is through conducting a prospective follow-up of traumatized individuals to detect the onset of the delayed cases.

Table 8.1 summarizes the studies that have addressed in one way or another the topic of delayed-onset PTSD. In only two of these studies, our own (Buckley, Blanchard, & Hickling, 1996) and that of Bryant and Harvey (2002), are the technical criteria for delayed-onset PTSD met (meeting the full criteria for PTSD six months or longer after the trauma). In all of the other studies delayed-onset PTSD is defined as not meeting the criteria for PTSD at various short intervals after the trauma (two weeks—Schnyder et al., 2001; one month—Green et al., 1993; Ursano et al., 1999a; three months—Mayou et al., 1993; Ehlers et al., 1998; four months—Freedman et al., 1999) but being positive at a later time, typically 12 to 18 months post-MVA.

TABLE 8.1
Summary of Research on Delayed-Onset PTSD Among MVA Survivors

Study and country of origin	Sample	When assessed (post-MVA)	Number of individuals with delayed-onset PTSD at 1 year or longer	% total sample with delayed-onset PTSD	% PTSD cases at 1 year + those who have delayed-onset	% sub-PTSD who develop delayed-onset PTSD	Risk factors for delayed-onset PTSD
Green et al. (1993) Australia	24 Hospitalized patients	1 week, 1 month, 18 months	5 at 18 months who were negative at 1 month	5/24 = 20.8%	5/6 = 83%	5/7 = 71.4%	Sub-PTSD at 1 month, high IES scores at 1 month, more depressed at 1 month
Mayou et al. (1993) United Kingdom	188 ER attendees 126 hospitalized	10 days, 3 months, 12 months	6 at 12 months who were negative at 3 months	6/171 = 3.5%	6/19 = 32%	N/R	N/R
Epstein (1993) United States	15 seriously injured (on trauma unit)	Few days, then every 10 weeks	2 at 9 months who were negative at 10 weeks	2/15 = 13.3%	2/6 = 33%	N/R	High IES avoidance scores initially
Buckley et al. (1996) United States	158 who sought medical attention (75% seen in ER)	1–4 months (X = 2 months), 8 months, 14 months	7 at 14 months who were negative at 6 months	7/132 = 5.3%	4/20 = 20%	7/43 = 16.3%	(see text)
Ehlers et al. (1998) United Kingdom	967 ER attendees (26% admitted)	8 days, 3 months, 12 months	34 at 12 months who were negative at 3 months	34/781 = 4.4%	34/129 = 26%	N/R	N/R
Freedman, Shalev, et al. (1999) Israel	62 (of 236) ER attendees (86% MVA)	1 week, 1 month, 4 months, 12 months	2 at 12 months who were negative at 4 months	2/62 = 3.2%	2/12 = 17%	Both cases had sub-PTSD	Sub-PTSD?

Study/Country	Sample	Assessment times	Delayed-onset cases				Predictors
Ursano et al. (1999a) United States	122 hospitalized patients	2–3 weeks, 1 month, 3 months, 9 months, 12 months	2(?) at 12 months who were negative at 1 month	2/86 = 2.3%	2/12 = 17%	N/R	N/R
Dougall, Ursano, et al. (2001) United States	115/122 from Ursano et al.	2–3 weeks, 1 month, 6 months, 12 months	3 (PTSD/sub) at 12 months who were negative at 6 months	3/75 = 4.0%	3/28 = 10.7%	N/R	N/R
Schnyder et al. (2001) Switzerland	121 hospitalized on ICU, 60.4% MVA (exclude pretrauma psychological diagnoses)	13 days, 12 months	2 at 1 year who were negative at 13 days	2/106 = 1.9%	2/2 = 100%	2/22 = 9.1%	N/R
Bryant & Harvey (2002) Australia	170 hospitalized patients	Within 1 month, 6 months, 2 years	5 at 2 years who were negative at 6 months	5/103 = 4.9%	5/28 = 17.8%	2/5 = 40%	High IES intrusion score, high heart rate at discharge, being female

Note. IES = Impact of Event Scale; N/R = not reported.

Examining the various percentages, one finds that from about 2 percent to 21 percent of the various total samples meet the varying criteria for delayed-onset PTSD. Our best estimate of the "true" value based on the studies of Buckley et al. (1996), Bryant and Harvey (2002) because of their methodology, and on Ehlers et al. (1998) because of its size is 4.4% to 4.9%.

Of those who meet criteria for PTSD one year or longer after the accident, we find from 17% to 100% had delayed-onset PTSD. Again, relying on the methodologically strongest studies (Buckley et al. (1996); Bryant & Harvey (2002); and Ehlers et al. (1998)) we find from 18% to 26% of those with chronic PTSD one year after the crash had a delayed onset.

Risk factors for delayed-onset PTSD include (a) being symptomatic enough to meet the criteria for subsyndromal PTSD in the month immediately after the MVA; (b) high Impact of Event Scale (IES; Horowitz et al., 1979) scores, especially high intrusion scores, at the initial assessment; (c) having an elevated heart rate at discharge from the hospital; and (d) being female.

Green et al. (1993), in their study of 24 Australian MVA survivors who were hospitalized because of injuries, found only one case of PTSD at the one-month follow-up point. At the 18-month follow-up they found five more cases. All five delayed onset cases had shown a subsyndromal form of PTSD (part of the total symptom complex but not enough symptoms to meet the full criteria) at the one-month assessment. Another factor that identified those who would eventually show an onset of PTSD were high scores on the IES at the one-month follow-up.

Mayou et al. (1993), in their prospective follow-up of British MVA survivors admitted to the ER found 14 cases of PTSD among 174 participants assessed at a three-month follow-up. At the 12-month follow-up, five of those cases of PTSD had remitted; more important for this chapter, there were six new cases of PTSD, representing 3.4% of the total sample. Thus, these six cases are examples of delayed-onset PTSD. No explicit information was provided on these cases.

In later five-year follow-ups on this sample, Mayou et al. (1997) identified nine cases of PTSD at the five-year point. Only one individual had had PTSD for the entire five years. The other eight cases were not positive for PTSD at the one-year follow-up interview but were at five years. They thus represent true cases of delayed-onset PTSD. No other information is provided on these individuals.

In Epstein's (1993) prospective follow-up of 15 seriously injured (admitted to shock-trauma center) MVA survivors it was noted that two of his six eventual cases of PTSD were not diagnosed until three to six months after the MVA. In both of these cases, the individuals had relatively high scores on the Avoidance subscale of the IES. Epstein noted that both patients initially denied reexperiencing symptoms. During the frequent follow-ups (interviews every 9 to 10 weeks), the intrusive memories finally emerged, leading to diagnoses of delayed-onset PTSD. Epstein (1993) stated that high initial levels of avoidance symptoms can interfere in the diagnosis, and he recommended frequent reassessments for seriously injured MVA survivors so that reexperiencing symptoms that may be masked by high levels of avoidance can be detected.

Bryant (1996) reported on two cases of seriously injured MVA survivors who had each suffered significant head injury and who eventually developed delayed-onset PTSD. In the first case, the individual suffered five weeks of posttraumatic amnesia (PTA). Approximately 10 months after the accident, the individual had begun lessons to learn to drive again. A near miss while he was a passenger triggered a prolonged (two-hour) dissociative episode. Over the next few days he acknowledged various reexperiencing symptoms, based on pictures he had seen of his accident and accounts he had heard of it. Although he had no direct memory of the accident, he clearly developed PTSD.

The second individual had a three-week period of PTA secondary to his head injury, an extensive subdural hematoma. Seventeen months after the MVA, a police report was released indicating that another person, who was killed in the crash, had probably been the driver instead of the patient. It is not clear whether accounts of the MVA he had been told led to his extreme reexperiencing and hyperarousal symptoms. In any event, he clearly met the criteria for delayed PTSD at this point.

Bryant's (1996) findings contradict the prevailing clinical wisdom (Middleboe, Andersen, Birket-Smith, & Friis, 1992) that head-injured patients who suffer from PTA do not develop PTSD because of the absence of memory for the traumatic event. We would agree that vicarious experience of the accident from photographs and accounts the MVA survivor is given can be a sufficient basis for developing PTSD. In fact, DSM–IV (American Psychiatric Association, 1994) allows for vicarious traumatization to serve as the stressor. We have observed this in two cases. However, this "vicarious traumatization" is based on accounts and pictures that occurred before the initial assessment (one to four months post-MVA) in our cases.

In their large prospective follow-up of MVA survivors who were emergency room attendees in Oxford, Ehlers et al. (1998) identified, using Foa et al's (1993) Posttraumatic Stress Scale (PSS Scale) plus questions on disability, 34 individuals, out of 781, who did not meet criteria for PTSD at three months post-MVA but did meet them at the 12-month assessment. These delayed-onset cases constituted 26% of the total 129 cases of PTSD identified at 12 months.

The only variable from the initial assessment of Ehlers et al. (1998) that predicted the delayed-onset cases was initial injury severity ($r = .17$). At the three-month assessment, there were several predictors of who was negative for PTSD at three months but positive at one year. These included persistent medical problems ($r = .17$), persistent financial problems

($r = .17$), the presence of anger ($r = .18$), and the presence of rumination about the MVA ($r = .17$). A multivariate analysis identified four independent predictors of delayed-onset PTSD: injury severity, rumination at three months, anger at three months, and pre-MVA emotional problems.

Freedman et al. (1999) reported on a 12-month follow-up on part (62 of original 236) of Shalev's Israeli sample (Shalev et al., 1998) of emergency room attendees (86% were from MVAs). They found, using the SCID PTSD module, two cases of PTSD at 12 months who had not met full criteria at a four-month post-MVA reassessment. Both had been subsyndromal PTSD at four months.

Ursano et al. (1999a) were able to follow-up 86 of 122 MVA survivors admitted to a trauma unit in the United States. They found two cases of PTSD at 12 months who had not been positive at one-month post-MVA. In another report on this sample Dougall et al. (2001) reported on 75 of the cases who were reassessed at 12 months. They took an unusual approach of combining the full PTSD and subsyndromal PTSD categories. Using their combined symptomatic group, they found five new cases (of 86) at six months who had been negative at one month. More important, they identified three cases (out of 75 assessed, 4.0%) who met their symptom criteria at 12 months who had been negative at six months. These three new cases represented 10.7% of their 12-month symptomatic sample.

Schnyder et al. (2001) followed up 106 of 121 severely injured Swiss accident victims (all had been admitted to the intensive care unit); 60.4% were victims of MVAs. They found two cases of PTSD at 12 months, both of whom had had subsyndromal PTSD at the initial assessment an average of 13 days postadmission. They constituted only 9% of the 22 cases with initial subsyndromal PTSD and yielded the lowest rate of delayed-onset PTSD at one year (1.9%) that we found.

In one of the best and most informative studies of delayed-onset PTSD, Bryant and Harvey (2002) reanalyzed the data from their two-year prospective follow-up of 170 Australian MVA survivors admitted to the hospital. At their two-year follow-up assessment, using the PTSD module from the Composite International Diagnostic Inventory (CIDI; Peters et al., 1996) on 106 cases, they found five individuals with delayed-onset PTSD who had not been positive at a six-month assessment. They compared three subgroups of their 106 cases, those who had been negative for PTSD at six months and two years ($n = 75$), those who had been positive for PTSD at six months and two years ($n = 23$), and the five delayed-onset cases.

At the initial assessment, those who developed delayed-onset PTSD had higher IES intrusion scores and a higher resting heart rate at hospital discharge (83 bpm versus 74.3 bpm) than those who never met criteria for PTSD. At the six-month assessment, even though they were still not positive for PTSD, the eventual delayed-onset subsample had higher Beck Depression

Inventory (BDI; Beck et al., 1961) scores, IES intrusion scores, and state anxiety scores than those who never developed PTSD. Their scores on these measures were lower than those individuals who met criteria for full PTSD at this six-month assessment.

Two other differences emerged: Those with delayed-onset PTSD were more likely to be female (100%) than those who developed PTSD acutely and more likely to meet criteria for subsyndromal PTSD (40%) at six months than those who never met criteria for PTSD (4%). Those who had met criteria for full PTSD at both assessments were more likely than the delayed-onset cases to have received treatment (70% for PTSD versus 20% for delayed-onset cases at two years).

Briggs (1993) presented a case report of a 46-year-old male who was severely injured in an MVA but, aside from distressing dreams while in the hospital, had made a full physical and psychological recovery. About 18 months later, immediately following extensive media coverage of a multi-injury and fatality train crash, he developed symptoms of major depression (which was treated with antidepressants) and probably PTSD. Subsequent treatment with the antidepressant and six months of psychotherapy revealed symptoms of full PTSD that were successfully treated.

There are no data on delayed-onset PTSD in the large-scale epidemiological surveys (NCS–Kessler et al., 1995; Norris, 1992).

THE ALBANY MVA PROJECT

Because of the use of the LIFE-type (Keller et al., 1987) interviews focusing on the 17 specific symptoms of PTSD at each of the follow-up interviews (6-month, 12-month), it became possible to track all 17 symptoms on a week-by-week basis. From this analysis, we identified seven individuals who met the criteria for delayed-onset PTSD (4.4% of the original sample, and 7.3% of MVA survivors who were initially negative for full PTSD). A detailed report of these findings can be found in Buckley et al. (1996). We should note that these seven participants continue to meet the criteria for PTSD if DSM–IV criteria are applied or if the scoring for CAPS items is shifted from our rule of 3 to the more stringent rule of 4. There was one other case in which onset of full PTSD occurred after our initial assessment but the total interval between trauma and onset was only four months.

Detailed demographic and other assessment information on these seven MVA survivors is presented in Table 8.2. As can be noted in the table, all seven of these individuals received a diagnosis of subsyndromal PTSD at the initial assessment. Thus, our results are similar to those of Green et al. (1993) in their Australian study and those of Freedman et al. (1999), Schnyder et al. (2001), and Bryant and Harvey (2002), in that those with delayed-onset PTSD are not initially unscathed; instead they are symptomatic, but not symptomatic enough to meet the full criteria for PTSD. The delayed-onset sample is entirely Caucasian, predominantly female (86%) rather than 67% in the initial sample, with an average age of 42.9 years, slightly older than our original sample's 35.4 years. The preponderance of females is similar to Bryant and Harvey's (2002) results.

Clinical Hint

It is of interest that not one MVA survivor classified as non-PTSD developed delayed-onset PTSD. (These individuals did not have any significant reexperiencing symptoms but may have had some avoidance or hyperarousal symptoms; see Table 4.5.) Whether this finding is idiosyncratic to our MVA sample or holds for all trauma victims is unclear. We believe the clinician can be fairly confident that an individual who survives the trauma of an MVA without developing at least the subsyndromal PTSD condition is *extremely* unlikely to develop PTSD at a later date.

In three of the cases there was a proximal (within four weeks of the week in which the individual met full PTSD criteria) traumatic event, but not in the other four. This finding lends support to the utility of the diagnosis of subsyndromal PTSD, in our experience, because 15.6% of the latter individuals deteriorate sufficiently over the course of a year to meet the full criteria for PTSD.

For purposes of categorizing those MVA survivors with delayed-onset PTSD, we compared these with delayed onset to the 38 other individuals initially diagnosed as subsyndromal PTSD who did not deteriorate on three sets of variables, pre-MVA variables, accident-related variables, and follow-up variables. For those variables that were significantly different, we then compared the delayed-onset PTSD cases with the acute onset PTSD cases ($n = 62$).

Delayed-Onset Versus Subsyndromals Who Do Not Deteriorate

We have compared the two groups on three clusters of variables, demographic, pre-MVA variables, and variables related to the accident and its immediate consequences. There were no differences on the demographic variables of gender, age, ethnicity, education status or marital status.

The pre-MVA variable comparison is presented in Table 8.3. This analysis shows that only two variables were significantly different: The subsyndromals who did develop PTSD had significantly *poorer* average relationships with their first-degree relatives. In fact, it was a whole scale unit (on a 1 to 5 scale) worse (see chapter 4, this volume). The overall level of pre-MVA functioning, as measured by the Global Assessment Scale (GAS;

TABLE 8.2
Demographics for the Delayed-Onset PTSD Subgroup

Case number	Age	Gender	Ethnicity	Initial CAPS score	Proximal stressor	Interval from MVA to meeting DSM–III–R criteria for PTSD (days)
123	37	Female	Caucasian	41	Onset of agoraphobia and social phobia, relapse of opioid use	228
175	50	Male	Caucasian	36	No	273
178	41	Female	Caucasian	40	No	347
190	56	Female	Caucasian	25	No	291
209	36	Female	Caucasian	60	No	307
261	42	Female	Caucasian	28	New legal suit filed against participant	288
285	38	Female	Caucasian	41	Loss of medical benefits	251

TABLE 8.3
Pre-MVA Variable Analyses for Delayed-Onset PTSD From MVAs

Variable	Mean or frequency		Statistic	Probability
	Delayed-onset PTSD	Controls[a]		
Pre-MVA relationships with first-degree relatives (social support)	2.9	1.9	$t = 3.12$ (43)	.003
GAS rating	69.7	82.1	$t = 3.09$ (43)	.004
Previous Axis II (no/yes)	5/2	35/3	Fisher's Exact	.166
Previous Axis I (no/yes)	3/4	23/15	Fisher's Exact	.433
Previous trauma (no/yes)	1/6	3/35	Fisher's Exact	.505

Note. From Table 2, "A Prospective Examination of Delayed-Onset PTSD Secondary to Motor Vehicle Accidents," by T. C. Buckley et al., 1996, *Journal of Abnormal Psychology, 105,* pp. 617–625. Copyright 1996 by the American Psychological Association. Adapted with permission.
[a]Initial subsyndromal PTSDs who do not deteriorate.

Endicott et al., 1977), was also lower for the subsyndromals who developed delayed-onset PTSD.

Table 8.4 presents the comparisons on a number of variables assessed at the initial assessment (thus, post-MVA). Four variables from the 11 examined were significantly different: total CAPS score (p = .004), score on PTSD symptom 6 (behavioral avoidance; p = .001), post-MVA family relationships (p = .005), and post-MVA major role functioning (p = .046). Variables of note that were not different were extent of physical injury (Abbreviated Injury Scale [AIS] score; American Association for Automotive Medicine, 1985) and degree of depression as measured by the BDI. The finding of higher avoidance scores is consistent with Epstein's (1993) report. It appears that family relationships did not change appreciably from before to after the accident; thus, it is not surprising that the pre-MVA difference continues. We did not find the higher intrusion symptom scores at the first assessment (IES intrusion or CAPS reexperiencing symptoms) that others have reported are a risk.

The accident clearly had a strong effect on performance of major role functioning because those who develop delayed-onset PTSD are a full scale unit lower (slightly below fair performance with some impairment) than the subsyndromal individuals who do not deteriorate (slightly below satisfactory performance with no impairment).

We also compared the two groups on variables that emerged during the follow-up. After identifying the mean month in which survivors with delayed-onset PTSD met criteria for PTSD (Month 7), we compared their physical injury quotients (PIQ), the variable quantifying relative degree of physical healing, for Month 7 of the two groups. (One should remember that the higher the value of PIQ, the less physical healing has occurred.) The delayed onset group had a significantly (p = .007) higher value (0.57) than the comparison subsyndromal group (0.22), indicating that the delayed-onset group was more physically symptomatic at Month 7. The two groups had not differed on initial AIS scores. It thus appears that the delayed-onset PTSD group was recovering physically at a slower pace.

The mean number of stressful events during the follow-up, defined as new MVAs, new legal issues, and any other events the participant identified as stressful, were compared. Those with delayed-onset PTSD had significantly more of these new stressors than the comparison group (2.9 versus 1.1, p = .002).

Delayed-Onset PTSDs Versus Acute-Onset PTSDs

We compared the seven individuals with delayed-onset PTSD to the 62 MVA survivors with acute-onset PTSD on all of the variables that

TABLE 8.4
Comparison of Variables Related to MVA and Status at Initial Interview for Delayed-Onset PTSD

Variable	Mean or frequency		Statistic	Probability
	Delayed-onset PTSD	Controls[a]		
Symptom 6 CAPS (avoidance)	3.86 (1.95)	1.05 (1.72)	$t = 3.88$ (43)	.001
Initial CAPS (total score)	38.7 (11.4)	28.2 (10.5)	$t = 3.09$ (43)	.004
Post-MVA family relationship	2.9 (1.1)	1.9 (0.7)	$t = 2.98$ (43)	.005
Post-MVA role functioning	3.3 (1.0)	2.2 (1.4)	$t = 2.05$ (43)	.046
Post-MVA GAS rating	59.9 (6.4)	68.4 (12.4)	$t = 1.77$ (43)	.084
Litigation (no/yes)	2/5	25/13	Fisher's Exact	.098
Fear of death in MVA	0.0 (0.00)	14.8 (31.60)	$t = 1.23$ (43)	.225
Driver/passenger	7/0	29/9	Fisher's Exact	.315
BDI	9.0 (5.6)	7.4 (6.6)	$t = .62$ (42)	.538
AIS score	3.71 (2.56)	3.37 (3.16)	$t = .27$ (43)	.786
Current psychopathology (no/yes)	5/2	25/13	Fisher's Exact	1.00

Note. AIS = Abbreviated Injury Scale; BDI = Beck Depression Inventory; CAPS = Clinical Administered PTSD Scale; GAS = Global Assessment Scale. From Table 3, "A Prospective Examination of Delayed-Onset PTSD Secondary to Motor Vehicle Accidents," by T. C. Buckley et al., 1996, *Journal of Abnormal Psychology, 105,* pp. 617–625. Copyright 1996 by the American Psychological Association. Adapted with permission.
[a]Initial subsyndromal PTSD individuals who do not deteriorate.

TABLE 8.5
Acute-Onset PTSD Versus Delayed-Onset PTSD Group Comparisons

Variable	Mean or frequency		Statistic	Probability
	Delayed-onset PTSD	Acute-onset PTSD		
Number of negative life events during follow-up	2.9 (2.0)	1.3 (1.6)	$t = 2.36$ (67)	.021
Pre-MVA family relationships	2.9 (1.1)	2.0 (0.8)	$t = 2.26$ (67)	.027
Pre-MVA GAS Rating	69.7 (12.7)	78.5 (11.19)	$t = -1.94$ (67)	.057
Post-MVA family relationships	2.9 (1.1)	2.3 (0.9)	$t = 1.48$ (67)	.145
Physical injury score (Month 7)	.51 (.30)	.37 (.26)	$t = 1.28$ (53)	.207
Symptom 6 CAPS (avoidance)	3.9 (2.0)	4.1 (2.6)	$t = -.24$ (67)	.814

Note. GAS = Global Assessment Scale. From Table 4, "A Prospective Examination of Delayed-Onset PTSD Secondary to Motor Vehicle Accidents," by T. C. Buckley et al., 1996, *Journal of Abnormal Psychology, 105,* pp. 617–625. Copyright 1996 by the American Psychological Association. Adapted with permission.

reached significance in the earlier comparisons to subsyndromal individuals who do not deteriorate. These comparisons are in Table 8.5.

We found two significant differences: Those with delayed-onset PTSD had more negative life events during the follow-up and they had poorer pre-MVA family relationships. There was also a trend ($p = .057$) for those with delayed-onset PTSD to be functioning less well overall before the MVA.

Clinical Hint

Our clinical impression from these individuals is that MVA survivors who are fairly symptomatic but do not quite meet the full criteria for PTSD are at risk to develop PTSD later, especially if they have relatively poor family relationships (low social support) and if they were functioning somewhat poorly before the MVA. These are the subsyndromal individuals most at risk to deteriorate.

Our other clinical impression, unsupported by our data analyses, is that new trauma, especially related to the MVA (a new MVA or even a relative's having an MVA), are likely to exacerbate new symptoms. Certainly, it is the case that those who develop delayed-onset PTSD report more total life stressors than those with subsyndromal PTSD who do not develop PTSD.

Longer Term Follow-Up

We were able to follow-up five of these individuals at the 18-month point. Two had remitted in part (back to subsyndromal PTSD) and one was essentially symptom-free. Thus, the overall time course for remission in this group is much like that of those with acute PTSD.

It is clear from the world's MVA survivor literature and from our own prospective follow-up data that delayed-onset PTSD is a real, and potentially sizable, problem that could easily be missed if one focused only on the first one to three months after the MVA. It also seems to represent only incremental deterioration—in other words, becoming positive for one additional symptom, rather than the case of someone who appeared psychologically unscathed suddenly developing noticeable symptoms. We do believe those MVA survivors, especially females, with noticeable reexperiencing and hyperarousal symptoms (our subsyndromal PTSD group) should be monitored periodically for possible deterioration to full PTSD.

9

THE ROLE OF PHYSICAL INJURY IN THE DEVELOPMENT AND MAINTENANCE OF PTSD AMONG MVA SURVIVORS

As reference to Table 2.1 will show, most people who are involved in motor vehicle accidents (MVAs) do not suffer notable physical injury; however, slightly more than three million Americans are injured in MVAs each year. For the most part, the MVA survivor populations, which have been studied, were MVA survivors who were physically injured. For example, a commonality among all of the MVA survivors who participated in the Albany studies was that they had sought medical attention as a result of their MVAs. In fact, for our Cohort 1, 94 were seen in the emergency room and released after examination and treatment and 24 more were actually admitted to the hospital for periods ranging from 1 to 90 days. The other 42 participants sought medical attention on their own within two days of their MVA.

If one examines the studies summarized in Tables 3.2 and 3.3, one finds that most of these studies involved a physically injured MVA survivor population. Thus, investigators are implicitly assuming that there is likely to be a connection between physical injury and psychological difficulty, or at least that one is more likely to find psychological problems in MVA survivors with some physical injury. To the best of our knowledge, this reasonable assumption has never been examined empirically.

An examination of the reports listed in Tables 3.2 and 3.3 reveals details on the degree of injury using the Abbreviated Injury Scale (AIS; American Association for Automotive Medicine, 1985) or a variant (Feinstein & Dolan, 1991; Green et al., 1993; Malt, 1988; Mayou et al., 1993). However, none of these report any relationship between degree of injury and posttraumatic stress disorder (PTSD) or extent of posttraumatic stress (PTS) symptoms.

In chapter 6 we reviewed this topic explicitly and summarized the results in Table 6.3. Looking strictly at severity of physical injury as a predictor of PTSD, the weight of evidence is clearly negative, with only three studies (including our own) finding a significant relation; eight different studies explicitly report that they found no significant relationship. However, if one looks at variables clearly related to the extent or severity of injury (such as whether the patient was admitted to the hospital, or the length of hospitalization), then three other studies find a relationship between injury severity and PTSD.

When one examines all six of the positive studies, one thing stands out: In five of the six positive studies the population included a mixture of those admitted to the hospital and those who were not seriously injured enough to warrant admission. For all of the seven studies that explicitly report no relationship, all of the participants were hospitalized. It could be that the absence of relationship in the latter studies is a result of an attenuated range of injury severity among hospitalized samples—that is, they had no cases with very low injury severity scores.

A report from another area, criminal assaults on women, by Kilpatrick et al. (1989), found a clear effect of physical injury on PTS symptoms. Data were collapsed so that extent of physical injury was not graded. Presence of physical injury was a strong independent predictor ($r = 0.34$) of whether the assault survivor developed PTSD or not.

If we move from examining the role of initial injury in the development of PTSD to examining what role continuing physical problems play in the maintenance of PTSD, the number of relevant studies is markedly reduced. Frommberger et al. (1998) found length of hospitalization predicted PTSD prevalence six months post-MVA; likewise, Jeavons (2000) found total days in the hospital predicted presence of PTSD at 12 months but not at 3 months.

By far the most systematic work on this topic comes from the large study by Ehlers et al. (1998) of MVA survivors who sought treatment in an emergency room in Oxford. These authors found that patient acknowledgment of persistent medical problems at three months predicted the diagnosis of PTSD at three months ($r = .31$), and at one year ($r = .31$). This variable also predicted delayed-onset PTSD ($r = .17$). Patient ratings of persistent medical problems at one year also predicted PTSD diagnoses at one year (r = .47).

In a three-year follow-up on 546 (of 888 who completed the initial and three-month assessments [61.5%]) of this sample, Mayou, Ehlers, and Bryant (2002) found 11% still suffering from MVA-related PTSD. Persistent medical problems at three months (r = .40) and at one year (r = .45) were both significant predictors of three-year PTSD diagnosis. It thus seems clear that the persistent physical problems appear to be maintaining the PTSD.

In the remainder of this chapter we examine our own data to address two points that have received little attention in the literature: (a) what is the relationship between extent of initial injury and the development of psychological symptoms, especially PTSD; and (b) what role does physical healing play in the maintenance of, or recovery from, psychological symptoms.

THE ALBANY MVA STUDY: ROLE OF INITIAL INJURY SEVERITY

As we mentioned in chapter 4, the initial physical injuries of our participants were scored using the AIS. This instrument provides scaled ratings from 1 to 6 for the injuries to each extremity, the trunk, and the head. All six ratings are summed for the total AIS score. For example, considering the left lower extremity (leg), a simple fracture of the fibia receives a score of 2, a compound fracture a score of 3, and crushing of the lower leg would warrant a 4.

In a preliminary report (Blanchard et al., 1995), using the data on our first 98 MVA survivors, we found that AIS score was significantly correlated with extent of PTS symptoms as measured by the Clinician-Administered PTSD Scale (CAPS; Blake et al., 1990a; $r[96]$ = .311, p = .017) and with whether the individual developed full PTSD or not ($r[96]$ = .302, p = .017). A multiple regression analysis found that both extent of injury and extent of fear of death at the time of the MVA were independent predictors of PTS symptoms (multiple R^2 = .349, p = .007).

Returning to Table 6.4, one can see that for the entire sample, this relationship continues to be present. The correlation of AIS and PTS symptoms (initial CAPS score) for the entire sample was 0.250, $p < .01$. Similarly, the point biserial correlation of AIS and whether a participant developed PTSD was 0.245, $p < .01$.

Additional confirmation of the importance of extent of physical injury in the development of psychological symptoms comes from the multivariate prediction work summarized in Tables 6.5 and 6.6. In both the logistic regression to predict development of PTSD (Table 6.6) and the multiple regression to predict severity of PTS symptoms (Table 6.5), initial AIS scores enter as significant independent predictors. It seems clear to us that the extent and severity of physical injuries do play a significant role in the development of psychological symptoms; it is likewise clear that extent of physical injury predicts only a portion of the variance in the psychological outcome of an MVA. Thus, there is a connection of physical injury and psychological symptoms at the beginning.

THE ROLE OF INJURY RECOVERY IN PTS SYMPTOMS

The second question is what role physical healing plays in mental recovery (and its converse, what role lack of healing plays in the prolongation of PTS symptoms). At our prospective follow-up interviews we assessed the participants' views of how well they had recovered from each of their physical injuries. For each separate injury they were asked its status and responses were scored on a four point scale: 3 = unchanged; 2 = improved but still causes difficulty (pain, lack of strength or flexibility, etc.); 1 = much improved but participant is still aware of injury with mild symptoms; 0 = completely healed, asymptomatic. Then using the LIFE technique (Keller et al., 1987) we traced the time course of change over the follow-up interval. From this we could generate an injury rating for each separate injury for each month.

Our next data reduction step was to calculate an average Physical Injury Quotient (PIQ) for each month in the following manner: For each separate injury the highest rating for that month is divided by the rating at the time of the initial assessment (this value was typically a 3, but could be a 2 or 1). Then all of these individual PIQs were summed (for one injury, two injuries, or more: such as broken ribs, broken arm, and whiplash injury with pain and reduced range of motion to the neck, shoulders, and upper back) and an average PIQ for the month was calculated. This was repeated for each month. For the participant who had shown essentially no recovery by the first month of follow-up, the PIQ score might be 1.0; by way of contrast, the individual with such injuries who healed quickly and who had had good physical therapy might have a PIQ of 0.11 by the sixth month of follow-up.

To examine the role of physical injury healing in psychological recovery, for those MVA survivors with an initial diagnosis of PTSD, we compared two subgroups, those who had shown partial remission (to subsyndromal PTSD) or full remission (to non-PTSD) by the six-month follow-up point ($n = 31$) and those who continued to meet the full PTSD criteria at six months ($n = 24$). The average PIQ scores for each month of these two subgroups are presented in Table 9.1.

We calculated a two-way repeated-measures MANOVA (subgroup × time). It yields a main effect of time ($p < .001$) and of subgroup ($p = .075$)

TABLE 9.1

Average Physical Injury Quotients for Initial PTSDs on a Month-by-Month
Basis for Those Showing Full or Partial Remission Versus No Remission

Group	Month of follow-up					
	1	2'	3'	4*	5'	6*
PTSD at 6 months	0.797	0.731	0.664	0.634	0.576	0.571
Sub- or non-PTSD at 6 months	0.716	0.587	0.526	0.469	0.435	0.404

Note. Differences are significant at $p < .05$ (*) or $p < .09$ (').

but no significant interaction. Between-group comparisons at each month revealed significant ($p < .05$) difference at Months 4 and 6, with trends ($p < .09$ or better at Months 2, 3 and 5).

Examining the mean PIQ scores in Table 9.1, it is apparent that the individuals who have remitted fully or in part are recovering physically at a more rapid rate. Their PIQ scores drop below 0.5 by Month 3 whereas those who do not improve psychologically are still above 0.5 even by Month 6.

We repeated this analysis on the sample ($n = 47$) available for the 12-month follow-up. The average PIQs for each month for Months 7 to 12 for each subgroup (remitter [$n = 31$] versus nonremitter [$n = 16$] are shown in Table 9.2.

The two-way repeated-measures MANOVA revealed a significant main effect of time ($p = .045$) but no effect of subgroup or interaction. Moreover, none of the between-group comparisons at individual months are significant.

Examining the mean PIQ scores in Table 9.2, it is apparent that our subgroup of individuals who continued to meet the criteria for full PTSD at 12 months had plateaued with regard to remission of injuries. There is slight (3 to 4%) variation month by month but no overall trend. The remitted groups did show a gradual improvement, but even they do not go to zero. It is as if the physical injuries in those who remain PTSD have ceased to improve. To some degree this factor mirrors the data in Figure

TABLE 9.2

Average Physical Injury Quotients for Initial PTSDs on Month-by-Month
Basis for Months 7 Through 12 for Those Showing Full or Partial
Remission Versus No Remission

Group	Month of follow-up					
	7	8	9	10	11	12
PTSD at 12 months	0.387	0.387	0.371	0.387	0.387	0.348
Sub- or non-PTSD at 12 Months	0.355	0.318	0.281	0.272	0.282	0.285

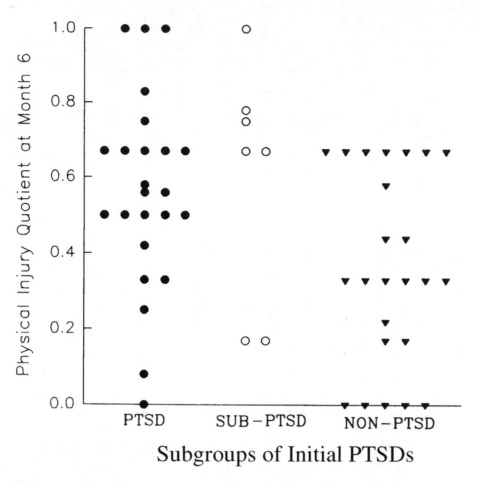

Figure 9.1. PIQ examination results at six months for three survivor subgroups with initial PTSD.

7.3, showing only slight continued psychological remission after six months in the group initially diagnosed with PTSD.

As a final way of examining the relationship, to see how well it held up on an individual case basis, we examined the six-month PIQs for three subgroups of MVA survivors with initial PTSD: those who had not remitted (full PTSD, n = 24), those with partial remission (subsyndromal PTSD, n = 7), and those who had fully remitted (non-PTSD, n = 24). This array is shown in Figure 9.1.

One can see that, although the array of PIQ scores for those who continue to meet the full criteria for PTSD spans the full range of scores, for those initial PTSDs who have remitted the arrays of scores are attenuated and cluster toward the recovery end of the axis (PIQ = 0). The few subsyndromals are scattered across the axis.

We also calculated correlation coefficients between individual six-month PIQs and six-months CAPS scores and change in CAPS scores from initial to six months: Whereas the correlation of six-month CAPS and six-month PIQ was significant ($r[53] = 0.301, p = .025$) the correlation between change in CAPS and PIQ at six months was not ($r[53] = -0.204, p = 0.14$). The direction is correct: The greater the change in the CAPS (representing more psychological improvement), the lower the PIQ score (representing more physical improvement). There is clearly not a strong dose–response relationship. Despite our failure to find a dose–response relationship, it seems clear from our data that there is a connection for MVA survivors such that the progress in psychological recovery or healing is tied in part to progress in physical healing.

At an anecdotal level, we have heard many patients with noticeable PTS symptoms explain that their physical injuries, with the concomitant pain and restricted range of motion and other limitations, served as a frequent reminder of the MVA and its psychological impact. In fact, it was an unavoidable reminder that would trigger arousal and anxiety (and sometimes anger or guilt). (This exposure did not seem to serve the therapeutic purpose of enforced exposure and subsequent extinction.) Thus, long-lasting, nagging injuries, especially the soft tissue injuries of whiplash, seem to impede psychological recovery.[1]

THE ROLE OF WHIPLASH INJURIES

As we were preparing the current revision of this book, we began to look again at the role whiplash injury might play in the natural history of MVA-related PTSD. Mayou and colleagues (Mayou & Bryant, 1996, 2002) have been the primary contributors to the world's literature on psychiatric consequences of whiplash injuries in MVAs. In the first report, Mayou and Bryant (1996) reported on the 12-month outcome for 74 patients from Mayou et al.'s (1993) prospective study who had whiplash injuries. Sixty-one participants were reassessed at three months and 57 (77.0%) at one year. Whereas 84% complained explicitly of neck pain at the initial evaluation (a mean of 25 days post-MVA), this was reduced to 51% at three months and 37% at one year. There were no special psychiatric outcomes for these whiplash patients with 18% qualifying as a "case" at three months and 12%

---

[1]We have assumed a causal direction: that physical injury and its healing influence psychological state. It is equally possible that the survivor's psychological state influences physical state and healing. For our measurement, especially, the patient's estimate of the degree of healing and of his or her physical state, it could well be that overall psychological state influences the patient's perception of his or her physical state and thus leads to a spuriously high correlation.

at one year on the Present State Examination (Wing et al., 1979). Moreover, psychosocial outcomes were predicted by variables other than the injury status, consistent with the overall results. The authors concluded "that the continuing report of neck symptoms at 3 months and 1 year is largely unrelated to any of the psychological and social variables assessed at, or soon after, injury or to compensation" (p. 621).

The second report (Mayou & Bryant, 2002) from these investigators is from the three-year follow-up data on the Ehlers et al. (1998) Oxford study. Of the 1,148 patients who were initially assessed, 278 (24.2%) had whiplash injuries. They were able to reassess, by questionnaire, 208 (74.8%) at three months, 187 (67.3%) at one year and 124 (44.6%) at three years.

The percentage of whiplash patients claiming moderate to very severe pain over time was three months, 37%; one year, 27%; and three years, 30%. These values exceed those for patients with other soft tissue injuries and are on par with those who had bone injuries. The fraction with any noticeable psychological difficulty was fairly consistent at 37% at three months, 35% at one year, and 35% at three years, and again was comparable to those with bone injury.

The only significant multivariate predictor of pain level at one year was whether the patient had filed a legal suit for compensation by three months. This seems somewhat akin to our finding in chapter 6 that having initiated litigation by two months post-MVA independently predicted PTSD status at that time. The authors concluded, "There is no special psychiatry of whiplash" (p. 654). Overall, they noted that the minority of whiplash patients have long-standing physical, and to some extent, social and psychological problems. Unfortunately, their presentations do not shed great light on our issue of the potential interacting the roles of physical recovery and psychological recovery.

Turning to the Albany Cohort 1, there were 87 patients who had initial diagnoses of either full PTSD or subsyndromal PTSD who were reassessed at both six-month and one-year follow-ups. We used their data because their diagnoses (and CAPS scores) gave them room for improvement. Among this subsample were 24 males and 63 females of average age 35.5 years. Any patient who complained of neck and upper back pain, tenderness or stiffness after their MVA, or any patient who had been told by their physician that they had a whiplash injury was counted as positive. Patients were counted as recovered from whiplash when they rated the problem as absent.

For dependent variables on this sample we had the CAPS score and whether they had improved categorically (for those with PTSD initially being rediagnosed as less than PTSD [subsyndromal PTSD] or non-PTSD; for those with sub-PTSD initially, being rediagnosed as non-PTSD).

TABLE 9.3
Relationship Over First Six Months of Follow-Up Between Change
in Clinical Status and Change in Whiplash Injury Status for
Cohort 1 MVA Survivors

Status of whiplash injury	Clinical status at 6 months	
	Improved	Unchanged
Never had whiplash	15	3
Whiplash remitted at 6 months	15	11
Whiplash has not remitted at 6 months	20	23

Initially, 69 of the patients reported whiplash injuries and 18 did not. Although the initial CAPS score for those with whiplash injury was arithmetically higher than that of those without whiplash, the difference was not significant. Over the first six months of follow-up, 26 (37.7%) of those with whiplash reported that the neck pain and stiffness had remitted. This allowed us to form three groups: those who never reported whiplash ($n = 18$), those who initially had whiplash but it had remitted by the six-month follow-up ($n = 26$), and those for whom the whiplash continued ($n = 43$). The clinical status of these three groups at the six-month follow-up as improved or not is presented in Table 9.3.

As can be seen, the percentage of the subgroups who had improved clinically ranged from 83.3% (never whiplash) to 57.7% (whiplash remitted) to 46.5% (whiplash not remitted). The overall array was significant by chi square ($p < .025$). A comparison of the clinical status for those who never had whiplash and those whose whiplash remitted to those whose whiplash continued was also significant ($p = .034$). Although the CAPS scores show significant improvement across the three subgroups from initial evaluation to the six-month point, there was no subgroup by time interaction.

It thus seems that again we find a concurrent relationship between physical healing (remission of pain and stiffness of whiplash) and psychological healing (improved psychological diagnostic status). Our data did not permit a fine-grained enough analysis to draw strong causal inferences.

This topic area is in need of more extensive research and of collaboration among orthopedists, physical therapists, and mental health professionals. As if to answer our earlier call (Blanchard & Hickling, 1997) for more research on this topic, Sharp and Harvey (2001) have recently published a theoretical paper in which they speculate about the possible mutual maintenance between PTSD and chronic pain. They noted the scattered reports of high levels of comorbidity between PTSD and chronic pain and go on to speculate on possible mechanisms by which these two problems reinforce each other. Chief among these are (a) that the pain serves as a reminder of the trauma, (b) that chronic levels of anxiety and arousal (from PTSD) make the sufferer more sensitive to painful stimuli, and (c) that both problems lead to efforts to avoid painful affect in PTSD and painful stimulation in those with chronic pain. We certainly agree with this formulation.

Clinical Hint

To jump ahead to treatment, in chapter 18 we describe our explicit strategy to "decouple" the chronic pain and chronic PTSD. In the cognitive–behavioral therapy (CBT) treatment regimen, we initially acknowledge and validate the lingering pain problems and other physical problems that the patients are experiencing but then, in essence, make them off limits by telling the patient that therapy is aimed at their PTSD, not their pain. We do add that the successful treatment of the PTSD may lessen the distress they experience from pain and other physical symptoms.

10

THE ROLE OF LITIGATION IN THE REMISSION OF MVA-RELATED PTSD

It is widely believed that litigation and its settlement play a large role in the natural history of psychological symptoms and disability among accident victims. Conventional clinical wisdom holds that individuals will continue their symptomatic complaints until after a suit is settled, ostensibly to enhance their chances of collecting a large settlement; a corollary is that once the suit is settled, one should expect to see a dramatic improvement, especially in psychological symptoms.

Reviewing this literature, much of modern thinking and conventional clinical wisdom seems to date to a presentation in 1961 by an eminent British neurologist, Henry Miller, at a distinguished invited address, the Milroy Lecture, which was subsequently published in the *British Medical Journal*. In that address, titled, "Accident Neurosis," Miller (1961) presented data on 50 accident victims (31 industrial accidents and 18 traffic accidents) followed up for two to four years after settlement of their compensation suits; the average interval from initial accident to settlement had been 26 months. Miller had found evidence for "gross psychoneurosis" in this sample when they were examined before settlement, including an "unshakable conviction (on the part of the patient) of unfitness for work" and "an absolute refusal to admit any degree of symptomatic improvement." Predisposition to neurosis was supposedly evident in only 15 of the 50 cases. When these patients were examined after settlement (either positively or negatively) of their claims, 41 of 45 who had worked previously had returned to work. Only two had had psychiatric treatment for their symptoms.

These findings led Miller (1961) to conclude, "The cause of accident neurosis is not the result of physical injury" but arises (a) "when the accident is due to someone else's fault" and (b) "has occurred in circumstances where payment of financial compensation is potentially involved." Miller stated unequivocally (p. 994), "In my opinion it (accident neurosis) is not a result of the accident but a concomitant of the compensation situation and a manifestation of the hope of financial gain. The condition is not encountered where this hope does not exist or where it has been finally satisfied or dissipated."

Almost all subsequent research and reviews disagree with Miller's (1961) conclusions. As noted in chapter 3, Mendelson (1981) followed up 101 accident victims (42 from motor vehicle accidents [MVAs], 59 from industrial accidents) after their compensation claims were settled. Thirty-five (25 MVA, 10 industrial) accident victims had resumed work before settlement. Forty-four of the remaining 66 had not returned to work 16 months after claim settlement. Likewise, Thompson (1965) in a study of 500 accident victims with posttraumatic neurosis (usually anxiety states [n = 406] with possible superimposed neurotic depression [n = 156]) found that "the effects of financial settlement on the course of the illness had negligible benefit."

Kelly and Smith (1981) sought to trace 100 accident victim patients seen by them whom they had diagnosed with posttraumatic syndrome to learn what happened after their compensation claims were settled. The average time from injury to settlement was 3.8 years. Fifty-one were located: 16 had returned to full work before the settlement, 4 to work after the settlement, 22 were not working (but apparently able), and 3 had incapacitating symptoms, 4 had died, and data were incomplete from 2.

In an elegant study, Tarsh and Royston (1985) followed up 35 of 50 patients they had assessed on medico–legal referral because of gross somatic symptoms for which no adequate physical basis could be established. The average time from injury to settlement was five years. Two patients never left work; two others returned before settlement. After settlement four (of 31) returned to the same work and four others to lighter duty work. These eight returns were scattered from one to five years postsettlement (with five within two years). Thus the majority (two thirds) never returned to work.

Reviewing this literature, Weighill (1983) was dismayed by the methodological problems plaguing it but seemed to agree that most of the published evidence disagreed with Miller's (1961) conclusions concerning the absence of return to work before settlement and relative high rate of return to work with settlement. He also called for studies of psychiatric patients with and without compensation cases and for prospective study of compensation cases.

More recently, Mayou and colleagues (Mayou, 1995, 2002; Mayou et al., 1993), in the course of conducting a prospective follow-up of 171 of 200 MVA victims seen in an emergency room in Oxford, have addressed the role of litigation and compensation among MVA victims. At a three-year follow-up, Mayou (1995) found 96 individuals had filed claims, and 75 had not. There were no differences in psychological distress between the two groups (Mayou et al., 1993). Of the 96, 56 (58%) were settled by the three-year point, whereas 21 (22%) had not settled, and 7 (7%) had dropped their suits. Mayou pointed out there were no effects of initiating or settling litigation: "Overall, there was no evidence that there were significant differences in any aspect of outcome between those who sought compensation and those who did not; further, there was no evident difference between those who settled early and those who settled late"; but at another point he noted, "This information (on individuals who settled after 1 year but by the third year) suggests that the subjects did report some improvement at this follow-up point compared to those who had still not settled" (p. 795). Unfortunately, no data to support these conclusions were presented in the paper.

In a six-year follow-up on the status of litigation and compensation of the Oxford sample, Bryant, Mayou, and Lloyd-Bostock (1997) were able to obtain data on 81 of 96 (84.4%) who had filed cases by the one-year post-MVA point. Five cases had not been settled, seven cases had been dropped, leaving 69 settled cases with data. The whiplash cases were settled earlier (82% by three years) than the other more severe injury cases (about 43% by three years). The median award for the severe injury cases was about 10,000 English pounds (about $16,000 USD), and for whiplash about half of that. Many of those involved were frustrated and angry over the slowness of the process and the modest size of awards. Many had also endured considerable financial hardship while the case was making its way through the system.

Again, contrary to Miller's (1961) assertion, there were no dramatic improvements in physical symptoms, mental state, or social functioning once the case was settled. Instead, the authors report continued anger and frustration, with some showing increased levels because of disappointing settlements.

Among those who did not seek compensation (n = 75), 18 (10.5% of the total) were convicted of various offenses related to the MVA (10 for "lack of due care" and 5 for excess alcohol).

Bryant and Harvey (2003) have investigated the litigation and compensation issue in their Australian sample of MVA survivors who were hospitalized because of their injuries. Of the 171 patients assessed initially within one month of the MVA, 134 were reassessed at six months and 106 (62%) at two years. The latter were the subject of study and were made up of 60 males and 46 females of average age 31. Ninety-three (87.7%) had initiated litigation within the first six months, whereas 13 (12.3%) did not. Of the 93, 20 (21.5% of litigants, 19% of total sample) had settled at two years, whereas 73 had not.

Comparisons across the three groups (nonlitigants, litigation settled, litigation ongoing at two years) on initial demographics and injury variables and measures of psychological distress at all three assessment points were all nonsignificant. Those who sought compensation did not differ from those who did not seek compensation, and those who had settled were no different from those whose cases were still pending. Litigants (ongoing plus settled cases) versus nonlitigants had higher percentages of Acute Stress Disorder (ASD) initially (18.3% versus 8%), and higher percentages of posttraumatic stress disorder (PTSD) at six months (27% versus 8%) and at two years (30% versus 0%). Our recalculations (not the authors' of the original study) show a trend ($p = .13$) at six months and a significant difference ($p = .021$) at two years for litigants to have more diagnosable psychopathology than nonlitigants, and the latter difference was significant. The two litigant groups did not differ diagnostically at any point.

Thus clearly, settling the litigation had no beneficial psychological effect on these MVA survivors. There was a slight (6.1 to 5.0) but significant ($p < .05$) decrease in mean number of PTSD symptoms across the whole sample from six months to two years, but no differential change by group.

THE ALBANY MVA PROJECT

From our project and the one-year prospective follow-up we had data pertinent to the litigation issue from 132 MVA survivors: 18 who settled litigation within the first 12 months of the follow-up; 49 who had initiated litigation by the time of our initial assessment but who had not settled by the 12-month follow-up; and 65 MVA survivors who never initiated litigation. Portions of the information to follow were published separately (Blanchard et al., 1998).

These categorizations were determined from the structured interviews administered initially and at the 6- and 12-month follow-ups. Initially, participants were asked if they had contacted a lawyer; if they answered affirmatively, they were scored as involved in litigation. Status of the potential litigation was assessed at each follow-up and dates of any settlements were obtained. Because New York has a no-fault automobile insurance law, the bulk of an MVA survivor's medical bills are paid by his or her own insurance company. Thus, suits solely to recover medical expenses are relatively rare. Demographic and diagnostic data on these three subgroups are contained in Table 10.1.

We compared the three patient groups on the variables summarized in the table. These analyses revealed no significant differences among our three groups on age, gender, or the distribution of initial diagnoses. There was a significant difference on extent of initial injury (Abbreviated Injury Scale [AIS] score; American Association for Automotive Medicine, 1985; p = .0013); follow-up tests revealed that the group who had settled the litigation within the year follow-up was more severely injured than the other two groups that did not differ. There was also a significant (p = .0004) difference in the extent of initial posttraumatic stress (PTS) symptoms as measured by the CAPS (Clinician-Administered PTSD Scale; Blake et al., 1990). Follow-up tests revealed that the nonlitigants had significantly (p = .05) lower PTS symptoms scores than the two litigant groups who did not differ.

It is of some interest to see that the presence of noticeable psychological distress, as indicated by a diagnosis of PTSD or subsyndromal PTSD, was not the sole (or even a primary) determinant of whether an MVA survivor became a litigant. Almost a quarter of the litigants were initially diagnosed as non-PTSD.

Change in Posttraumatic Stress Symptoms Over Time

Our primary indicator of psychological status over time was the CAPS interview. The mean CAPS score for each group at each point in time are given in Table 10.2.

A repeated-measures MANOVA revealed a main effect of group (p < .001) and of time (p < .001) but no interaction between these two variables. Because of the slightly different slope between the 6- and 12-month follow-up points for the group whose litigation was settled in comparison to those of the other two groups, we reanalyzed the data for the two follow-up points, using the initial score as a covariate. Again, there was no interaction.

To explore further whether there were possibly litigation settlement effects among those who initially were more symptomatic, we repeated the analyses on only those members of the three groups who met criteria for PTSD and also for the combination of those who initially met criteria for PTSD and subsyndromal PTSD. These analyses yielded the same results, main effects of Group and Time, but no interaction.

A follow-up one-way ANOVA on CAPS scores at 12 months was significant (p = .0005). Follow-up tests revealed that the nonlitigant group was significantly (p = .05) lower than the group whose litigation was still pending; the group who had settled was in between these two groups and

TABLE 10.1

Group Mean Demographic and Diagnostic Data on Three Groups of MVA Victims

	Litigation settled within 12 months (n = 18)	Litigation not settled within 12 months (n = 49)	Nonlitigants (n = 65)
Age (SD)	42.1 (13.8)	35.0 (11.1)	35.8 (13.7)
Gender (male/female)	7/11	15/34	21/44
Pre-MVA employment status:			
Employed	13 (72%)	39 (80%)	44 (68%)
Unemployed	2 (11%)	0	2 (3%)
Homemaker	1 (6%)	3 (6%)	5 (8%)
Student	1 (6%)	3 (6%)	13 (20%)
Disabled	1 (6%)	2 (4%)	0
Retired	0	2 (4%)	1 (2%)
Initial diagnostic status			
PTSD	8 (44%)	23 (47%)	18 (28%)
Sub-PTSD	5 (28%)	15 (31%)	22 (34%)
Non-PTSD	5 (28%)	11 (22%)	25 (38%)
Initial CAPS score (SD)	40.7 (29.5)	43.7 (27.5)	25.6 (20.4)
Initial abbreviated injury scale score (SD)	9.2 (11.3)	5.1 (4.3)	3.5 (4.2)

TABLE 10.2
Mean CAPS Scores for Initial Assessment and Follow-Up Points for All
Litigation Groups

	CAPS score		
Group	Initial	6-month follow-up	12-month follow-up
Nonlitigant	25.6 (20.4)	12.7 (23.6)	8.2 (15.0)
Litigation settled by 12 months	40.7 (29.5)	22.6 (22.2)	15.3 (19.6)
Litigation not settled	43.7 (27.5)	26.5 (24.1)	23.4 (24.9)

Note. CAPS = Clinical Administered PTSD Scale.

did not differ from either. All three groups had significantly ($p = .01$) lower CAPS scores at the 12-month follow-up point than they had initially, including the litigants whose suits were pending. Thus, it seems clear that even those litigants with pending suits are significantly less symptomatic over time.

Other Measures of Subjective Distress

The psychological tests used in our study were additional measures of subjective distress. Some litigants settled before the six-month follow-up assessment, and others settled after that time but before the 12-month assessment. The six-month follow-up assessment values for the litigation-settled group are thus partially confounded. To avoid this confound, and to detect possible litigation settlement effects, we analyzed the data from the unconfounded points, those from the initial assessment and from the 12-month assessment. Values for these two points for each group for each test are summarized in Table 10.3.

These were subjected to an overall group × time MANOVA, followed by tests on each of the individual variables. Results of those individual tests are also presented in Table 10.3. The overall MANOVA yielded a main effect of groups ($p < .001$) and of time ($p < .001$) but no interaction.

Examining Table 10.3, one can see that for three variables (Beck Depression Inventory [BDI]; Beck et al., 1961) state–anxiety, and Impact of Event Scale (IES; Horowitz et al., 1979), there are main effects of group and time but no interaction. In each of these instances, follow-up analyses revealed that the nonlitigants were less distressed than the two litigant groups, which did not differ at the initial assessment. At the 12-month assessment for three of the measures (state anxiety, trait anxiety, and the IES), the same pattern of results obtained: the nonlitigant group was significantly ($p = .05$) lower than either of the two litigant groups, which did not

TABLE 10.3
Values for Psychological Tests for All Litigation Groups at Initial and 12-Month Assessments on Each Psychological Test

Measure	Group	Initial assessment	12-month assessment	Group	Time	Group × time
				F and *p* values		
Beck Depression Inventory	Nonlitigant	7.7 (7.5)	5.1 (8.1)	4.87, .009	8.29, .005	1.03, ns
	Litigation settled	10.7 (6.0)	7.6 (7.8)			
	Litigation pending	11.5 (9.9)	10.4 (10.0)			
STAI–State Anxiety	Nonlitigant	49.8 (16.0)	44.4 (13.0)	4.97, .008	3.54, .06	1.17, ns
	Litigation settled	57.1 (20.4)	54.8 (17.7)			
	Litigation pending	56.6 (19.9)	56.0 (21.9)			
STAI–Trait Anxiety	Nonlitigant	50.8 (13.4)	46.2 (14.6)	1.82, ns	0.35, ns	3.16, .046
	Litigation settled	52.3 (15.7)	54.5 (16.4)			
	Litigation pending	53.4 (16.4)	54.3 (20.8)			
Impact of Event Scale	Nonlitigant	14.0 (15.7)	7.4 (10.9)	12.84, <.001	19.25, <.001	.19, ns
	Litigation settled	24.9 (19.6)	19.8 (20.9)			
	Litigation pending	28.6 (17.3)	20.1 (17.8)			

Note. ns = not significant.

differ. For the BDI, however, the group with the litigation pending was significantly (p = .05) more depressed than the nonlitigant group, and those whose litigation was settled were intermediate and not different than either of the other two groups.

For trait anxiety, there were no main effects, only the interaction. Whereas the nonlitigants did score lower at follow-up, the two litigant groups increased slightly. The two litigant groups did not differ at either assessment.

Role Functioning Variables

Table 10.4 presents the values for the variables assessed with the LIFE-Base and LIFE (Keller et al., 1987) related to role functioning. We present three points in time, pre-MVA, initial assessment (post-MVA) and 12-month follow-ups, for the three groups of accident victims. For the reasons mentioned earlier with the psychological tests, the analyses did not use the six-month assessment values.

(As noted in chapter 4, we remind the reader that our variable, major role function, is derived hierarchically [in line with the varying status of participants shown in Table 10.1]: If the participant was working 30 hours per week or more, then rating values for work are used; if the participant was a full-time student, then ratings for school performance are used; finally, if the participant did not work outside of the home, then the rating values for homemaking were used. For relationship with family, we have averaged the individual ratings for all first-degree relatives and spouse or partner.) All variables are rated on 1 to 5 scales, with 1 being best and 5 best worst; the scales are defined in chapters 4 and 5.

These variables, which define role functioning and role impairment, were subjected to an overall repeated measures MANOVA (group × time), followed by analyses on each variable separately and then follow-up tests. The overall MANOVA yielded a main effect of group (p < .001), a main effect of time (p < .001), and an interaction of group × time (p = .05).

One sees from Table 10.4 that there are no significant effects of litigation status (group) nor the passage of time (or settlement of litigation) on average relationships with family. The average overall relationship is rated as "good" across all points in time.

For the performance of major role function and relationships with friends, however, there are main effects of group and of time as well as significant (p < .05 or better) interactions for each variable. Follow-up analyses reveal, for relationship with friends, no difference among the groups before the MVA, with a significant (.05) difference (relationships were better for nonlitigants) at the initial assessment between those involved in litigation versus the nonlitigants. At the 12-month follow-up, the nonlitigants have significantly (p < .05) better relations with friends than those

TABLE 10.4
Role Functioning Variables for All Litigation MVA Victim Groups at All Assessment Points

Variable	Group	Assessment points			Statistics F/p		
		Pre-MVA	Initial assessment (post-MVA)	12-month follow-up	Time	Group	Group × time
Major role functioning (work, school, homemaking)	Nonlitigant		2.2	1.6	24.5, <.001	6.20, .003	3.50, .033
	Litigation settled		2.3	1.8			
	Litigation pending		3.2	1.9			
Family relationships	Nonlitigant	2.1	2.1	2.0	1.02, ns	.03, ns	0.0, ns
	Litigation settled	2.1	2.2	2.1			
	Litigation pending	2.0	2.1	2.1			
Relationship with friends	Nonlitigant	1.6	1.6	1.6	5.17, .025	6.76, .002	3.19, .045
	Litigation settled	1.9	2.6	1.8			
	Litigation pending	1.8	2.1	2.1			
Participation in recreation	Nonlitigant	1.6	2.2	1.7	31.4, <.001	11.76, <.001	1.25, ns
	Litigation settled	1.8	2.9	1.9			
	Litigation pending	1.6	3.2	2.6			

Note. ns = not significant.

whose suits are still pending. Those litigants whose suits are settled lie in between and are not statistically different on quality of friendships from either of the two groups.

For performance on major role function at the initial assessment, those litigants who have not settled their suits within the first 12 months are performing noticeably poorer ($p = .05$) than either the nonlitigants or the litigants who settle. In fact, the difference is a whole scale unit (between satisfactory performance with no impairment to fair performance with mild impairment). At the 12-month assessment, the three groups are all functioning significantly better with no difference in functioning among them. Thus, those litigants whose suits are still pending have *improved* markedly (average of 1.3 scale units) over the year.

For participation in recreation, the nonlitigants were significantly more involved at the time of the initial assessment than the litigant groups who did not differ. At the 12-month follow-up, the nonlitigant group and those whose litigation was still pending were significantly different; those litigants who had settled were intermediate but not significantly different from either of the other two groups.

Return to Work

Table 10.5 tabulates the frequencies of each group who were working full-time or part-time at the time of the MVA (96 of 132, 72.7%) and their employment status at the 12-month follow-up.

We compared the status of those from each group who had been working full-time before the MVA as to whether they were working at all

TABLE 10.5
Employment Status of Members of All Litigation Groups Who Were Employed at the Time of the Accident

Group and pre-MVA employment status	12-month employment status			
	Employed			
	Full-time	Part-time	Unemployed	Disabled
Nonlitigant ($n = 44$)				
Full-time ($n = 38$)	34	3	1	—
Part-time ($n = 6$)	1	3	2	—
Litigation pending ($n = 39$)				
Full-time ($n = 36$)	24	6	3	3
Part-time ($n = 3$)	2	1	—	—
Litigation settled ($n = 13$)				
Full-time ($n = 11$)	9	2	—	—
Part-time ($n = 2$)	—	—	—	2

(full-time or part-time) at the 12-month follow-up. The X^2 ($p = .05$] was significant; those whose suits were still pending were less likely to be working at the 12-month follow-up, partially supportive of Miller's (1961) position.

Initial Differences Between Litigant Versus Nonlitigant MVA Survivors

One question to ask about this topic is whether litigants at the initial assessment were different from the nonlitigants. The answer is generally yes. Litigants had higher PTS symptom scores as measured by the CAPS, they showed higher levels of subjective distress as indicated on the standardized psychological tests, and their role performance was more impaired with regard to major role function, relationships with friends, and use of leisure time as indicated by participation in recreational activities. Average relationships with family members were not different. They also had more severe physical injuries as measured by AIS scores.

Unfortunately, one cannot determine the direction of causality from these data. It could be that because of greater subjective distress, greater role impairment, and a higher level of PTS symptoms, these MVA survivors decided to seek compensation through litigation. Alternatively, it could be that, having decided to initiate litigation, these litigating MVA survivors portrayed themselves at the assessment (which occurred after litigation had been initiated) in a more distressed and impaired light.

Support for the former interpretation comes from the greater average degree of physical injury, as measured by AIS scores, for the litigating group. In fact, it could be that the extent of injury is the causal variable; that is, those who are more injured are more likely to initiate litigation, even though their health care is being paid by the no-fault insurance trust.

Follow-Up Differences Between Litigants Who Settle Versus Litigants Whose Cases Are Still Pending

Miller's (1961) prediction on this point is fairly clear: Those whose litigation is still pending should be more distressed and more impaired. Although the direction of the group means in our data generally support Miller's viewpoint (that is, the group mean scores show less distress and impairment for litigants who have settled versus litigants whose suits are still pending), in no instance is this effect statistically significant. Thus, on balance, we do not show differences at follow-up between litigants who have settled versus those whose suits are still pending.

At the 12-month follow-up, the general finding is that the values for the litigants who have settled are not different from those who never initiated litigation on role functioning variables and degree of PTS symptoms. However, on other measures of psychological distress, state and trait anxiety and on the IES scores, the litigants who have settled remain more distressed than those who never initiated litigation.

More important, those litigants whose suits are still pending at 12 months show consistently more psychological distress and role impairment, as well as higher PTS symptom scores, than those who never initiated litigation. Again this is consistent with Miller's view that such individuals would continue to be symptomatic until after their suits are settled.

Improvement Over the Follow-Up Interval

For the most part, all three MVA victim groups improve over the 12-month follow-up interval: The two exceptions are in relationships with family members (which do not deteriorate after the MVA and thus remain at the "good" level throughout) and trait anxiety scores.

When we examined the specific within-group change for each group from the initial assessment to the 12-month follow-up point, we find the nonlitigant group improved significantly on all variables except family relationships. Likewise the litigants whose suits were settled improved significantly on all role functioning variables except family relationships but had no significant change on any psychological distress measure. For the crucial group, those litigants whose suits have not been settled by 12 months, we find significant reduction in measures of PTS symptoms (i.e., CAPS scores, IES scores—which are highly correlated—and in major role function and participation in recreation). However, relationships with friends do not improve nor do the measures of psychological distress, BDI, or state anxiety and trait anxiety.

These latter results thus partially support Miller's (1961) contention that on some variables there is no improvement before settlement, whereas on other variables there is significant improvement. In fact, on the most crucial variables, impairment in major role function, such as work performance, and presence of posttraumatic stress symptoms, those litigants whose suits are still pending do show significant improvement over the year. It is only on other measures of generalized psychological distress that no improvement was shown.

On the crucial functional variable of return to work for those who were employed full-time at the time of the accident, we find 83% of those whose legal suits are still pending are back at work full-time ($n = 24, 66.7\%$) or part-time ($n = 6, 16.7\%$). These data clearly contradict Miller's (1961) assertion that such individuals do not return to work until after the suit is settled. We do find that 100% of those who had been employed full-time at the time of the MVA and whose suits have been settled are back at work.

The only finding partially supportive of Miller's (1961) contentions is that significantly fewer of those whose suits are still pending and who had been working full-time at the time of the MVA have returned to work. Thus although he expected none to return, we find a great majority have returned to full-time employment. However, the fraction of this group who have not returned to work is arithmetically, but not statistically, less than the fraction found in the other two groups.

Overall, our data are consistent with most of the work published since Miller's (1961) paper—that is, not supporting his view about accident neurosis. Those who have suits pending are generally back at work either full-time (67%) or part-time (16%) and generally have substantially reduced levels of PTS symptoms and of role impairment. However, there are trends in our data that are supportive of the notion that those with pending suits do more poorly than those who never file suit or those who have settled suits. Those with pending suits are consistently more distressed and functioning less well than those who never filed suits and show nonsignificant differences from those whose suits are settled. It could be that with larger samples, those differences might reach significance.

Speculation

There are two final points related to litigation on which we would like to speculate, based on anecdotal, rather than systematic, data. The first point is that the process of litigation can result in retraumatization and that such an ongoing process could account for our trends for those who are still in litigation to be doing less well. Pitman, Sparr, Saunders, and McFarlane (1996) and Napier (1991) have pointed out that the potential impact of the process of litigation may be to perpetuate or exacerbate. Pitman et al. (1996) have suggested that the very act of litigation may also be a factor affecting PTSD symptoms through what they describe as "retraumatization." They stated that the need to confront the traumatic history through interviews with attorneys, depositions, and courtroom testimony thwarts the victim's characteristic efforts at avoidance, and predictably results in the resurgence of intrusive ideation and increased arousal. Further, this is done in a system many view as adversarial, pitting the plaintiff against the defendant, who through the occurrence of the traumatic event may already be seen as the "enemy." Patients as participants in the process may come to see that even though they perceive themselves as the victims, they are now the ones placed on trial, exacerbating their sense of vulnerability and victimization. In addition, although the MVA survivor may have already suffered a major loss financially as a result of the traumatic event, pursuit of litigation necessitates additional financial risk and anxiety, because the positive outcome is not assured. Pitman et al. (1996) found that accident survivors are seeking understanding (and justice) more than financial gain.

Our own unsystematic observations are that formal contact with the litigation process, especially giving depositions and appearing in court, do lead to increase in PTS symptoms. (To some extent this is to the MVA survivor's advantage because the nonverbal communication of distress is heightened.)

The second point on which we wish to speculate is the broad one of *malingering*. It is always possible for the clever individual with the appropriate MVA and physical injury history to give biased (in terms of portraying more distress than is present) or even false answers, to us and to everyone else involved in the litigation process.

We made no effort to check on the veracity of our research participants' reports, either details of the accident or their reports of their psychological symptoms at any point in the follow-up. The interviewers were all experienced clinicians and probed when answers were inconsistent with each other or when the nonverbal behavior was not consistent with the verbal content. We had no instances for which we felt we had been misled.

However, when serious financial rewards are at stake, it is possible that individuals will not tell the truth but instead may malinger. In chapter 13, we present our efforts to learn how well individuals can fake a presentation consistent with PTSD.

11

ACUTE STRESS DISORDER AMONG MVA SURVIVORS

The reintroduction of the posttraumatic stress disorder (PTSD) diagnostic category in the *DSM–III* (American Psychiatric Association, 1980) provided a category with which to diagnose and code individuals who had been exposed to a traumatic event and then were experiencing avoidance, numbing, hyperarousal, and reexperiencing symptoms over the next month or more. Before the one-month point, individuals who were clearly distressed and symptomatic could only be diagnosed and coded with adjustment disorder. The latter diagnosis seemed an understatement for rape survivors and others who were acutely distressed in the days following the trauma up until they crossed the temporal threshold that allowed a formal diagnosis of PTSD.

The publication of the *DSM–IV* (American Psychiatric Association, 1994) and its inclusion of a new diagnostic category, acute stress disorder (ASD), was in part an attempt to remedy this diagnostic situation and to provide a more meaningful diagnostic label for distressed trauma victims during the days immediately following the trauma. Moreover, the introduction of ASD provided a category to highlight the frequent occurrence of dissociative symptoms as part of the acute response to trauma.

There is great overlap in the diagnostic criteria for ASD and PTSD; however, there are some important differences. Exhibit 11.1 compares the diagnostic criteria.

EXHIBIT 11.1
Comparison of *DSM–IV* Diagnostic Criteria for Acute Stress Disorder and Posttraumatic Stress Disorder

Acute stress disorder	Posttraumatic stress disorder

A. Person exposed to traumatic event in which:
  1. Person is exposed to actual or threatened death or serious injury for self or others.
  2. Person's response involved intense fear, helplessness, or horror.
B. Either while experiencing traumatic event or after the event, person has three or more dissociative symptoms:
  1. Sense of numbing, detachment, absence of emotional responsiveness.
  2. Reduction in awareness ("being in a daze").
  3. Derealization.
  4. Depersonalization.
  5. Dissociative amnesia.
C. At least one reexperiencing symptom.
D. Marked avoidance of stimuli that remind person of trauma.
E. Marked hyperarousal symptoms.
 	
F. Marked distress or role impairment.
G. Disturbance lasts for two days to four weeks.
	A. Person exposed to traumatic event in which:
	  1. Person is exposed to actual or threatened death or serious injury for self or others.
	  2. Person's response involved intense fear, helplessness or horror.
	
	B. At least one reexperiencing symptom.
	C. At least three avoidance or psychic numbing symptoms.
	D. At least two hyperarousal symptoms.
	E. Marked distress or role impairment.
	F. Disturbance lasts for at least one month.

Examining the two disorders we see that the differences are the necessity of dissociative symptoms in ASD (but not in PTSD), fewer avoidance and numbing symptoms in ASD than in PTSD, and the temporal difference (two days to four weeks for ASD versus at least one month for PTSD).

HARVEY AND BRYANT'S WORK ON MVA-RELATED ASD

Although there was very little research available on ASD per se when the first edition of this book was written in mid-1996, much less research on ASD among motor vehicle accident (MVA) survivors, that situation has changed over the past six years, thanks in large part to the research efforts of two Australian psychologists: Richard Bryant and Allison Harvey.

In fact, the two have written a very good book on this topic, *Acute Stress Disorder* (Bryant & Harvey, 2000).

In the one report on MVA survivors and acute stress, Bryant and Harvey (1995a) studied acute stress responses among two groups of MVA survivors, 38 who had had a mild head injury (Glasgow Coma scale scores of 13 to 15 and posttraumatic amnesia of fewer than 24 hours) and 38 non-head-injured MVA survivors. They were assessed 1 to 15 days post-MVA. Although the participants were given a structured interview used to diagnose PTSD (PTSD–I; Watson, Juba, Manifold, Kucala, & Anderson, 1991), no formal diagnostic judgments were presented.

Comparisons of the two groups revealed greater subjective fear, higher levels of PTSD symptoms, higher total Impact of Event Scale (IES; Horowitz et al., 1979) scores and IES intrusion scores among the non-head-injured group than those with mild head injury. No assessment of dissociative symptoms was reported. It is clear that the non-head-injured were very acutely distressed, having an average IES score of 25.7 and state anxiety score of 46.6. It is not clear what a PTSD–I scale score of 45 might mean.

More recent reports by this research team include parallel sets of studies on head-injured and non-head-injured samples assessed over the same 10-month time span among MVA survivors whose injuries led to admission to a regional trauma center. For the non–head-injured sample Harvey and Bryant (1998b) assessed 61 males and 31 females who ranged in age from 17 to 63 (mean 33.3) and who were hospitalized for an average of 7.6 days (mean injury severity score was 4.4). Initial assessment took place between 2 and 26 days post-MVA (mean 6.9 days). Seventy-one of these individuals (77%) were reassessed six months later using the PTSD module of the Composite International Diagnostic Interview (CIDI; Peters et al., 1996).

Of the 92 initial participants, 12 (13%) met full criteria for ASD, 19 (20.7%) met criteria for subclinical ASD, and 61 (66.3%) had no diagnosis. They defined subclinical ASD as meeting three of the four of *DSM–IV* criteria, B, C, D and E. Most (79%) of those with subclinical ASD did not meet the dissociative symptom (Criterion B) category.

Clinical Hint

These assessments of ASD were done with a structured interview developed by this research team (Acute Stress Disorder Interview [ASDI]; Bryant, Harvey, Dang, & Sackville, 1998). If one is interested in assessing acute MVA survivors for ASD, we would recommend this interview. It has good psychometric properties.

* * *

Of the nine full ASD cases (75%) that were reassessed, seven met criteria for full PTSD (77.8%) and two had essentially remitted. Of the 15 sub-ASD cases (79%), nine met criteria for full PTSD (60%), three for subsyndromal PTSD (20%), and three (20%) had remitted. Among the original 61 with no ASD, 47 (77%) were reassessed. Two (4.3%) met criteria for PTSD, four for subsyndromal PTSD (8.5%), and 41 (87.2%) had no diagnosis. Thus, meeting criteria for either full ASD or sub-ASD is a strong risk factor (about an 80% chance) for having diagnosable posttraumatic stress difficulties six months later. Harvey and Bryant (1998b) concluded that the dissociative symptom cluster has relatively strong positive predictive power (presence of PTSD at six months when Criterion B was met at initial assessment [0.71]), and all four symptom clusters have strong negative predictive power (absence of PTSD at six months when criterion not present at initial assessment).

Much to their credit, Harvey and Bryant (1999c) followed-up and reassessed 56 of the original 92 (61%) two years post-MVA (this represented 79% of those assessed at six months), again using the CIDI. Of those with full ASD who were positive for PTSD at six months ($n = 7$), six were reassessed and five of these (83%) were still positive for PTSD. Overall, five of eight (62.5%) full ASD participants still met criteria for PTSD at two years. Of those initially meeting criteria for sub-ASD, 10 of 19 were reassessed; 7 of the 9 (78%) who had met criteria for full PTSD at six months were still positive. Overall, 7 of 10 (70%) sub-ASD cases were positive for PTSD at two years. Among those with no initial diagnosis, 38 were reassessed. Four (of 38 reassessed, 11.1%) who had been negative for PTSD at six months now met criteria for PTSD (genuine delayed-onset cases of PTSD; see chapter 8). One of the two cases positive at six months for PTSD was still positive. Overall, 5 of 38 (13%) of individuals with no diagnosis acutely met criteria for PTSD at two years. The dissociative symptom cluster (Criterion B) continued to have good (0.73) positive predictive power for PTSD at two years. Overall, 17 of 56 (30.4%) of hospitalized, non-head-injured MVA survivors still met criteria for PTSD two years after the accident.

In the companion studies on a hospitalized MVA survivor sample with mild traumatic brain injury (defined as a period of posttraumatic amnesia of less than 24 hours), Harvey and Bryant (1998a) assessed 79 adults (55 men, 24 women) of average age 29 (range 16–60) who had been hospitalized for an average of 11.6 days, again within 2 to 24 days after the MVA. They found 11 cases (13.9%) of full ASD and 5 cases (6.2%) of sub-ASD. Those who met full criteria for ASD had shorter hospitalizations and less severe ISS injury scores (5.9 versus 10.1). Those with ASD were significantly more likely to have had previous psychiatric treatment (54.5%).

In the six-month follow-up study, Harvey and Bryant (1998a) reassessed 63 of 79 (79.7%) of the sample with the PTSD module of the CIDI. Of those 11 with full ASD, all were followed up. Nine (81.8%) met criteria for PTSD and two did not. Of the 52 who did not meet full ASD, 6 (11.5%) met criteria for PTSD and 46 (88.5%) did not. Unfortunately, no details about the sub-ASD cases were presented.

Comparing the head-injured to non-head-injured participants, 81.8% of the head-injured with ASD met criteria for PTSD at six months compared to 77.8% of the non-head-injured. Of those head-injured without ASD, 11.5% met criteria for PTSD versus 17.7% of those without head injury. It seems clear that mild traumatic brain injury (TBI) does *not* prevent MVA survivors from developing PTSD; 23.8% of those with TBI had PTSD six months later.

In the two-year follow-up, 50 (31 male, 19 female) of the original 79 (63.3%) were reassessed. Eleven cases of PTSD (22% of sample) were identified at two years. Of 10 individuals initially diagnosed with ASD (out of 11) who were reassessed, 8 (80%) met criteria for PTSD at 2 years. Of the 40 who did not initially meet criteria for ASD, only 3 (8%) met criteria for PTSD at the reassessment.

Comparing these results to those for the non-head-injured individuals who were reassessed at two years, for those who initially met full ASD, 80% of the head-injured participants met criteria for PTSD versus 63% of the non-head-injured (but only 8 of 12 were followed up). For those without ASD, 8% of the head-injured individuals met criteria for PTSD versus 15.6% of those who were not head-injured. Thus, at this longer term follow-up, the non-head-injured are twice as likely to meet PTSD criteria as the head-injured.

Unfortunately, in the reports on the head-injured MVA survivors, no use was made of the subsyndromal PTSD category nor of the sub-ASD category. These two categorizations yielded important information in the non-head-injured studies.

This prolific research team has made many more contributions to our understanding of the psychological sequelae of MVAs. At other places in this book we will summarize their work on the cognitive–behavioral treatment of ASD (chapter 15) and the role of acute psychophysiological responses, especially heart rate, in predicting later PTSD (chapter 12).

In a last prospective study involving severe (rather than mild) traumatic brain injury, Bryant, Marosszeky, Crooks, and Gurka (2000) assessed 96 individuals (77 male, 19 female) of average age 34.3 years, who had been admitted to a brain injury rehabilitation unit. Most were the survivors of MVAs. The mean length of posttraumatic amnesia was 37 days with a range of 7 to 143; the mean Glasgow Coma Scale score was 8.0 (SD = 3.8). Assessments took place five to seven months posttrauma.

Using the Posttraumatic Stress Disorder Interview of Watson et al. (1991) and *DSM–III–R* criteria, they found 26 patients (27%) met criteria for PTSD. Especially salient symptoms, with high positive predictive power for PTSD, were intrusive memories, nightmares, and sense of reliving the trauma. Although all three of these intrusion symptoms were present in only a small minority of PTSD cases, they were highly predictive.

Harvey and Bryant (1999c) examined a consecutive series of patients hospitalized from injuries as a result of various traumas including MVAs (n = 32), industrial accidents (n = 25), severe burns (n = 20), and assaults (n = 25) to determine the rate of ASD and of sub-ASD in these different trauma populations. Rates of ASD were: MVA (12.5%), assault (16%), burns (10%), industrial accidents (12%). For subclinical ASD (as usual meeting three of four symptom criteria with dissociation being the most common missing cluster [14/16 = 87.5%]), the rates were MVA (18.8%), assault (12%), burns (16%), and industrial accidents (16%). There were few differences across types of trauma. The total level of patients with noticeable acute distress ranged from 32% to 26%, with this new sample of MVA survivors replicating previous work.

A Danish investigator, Annette Fuglsang (2001), has reported on the presence of ASD in an MVA population seen in the emergency departments of two Danish hospitals. Of 236 eligible MVA survivors, 122 (52%) returned copies of the Acute Stress Disorder Scale (ASDS; Bryant et al., 2000) that had been sent to them the same week as the emergency department visit. Men were more likely to refuse participation than women. Using Bryant and Harvey's (2000) suggested cut-off scores, Fuglsang found 34 (28.1%) cases of ASD. Women were more likely (p < .01) to meet criteria for ASD than men. When questions related to Criterion A-2, subjective response to trauma, were added, the rate of ASD dropped to 14%, similar to the rate found by Harvey and Bryant (1998b)—in other words, 13% of hospitalized MVA survivors.

Working with various ASD populations, Bryant and Panasetis (2001) have found that trauma survivors who meet criteria for ASD or subclinical ASD are more likely to report panic symptoms and to meet criteria for a panic attack (53%) during the trauma than those without ASD. These investigators also found a strong association (R^2 = .42) between report of panic symptoms and report of dissociative symptoms during the trauma (Bryant & Panasetis, 2001). Furthermore, Nixon and Bryant (in press) found, in a trauma population with no history of panic attacks, that those who met criteria for ASD were more likely to experience a peritraumatic panic attack (100%) than those without ASD (53%) and more likely to have persistent panic attacks (93.3%) than those without ASD (6.7%). Finally, Bryant and Panasetis (2003) found that those with ASD or subclinical ASD were more likely to have persistent dissociative experiences than trauma victims without ASD. Persistent dissociation was more strongly related to severity of ASD than peritraumatic dissociation.

In a valuable methodological paper Harvey and Bryant (2000a) compared the reports of the presence or absence of the four symptom clusters that make up ASD (see Exhibit 11.1) as originally reported in the initial assessment (about eight days post-MVA, and as recalled from that earlier time at their two-year reassessment). Fifty-six of the original 92 hospitalized MVA survivors took part. Twelve patients had met criteria for ASD at the initial assessment; 17 (30%) met criteria for PTSD at two years.

They found no recall errors in only 25% of cases. Fifty percent incorrectly recalled one symptom cluster, 18% incorrectly recalled two symptom clusters, 3.6% three clusters, and one individual (2%) made mistakes on all four clusters. Patients were significantly more likely to be correct on the dissociative, reexperiencing, and avoidance symptoms, but not the hyperarousal symptoms. For dissociation, reexperiencing, and avoidance the more common errors were of omission—that is, failing to recall the acute symptom at the follow-up. For the arousal symptoms, it was more common for the patient at two years to report a symptom that had not been reported initially. In a useful correlational analysis, the authors showed a highly significant negative correlation ($r = -.56$) between errors of omission and PTSD severity and positive correlation ($r = .43$) between PTSD severity and errors of addition.

Clinical Hint

These correlations mean that the more distressed the patient is at a time distant from the trauma, the more likely his or her retrospective report of how he or she was at the time of the trauma will be mistaken in terms of reporting symptoms that were not present initially; this is especially true of the arousal symptoms. Furthermore, the less symptomatic the patient is at a distant time, the more likely his or her retrospective report will omit symptoms that were present initially. Thus, diagnosing ASD retrospectively, at least two years after the trauma, is fairly likely to lead to error, with the kind of error being determined in part by the patient's clinical state at the distant point.

These findings cast some doubts on the retrospective diagnoses of ASD in some of the early research on the area, especially research linking current PTSD to earlier ASD and the absence of current PTSD to an earlier absence of ASD.

PROVISIONAL PTSD

Keane and colleagues (Keane et al., 2000) have recently reviewed the literature on the role of dissociative symptoms and ASD in the subsequent development of PTSD, using some of the studies reviewed. Starting from the point made in Exhibit 11.1 of the high degree of symptom overlap between ASD and PTSD (except for the dissociative symptoms), they conclude that the reexperiencing, avoidance, and hyperarousal symptoms of ASD combined (essentially, Harvey and Bryant's sub-ASD) are good predictors of subsequent PTSD and that the dissociative symptom cluster adds little incremental utility. They thus advocate for a "provisional PTSD" diagnosis—that is, meeting the symptomatic criteria for PTSD (and probably subsyndromal PTSD) except for the duration criterion; they see this "diagnosis" as having more value and utility for prediction of later PTSD. Our own results on ASD among MVA survivors, to be summarized later in this chapter, is in agreement with Keane et al.'s (2000) views. Only additional research such as that of the Australian team will provide a definitive answer.

Two research teams working with MVA survivors have taken this different approach to early diagnosis by diagnosing PTSD and subsyndromal PTSD, provisionally, by relaxing Criterion E, the one-month duration of symptoms. Delahanty et al. (1997) assessed 130 MVA survivors admitted to a trauma hospital who were hospitalized for 10 days or fewer. These represented about half of those approached at the hospital and about 25% of those referred by the police. They were initially assessed 14 to 21 days post-MVA using the Structured Clinical Interview for *DSM–III–R* (SCID), including the SCID module for PTSD. Eighty participants (61.5%) completed 6-month and 12-month reassessments.

Participants were divided into those who were responsible for the accident (*n* = 34) and those whose MVA was someone else's responsibility (other responsible; *n* = 46); 17 cases who were passengers or whose attribution of responsibility was ambiguous were eliminated. For the self-responsible group, 19% (*n* = 6) met criteria for provisional PTSD while 22% (*n* = 8) were subsyndromal PTSD. By way of contrast, among those who were other-responsible, 29% (*n* = 13) met criteria for provisional PTSD and 32% (*n* = 15) were subsyndromal PTSD. These rates of provisional PTSD showed a trend (*p* = .08) toward being different.

Although rates of PTSD and sub-PTSD for each group were presented for each follow-up point (6 months: self-responsible, 8% PTSD, 16% sub-PTSD; other-responsible, 22% PTSD, 24% sub-PTSD; 12 months: self-responsible, 5% PTSD, 9% sub-PTSD, other-responsible, 15% PTSD, 27% sub-PTSD), there was no tracking of individual cases, so that one cannot tell whether provisional PTSD at two weeks predicts full PTSD at 6 months or 12 months. It is clear that the other-responsible group were more distressed than the self-responsible on psychometric measures and in terms of meeting diagnostic criteria during follow-up.

A reanalysis of our follow-up data on Albany Cohort 1 (Hickling, Blanchard, Buckley, & Taylor, 1999) subdividing on the responsibility variable replicated the findings of Delahanty et al. (1997) about the importance of the attribution of responsibility variable.

Clinical Hint

When the MVA survivor has been the victim of someone else's negligence or carelessness, he or she seems to have a harder time recovering from the psychosocial difficulties than if the survivor was him- or herself responsible for the MVA. It is as if the self-responsible driver says, "I was careless but I can correct my own poor driving." The other-responsible is faced with the knowledge that there are careless drivers on the roadways and that there is little or nothing he or she can do about the other drivers' behavior, except be on guard. The other-responsible survivor is thus more reluctant to return to traveling.

* * *

Schnyder et al. (2001), working with severely injured accident survivors (60.4% MVA) who were admitted to an intensive care unit (Injury Severity Scale score of 10 or greater), assessed 121 patients an average of 13 days after the accident using the CAPS and assigned provisional diagnoses. For some reason, 16 patients who had preexisting psychiatric disorders were excluded. Our research (Blanchard, Hickling, Taylor, Loos, & Forneris, 1996) and that of others (Ehlers et al., 1998) has shown that preexisting psychiatric disorders, especially past major depression and past PTSD, are a strong risk factor for developing PTSD after a personal injury accident. Schnyder et al.'s (2001) exclusion could explain their very low rate of PTSD at one year.

Five patients received provisional diagnoses of PTSD and 22 patients had provisional subsyndromal PTSD diagnoses. At a reassessment 12-months later, 106 patients were available. Their clearly presented results showed that all five cases of provisional PTSD had remitted fully ($n = 3$) or in part ($n = 2$). For their 22 cases of provisional subsyndromal PTSD, 15 (68%) had remitted, 5 (23%) were unchanged, and 2 (9%) had worsened so that they met criteria for full PTSD. There does seem to be some utility to the provisional PTSD diagnosis in that it identifies accident survivors who are likely to be having diagnosable difficulties a year later.

In another study of Australian MVA survivors admitted to the hospital, McFarlane, Atchison, and Yehuda (1997) provided data on 26 who were assessed at Day 2, Day 10, and six months after the accident. At the six-month reassessment, they found seven cases of PTSD (17.5%), seven cases of major depressive disorder (MDD; 17.5%), and 12 with no disorder (30%). The other 35% had other diagnoses. There were no differences at Day 2 in IES scores or a measure of acute stress response Stanford Acute Stress Reaction Questionnaire (SASRQ; Cardena et al., 2000). At 10 days there was a difference on the flashback subscale of the SASRQ with the PTSD group scoring higher. There were no predictive values for later diagnosis of PTSD from the Day 2 or Day 10 measure. There was a Day 2 difference in serum cortisol between those who eventually met criteria for PTSD versus those with MDD (with the eventual PTSDs lower). However, it disappeared when corrections for time of accident and time of blood sample were partialed out.

ALBANY MVA PROJECT

Because of the detailed records of the participants' reactions to their MVAs, we were able, after the fact by chart review, to identify 14 cases of ASD from among our 62 initial cases of PTSD. A graduate research assistant[1] reviewed all of the records, searching for descriptions of dissociative phenomena in the patient's account of the accident and its immediate aftermath. Those cases that were potentially positive were reviewed by one of the senior clinician–interviewers to confirm the presence of dissociative symptoms. Examples of dissociative phenomena were time distortion, feeling as if everything was happening in slow motion; depersonalization, feeling as if the MVA survivor were watching the accident occur from a removed position; being dazed (without head injury), and so forth.[2]

These data have been reported in detail in Barton, Blanchard, and Hickling (1996). To examine these subjects, we randomly selected two other PTSD cases, thus controlling for diagnosis and overall posttraumatic stress symptom severity, matched for gender and age (within five years) to the ASD cases. We then compared the 14 cases of ASD to 28 matched cases of PTSD on several families of variables, similar to the comparisons in chapter 8 on delayed-onset PTSD. We made comparisons on (a) pre-MVA variables including preexisting psychopathology; (b) post-MVA comorbidity and psychosocial functioning, as well as psychological test scores; and (c) six-month follow-up data.

---

[1] We acknowledge Kristine Barton's crucial role in the research reported in this chapter.
[2] Although the diagnoses of ASD were made retrospectively, and thus are subject to the potential biases Harvey and Bryant (2000a) identified, we believe they are reasonable because the delay interval was only about five weeks (compared to two years in Harvey and Bryant) and because *all* participants had current acute PTSD and thus all would have the same state-dependent recall biases.

TABLE 11.1
Comparison of MVA Survivors With Acute Stress Disorder to PTSDs on
Preexisting Conditions and Past Psychopathology

Variable	Acute stress disorder (n = 14)	PTSD (n = 28)	p
Previous trauma	12 (85.7%)	18 (64.3%)	.14
Number of previous traumas	2.00	1.07	.02
Past PTSD	6 (42.9%)	3 (10.7%)	.02
Past anxiety disorder (other than PTSD)	6 (42.9%)	6 (21.4%)	.15
Past mood disorder (other than MDD)	4 (28.6%)	0	.003
Past alcohol/substance abuse, or dependence	2 (14.3%)	1 (3.6%)	.20
Any past AXIS-II disorder	5 (35.7%)	1 (3.6%)	.005

Note. MDD = major depressive disorder. From Table 2, "Antecedents and Consequences of Acute Stress Disorder Among Motor Vehicle Accident Victims," by K. A. Barton et al., 1996, *Behaviour Research and Therapy, 34*, pp. 805–813. Copyright 1996 by Elsevier Science Ltd. Adapted with permission.

Pre-MVA Variables

Table 11.1 gives values for the ASD group and the PTSD comparison group on psychiatric variables, which occurred before the MVA. Consistent with Spiegel and Cardena's (1991) findings, and also those of Harvey and Bryant (1996, 1999b) we do find higher levels of previous trauma and previous PTSD among our MVA survivors who meet the criteria for ASD. We also find those with ASD were more likely to have met criteria for previous mood disorders other than major depression, again consistent with Harvey and Bryant (1996, 1999b). The latter study (1999b) found previous psychiatric treatment and previous PTSD were significant predictors of overall ASD symptom severity scores at the initial assessment. Finally, more than one third of our ASD subgroup meet the criteria for one or more personality disorders.

Initial Assessment Variables

The next set of comparisons are on variables assessed after the MVA at our initial assessment (one to four months post-MVA). These are tabulated in Table 11.2.

Examining the large array of variables in Table 11.2, we find *no* significant differences between those MVA survivors with PTSD who earlier met criteria for ASD and similar MVA survivors with PTSD who did not meet criteria for ASD. From our data, meeting criteria early on for ASD does

TABLE 11.2
Comparison of MVA Survivors With Acute Stress Disorders to PTSDs on Initial Psychiatric Psychological and Psychosocial Data

	Acute stress disorder (n = 14)	PTSD (n = 28)	p
BDI	17.2	15.8	.58
State–Anxiety	65.1	66.4	.82
Trait–Anxiety	67.2	59.7	.10
IES	41.1	34.8	.26
CAPS	66.1	58.3	.26
GAS	56.2	57.6	.69
Participant's estimate of present functioning	64.6	53.2	.42
Participant's satisfaction with recreational activities	3.7	3.0	.23
Participant's overall life satisfaction	3.4	3.3	.82
Major role functioning impairment	3.3	3.1	.65
Current major depression	9 (64.3%)	15 (53.6%)	.51
Current mood disorder other than MDD	1 (7.1%)	1 (3.6%)	.61
Any current Axis I disorder	9 (64.3%)	17 (60.7%)	.82

Note. BDI = Beck Depression Inventory; CAPS = Clinical Administered PTSD Scale; GAS = Global Assessment Scale; IES = Impact of Event Scale; MDD = major depressive disorder.

not seem to lead to a better or worse psychological picture one to four months postaccident.

Follow-Up Data

One of the primary reasons for noting the appearance of ASD and its associated dissociative symptoms is the observations (after the fact or retrospectively) by Marmar et al. (1994) that individuals with PTSD and dissociative symptoms tend to have a poorer outcome than those with PTSD and no dissociative symptoms.

Table 11.3 lists the primary measures on the two samples (ASD and PTSD controls) from the six-month follow-up assessment. (Details on the follow-up procedures are in chapters 4 and 7.)

One can see that the two groups show similar rates of remission and similar average CAPS scores at the six-month follow-up. Thus, on the primary variables of interest, meeting the criteria for ASD early on makes no apparent difference at six months. Comparisons on all of the other variables assessed at the six-month follow-up point are presented in Table 11.4.

TABLE 11.3
Six-Month Follow-up Data on Acute Stress Disorder MVA Survivors

Diagnostic measures	Acute stress disorder (n = 11)	PTSD (n = 25)	p
PTSD at 6 months	5 (45.5%)	12 (48%)	0.89
Dropout rate	3 (21.4%)	3 (10.7%)	0.35
6-month CAPS scores	45.7 (34.2%)	41.9 (32.1%)	0.75

Note. From Table 5, "Antecedents and Consequences of Acute Stress Disorder Among Motor Vehicle Accident Victims," by K. A. Barton et al., 1996, *Behaviour Research and Therapy, 34*, pp. 805–813. Copyright 1996 by Elsevier Science Ltd. Adapted with permission.

TABLE 11.4
Six-Month Follow-Up Data on Psychological, Psychiatric, and Psychosocial Variables for MVA Survivors With Acute Stress Disorder

Variable	Acute stress disorder (n = 11)	PTSD (n = 25)	p
BDI	18.0	15.4	0.56
State–Anxiety	62.4	64.1	0.84
Trait–Anxiety	67.2	63.6	0.56
GAS	63.4	61.2	0.66
IES	33.9	28.2	0.46
Individual's satisfaction with recreational activities	2.5	2.6	0.86
Major role function impairment	2.6	2.4	0.75
Current major depression	3 (27.3%)	9 (36%)	0.61
Current mood disorder other than MDD	2 (18.2%)	1 (4%)	0.16
Current alcohol/substance abuse or dependence	1 (9.1%)	0	0.13
Current Axis-I disorder	7 (63.6%)	13 (52%)	0.52

Note. BDI = Beck Depression Inventory; GAS = Global Assessment Scale; IES = Impact of Event Scale; MDD = major depressive disorder. From Table 4, "Antecedents and Consequences of Acute Stress Disorder Among Motor Vehicle Accident Victims," K. A. Barton et al., *Behaviour Research and Therapy, 34*, pp. 805–813. Copyright 1996 by Elsevier Science Ltd. Adapted with permission.

As with the initial assessment data, the six-month follow-up reveals no significant differences on any of the variables in Table 11.4 between those with ASD and the PTSD comparison group. Thus, we can find no follow-up effects of initially meeting the criteria for ASD in comparison to a matched group of MVA survivors.

We cannot speak, within our analyses, of whether initial dissociative symptoms predict later PTSD or not. Our initial assessment was not attuned to that question. The work of Harvey and Bryant (1998b, 1999c) in Australia indicates strong positive predictive power for the dissociative symptom cluster; however, Keane et al.'s (2000) detailed reanalysis of their work and other prospective studies casts some doubt on the specificity of the dissociative symptoms. It is also possible that we missed some cases of ASD among our sample, again because of the nature of the initial interview. We did not focus explicitly on the presence of dissociative symptoms during or after the MVA. Thus, we might have missed some cases. We do believe, however, that the cases we identified were positive for ASD because the dissociative symptoms were pronounced enough for the participant to mention them.

Based on our small, and retrospectively identified sample, we do not find that meeting the criteria for acute stress disorder within the month following the MVA is at all predictive of short-term (six month) outcome over and above a diagnosis of PTSD two months after the accident. Those individuals who are involved in serious MVAs, and who are likely to have the dissociative symptoms necessary to warrant the diagnosis of ASD, were different in some ways before the accident than MVA victims who develop PTSD but do not develop ASD.

12

PSYCHOPHYSIOLOGICAL ASSESSMENT WITH MVA SURVIVORS

Beginning with the early studies by Blanchard, Kolb, Pallmeyer, and Gerardi (1982) and Malloy, Fairbank, and Keane (1983), psychophysiological assessment has been an integral part of research on posttraumatic stress disorder (PTSD) in Vietnam War veterans. A large-scale multisite study of the potential role of psychophysiological assessments in the overall evaluation of Vietnam War veterans (CS–334; Keane, Kaloupek, Blanchard, et al, 1988) has been completed.

What seems clear from that research is that individuals with PTSD show a distinctive pattern of probably sympathetically mediated arousal when the participant with PTSD is exposed to cues reminiscent of the trauma. This finding appears robust enough with heart rate (HR), and perhaps electrodermal activity (EDA), to have utility at the level of the individual subject. For a comprehensive (though somewhat dated) review of this research, see Blanchard and Buckley (1999).

Research with other traumatized populations such as sexual assault victims (Forneris, Blanchard, & Jonay, 1996) and civilian populations exposed to mixed trauma (Shalev, Orr, & Pitman, 1993) have replicated the general findings, which emerged from the Vietnam War veteran research.

STUDIES OF MOTOR VEHICLE ACCIDENT SURVIVORS: EARLY STUDIES OF PSYCHOPHYSIOLOGICAL ASSESSMENT

In an early report from our center, we (Blanchard, Hickling, & Taylor, 1991) assessed four motor vehicle accident (MVA) survivors (one male and three females) with PTSD with measures of heart rate, systolic and diastolic blood pressure (BP), and skin-resistance level as a measure of electrodermal activity (EDA). Procedures included exposing participants to three stressors, mental arithmetic and imagining two idiosyncratic scenes reminiscent of their own MVA, separated by 5-minute baselines. The scripts for the scenes were similar to the procedure of Pitman, Orr, Forgue, deJong, and Claiborn (1987).

Participants showed heart rate increases to each of the MVA descriptions ($n = 8$) averaging eight beats per minute (BPM). On five of the eight trials (and at least once for each participant) there was a systolic blood pressure increase. Only two of four participants showed EDA responses. These data support the value of the heart rate (HR) response to idiosyncratic descriptions of their own MVAs as a useful assessment tool for assessing PTSD in MVA survivors.

Shalev et al. (1993) assessed an Israeli civilian population ($n = 26$) who had earlier experienced various civilian traumas, including 10 who had been in MVAs. (Unfortunately, for our purposes, separate data on MVA survivors were not available.) Half ($n = 13$) of the sample met the DSM–III–R criteria for PTSD, half did not. Average age was 35 for the PTSD group, 28 for the non-PTSD. Average time since the trauma was 4.3 years for the PTSD group, 5.6 years for the non-PTSDs. Among the MVA survivors, four met criteria for PTSD, six did not.

The research team used the idiosyncratic scripts procedure of Pitman et al. (1987). Results from between-group comparisons of those with PTSD to those without it during the personal traumatic imagery revealed significant differences on HR (13.9 BPM increase versus 2.0 BPM increase [$p = .003$]) and on frontal electromyogram (EMG; $p = .01$) but not on skin conductance, although there was a baseline difference ($p = .04$) between the groups on this measure. The HR finding is consistent with much of the research on Vietnam War veterans with PTSD.

Bryant, Harvey, Gordon, and Barry (1995) assessed initial eye fixations and orienting responses (electrodermal activity) of MVA survivors ($n = 10$) with PTSD in comparison to age and gender-matched controls. Those with PTSD satisfied DSM–IV (American Psychiatric Association, 1994) criteria based on a structured interview and the Impact of Event Scale (IES; Horowitz et al., 1979). Mean time since the MVA was 38.6 months. Research participants were asked to look at four words (in quadrants around a fixation point), which on certain trials included "threat words" (e.g., "blood", "ambulance") or neutral words. Only half of the PTSDs were used in the electroder-mal data analysis. The remaining five PTSDs showed more orienting re-sponses overall than the controls but did not respond differentially to the threat words. Thus, in terms of psychophysiological responding, the MVA survivors with PTSD were more responsive, but the responsivity was not necessarily to cues reminiscent of the trauma.

VERY EARLY BASAL PSYCHOPHYSIOLOGICAL RESPONSES AS PREDICTORS OF PTSD

Numerous studies have shown that individuals and groups of individuals with PTSD, when exposed to cues reminiscent of the trauma, demonstrate greater psychophysiological responding than groups who have been exposed to the trauma but who did not have PTSD. Several studies of MVA survivors have recently taken a different approach by examining basal responses, measured early after the trauma, to see if these responses are an early indicator of who will eventually develop PTSD. Certainly, there was early evidence, summarized by Blanchard (1990) that baseline heart rate (HR) and blood pressure (BP) were elevated among Vietnam veterans with PTSD who were about to undergo a psychophysiological assessment in comparison to other veteran groups.

Shalev et al., 1998

In the first study, Shalev, Sahar, Freedman, et al. (1998) followed up 86 trauma survivors who attended the emergency department (ED) but who were not admitted to the hospital with assessments in the ED and then at one week, one month, and four months posttrauma. These constituted part of the total sample of trauma survivors (n = 239 who agreed to the study and n = 91 who completed all follow-ups). The sample included 70 MVA survivors (81.4%), as well as six survivors of terrorist attacks, five survivors of work-related accidents, and four who were injured in accidents at home. There were 34 women and 52 men of average age 27.3 years. Thirty-three (38.4%) met criteria for PTSD, based on the Clinical Administered PTSD Scale (CAPS), at one month; 20 (23.3%) met criteria at four months.

HR and BP were measured in the ED using a Critikon Dynamapp for routine vital signs. At the follow-up points, these variables were measured in a psychophysiology laboratory over a 5-minute period after a 5-minute adaptation phase.

Comparisons of two groups based on four-month PTSD diagnoses yielded significant differences in an emergency department HR (PTSD: 95.1 bpm, non-PTSD: 84.7 bpm, p < .002). At the one-week assessment there was a trend (p = .09) for the laboratory values to differ (PTSD: 77.3 bpm, non-PTSD: 72.6 bpm). The two groups did not differ at one month or four months. No systematic data were presented on BP. Males had higher ED HR values (88.6 bpm) than females (82.9 bpm). There was no sex × PTSD status interaction.

The most intriguing parts of the results were that four-month PTSD status was significantly predicted by status of the traumatic event with an additional significant increment in prediction of ED HR (p = .005) after being controlled for age, sex, trauma history, and degree of initial dissociation. At the level of the individual case, with an ED HR of 90 bpm or greater, 15 of the 20 cases of PTSD (75%) are correctly classified. Sixteen of 66 cases of non-PTSD (24%) are misclassified. Conversely, only 5 of 20 (25%) PTSD cases have ED HR of less than 90 bpm as compared to 50 of 66 (76%) cases of non-PTSD.

Bryant et al., 2000

The second study was conducted in Australia on a sample of hospitalized MVA survivors. As noted earlier (chapter 11), Bryant, Harvey, and colleagues (Bryant, Harvey, Guthrie, & Moulds, 2000) assessed 146 hospitalized MVA survivors for possible Acute Stress Disorder (ASD) either while hospitalized or within a month of admission. At six months post-MVA they were able to reassess 113 of the participants (77%) for PTSD, using the Composite International Diagnostic Interview (CIDI; Peters et al., 1996). The sample of 113 was made up of 67 males and 46 females. Resting HR and BP were measured with an Omnicare monitor on day of discharge as the patient lay on a hospital bed. This was on average 7.7 days after admission.

Of the 113 who were reassessed, 17 initially met criteria for ASD, 17 for subclinical ASD, and 79 for no ASD. At the six-month assessment, 24 (21.2%) met criteria for PTSD, whereas 89 did not.

The BP data yielded no significant differences. Comparisons of the three ASD groups showed that those with sub-ASD (85.6 bpm) had higher discharge HRs than those with ASD (77.1 bpm) or non-ASD (76.2 bpm). A comparison of discharge HR for those with six-month PTSD (82.9 bpm) versus non-PTSD (76.3 bpm) was significant (p < .01).

The authors found that discharge HR added a significant increment (4% of variance) in predicting six-month PTSD status over that found with the ASD diagnosis (31% of variance). They found resting HR above 90 bpm was the best predictor.

These results have led some to speculate that very early sympathetic nervous system arousal, as indexed by elevated HR, might be associated with developing PTSD. They further reasoned that, if one could block this early arousal pharmacologically, then the development of PTSD might be prevented.

A small-scale double-blind placebo-controlled trial of propranolol as a beta adrenergic blocking agent was tried by Pitman, Sanders, Zusman, et al. (2002). Forty-one ED attendees who had suffered a trauma (Criterion A.1) and had the required subjective distress (Criterion A.2) and who had resting HR of 80 bpm or higher were randomized to 160 mg/day (in four 40-mg doses) of propranolol (n = 18) or comparable placebo (n = 23) for 10 days followed by a 9-day taper period. The drug group had 8 males and 13 MVA survivors (72.2%), whereas the placebo group had 12 males and 16 MVA survivors (69.6%).

Assessments with the CAPS were done at one month and three months. Eleven propranolol (61%) and 20 placebo (87%) recipients were assessed at one month. (There was a trend [p = .08] for greater dropout in the drug group.) Nine propranolol and 15 placebo patients were assessed at three months.

PTSD rate at one month was 6 out of 20 (30%) in the placebo condition and 2 out of 11 (18%) in the active drug (ns). At three months, there was one case of PTSD (11%) in the drug arm and two (13%) in the placebo arm. Despite the guarded optimism of the authors (p. 192), we do not find any evidence of a secondary prevention of PTSD effect for early beta blockade with propranolol.

Albany MVA Project: ED Vital Signs and PTSD

Blanchard, Hickling, Galovski, and Veazey (2002) have taken a somewhat different approach to this issue by retrieving vital signs information, taken at the ED shortly after the MVA, on 76 MVA survivors (62 female, 14 male) who were a part of our Cohort 2 treatment seekers. No one who was approached about the study declined permission to retrieve vital sign data. The average age of the sample was 38.7 years; the ethnic mix was 64 Caucasian (84.2%) and 12 minority (15.8%).

We obtained diagnoses of PTSD or not at two points in time, for the month following the MVA and for the month just passed (current). On average the participants were 13 months post-MVA. Diagnoses were on the basis of the CAPS (n = 68) or the PTSD Checklist (PCL; Weathers et al., 1993; n = 8) used as a structured interview. We found 50 of 76 (65.8%) met criteria for current PTSD, whereas 58 (76.3%) met criteria one month after the MVA.

Comparisons of ED vital signs, based on current diagnostic status, revealed significantly ($p < .05$) higher ED HR values and diastolic blood pressure (DBP) values for those without current PTSD than those with current PTSD (HR: current PTSD—83.4 bpm, non-PTSD—89.5 bpm; DBP:

current PTSD—79.8 bpm Hg, non-PTSD—86.4 mm Hg). The systolic blood pressure (SBP) values were in the same direction but not significant. None of the comparisons based on one-month PTSD status were significant, but all showed the same directional trend for the non-PTSD group to have higher ED vital sign readings than the PTSD group (e.g., HR PTSD: 84.5 bpm; non-PTSD: 88.7 bpm).

When the sample was subdivided on the basis of Shalev's value of ED HR of 85 bpm or greater as predictive of PTSD one-month post-MVA, we found significantly ($p < .05$) higher current CAPS scores for the low HR group (low HR CAPS: 67.6; high HR CAPS: 50.6. There was also a trend ($p < .10$) for the one-month post-MVA PCL scores (gathered retrospectively), to be higher for low HR participants (low HR PCL: 54.1; high HR PCL: 48.8).

Examining the data categorically, the low HR group ($n = 43$) showed 79.1% positive for PTSD currently versus 48.5% of the high HR ($n = 33$) group ($p < .01$). For the one-month diagnostic status, 90% of those with low HR values were positive for PTSD versus 71.4% of those with high ED HR values.

Thus, our data directly contradict those of Shalev et al. (1998) and Bryant et al. (2000). There are several differences between the samples that might account for the differences: (a) a majority of our sample was female (81% versus 39.5% in Shalev et al. and 36.3% in Bryant et al.); when we covaried sex, the results still hold up; (b) our sample was older (38.7 years versus 27.3 years in Shalev and 31.0 years in Bryant). When one covaries age, the results still hold up. Our sample was 86.5% Caucasian; ethnicity was not available on the other two samples. Our sample was all treatment-seeking, whereas the other two were receiving routine care for their traumatic physical injuries.

We are left with the conclusion that elevated HR values taken in the ED, or by emergency personnel at the MVA scene, are *not* predictive of short-term or longer term PTSD status. If anything, lower HR values are more likely associated with later PTSD. Clearly, more research is needed on this interesting topic to resolve the discrepancy and before one bases a secondary prevention treatment trial on ED vital signs.

THE ALBANY MVA PROJECT: COHORT 1

Psychophysiological testing was an integral part of the overall assessment of the MVA survivors in the Albany MVA project. The results from Cohort 1 have been reported twice: the first paper (Blanchard, Hickling, Taylor, Loos, & Gerardi, 1994b) described the results for the first 50 MVA survivors and 40 non-MVA controls. The second paper (Blanchard et al.,

1996) reported on a replication of the initial results with an additional 105 MVA survivors and 54 additional controls. The second paper also reported one-year reassessment data on the whole MVA sample ($n = 125$) as well as some other analyses on the combined sample.

Psychophysiological Responses

In our initial report we included skin resistance level as a measure of EDA. It was dropped from the replication because of equipment difficulties and undetected electrode failure. It was measured from 1 cm silver/silver chloride electrodes filled with Beckman electrode paste and attached to the ventral surface of the index and middle finger, which had previously been cleaned with isopropanol. We used a Grass Model 7 Polygraph and a 7-P1 Preamplifier. Once per minute the bridge circuit was calibrated to zero and the level of skin resistance read from the dials.

Clinical Hint

Although EDA has not proved to have the discriminating power of HR in our work with PTSD, based on its value in other studies we recommend it be included as a second response (after HR) if one is going to use more than one response measure. If only one measure is to be taken, we strongly urge the use of HR.

*   *   *

We measured HR, SBP, and DBP with a Dinamapp Critikon 1990, which was programmed automatically to take readings of the responses once per minute. It uses an inflatable cuff and microphone over the brachial artery, at the level of the heart, to detect Korotkoff sounds (K sounds) for determining SBP (onset of K sounds) and DBP (offset of K sounds). It measures interbeat interval during this period and converts that to HR in BPM. These values are displayed digitally.

Forehead electromyogram (EMG) was measured with Grass precious metal electrodes filled with Grass electrode paste. After cleaning the forehead with Brasivol and then isopropanol, the active sensors were attached to the forehead about 2½ cm above the eyebrow, centered on the pupil. The ground was placed midway between them. The response was detected by a Grass 7-P3 preamplifier and integrated with a 7-P10.

Clinical Hint

Forehead or frontal EMG has proven of little utility in this work and that of others working on the psychophysiology of PTSD. We *do not* recommend using it.

Assessment Procedures

All of our assessments were done with the participant comfortably seated in an upholstered chair with good support for the neck and head (a few assessments were done on individuals who were still in a wheelchair because of injuries). Feet were on the floor. The room was dimly lit. The participant was alone in the room in voice contact with the technician over an intercom. (In Blanchard et al., 1991, the experimenter was in the room with the participant.)

The conditions and verbatim instructions are contained in Table 12.1.

As one can see, there are four stressors, each lasting about 3 minutes, separated by baseline phases of 5 minutes.

The mental math is seen as a standard stressor, which elicits a pressor response (increased BP and HR) in most individuals.

The idiosyncratic audiotapes attempted to capture the participant's MVA as he or she had described it at the initial assessment. There was a brief lead-in setting the date, time of day, and situation. Then elements of the MVA were described, including actions by the survivor, thoughts, feelings and sensations, with special attention to emotional responses. Two slightly different descriptions were made by the assessor so that the survivor was asked to imagine his or her own MVA twice.

Exhibit 12.1 presents a verbatim transcript of part of the idiosyncratic script used in the assessment.

The final stressor was a 3-minute videotape, depicting several car crashes, some viewed from inside the vehicle. There was little depiction of blood and serious injury. It was a composite from available materials.

We used a single fixed order of experimental conditions. With hindsight, we might have had a tighter study had the order of stressors been randomized or varied by a Latin square. This would have controlled for possible order effects.

Results for Heart Rate

By far the most consistent and most powerful results came from HR, with SBP a distant second. The interaction of groups (MVA survivors with PTSD, subsyndromal PTSD, non-PTSD, and non-MVA controls) by conditions [see Table 12.1] was significant for HR and SBP but not for DBP or EMG. The most valuable data came from HR response to the first audiotape. We calculated a reactivity or response score by subtracting the preceding baseline value from the value for the stressor.

The average HR reactivity values for this condition for each of the four groups, along with the initial baseline HR value, are presented in Table 12.2.

TABLE 12.1
Psychophysiological Test Conditions

Adaptation 2–7 minutes
  Polygraph is calibrated
  Dynamapp is calibrated
  SUDS* rating is elicited

Baseline (BL) 5 minutes
  "Please sit quietly with your eyes closed."
  Data sampled = mean minutes 2–4.

Mental math 3 minutes
  "Please count backwards by 7's starting at 250."
  SUDS, "How anxious do you feel right now?"
  Data sampled - minute 2

Return to BL: #1 5 minutes
  "Please sit quietly with your eyes closed."
  Data sampled = mean minutes 2–4

Return to BL: #2, #3, #4

Audiotape #1: 3 minutes
  "Please listen to this audiotape."
  SUDS, "How anxious do you feel?"

Return to BL: #2: 5 minutes (same instructions as return to BL #1)

Audio #2: 3 minutes (same instructions as Audiotape #1)

Return to BL: #3: 5 minutes (same instructions as return to BL #1)

Eyes open 2 minutes
  Please sit quietly with your eyes open."
  Data sampled = mean minutes 1 and 2 used in lieu of return to BL #3

Videotape: 3 minutes
  "Please watch this video."
  SUDS, "How anxious do you feel?"
  Data sample = minute 2

Return to BL: #4: 5 minutes (same instructions as return to BL #1)

Relax: 2 minutes
  "Please take a deep breath and let yourself begin to relax. (Pause) And take a
  deep breath and let yourself sink more deeply into the chair. (Pause) Just let
  your muscles become more and more heavy as you sink more deeply into the
  chair. (Pause) As you become more and more relaxed I'd like you to imagine as
  vividly as you possibly can that you are . . ." (describe back a specific scene
  elicited during set up. This is a scene describing a specific instance when
  participant was warm and relaxed. Examples include lying on beach, lying in tub
  of warm water, fishing, or looking out over a mountain valley.)
  Data sampled = mean minutes 1 and 2

Return to BL #5: 15 minutes
  "Please sit quietly with your eyes closed, enjoying your relaxed feelings."
  Data sampled = mean minutes 2–4

Note. From Table 1, "The Psychophysiology of Motor Vehicle Accident Related Post-Traumatic Stress Disorder," by E. B. Blanchard et al., 1994b, *Behavior Therapy, 25*, pp. 453–467. Copyright 1994 by Association for Advancement of Behavior Therapy. Adapted with permission.
*Subjective Units of Discomfort (SUDS): 0–100, 0 = not at all anxious, 100 = the most one can imagine.

EXHIBIT 12.1
Idiosyncratic Script Used in Assessment

You are on your way home from work, you are in a hurry. As you are driving down a very familiar road, a road you have driven many times before, you come upon a car. This car is driving at about 40 MPH You want to pass this car and you begin to do so when you enter a passing zone. You are half way passing this car, you notice that there is another car, an oncoming car in your lane now. You have been taking your time to safely get around the car. You increase you speed, in part because the car you are passing has also increased her speed. As you pull back in you oversteer, you begin to go off the road. You overcorrect, as you swerve you cross the yellow line, you overcorrect again, you swerve and you are coming back into the lane that you had been driving in. You are not able to keep the car on the road. You are traveling at about 60 MPH. You go off the road. You hit a ditch. You go end-over-end. Your next memory is laying on the ground. You are taking your time to think about what has happened to you. You want to check your movement. You move your head. You move your arms, but you cannot move your legs.

TABLE 12.2
Initial Assessment Heart Rate Reactivity Scores: All Diagnostic Groups at All Four Stressors and Initial Basal Values

Stressor	Diagnostic groups			
	PTSD	Subsyndromal PTSD	Non-PTSD	Non-MVA
Mental arithmetic	7.7	6.0	8.5	8.8
	(7.3)	(7.6)	(6.89)	(9.59)
Audiotape #1	4.2[a]	0.3[b]	0.8[b]	−0.6[b]
	(6.7)	(5.2)	(5.30)	(4.29)
Audiotape #2	1.9	1.1	1.2	0.3
	(3.9)	(4.3)	(3.34)	(3.17)
Videotape	−1.6	−2.0	−2.8	−1.6
	(6.6)	(4.0)	(3.52)	(3.80)
Baseline - 1	73.0 (10.7)	71.0 (9.3)	70.0 (10.7)	70.3 (10.9)

Note. Means in a row that share a superscript are not different at the p = .01 level by Duncan's Multiple Range Test. From Table 2, "Psychophysiology of Post-Traumatic Stress Disorder Related to Motor Vehicle Accidents: Replication and Extension," by E. B. Blanchard et al., 1996, *Journal of Consulting and Clinical Psychology, 64*, pp. 742–751. Copyright 1996 by the American Psychological Association. Adapted with permission.

The one-way ANOVA across groups for the reactivity scores was highly significant (p = 0.0003). Post hoc comparisons (Duncan's Multiple Range Test at p = .01) showed that the PTSD group had a greater response than any of the other groups, which did not differ.

The baseline HR values did not differ, contradicting the finding reported by Blanchard (1990) in his review of the Vietnam War veteran literature that veterans with PTSD have higher resting HRs (by about 5 to 10 BPM) than other comparison groups of veterans. The combined individual subject data from our two reports are shown in Figure 12.1.

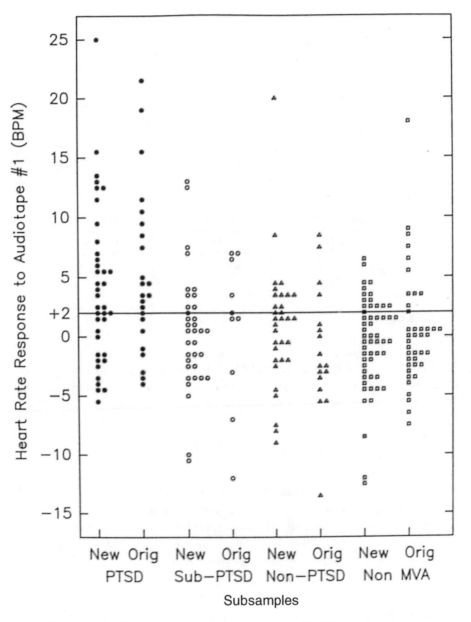

Figure 12.1. Heart rate response to audiotape #1 (BPM): subsamples.

Examining these combined data, we find that a cut-off score of +2 BPM—that is, an increase in HR from return to baseline #1 to audiotape 1 of 2 BPM or greater discriminates among the groups (PTSD and other [sub-PTSD, non-PTSD, and non-MVA]) fairly well, with a sensitivity of 65.6 and specificity of 68.6 and a diagnostic efficiency of 67.9.

TABLE 12.3
Psychological Test Scores of MVA Survivors With PTSD Who Show, or Fail to Show, Heart Rate Response to Audiotape #1

Test	HR responders (n = 40)		HR nonresponders (n = 21)		
	X	(SD)	X	(SD)	p
Total CAPS score	61.5	(23.3)	55.4	(17.8)	ns
CAPS score for item #17 (physiological reactivity)	4.2	(2.0)	3.3	(2.3)	.066
BDI	16.5	(10.4)	13.5	(4.0)	ns
STAI–Trait	61.9	(13.6)	57.0	(13.3)	.096
STAI–State	67.3	(17.2)	58.9	(18.4)	.040

Note. BDI = Beck Depression Inventory; CAPS = Clinical Administered PTSD Scale; HR = heart rate; ns = not significant. From Table 4, "Psychophysiology of Post-Traumatic Stress Disorder Related to Motor Vehicle Accidents: Replication and Extension," by E. B. Blanchard et al., 1996, *Journal of Consulting and Clinical Psychology, 64*, pp. 742–751. Copyright 1996 by the American Psychological Association. Adapted with permission.

Clinical Hint

We believe this level of separation on a single measure has clinical utility at the level of the individual MVA survivor. Group mean differences are useful for hypothesis testing but one needs a simple, convenient measure, instead of a complex multivariate discriminate function, to have clinical utility.

Nonresponders

Although correctly classifying two thirds of the instances of PTSD among MVA survivors is useful, one might ask if there are differences between HR responders and HR nonresponders. We compared these two groups on a number of psychological measures of anxiety, depression, CAPS total score, and CAPS score on the physiological reactivity item. These values are presented in Table 12.3.

The only between-group difference was on state anxiety, with the HR responder group more anxious (p = .040) and about 8 units higher (67.3 vs. 58.9).

Follow-Up Results

As mentioned earlier, we were able to reassess 125 MVA survivors at the one-year follow-up, including 45 who had initially been diagnosed with PTSD. Of these 45 initial PTSDs, 15 still met the criteria for PTSD and 30 did not. Analyses of their psychophysiological data (especially HR) show a decrease in reactivity for all participants for all stressors; however, those who do not remit (remain full PTSD at one-year) continue to show a positive HR response to audiotape #1.

Determining if Initial Psychophysiological Data Predict 12-Month Clinical Status

Our final task in using these data was to determine if initial psychophysiological data predict 12-month clinical status. We had initial psychophysiological data on 48 PTSDs who were assessed at the 12-month follow-up (three refused the follow-up psychophysiological assessment). Among this group, 16 still met the criteria for full PTSD, 7 for subsyndromal PTSD and 25 for non-PTSD (essentially full remission).

For these HR data, we used a transformation that we previously used with Vietnam War veterans: From the audiotape #1 reactivity score (our best discriminating condition) we subtracted the reactivity to mental arithmetic as a way of correcting for overall tendency to respond to stressors with an increase in HR. The group mean values for this transformed response were PTSD: +2.2; subsyndromal PTSD: −6.5, non-PTSD: −5.2. The PTSDs are significantly greater on this parameter ($p = .027$) than the other two groups (full or partial remitters) combined.

When we examine the individual results, using a cut-off of 0 (equal response to mental arithmetic and audiotape #1), we correctly identify 11 of 16 initial PTSDs who have not remitted and 26 of 32 remitters, for a total correct classification (diagnostic efficiency) of 37 of 48 (77.1%). This represents an improvement on base rates of 66.7%.

It thus appears that psychophysiological assessment results obtained 1 to 4 months after the MVA have clinical utility, not only initially in helping to confirm the diagnosis but also as a predictor of how the patient will be functioning 12 months later. For these reasons, we believe that psychophysiological assessment has a truly useful role to play in the overall assessment of MVA survivors.

Our speculation is that the finding of greater psychophysiological reactivity among nonremitters with initial PTSD could represent a stronger conditioned emotional response (see Keane, Zimering, & Caddell's [1985] behavioral model of PTSD) or a more entrenched cognitive fear structure (as postulated by Foa, Steketee, & Rothbaum [1989] cognitive model of PTSD).

THE ALBANY MVA PROJECT: COHORT 2

We continued to include the psychophysiological assessment as part of the total assessment for participants in Cohort 2. The procedures and equipment used with this treatment-seeking population were more or less the same, with three notable exceptions: (a) given the lack of physiological responsivity to the videotape of crash scenes, it was eliminated. (b) Given the lack of discrimination among groups provided by frontal EMG, this response was eliminated. (c) We reinstituted use of the EDA measure, and measured skin resistance level (SRL), as described earlier. The results of this assessment are summarized in Veazey, Blanchard, Hickling, and Buckley (in press).

Participants

We completed initial psychophysiological assessments on 132 MVA survivors who were seeking nondrug treatment for distress related to the accident. As noted earlier, this population had to meet three screening criteria: (a) They had received medical attention for MVA-related injuries within two days of the accident; (2) they were 5 to 24 months post-MVA (with an average of 12.4 months, they were much more chronic than Cohort 1); and (c) at a telephone screening interview they indicated enough current symptoms that they would probably meet criteria for subsyndromal PTSD.

From the 78 MVA survivors who completed the initial treatment or wait list, we were able to obtain a posttreatment psychophysiological assessment on 73. Results from these pre–post assessments are presented in chapter 17, which describes the treatment study outcome.

Based on CAPS interviews, we had a sample of 92 individuals with PTSD, 23 with subsyndromal PTSD, and 17 non-PTSD. Demographic data on this subsample from Cohort 2 are presented in Table 12.4. (With the exception of CAPS scores, the three groups did not differ.)

Results

Because preliminary analyses again showed no significant differential responding among the groups to blood pressure and EDA responses, we focused solely on heart rate (HR). As described earlier in Cohort 1, we calculated reactivity scores by subtracting the preceding baseline value of HR from the average value of HR during the stressor (that is, for mental arithmetic, we subtracted the average value for the initial baseline from the average value for mental arithmetic). The mean HR reactivity scores for each group for each condition are contained in Table 12.5.

These values were subjected to groups × stressors repeated-measures ANOVA that yielded a main effect of group ($p = .04$), a main effect of

TABLE 12.4
Characteristics of MVA Survivors by Diagnostic Group

Characteristics	PTSD	Subsyndromal	Non-PTSD
N	92	23	17
CAPS score			
M	72.4	36.3	16.8
SD	20.4	11.4	7.7
Gender (male/female)	23/69	9/14	3/14
Ethnicity (White/non-White)	84/8	19/4	15.2
Age			
M	39.7	41.9	43.4
SD	11.1	13.2	12.6
Months since MVA			
M	12.7	12.3	10.7
SD	8.8	7.7	7.0
Baseline heartrate (BPM)			
M	73.0	70.9	77.0
SD			

TABLE 12.5
Mean Physiological Reactivity Scores for Heart Rate for All Diagnostic Groups for All Stressors

	PTSD		Subsyndromal		Non-PTSD	
Condition	M	SD	M	SD	M	SD
Mental arithmetic	9.2[a]	6.5	9.7[a]	7.3	9.3[a]	4.9
Audiotape 1	7.0[a]	7.0	1.4[b]	4.0	3.9[b]	4.0
Audiotape 2	5.2[a]	4.4	3.5[a]	5.0	3.3[a]	3.7

Note. Means that share a superscript are not different at the .05 level.

stressor (p = .001), and very importantly an interaction of group × stressor (p = .002), indicating differential responding by the three groups of MVA survivors to the different stressors.

Follow-up analyses showed no difference in responding to mental arithmetic and only a trend (p = .10) for differential responding to audiotape #2. As shown in Table 12.5, the significant differential responding was to audiotape #1 (p < .001). Those with current PTSD, a year after the MVA, responded greater to audiotape #1 (X = 7.0 bpm) than either those with subsyndromal PTSD (X = 1.4 bpm) or the non-PTSD group (X = 3.9 bpm). The latter two groups did not differ.

Thus, the results from Cohort 1 with MVA survivors about two months post-MVA are replicated with this treatment-seeking sample who are more than 12 months post-MVA.

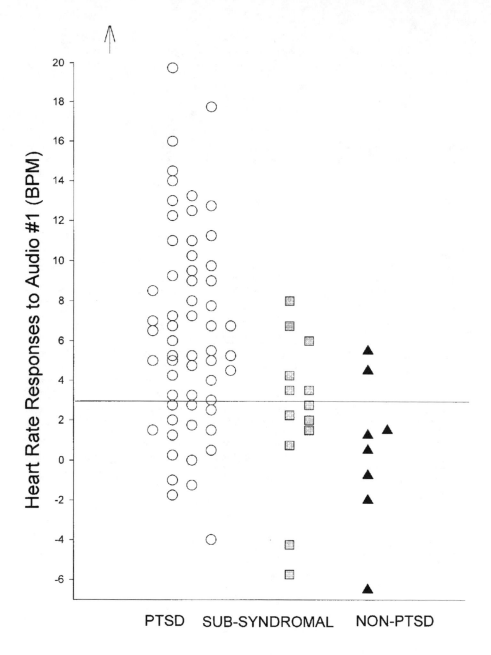

Figure 12.2. Heart rate response to audiotape #1 (BPM): diagnostic status.

Clinical Hint

This finding seems to indicate that the psychophysiological responding is a fairly robust one that holds up, on a group basis, over time.

Individual Subject Data

As we have done in the past, we examined the audiotape #1 HR reactivity data at the level of the individual participant. These results are in Figure 12.2.

If we take the cut-off score developed on Cohort 1 of audiotape #1 of + 2.0 bpm, we find that 71 (77%) of those with PTSD are responders and 18 (23%) nonresponders. This is slightly better separation (66% responder versus 34% nonresponder) than we found for those from Cohort 1 with acute PTSD.

The use of psychophysiological responses in identifying MVA survivors with PTSD could present a partial answer to the issue raised in chapter 10 about detection of malingering. We say partial answer for two reasons: With our current psychophysiological work described in this chapter, we find positive responses in about two thirds of cases (overall diagnostic efficiency of 67.9) acutely, which means we misdiagnose in almost a third of cases. With more chronic cases we find a positive response in about three quarters of cases. That level of potential error would probably not stand up in a legal setting. Second, at this point we do not know how well an MVA victim without PTSD could simulate the psychophysiological profile of an MVA survivor who did suffer from PTSD. We provide preliminary new research to answer the latter issue in chapter 13.

Despite these shortcomings, we believe psychophysiological responses, because they are a non-self-report measure and thus are not as readily faked, have potentially a strong role to play in the comprehensive assessment of the MVA survivor.

13

CAN YOU DETECT MALINGERED MVA-RELATED PTSD? THE ALBANY MVA PROJECT'S ANSWER

One concern that arises in both research and clinical practice (both treatment and forensic settings) is the veracity of symptoms presented. Because of the nature of personal injury law, it is often the case that some question might be raised over whether an individual might be malingering or exaggerating their symptoms for purposes of financial gain. Excellent reviews about malingering and detection of malingering can be found in the recent literature (e.g., Resnick, 1997; Rogers, 1997a).

However, as discussed earlier in chapter 9, Miller's assertion that most individuals who are presenting injury-related symptoms would improve markedly once they have been compensated has not been supported by the literature. In fact as discussed, it has been documented instead that even after most litigants have received payment, their lives are little changed and symptoms continue unabated.

Due to its link with a causal factor and the psychological distress that follows, posttraumatic stress disorder (PTSD) has increasingly become a diagnosis for which the potential for legal recourse and financial compensation for the psychological distress seem plausible. This has led to a growing concern about whether an individual might be exaggerating or lying about his or her disorder. Often, the authenticity of the diagnosis, as pointed out by Resnick (1997), is largely based on observable behaviors and a subjective history. This type of information is more open to a challenge than physical disorders, which usually can be supported with physical and biological evidence.

Although there have been concerns about the ability of clinicians to detect malingering for reasons of low index of suspicion, issues of legal liability, and limited data from which to draw a conclusion, other assessments such as psychological testing and psychophysiological assessment have also been found to be problematic.

Testing has been found to limit capability for detecting feigned PTSD. The MMPI–2 has been used in a number of studies, using both the clinical scales and special scales developed for the detection of malingering. Although useful for assessing clinical conditions, both types of scales have been found to be of limited use in discriminating true cases of PTSD from simulated efforts (Greene, 1991).

The same concern over limited sensitivity and failure to discriminate groups has been noted for psychophysiological assessments. Although PTSD is unique among many of the psychological disorders in that there is a physiological component that is required to be present for diagnosis, not all cases of PTSD present with the same pattern of response. In fact some individuals are quite capable of blocking uncomfortable physiological arousal as a way of coping with their distress. As reviewed earlier, our studies have found that only about two thirds of the motor vehicle accident (MVA) survivors with PTSD can be correctly identified as having PTSD on the basis of heart rate response alone (see chapter 12). Thus, the results of the psychophysiological assessment must be viewed within the context of the overall assessment. The purpose of the psychophysiological assessment is not to assess truthfulness or even reach a definitive diagnosis, but rather it is to assist in the assessment of some of the PTSD symptoms. The presence or absence of physiological reactivity is neither sufficient nor necessary for a diagnosis to be made.

Resnick (1997) pointed out that perhaps one of the better-recognized ways to detect malingering is the clinical interview. Within the interview, he stated that there are several things that can help to detect malingering. The first is to determine if there is an understandable motive to malinger. These can include seeking compensation, avoiding punishment, or gaining admission to a hospital. He has suggested a series of questions that can be asked when a clinician is investigating the possibility of malingering after a traumatic event. These include questions investigating a poor work record; previous "incapacitating" injuries; markedly discrepant capacity for work and recreation; unvarying, repetitive dreams; antisocial personality traits; overidealized functioning before the trauma; evasiveness; and inconsistency in symptom presentation. Resnick goes on to suggest that for a clinician to make a decision about malingering, there should be a clear motivation and at least two of the associated characteristics (e.g., irregular employment, previous claims, capacity for recreation but not work, evasiveness, etc.) during the evaluation and strong confirmatory evidence of malingering before the possibility is even raised.

Recent articles have gone so far as to caution that coaching of psychological symptoms may take place before an evaluation. Rogers (1997b) has argued it is impossible to have a naive individual tested in today's world for reasons of informed consent and the ready access to information about psychological evaluations, including information on detection of malingering. Recent articles have even reported on lawyers coaching clients on how to fake symptoms for a psychological evaluation (Youngjohn, 1995).

INITIAL STUDY

The Albany Motor Vehicle Project presented what we saw as a unique opportunity to explore some of the concerns found in forensic evaluations of MVA victims involved in personal injury lawsuits. Because the project had a steady flow of potential research participants evaluated for entry in a number of studies, the opportunity for examining comparison groups of simulating participants and matching them with "true" cases became possible.

The project had an easily accessible comparison group of people who were in MVAs but did not develop PTSD or other comorbid symptoms. We then had the opportunity to coach these post-MVA individuals in the simulation of PTSD (which would be comparable to a real-world comparison of facetious disordered individuals who might be exaggerating the psychological symptoms for financial gain). We could also obtain (though not as easy as one would think) a group of individuals who were not in a recent MVA and then coach those individuals in the occurrence and presentation of PTSD following MVAs. We could also examine if the amount of information increased or decreased the skill in replicating PTSD and other psychological disorders of interest. The amount of information each group received, either coached (trained) or uncoached (naive) could then be used as a possible comparison for answering the question of whether or not individuals with varying amounts of information could successfully respond on psychological tests in a fashion similar to "true" (i.e., no reason to suspect malingered or facetious symptoms) cases of PTSD. The first study examined these concerns, and is summarized next (Hickling, Taylor, Blanchard, & Devineni, 1999).

Participants

Participants in the first study were 130 community dwelling adults and students (mean age = 29.3, 58.3% male, 41.7% female). Participants were asked to complete a short battery of standard psychological tests after being instructed in one of two conditions.

The first condition involved training in *DSM–IV* (American Psychiatric Association, 1994) criteria for major depression disorder (MDD) and PTSD. Participants were provided some background on the occurrence of these disorders following MVAs and a rationale that we did not have knowledge about how people might try to fake the questionnaires and hoped that their participation would help in that area. Participants were told of a typical personal injury MVA made from a composite of MVA survivors' experiences and provided handouts on *DSM–IV* criteria for MDD and PTSD. They were then asked to complete a battery of psychological tests as they thought a distressed MVA victim might respond.

The second condition involved participants who were instructed to simulate or fake how they thought an MVA survivor would respond on the questionnaires but were not provided any explicit instruction or training in the psychological disorders that might follow an MVA. They were provided the same description of the MVA given to coached participants, but no other information.

As part of the solicitation from the ongoing MVA project, a portion of the simulators had been assessed as part of that project, and found to be negative for PTSD or MDD. Thirty-two percent of the simulators had in fact been involved in a serious MVA (51.8% of the "trained" participants, 48.8% of the untrained). A serious MVA as defined for our ongoing project was one that led a volunteer to seek medical attention because of physical injury following their MVA. We then used this sample as a comparison of whether or not having survived an MVA without psychological injury facilitated the ability of a participant to fake psychological disorders following an MVA.

The diagnosis of the MVA PTSD-positive group was determined by use of the Clinical Administered PTSD Scale (CAPS) and extensive clinical interviewing. Participants were diagnosed as having PTSD from 6 to 24 months after their MVA. Sixty-one of the PTSD-positive patients were involved in litigation at the time of their assessment. This was also used as a comparison between groups.

Procedure

Participants were provided information while in groups of 1 to 10. All participants received the same protocol. Each group received the same standard description of an MVA survivor's experience constructed from a composite of case material obtained from participants who had participated in the MVA research project. Both groups of simulators were instructed to respond to the same self-report inventories as if they were suffering from PTSD and major depression as the result of the MVA. Scores from the PTSD-positive group were randomly drawn from the ongoing MVA project participant pool.

Dependent Measures

Tests used included the PTSD Checklist (PCL; Weathers et al., 1994), the Beck Depression Inventory (BDI; Beck et al., 1961), the State Trait Anxiety Inventory (STAI; Spielberger et al., 1970), and the Impact of Event Scale (IES; Horowitz et al., 1979). Descriptions of the tests can be found in chapter 5, along with a brief description of their content and psychometric properties.

Results

A 2 (training versus no training) × 2 (male versus female) × 2 (previous MVA or no previous MVA) ANOVA was calculated. There were no main effects found for gender or previous MVA experience, nor were there any interactions of either of these two variables found with each other or with the training variable for any dependent variable.

There was a main effect found for $DSM–IV$ training. Significant statistical results using a .05 level was found for each of the following psychological test measures: BDI, $p < .001$; PCL, $p < .001$; State Anxiety, $p < .01$; Trait Anxiety, $p < .01$; overall IES, $p < .001$; IES Intrusion subscale, $p < .001$; and IES Avoidance subscale, $p < .01$. The pattern of scores for each cell mean showed the $DSM–IV$ trained groups were significantly higher on all of the psychological scales compared to the naive, untrained group

DSM–IV Trained Simulators Versus PTSD Positive Patients

One of the main purposes of this study was to examine the impact of training or coaching on subsequent simulation of PTSD and related psychopathology. Subsequently, theoretically driven, pairwise comparisons were made for the mean scores of all of the dependent variables between trained and naive simulators and a group of PTSD-positive patients. Because of the number of comparisons, the probability of Type I error was maintained at the overall alpha level of .05 by Tukey's honestly significant difference (HSD) procedure. The mean scores on the BDI, IES, and IES Intrusion and Avoidance subscales were significantly greater for trained simulators

TABLE 13.1
Mean Scores on Psychological Tests for Simulation and PTSD-Positive
Groups by Diagnostic Training, Gender, and Previous MVA Experience
and by Experimental Condition

| Condition | Simulation sample (N = 130) | | | | PTSD-positive sample (N = 56) | |
| | Informed | | Naïve | | | |
Gender	Males	Females	Males	Females	Males	Females
Previous MVA						
N	12	9	8	12	13	43
Age (years)	28.3	34.9	31.1	36.3	37.5	36.2
BDI	29.9	40.6	21.0	13.5	29.5	28.6
State anxiety	55.3	56.8	50.5	45.7	61.8	60.7
Trait anxiety	51.8	56.6	49.6	45.4	61.4	59.8
IES total	51.3	57.7	47.0	44.3	43.2	43.2
IES avoidance	24.4	30.2	25.4	22.4	21.4	22.7
IES intrusion	26.9	27.4	21.6	21.8	21.8	20.6
PCL	60.3	69.9	45.0	43.0	61.5	60.5
No Previous MVA						
N	21	22	23	23		
Age (years)	23.0	24.4	22.6	23.1		
BDI	33.6	39.7	15.7	21.7		
State anxiety	57.3	49.8	46.4	47.0		
Trait anxiety	58.6	50.4	47.8	47.1		
IES total	53.3	54.8	38.7	48.3		
IES avoidance	26.9	27.9	20.1	24.6		
IES intrusion	26.4	26.9	18.7	23.7		
PCL	60.6	64.9	45.3	51.8		

Note. BDI = Beck Depression Inventory; IES = Impact of Event Scale; PCL = PTSD Checklist.

when compared to the PTSD positive group and significantly lower on the State and Trait anxiety scales. PCL mean scores did not differ for the two groups. Mean scores can be found in Tables 13.1 and 13.2.

Trained simulators were then compared with PTSD-positive patients for each item on the PCL (i.e., the 17 PTSD symptoms). Again, controlling for multiple comparisons, trained simulators were found to have higher scores on item 8 (dissociative amnesia) and marginally higher scores for item 7 (behavioral/situational avoidance) and had significantly lower scores for items 9 (anhedonia) and 10 (emotional detachment/estrangement). Mean scores for the other two groups did not differ on any items.

Trained simulators' scores did not differ from PTSD-positive patients as a function of age, gender, or previous MVA experience.

Litigation was then examined as a possible variable by defining the presence or absence of litigation occurring or expected as a result of the MVA as stated at the time of the MVA interview. PTSD-positive patients

TABLE 13.2
Means and Tukey HSD Comparisons for Psychological Tests for Trained and Naïve Simulators and PTSD-Positive Patients

| Measure | Simulators | | PTSD-positive patients $n = 56$ |
	Trained $n = 64$	Naïve $n = 66$	
PCL	63.3[a]	47.1[b]	60.7[a]
IES	54.1[a]	44.1[b]	43.2[b]
IES-avoidance	27.3[a]	22.7[b]	22.4[b]
IES-intrusion	26.8[a]	21.3[b]	20.8[b]
BDI	35.9[a]	18.1[b]	28.8[c]
State anxiety	54.3[a]	46.9[b]	60.9[c]
Trait anxiety	54.3[a]	47.4[b]	60.2[c]

Note. Means in the same row that do not share superscripts differ at $p < .05$ by Tukey HSD procedure. BDI = Beck Depression Inventory; HSD = honestly significant difference; IES = Impact of Event Scale; PCL = PTSD Checklist.

who were involved in litigation did not differ from nonlitigating PTSD-positive patients on age, gender, or measures of psychological functioning.

When PTSD-positive patients involved in litigation had their scores compared with *DSM–IV* trained simulating participants, they did not appear significantly different. Moreover, litigating PTSD patients did not differ significantly when compared with nonlitigating PTSD-positive patients. Trained simulators did have more years of education than PTSD-positive patients. However, psychological test scores were not significantly correlated with years of education for either the trained group or the PTSD positive group.

Discriminate Analysis

Discriminate analyses were conducted to determine if combining the five psychological test scores (BDI, PCL, IES, State and Trait anxiety scores) could reliably distinguish the trained simulators from the positive PTSD patients. A complete description of the analyses can be found in Hickling et al. (1999). Table 13.3 presents the within-group correlations (discriminate loadings) between the predictors and the discriminate function as well as the standardized weights (canonical discriminate coefficients). The discriminate function was interpreted as representing a pattern of responses, which distinguished simulator responses from the pattern found in positive PTSD patients. BDI and IES had a relatively large positive correlation, and scores on the STAI had a negative relationship.

Mean scores for the psychological tests were consistent with this interpretation. Trained simulators tended to have significantly higher BDI and IES scores than PTSD-positive patients, whereas the simulators had

TABLE 13.3
Standardized Coefficients and Correlations of Predictor Variables With the Discriminant Function (Summary of Interpretative Measures for the Discriminant Analysis)

	Standardized coefficient	Structure correlation
Predictor variable		
IES total	.89	.57
BDI	.80	.39
State anxiety	−.29	−.37
Trait anxiety	−.50	−.36
PCL total	−.75	.13

Note. Structure correlation (discriminant loading) refers to the simple linear correlation between each predictor variable and the discriminant function. *Standardized coefficient* refers to the standardized discriminant weight assigned to each variable in computing the discriminant function. Variables are listed in rank order of their relative discriminating power in the model based on the absolute size of the structure correlations. By convention, a variable exhibiting loadings ± .30 or higher is considered significant. BDI = Beck Depression Inventory; IES = Impact of Event Scale; PCL = PTSD Checklist. From Simulation of Motor Vehicle Accident-Related PTSD: Effects of Coaching With *DSM–IV* Criteria, by Hickling et al., *Road Traffic Accidents and Psychological Trauma.* Copyright 1999. Elsevier Science Ltd. Adapted with permission.

significantly lower scores for the anxiety scales than the positive PTSD group. Based on the loadings, the IES had the highest discriminative power, and the PCL had the least. This can be viewed as showing that the *DSM–IV* trained simulators, when instructed on how to adopt a malingering or simulating response style for PTSD, tended to have higher scores on the BDI and IES but were also more likely to have lower scores on the STAI than true cases of PTSD.

These results allowed us to correctly classify 76.3% (72% with cross-validation) of individuals in our sample when assuming homogeneity of covariance matrices and 74.6% when not assuming homogeneity. The corresponding kappa (k) value (an index that corrects for chance agreements) was .53 and .50, respectively. Conventional use of these values would indicate that there was a moderate rate of accuracy in the prediction of group membership.

Overall, we felt that the study supported the idea that explicit training in *DSM–IV* diagnostic categories for PTSD and MDD can aid an individual wishing to simulate the disorders. However, the data suggested that there might be a discernible pattern of scores obtained during the deception that might aid in the detection of simulators and lend support for determination of true cases of PTSD. We obviously cannot say how well our briefly trained simulators would represent a true malingerer or exaggerator of PTSD symptoms. As found earlier in this text, norms for MVA survivors with and without PTSD exist. As we will discuss later in the chapter, the careful, open-minded, and at times cautious and skeptical attitude of an examiner needs to be used when concerns of malingering occur. It is speculated that this use of commonly used psychological tests may aid in the determination.

The finding that faking or exaggerating individuals may lead to overreporting of symptoms has been noted by forensic examiners in other studies (e.g., Greenberg & Shuman, 1997).

One strength of this study was the use of MVA victims who, following our comprehensive examination, were found to be without diagnosable psychological disorders. To ask these individuals to simulate how they think someone with a psychological disorder might present is a strong comparison group in our opinion. They have suffered a comparable traumatic event. The event also led them to seek medical attention. Such individuals appeared to be exactly the group of individuals one might suspect could try to simulate a response to gain financial advantage in a personal injury lawsuit. These MVA survivors seemed a more realistic comparison group than college undergraduates or individuals who had not suffered a recent MVA. Furthermore, the context of a car accident is a familiar and applicable scenario for simulation. It can be argued that this event is more common than the other psychological disorders such as psychosis that simulators have been requested to fake in other studies. The data suggest that individuals who had survived a serious MVA did not fake any better than people who had not been in serious accidents.

The presence of ongoing litigation did not seem to lead to any significant differences between the groups. Our MVA project has not led to a significant number of individuals who we have believed significantly exaggerated or malingered their symptoms. This could be true for several reasons. First, given the extensive nature of our evaluation, and the unknown outcome of the assessment, individuals, who are concerned that they might be discovered as faking, do not volunteer for our study. We have had a number of patients who, following their initial call, were cautioned by their attorneys not to participate in our study for such reasons. Second, patients who are referred have already been screened by physicians and other health professionals. Third, we routinely use collateral sources in assessments and treatment, which we have found can lend considerable credence to the overall presentation. Close friends and families will come to an interview and not be sure why they were included. They quickly are given an opportunity to describe the behavioral and psychological functioning of the participant. This type of validation has at times been extremely useful in treatment and adds a type of consensual validation to patient report, clinician judgment, psychological tests, and psychophysiological assessment.

Detection of Professional Actors Trained to Simulate MVA-Related PTSD

Given our preliminary success in detecting group differences between trained and untrained simulators of PTSD and those with true cases of

PTSD, we again considered the uniqueness of our center and our ongoing screening for treatment of PTSD (Hickling, Blanchard, Mundy, & Galovski, 2002). Experts in the area of forensic evaluations and simulation studies have historically suggested that experiments should use highly trained individuals as simulators who could present to different clinicians with a standardized presentation of a feigned disorder (Rogers, 1997b). We used that model in this investigation of the ability of trained assessors to detect faking by trained simulators on an individual basis.

In keeping with many of our investigations, we tried to approximate conditions that can be found in a clinical setting. In the Albany MVA Project, we typically use very well trained, advanced doctoral students in clinical psychology, who, over their training, became experienced, well-supervised diagnosticians in the disorders of interest (i.e., PTSD, Acute Stress Disorder [ASD], MDD). Unlike forensic settings, self-referred patients are not met with undue suspiciousness about their self-reported symptoms, because those are the very things they are trying to change. It is why they are seeking help. Although the possibility of secondary gain and malingering is part of each evaluator's training, and the possibility of a court appearance necessitating the defense of their decisions is raised routinely, in our setting a high level of suspiciousness is the exception rather than the rule. However, each assessor is routinely asked about the degree of certainty of each diagnosis and doubts of truthfulness as part of the CAPS. Each new case is also discussed with supervising staff and shared among all members of the MVA project at weekly staff meetings.

This became the backdrop for the study. After gaining approval from the University at Albany's IRB, a deception-based investigation was run. Without previous knowledge on the part of the evaluators, trained simulators gained entry to the study, were assessed, and if appropriate, entered into the ongoing treatment study. It was hypothesized that even very well trained simulators would not be able to reproduce the constellation of symptoms and test results that occur in true cases of PTSD and that the evaluation process would be sensitive to identifying the feigned symptoms or reports of the simulators.

Participants

Six doctoral students in clinical psychology (5 female, 1 male) were the primary participants. All of the students had received extensive training in all instruments, the standardized assessment of MVA survivors as outlined in chapters 4 and 5. They had also all received training in psychophysiological assessments and had a minimum of 1½ years of experience in assessing and working with MVA survivors as part of the Albany MVA Project.

Experimental Condition

A group of six professional actors and actresses were instructed in *DSM–IV* criteria for PTSD and MDD. This was our simulation condition. The actors were instructed about the varied psychological disorders that can follow an MVA and provided a context for the need to discover malingering individuals from true cases of PTSD. A method acting coach known to the actors was in attendance at the meeting and helped the actors practice portrayal of MVA victims for the study. Scenarios were constructed for each actor/actress in an effort to help him or her realistically fake how he or she would act if psychologically affected from an MVA. The actors were instructed to draw, if at all possible, from their own experiences, and to improvise as necessary to reach criteria for entry into the study on the telephone screen. Each simulator was then given the phone number to call for screening into the MVA Project. It was necessary to pass the telephone screen to gain access to the comprehensive screening used in the MVA Treatment Study.

The actors were not provided any specific information about tests, questionnaires, or interview questions but were instructed in how to stay in role and respond how they thought necessary to present as if they had PTSD or MDD and to intentionally mislead the interviewer. Actors were paid $50 each for their participation at the start of the study, and an additional $75 at the completion of the study.

The comprehensive interview is discussed in chapter 4, as are the psychological tests and the psychophysiological procedures that each actor completed in role. If an actor reached criteria for PTSD and following blind review by the project director (the first author, who was blinded to the identity of the actors/actresses) and evaluator, he or she would be randomly assigned to treatment.

Procedure

Actors were covertly entered into the project over a four-month period of time. Only one of the investigators (the second author) and the clinic secretary knew of the identity of the actors. The project director was kept blind to the identity of the actors, as were the doctoral student evaluators. Following the assessment, if the actor met criteria for entry into the ongoing treatment study (see chapter 17), a treatment condition was randomly assigned and the simulator was provided the name of his or her treating psychologist. At that time, the nonblind psychologist (the second author) contacted the psychologist to whom the case was assigned and clarified the simulator condition to the psychologist. Treating psychologists provided care in a location several miles away, and other than with the second author had limited contact with the doctoral students. This allowed for information to be easily controlled and the evaluators (wrongly) reassured that treatment referrals had been made.

Once all of the actors had completed their role in the study, the six evaluators were made aware that a deception had been ongoing. However, rather than just reveal the names of the actors, the evaluators were requested to make a guess about whom they thought might be a simulator among the cases they had seen in the past six months. They were not told how many simulators each assessor had seen, but only that they had each seen at least one. The evaluators made nominations about whom they thought might have been a simulator. Each evaluator was then asked to collect all the charts of the patients they had seen over the past six months. They were then asked after their review to guess again who might have been a simulator. This was done to see, when given all possible information, how well they did in discovering the simulator. There had been 23 evaluations done during this time period for the six evaluators in total.

Results

The six simulators were examined as a series of case studies, which used multiple measures. This allowed for a case-by-case comparison of clinical expertise to be made. Following the case approach, group comparisons were made with true PTSD patients and true MVA survivors without PTSD where appropriate. We fully recognized that, given the small sample size of actors, and the number of measures taken, there was much chance for significant error. Thus the results could only be viewed as a preliminary estimate of how the groups compared on the selected measures.

Diagnoses

All of the simulators were originally diagnosed with PTSD. None received a CAPS validity rating, which would have suggested a concern about the truthfulness of the participant. When the assessors were first informed, three of the actors were identified as simulators. Three of the actors were also diagnosed to have MDD. An average of 2.0 diagnoses were given to the actors, and true MVA survivors with PTSD had on average 1.8 diagnoses. This difference was not statistically significant. However, the difference between the actors' number of diagnoses and MVA survivors who did not develop PTSD (0.64) was significantly different ($p = 0.01$) as was the difference with MVA survivors who developed PTSD ($p < 0.001$). It was also noted that three of the actors met criteria for generalized anxiety disorder (GAD), which, although common to MVA survivors, was not a disorder they had received any training in or asked to fake.

TABLE 13.4
Correct Identification of Malingering MVA Survivors With PTSD

	#545	#546	#547	#548	#554	#557	False positives
Initial interviewer guess		Y	Y			Y	3
Interviewer + chart review	Y	Y	Y		Y	Y	1
Objective chart review (by interviewer who had not interviewed participant)		Y	Y		Y		4

Note. Y = correct guess that the participant was simulating his or her symptoms. Blank cell means simulating participant was not identified.

As stated, the original request to identify simulators led to a 50% rate of identifying the actors. However, there were also three false positives. When asked to review all possible data, including test data, psychophysiological testing, and chart notes, the correct identification rose to 83% with only one false positive.

When a second set of experienced doctoral students were given the same charts and test results and asked to find the simulators for whom they had not done the clinical interview, the correct identification rate dropped to 50%, with four false positives. These results are summarized in Table 13.4.

An alternative way to view the results is to examine the rate of correct identification, for selecting both simulators and true cases. As can be seen in Table 13.5, the overall base rate of correct identification (hit rate) of true cases and simulators is 73%. When the suspiciousness instructions are given to the evaluators, the overall hit rate is unchanged, with three simulators correctly identified but three other cases were wrongly labeled fakers. When assessors had access to all of their information, the overall hit rate improved to 91%. However, when trained evaluators who had not interviewed the patients but only reviewed charts and information in the charts made the determination, the correct rate of identification was only 70%.

In our larger sample of more than 400 participants, only two participants had been identified as having faked or exaggerated their symptoms. Thus the base rate for malingering in our sample is extremely low (or so we believe). The occurrence of PTSD in our treatment-seeking sample is 69.1% ($n = 112$), 15.4% ($n = 25$) for subsyndromal PTSD, and 15.4% for non-PTSD ($n = 25$). In this larger sample of MVA survivors who were assessed for PTSD and had litigation data ($n = 160$), 94 were undergoing litigation.

A preliminary group comparison was then made between the actors, true PTSD MVA survivors and non-PTSD MVA survivors. Comparisons were made on psychological test scores, diagnostic formulations (CAPS),

TABLE 13.5
Overall Rate of Correction Identification When Simulators and True Cases
of PTSD Are Combined

| | Diagnostic decision | | | | |
| | Actors | | Patients | | |
Condition	Simulator	Legitimate case	Simulator	Legitimate case	Hit rate
Without suspiciousness instructions	0	6	0	17	73%
With suspiciousness instructions but no chart review	3	3	3	14	73%
With suspiciousness instructions and chart review	5	1	1	16	91%
Outside raters with suspiciousness instructions and chart review but no patient contact	3	3	4	13	70%

and psychophysiological measures. No significant differences were found between the actors and PTSD MVA survivors except on the CAPS criterion D category, with the MVA PTSD group having more symptoms endorsed. Significant differences were found between the actors and the non-PTSD MVA survivor group on age, PCL, BDI, IES, STAI, and CAPS scores.

On a case-by-case basis few of the actors look different than true MVA survivors on many of the measures (see Table 13.1). None of the CAPS validity scores would raise concerns about the performance at this point of the assessment.

The psychological test scores do support the findings of the initial study. The results of the six actors' scores suggest that, with coaching, participants can produce scores that are comparable with true PTSD patients on psychological tests. However, on a case-by-case basis, the pattern analysis found in the initial study did not occur and would have only identified one of the actors.

On psychophysiological measures, heart rate response showed marked variability, with two of the simulators showing significant heart rate increase to stimulus number 1, and four could show a reaction to stimulus 2.

As per Roger's recommendations, the actors were debriefed, and the actors reported that they felt they had complied with the instructions they had been given. The actors appeared motivated to succeed and did not report any disincentive in their portrayal of an MVA victim.

Discussion

We believe that this study pitted the best simulators we could obtain against very experienced, qualified evaluators. Overall, if one considers the 91% successful identification rate, the clinicians did well in correctly ascertaining who were actors and who were simulators. The interview, despite cautions by forensic evaluators, remains the gold standard for diagnosis of PTSD. The findings of this study would support the belief that clinicians, who are well trained in their area, can do a credible job in discerning malingerers or individuals who might be exaggerating their symptoms.

Psychological tests and psychophysiological testing are still quite unreliable as definitive tests for the diagnosis of PTSD. However, if one looked at any change in heart rate or diastolic blood pressure, four of the six simulators would have been identified. Multifaceted assessment does seem to add a great deal to the correct diagnosis of the disorder.

It is important to state that we are not sure if trained actors can fake symptoms as well as sociopathic individuals or people who malinger or exaggerate symptoms for financial or psychological gain. It can be argued that they can portray roles much better than most of us, and do so as part of their professional livelihood and training. In addition, the actors used in this study had, in fact, received earlier training in the simulation of both mental and physical diagnoses as part of an ongoing collaboration between the Health and Rehabilitation Medicine Departments of a local college and the Theater Arts Department. The actors had all received personalized coaching from a professional method coach, and each felt comfortable in carrying out the deception throughout the study. Thus, we believe that these actors were at least as good fakers as we can construct from a nonpathological population. In fact, it might be possible to argue that they could fake better than untrained individuals. The difficulties in ever determining true malingerers and individuals who are exaggerating symptoms are beyond the scope of this chapter. We do believe that this study provides support for the ability of experienced clinicians to detect simulation of PTSD with the tools and information found in everyday practice.

Clinical Hints

The following clinical hints have been developed over the past decade. Some have empirical validation, and others are supported from experience with other health professional, attorneys, courts, and our own clinical experiences.

Assessment

We suggest that the evaluation should include several standardized procedures. Although a clinical interview can be capably performed by experienced clinicians in an unstructured format, the material obtained from structured questions allows the systematic collection of information that assures that nothing has been left out that is important. For a similar reason we suggest the use of a standardized assessment of PTSD using an instrument such as the CAPS. This provides a good record for the chart and a structure for the reporting of individual symptoms that can be compared over time and placed in a formal report.

We find the use of a short test battery extremely helpful. This can include the PCL, the BDI, the STAI, and the IES. Other inventories can be added according to the needs of the case and judgment of the clinician. Again, this material rounds out an assessment and gives the clinician a foundation for both clinical and forensic assessment. We have selected instruments that have been well established within the literature and allow for comparisons with data such as those found in this book.

As you may note, we do not routinely use the MMPI–2 or other tests that might add validity measures or test of malingering to the assessment. First, as our studies show, we believe the clinician is a good source of reaching these conclusions. Second, the instruments available at this time have not yet shown the ability to correctly identify suspected malingerers in this population at a sufficient level to be a part of routine practice. The MMPI–2, although one of our better empirically derived tests, has shown it can be faked successfully and is sensitive to many medical conditions such as head injuries and lingering pain, both of which are common to an MVA population. Studies have also shown that the PTSD population, even when honestly completing the test, can raise many of the scales to a level that might look as if the test was completed in an invalid fashion.

As a consequence, it is much like the use of psychophysiological testing; although we collect this information as part of our study, we do not yet know what to make of individuals who we firmly believe have PTSD but may not have a psychophysiological reaction that would support it. As clinicians we realize this does not invalidate the diagnosis, but it now makes it potentially necessary to explain this discrepancy to others. Our advice is to use validity scales prudently. We fully appreciate that neuropsychological assessments routinely add in tests of malingering. We also acknowledge that the level of base rates, expected response rates with well-defined clinical populations for these tests at this point in time, allow their use with great confidence in the conclusions reached by poor performance. Unfortunately, similar conclusions cannot yet be reached using the psychological tests we are aware of with the population of individuals who present with PTSD following an MVA. We are not aware of any test that would lead to a definitive conclusion that a patient is malingering or exaggerating. Until the time when such a test is developed, we believe that our data provide some support for the belief that an experienced clinician is a fairly sensitive discriminator of feigned symptoms in this population.

We have found that the use of collateral information is extremely important. The significant other or family member can provide a great deal of information about the patient. Although we typically do not use this individual as a source of accident-related data, collateral sources are often useful in providing premorbid information, information about how the accident has affected the interpersonal relationship, how the patient is driving, changes in eating, sleeping, and social situations; all of this information can validate and support the understanding gained by interview and other assessment procedures listed.

As part of the MVA Project, we did not collect medical records on our patients. This was a decision made for purposes of completing our studies. In clinical practice, it is strongly recommended that any and all information be obtained. This should include notes and reports from any treating or evaluating health professionals.

Report Writing

In writing reports, we tend to err on the side of overcompleteness. Our logic has been to try to provide as clear a description of the MVA from the patient's perspective, and the psychological reaction to the accident, as possible. In addition to fully describing the MVA, we also elaborate the findings of the CAPS and other tests administered. Each symptom, symptom cluster, and the determination of how diagnoses were reached is provided. This was originally done to help evaluators in the prospective studies determine how a diagnosis was derived for each point in time. However, it has been found to be extremely useful in clinical practice for other reasons as well. For example, when records are reviewed as part of an independent medical examination or in defending conclusions in a court of law, the more descriptive and complete the record, the easier to support a conclusion that may have been rendered several years earlier (on average the time from MVA to settlement/court has been between 2½ and 3 years for our clinic). Our belief is that the honest portrayal of our methods and results is supported by standards of practice based on empirical evidence. We endeavor to maintain objectivity, letting the data speak for themselves.

We have also had the opportunity to review other clinician's records, and at times have been unable to support or help them defend the conclusions reached, because the notes or reports were too incomplete. Although it is easy to have missed some aspect of presentation or history that later becomes important in forensic or clinical matters, the use of the standardized format listed earlier will minimize, one hopes, this possibility. Reports typically will also include a psychosocial history, a medical history, history of previous trauma, diagnoses on all five axes, summary, and recommendations. Clinical reports also routinely include how and why a patient was referred.

We believe that the data in this chapter can help professionals who are asked to testify during a personal injury trial. The information in this series of investigations addresses some of the concerns about symptom magnification and malingering in as good a comparison group as possible in the circumstances. We compared individuals who we believed with a great deal of certainty had PTSD to individuals who had been in accidents but did not have PTSD. These MVA victims were then asked to simulate PTSD. This is one group that would be exactly the type of individuals who were suspected to be faking their symptoms in an effort to gain financial rewards. We compared individuals who had been diagnosed with PTSD and who were in litigation with victims who had PTSD and who were not in litigation. This again allowed us to try to tease out the importance that litigation may have in the presentation of symptoms. We compared coached individuals with those who were naive to the symptoms of PTSD. This addresses the concern that lawyers may be coaching individuals on how to fake symptoms before psychological evaluations. Although these are still preliminary studies, overall, the data they provide should add to the professional's degree of certainty when asked (a)if he or she considered an individual might have been malingering the presentation of PTSD symptoms or (b) whether he or she believed it was possible to determine the presence of PTSD in someone who indeed is suffering from PTSD following their MVA.

III

TREATMENT FOR SURVIVORS

14

THE TREATMENT OF MVA-RELATED PTSD: A REVIEW OF THE EARLY LITERATURE

At the time the first edition of this book was written (1996) there was clearly a growing body of research exploring the psychological consequences of motor vehicle accidents (MVAs); however, at that time little had been reported in the literature dealing with the treatment of posttraumatic stress disorder (PTSD) following an MVA, and most of that was uncontrolled case reports. The earliest mention of psychological consequences of MVAs, rather than addressing PTSD treatment, focused instead on a posttraumatic phobic response, typically to driving. Whether any of these cases may have, in fact, been a case of PTSD is impossible to determine from retrospective review of the literature. The earlier cases, in actuality, could not have been diagnosed as PTSD, as per *DSM–III* (American Psychiatric Association, 1980) because 1980 was the year codification of the disorder became uniform. However, as a matter of historical interest, and as a prelude from which to gain perspective on today's conceptualization of treatment issues, selected examples are offered as part of this literature review.

This chapter reviews the literature dealing with accident phobias and the controversy of making such a diagnosis when the survivor has a diagnosis of PTSD. The limited case report literature on the treatment of MVA survivors up until 1996 is reviewed for both the treatment of accident phobia and for PTSD.

251

ACCIDENT PHOBIA

Taylor and Koch (1995) in their review of anxiety disorders following MVAs describe the history of accident phobia. As they point out, although many terms have been used to describe MVA-related phobias, including driving phobia and travel phobias, they reserved the term *accident phobia* to describe phobias arising from MVAs. They correctly pointed out that accident phobia is not limited to the drivers of vehicles but can also afflict passengers, pedestrians, motorcyclists, or anyone involved with motor vehicle collisions.

The differential diagnosis between accident phobia and PTSD is important for several reasons. Perhaps the most central is that the diagnosis leads to a model on which to base treatment. Kuch et al. (1991, 1994) defined accident phobia as comprising three main features: (a) *DSM–III–R* (American Psychiatric Association, 1987) or *DSM–IV* (American Psychiatric Association, 1994) diagnostic criteria for simple phobia (called *specific phobia* in *DSM–IV*), (b) onset and content of the phobia are related to a MVA, and (c) anxiety symptoms and avoidance center around excessive fears of repetitions of the accident. According to the *DSM–IV*, one *cannot* diagnose a simple or specific phobia if the patient also meets criteria for PTSD (American Psychiatric Association, 1994, p. 411). It is in fact a hallmark of the PTSD patient that he or she by definition *should be* avoidant and fearful of the situation that was traumatic and life-threatening.

Although the issues of assessment were dealt with in earlier chapters in this book (e.g., chapters 3, 4, 5), the issue becomes important when viewing earlier research. The disorder of PTSD did not become codified until 1980 in *DSM–III*. It is therefore certainly possible that earlier conditions may have been conceptualized and treated as a phobic response, when they may, in fact, have been cases of posttraumatic stress disorder. With the nosology changing over time, the critical issue becomes whether the treatment methodology used in those cases adds to an understanding of how to help our MVA survivors at the time of this review.

The Treatment of Accident Phobia

The earliest report we could find in our literature searches was that of Wolpe in 1962. His work and the work of Kraft and Al-Issa (1965) both reported use of systematic desensitization for the treatment of MVA-related phobia. Inspection of the studies, however, suggests more complex interventions in fact occurred.

The nature of the MVAs for the two survivors was quite different. The MVA survivor treated by Wolpe (1962) involved a car being struck by a truck when going through an intersection, rendering the victim, a 39-

year-old woman, unconscious. She was subsequently transported to the hospital by ambulance. She spent one week in the hospital for injuries to the knee and neck. It was discovered on the way home from the hospital that she became "unaccountably frightened." She reported heightened anxiety when driving, which worsened when a car approached her from either side. Previous traumatic experiences included an MVA at age 10 when a tractor crushed the side of the car in which she was a passenger. She was in London during World War II during the air blitz. At this time she lost her fiancé, a pilot who was killed. Treatment was based on conditioning theories using prolonged exposure, believing that imaginal or in vivo exposure should produce a reduction in perceived anxiety and phobic avoidance. The earlier treatments combined relaxation training and used graded imaginal exposure as well as in vivo exposure. Wolpe, in fact, conducted more than 57 desensitization sessions and also used hypnosis within the treatment session as part of the imaginal desensitization procedure. The patients reportedly became completely at ease in all normal traffic situations, and two near misses while driving had no lasting consequence emotionally.

Kraft and Al-Issa (1965) treated a 37-year-old male who had experienced two accidents as a road worker painting white lines on the road. The first accident occurred at age 30, the second at age 35. There was a previous history of a medical discharge from the army at age 17 for complaints of headaches and dizziness, and a marriage from age 24 to 29 with reported sexual maladjustment. Following his second MVA he was unemployed for a period of nine months and then was admitted to a psychiatric hospital for six weeks. He had been tried on a number of medications without resolution of the phobic response. Kraft and Al-Issa (1965) used three sessions of hypnotherapy, 22 sessions of desensitization (1½ hours each), and 10 follow-up sessions. A follow-up at six months showed the patient to be free of symptoms. It was also noted by the authors that the patient's symptoms remitted before a legal settlement, lowering the consideration of secondary gain from monetary compensation of this case. The desensitization sessions took place over a three-month period of time. Quirk (1985) has also shown a reduction in MVA-related anxiety using similar techniques.

As Taylor and Koch (1995) pointed out, systematic desensitization and other methods of imaginal exposure have been found useful for exposing patients to those aspects of the MVA that cannot be reproduced through in vivo exposure. Recent studies have treated accident phobia with a combination of imaginal exposure and in vivo exposure. Blonstein (1988) treated an accident-phobic individual over 33 sessions, using 22 weeks of imaginal exposure, followed by 11 weeks of graduated in vivo exposure. Treatment was conducted by the therapist directing five of the imaginal sessions, with much of the remaining sessions being completed as directed homework assignments. The imaginal exposure exercise involved 30 to 45 repetitions of a one-minute, endless loop audiocassette description of anxiety-provoking driving scenarios. In vivo exposure involved frequent exposure to the scene of the MVA. The patient drove past the scene 7 to 13 times per exposure episode, taking between 15 to 60 minutes, three days per week, for 11 consecutive weeks. Fear and avoidance were reportedly significantly reduced as measured by self-report rating scales. Several other case studies have also used similar approaches, including Horne (1993), Levine and Wolpe (1980), and Rovetto (1983). The latter two cases used in vivo desensitization through radio contact; Rovetto, in fact, telemonitored psychophysiological responsiveness as well as having verbal reports of subjective functioning from the research participant.

An extremely dangerous startle reaction was treated by Fairbank, De-Good, and Jenkins (1981) for an MVA victim who was also described as having a driving phobia. The startle response was so dramatic as to cause a potentially dangerous driving situation, when the patient would become highly anxious and abruptly jerk the steering wheel to the right at the sight of an approaching vehicle in the left lane. Following her MVA, the patient had, in fact, swerved off the road several times as a result of this involuntary startle response. The patient was treated first with three sessions of progressive muscle relaxation and autogenic training, which was followed by two weeks of daily in vivo exposure. In vivo exposure consisted of the patient driving twice per day along a mile-long segment of heavily traveled two-lane highway. As measured by self-reports of anxiety and frequency of startle response, the patient improved significantly, with gains being maintained at a six-month follow-up visit.

TREATMENT OF PTSD

In one of the earliest reports of the treatment of accident-related PTSD, McCaffrey and Fairbank (1985) used a broad-spectrum assessment and treatment package for two individuals who had met *DSM–III* criteria for a diagnosis of PTSD secondary to transportation accidents. One of the survivors had two traumatic accidents related to helicopter crashes, and the second victim involved a 28-year-old female who presented with a host of PTSD-related symptoms following four automobile accidents over a 14-month period of time.

Treatment consisted of three components: relaxation training, flooding in imagination to fearful stimulus, and self-directed in vivo exposure to the feared stimulus. The first two weeks of treatment involved relaxation with homework practice followed by imaginal flooding, which was preceded and ended by therapist-led relaxation exercises. The imaginal flooding focused on having each patient describe (using all five sensory modalities), the physical characteristics (i.e., symptom-contingent cues) associated with the trauma. Subsequent sessions focused on a combination of symptom-contingent cue presentations and the use of hypothetical cues associated with the traumatic events (viz. fear of bodily injury, dying, aggressive behavior, rejection, and punishment of wrongdoing). The first research participant was treated with four imaginal flooding sessions, each approximately two hours in length. Sessions focused on the participant's guilt about a friend who had died in the crash and fear he too would die in a similar crash. The patient was then seen for four additional sessions during which other aspects of the trauma were presented in imagination and a graded series of imagined events portrayed. The patient was also encouraged to engage in as much self-directed in-vivo exposure as possible.

The second participant, the one who had experienced the multiple MVA trauma, was treated with a combination of symptom-contingent cues (e.g., the patient being responsible for the accidents), and hypothetical cues (e.g., fear of causing the death of an innocent person or her own death) during the first four imaginal flooding sessions. At that point she had a slight reduction in anxiety during the sessions, but little decrease in the associated symptoms of PTSD; in fact, she reported a worsening of her sleep difficulties. The authors reported a change in treatment strategies at that point because of the patient mentioning that her mother, who had been extremely upset with the patient because of the accidents, had, in fact, deserted the family for more than three years when the patient was 10 years old. Reportedly, the stepfather told the patient that the reason the mother left was because the patient was a "bad child." Issues related to the mother and the patient's relationship with her mother were also focused on in treatment as well as three imaginal flooding sessions dealing with the same contingent cues and the hypothetical cues related to fears and guilt about perceived responsibility. Gains as measured by self-report of symptoms related to PTSD were shown for both patients and reported to be sustained at 12-month follow-up.

Kuch et al. (1985, 1987) at about the same period of time reported on their experience with the assessment and treatment of PTSD after car accidents. Kuch et al. (1985) studied 30 participants (22 female, 8 male), with 12 being treated, and the remaining 18 were assessed for medico-legal opinions. The 12 treatment participants were provided 4 to 12 hours of imaginal flooding, with images of their accident and in vivo exposure to driving or being driven for no less than one and up to three hours per session for four sessions. Six of the 12 participants were reported to have marked improvement, with 4 others improving on their ability to drive following the provision of lorazepam or diazepam in declining dosages during exposure and after receiving several hours of cognitively oriented therapy. Two participants received no benefit and remained unable to drive. Because the study participants reportedly had found a high incidence of phobic avoidance, the authors suggested that treatment could be offered with effectiveness, despite the fact that litigation might be ongoing. In a later paper Kuch (1989) shared his impression that a conditioning paradigm guides his work with accident survivors, particularly with the occurrence of posttraumatic phobia. He also reported how "worries" about illness may obscure specific phobias and become the presenting complaint, particularly with whiplash survivors. Kuch also reported on the common occurrence of anger in survivors and how many survivors feel "victimized by the system." Treatment reportedly used primarily an exposure-based intervention, with patients first being desensitized to the role of a passenger and then to the role of driver. Kuch reported a preference for in vivo to imaginal exposure, but adds the two may be used in combination successfully. Kuch ends with a concern that chronic pain may interact with the presentation of PTSD, with pain often remitting as driving-related anxiety decreased in reported intensity.

Muse (1986) has also reported on anecdotal cases of PTSD and the effect of chronic pain. He reportedly treated three cases of MVA-related PTSD who also suffered injuries resulting in lingering pain. Patients were treated with a pain management program (which included physical exercise, biofeedback, supportive counseling, and medication). Although this program was somewhat effective in reducing the level of the patient's pain, there appeared to be little impact on the symptoms of PTSD. The patients were then treated with between 11 to 16 sessions of systematic desensitization followed by two sessions of in vivo exposure. At that point symptoms of PTSD began to decline, with treatment gains continuing four to seven months later during follow-up evaluations.

In an earlier work, Hickling, Blanchard, Schwarz, and Silverman (1992) treated 20 posttraumatic headache patients, 10 of whom had PTSD as a comorbid condition to the posttraumatic headache. Although both groups responded equally well to the combination of treatments provided (cognitive–behavioral, relaxation, biofeedback, and exposure), those with PTSD required significantly ($p < .05$) longer to show treatment results (26 versus 11 sessions on average). Moreover, treatment did not show positive results for the headaches until symptoms for PTSD had been addressed.

McMillan (1991) has reported on the unusual presentation of a case of PTSD where the patient had a severe head injury but no recollection of the MVA. The patient reportedly had been unconscious for three to four days following the accident and suffered posttraumatic amnesia for six weeks. A close friend of the MVA victim had been killed in the MVA. During recovery from the accident, the patient experienced increasingly intrusive thoughts of the friend who had been killed in the accident. Treatment for the PTSD began 14 months after the MVA. Treatment consisted of weekly sessions, lasting more than four months in total. Treatment included imaginal exposure using both verbal and written material and in vivo exposure to contingent cues of the MVA including visiting the friend's grave. Treatment used therapist-assisted exposure, self-directed exposure, and development of a close relationship with a friend–confidante outside of the treatment sessions. Symptoms of PTSD were reduced according to self-report, and lasted through at least a four-month follow-up period of time.

Horton (1993) also reported a case study of an MVA victim who suffered PTSD and mild neuropsychological impairment. Treatment consisted of 12 weekly sessions of behavior therapy, which used systematic desensitization and self-directed exposure. Treatment again was found to be positive, as measured by a decrease on the Willoughby Questionnaire (Wolpe, 1973), and by self-reported PTSD symptoms.

Horne (1993) has reported on three case studies, all of whom suffered from psychological problems lasting more than six months from the time of the MVA. Treatment included imaginal exposure to a hierarchy of car-travel scenes, in vivo exposure, relaxation training, cognitive–behavioral therapy, and contact with significant others as indicated. Treatment length ranged from 14 sessions to more than 30 sessions (> 1 year in time, for the two cases where length of treatment was reported). Positive treatment results were reported for each case, although it is important to note that although formal treatment had ended, there were still considerable residual problems reported by Horne for the treated survivors.

Lyons and Scotti (1995) report on a case of Direct Therapeutic Exposure (DTE; a term sometimes used for imaginal flooding), illustrating a treatment methodology using both imaginal and in vivo flooding and implosive therapy. Their paper describes the clinical application of DTE in some detail, as a case study example of application to the larger clinical problem of MVA survivors. As their case illustrates, the patient showed reduced anxiety and depressive symptoms, reexperiencing (e.g., intrusive thoughts and images, flashbacks, nightmares), physiological arousal, and lessened avoidance. The case illustrated how depression, substance abuse, anger, and aggression were not exacerbated during the provision of DTE; however, these problems reappeared and returned to baseline level when outpatient sessions were not held regularly. The authors speak to the (at times) important adjunctive treatment methods including problem solving, communication, anger control, marital or family therapy, or other treatments to attend to the individualized needs of this clinical population. Finally, they comment on the importance of the therapeutic relationship as developed by the therapist listening to the patient's report of the trauma. They believe the role of an empathic response to the often horrific material is one of the keys to rapport building. They conceptualize treatment as attending to distorted or repressed memories, delusions regarding guilt and fear of punishment, and even hallucinatory behavior. All of these symptoms are treatment issues traditionally thought to extend beyond the realm of behavior therapy at first glance. For their illustrative case, they also saw the factors of pharmacotherapy, problem solving, and relaxation training as important adjuncts to the DTE. The case in summary appears to incorporate many cognitive, supportive, and interpretative elements besides a strictly behavioral approach to the treatment.

Best and Ribbe (1995) have also recently shared their approach to treatment for survivors of accidental injury, using an illustrative case of a 23-year-old male who had been in a serious MVA six months before seeking treatment. Their overviews of treatment techniques include attention to physical, cognitive, and behavioral fear responses. They believe effective treatment should include a combination of relaxation training (e.g., Jacobsonian deep-muscle relaxation, controlled breathing), cognitive interventions (e.g., thought stopping, activation-belief-consequences [ABC] training, rational emotive therapy and behavioral techniques (role playing, exposure therapy, stress inoculation therapy). They further commented on special issues for therapy with accident survivors that include perceived life threat, the extent of physical injury and its lasting impact–reminder on the patient, differences on when the patient presents to treatment (immediately after the trauma versus years later), and finally the role of the therapist as advocate for the patient. Meichenbaum (1994), in his review of civilian posttraumatic stress disorders, shares his own considerable work in this area and comments on how in "virtually every case of significant trauma, the patient struggles with shattered fantasies about fairness, justice, security and the meaning of life" (p. 662). Some patients are therefore forced to view their own mortality and vulnerability, coming to perceive themselves as different from the rest of the world as a result of the trauma. Existential struggles with the search for meaning, rather than alleviation of symptoms, may be a productive direction for treatment. Meichenbaum's (1994) own work has reported on the positive anecdotal outcome of treatment through antidepressant medications and traditional psychotherapy and behavioral therapy.

Koch and Taylor (1995) have also reported on their ideas related to the assessment and treatment of PTSD following MVAs. In a recent paper they use anecdotes to support their belief in the provision of cognitive and behavioral interventions, primarily in vivo exposure and work to change cognitive beliefs about driving phobia. Here they see the overprediction of danger and underprediction of safety as important targets for cognitive restructuring in combination with the therapeutic exposure. Within their paper they discuss what they view as important issues regarding the sequencing of treatment (i.e., which comorbid psychological disorder or pain disorder to treat first). Although in general they suggest treating pain complaints before treating phobic complaints, they do not see this as a hard-and-fast rule.

Burstein (1986b) in an earlier study compared treatment characteristics of patients with PTSD who were successfully treated within a short period of time (three months or less), with those who were in treatment for greater than 12 months. Although both groups had a wide range of traumatic stressors, 7 out of 13 in the short-term group and 9 out of 15 in the long-term group had an MVA as their traumatic stressor for PTSD. All of the patients received medication (usually an antidepressant, imipramine or an MAOI [monoamine oxidase inhibitor], or phenelzine), and individual supportive psychotherapy. Goals of treatment were to decrease phobic avoidance and facilitate confrontation of the phobic situation in vivo. Ancillary issues such as preexisting PTSD and current marital issues were treated within the individual sessions. The patients were selected from a retrospective review of 84 records. Inclusion in the study was based on a successful outcome as determined by the absence or near absence of PTSD during a two-week period of no-treatment. Cases that had terminated prematurely or were still active in treatment were not used within the study. There did not appear to be any significant differences reported for the type of stressor, reported symptom distress, possible compensation factors, or time from trauma to intervention. The long-term treatment group were reported to require higher daily dosages of a tricyclic antidepressant. This research is summarized in Table 14.1. A summary of our own uncontrolled studies is contained in chapter 16.

In summary, these case study reports on the treatment of PTSD following MVAs are encouraging, and in general follow a cognitive–behavioral model. As shown in this chapter, the case studies have in general followed a similar model of cognitive–behavioral treatment. Behavioral treatment using imaginal and in vivo exposure has been reported for more than two decades. Cognitive models suggest using a variety of techniques including thought stopping, cognitive reappraisal, and reframing. Special issues of driving phobia, mortality, and impact of pain and lingering physical injury also are thought to complicate the clinical picture.

Comprehensive treatment models have begun to be proposed, such as those of Best and Ribbe (1995) and Lyons and Scotti (1995). Treatments that sound limited (e.g., systematic desensitization) on review, in fact, seem to comprise several elements that again speak to a comprehensive treatment package (e.g., Best & Ribbe, 1995; McCaffrey & Fairbank, 1985). It is of interest that, although treatment, even in behavioral models, addresses the implications of one's life's meaning and the interpretation of events, there does not yet appear to be anecdotal material reflecting these treatment

TABLE 14.1
Uncontrolled Treatment Studies of MVA-Related PTSD

Study	Description of study	Number of sessions	Results
McCaffrey & Fairbank (1985)	2 accident-related survivors; 1 with MVA. Treatment for MVA consisted of relaxation training, imaginal, and in vivo exposure, relationship issues with mother.	15	Drop in symptoms for PTSD. Continued ratings of fear, drop in skin conduction with exposure posttreatment.
Kuch, Swinson, & Kirby (1985)	12 MVA survivors received treatment consisting of 4–12 hours of imaginal and in vivo exposure.	N/A	6 of 12 showed marked improvement. 4 additionally improved with medication and cognitive therapy.
Muse (1986)	3 MVA survivors who suffered PTSD and chronic pain. Treatment included: (a) pain treatment [exercise, biofeedback, supportive counseling and medications] (b) systematic desensitization and in vivo exposure.	11–16 for PTSD treatment	Pain, no treatment effect for PTSD with exposure, drop in PTSD symptoms.
Hickling et al. (1986)	8 of 12 MVA survivors with PTSD and postconcessive headache. All received treatment consisting of relaxation training, cognitive–behavioral treatment, and supportive counseling. One case used antidepressant medication.	8–40	Patients with PTSD required almost 2.5 times as much treatment as those without PTSD.
Burstein (1986b)	28 survivors of civilian trauma were reviewed retrospectively to determine differences between short- and long-term treatment variables. 16/28 were MVA related survivors.	N/A	Long-term patients required antidepressant medication treatment. Type of psychological treatment was not readily discernible.
Burstein et al. (1989)	2 cases examples illustrating differences between chronic Vietnam PTSD and acute civilian PTSD.	N/A	N/A
McMillan (1991)	1 MVA survivor. Case study treating PTSD that involved no recollection of MVA. Treatment used imaginal and in vivo exposure and social involvement.	16	Drop in PTSD symptoms.

Study	Description		
Horton (1993)	1 MVA survivor. Case study of mild head injury and MVA related PTSD. Treatment consisted of behavior therapy, systematic desensitization and self-directed in vivo exposure.	12	Drop in PTSD symptoms.
Horne (1993)	3 MVA survivors treated with imaginal and in vivo exposure, relaxation training, and cognitive–behavioral treatment. Collateral therapy occurred at least once with each survivor.	14–30	Positive gains overall. However, residual problems were still reported.
Lyons & Scotti (1995)	1 MVA case study illustrating direct therapeutic exposure (DTE). DTE may involve imaginal and in vivo exposure, problem solving, anger management, relaxation therapy, use of medication, relapse prevention and cognitive scenes. Audiotape homework of DTE scenes. Case involved 13 inpatient DTE scenes and 4 as outpatients. Case prematurely terminated due to distance.	17 (DTE)	Case closed prematurely due to failure to report to treatment.
Best & Ribbe (1995)	2 case examples illustrating treatment and assessment issues of MVA-related PTSD. Treatment included relaxation, cue controlled breathing, imagery, RET, cognitive restructuring, SIT, thought stopping, role playing, and exposure therapy. Issues of life-threat and physical injury were discussed.	N/A	N/A
Koch & Taylor (1995)	3 case examples. Treatment used exposure and cognitive therapy.	N/A	N/A

Note. DTE = Direct Therapeutic Exposure; N/A = Not available; RET = rational emotive therapy; SIT = stress innoculation therapy.

approaches for MVA survivors. The literature certainly is available for PTSD treatment in other populations (e.g., rape and physical assault).

In the next chapter we summarize the more recent literature on the treatment of MVA survivors. Almost all of this work was in the form of randomized controlled trials.

15

THE TREATMENT OF MVA-RELATED PTSD: A REVIEW OF THE RECENT CONTROLLED LITERATURE

The earlier literature on the psychological treatment of MVA survivors, summarized in chapter 14, was mostly uncontrolled case reports or uncontrolled series of patients and dealt with both accident phobias and PTSD. The most recent work, all of which with one exception was published after the first edition of this book, has been mostly randomized controlled trials. This represents the usual evolution of a field, from positive uncontrolled case reports that point the way to potentially useful treatment techniques to controlled evaluations of those techniques that signify the maturing of a subfield of clinical psychology.

The literature on the psychological treatment of MVA survivors can be subdivided into early intervention studies for which treatment began within the first month following the MVA and later intervention studies for which the populations were three months or more post-MVA. The early intervention studies can be further subdivided into those with a single session, akin to psychological debriefing, and those with two or more sessions that spread treatment over some period of time. These seven studies are summarized in Table 15.1.

TABLE 15.1
Results of Controlled Treatment Trials for MVA Survivors

Study and country of origin	Sample description	When treated	When reassessed	Number of sessions	Duration	Content	Pre–post IES	Pre–post CAPS	Fraction of sample improved
Hobbs et al. (1996) United Kingdom	106 hospitalized MVA survivors, 54 treated, 52 controls	24–48 hours post-MVA	4 months post-MVA	1	1 hour	Review experience; encourage emotion, expression; encourage graded return to travel; promotion of cognitive processing; information leaflet	Treated 15.1–15.9 Control 15.3–12.9	N/R	N/R Loss at Reassess 22% Treated 6% control
Mayou et al. (2000) United Kingdom	3 years follow-up of Hobbs et al. 30 treated 31 controls	Same as above	3 years post-MVA	1	1 hour	Same as above	Treated 14.9–16 Control 15.9–13.1 High initial IES Treated 35–26 Control 31–12	N/R	Treatment shows higher GSI than control
Conlon et al. (1999) United Kingdom	40 ER attendees for MVAs; none admitted Treated-18 Controls-22	7 days post-MVA	3 1/2 months post-MVA	1	30 minutes	Education of PTSD, encourage emotion, expression and details of MVA. Education on coping techniques; information leaflet.	Treated 35.0–15.8 Control 28.5–16.1	Treated 37.8–11.2 Control 27.0–17.2	Treated 2/18 PTSD Control 4/21 PTSD

Study	Sample					Treatment	Treated	Treated > control on reduction of trauma symptoms	N/R
Brom et al. (1993) Netherlands	738 survivors of moderate to severe MVA. Treated-68, Control-86 16% agreed to treatment 36% agreed to controls	1 month post-MVA	6 months post-MVA	3–6	N/R	Confront experience; practical help; support; education on symptoms; reality testing; mobilize social support	Treated 21.9–9.3 Control 17.4–7.4	Treated > control on reduction of trauma symptoms	N/R
Bryant et al. (1998b) Australia	14 MVA + 10 industrial accidents, hospitalized for injury, met criteria for ASD Treated-12, Control-12 (11 dropouts)	10 days post-MVA	Post-treatment 6 months post-accident	5	90 minutes	Education about trauma; relaxation training; imaginal exposure; graded in vivo exposure; cognitive restructuring. Controls education on trauma, general coping skills, support	Treated 53.5 15.5 15.6 Control 53.7 37.2 37.3	N/R	Treated– 11/12, 92% Control– 2/12, 17%
Bryant et al. (1999) Australia	21 MVA + 24 nonsexual assault, some hospitalized, met criteria for ASD 11 dropouts, Treatment-1:15, Treatment-2:14; Control-16	2 weeks post-trauma	Post-treatment 6 months post-treated	5	90 minutes	Treatment-1-education about trauma, *relaxation training*, imaginal exposure, in vivo exposure, cognitive restructure. Treatment-2-education about trauma, imaginal exposure, in vivo exposure, cognitive restructure. Controls-education about trauma, problem solving, support	Treatment-1 54.9 23.5 18.9 Treatment-2 54.1 16.5 19.4 Control 49.2 44.1 35.7	Treatment-1 — 25.7 29.6 Treatment-2 — 21.2 27.4 Control — 43.1 55.5	Treatment-1 10/13 = 77% Treatment-2 11/13 = 85% Control 5/15 = 33%

(continued)

TABLE 15.1 (Continued)

Study and country of origin	Sample description	When treated	When reassessed	Number of sessions	Duration	Content	Pre–post IES	Pre–post CAPS	Fraction of sample improved
						Treatment conditions			
Gidron et al. (2001) Israel	17 MVA survivors admitted for 1 day, had high heart rate Treated-8, Control-9	2 days post-MVA	3–4 months	2	Telephone sessions about 1 hour	Structured recall of MVA, restructuring, practice telling narrative to their friends	Used PTSD scale at 3 months Treated 18.5 Control 8.1	N/R	Meet PTSD Controls 4/9 = 44% Treated 1/8 = 13%
Fecteau & Nicki (1999) Canada	23 MVA survivors Treated-10, WL-10 (3 dropouts)	3–95 months post-MVA average 19 months	Post-treated 3 month follow-up 6 month follow-up	4	120 minutes	Education about trauma, relaxation training, imaginal exposure, graded in vivo exposure, cognitive restructuring and reappraisal Controls-Supportive listening.	Treated 45.1 15.5 13.0 Control 8.3 Control 51.3 48.8 — —	Treated 70.9 37.5 — — Control 77.3 74.6 — —	Treated 5/10 = 50% WL 0/10 = 0%
Ehlers et al. (2002) United Kingdom	85 MVA survivors attended ER Treated-28, Control-1-28, Control-2-29	3–6 months post-treated	Post-treated 3 months 6 months	N/R	N/R	Treated-cognitive-behavioral therapy Control-1 self-help book Control-2 wait list	Used PSS (see below)	Used PSS (see below)	N/R

Used PSS

	Treated	Control-1	Control-2
pre	26	28	27
post	8	22	24
3 months	8	23	23
6 months	9	22	22

Note. ASD = Acute Stress Disorder; CAPS = Clinician-Administered PTSD Scale; GSI = Global Severity Index; IES = Impact of Event Scale; PSS = Posttraumatic Stress Scale; WL = Wait List.

EARLY INTERVENTION STUDIES: SINGLE SESSION

In the first debriefing trial, Hobbs, Mayou, Harrison, and Worlock (1996) randomly assigned 106 MVA survivors who attended a British Emergency Department to either a one-hour debriefing session (n = 54) or assessment-only control condition (n = 52). They had excluded those with head trauma who could not remember the accident and those with no psychological symptoms. Eight eligible MVA survivors (8/114 = 7.0%) declined participation. The overall sample was 62.3% (66/106) male, with a median age of 27. The vast majority had been drivers (86.8%). The median number of days in the hospital was significantly higher for the treatment group (7.7) than for the controls (3.7).

The treatment session lasted about one hour and took place usually on the second day after the MVA. It covered (a) a review of the traumatic experience; (b) encouragement for the participant to express emotions related to the MVA; (b) advice about the usual emotional reactions to trauma; (d) encouragement to think about and talk about the experience; and (e) the promotion of an early, graded return to normal road travel. Treatment participants also received a written summary of the advice.

Ninety-one (42/54 from treatment, 78%, and 49/52 from control, 94%) were reassessed by telephone interview and self-report measures approximately four months later. There were no significant differences on total Impact of Event Scale (IES; Horowitz et al., 1979) score, although arithmetically the controls were doing better. In fact, there were no significant reductions on IES, clinical ratings of mood disturbance, presence of PTSD, travel anxiety, or of intrusive thoughts. The Global Severity Scale (GSI; scores from the Brief Symptom Inventory (BSI; DeRogatis, 1993) used as a measure of overall psychological distress, were unchanged, statistically; however, those in the intervention group went up (0.50 to 0.62) whereas the controls showed a slight decrease (0.42 to 0.38). On two scales of the BSI, the treatment group had a worse outcome than those in the control condition. Clearly the brief, early intervention was ineffective, and possibly led to an overall poorer early outcome.

Much to this research team's credit, they were able to obtain three-year follow-up data on 62 (30 treatment, 31 controls, 58.5% of total) of the 106 participants (Mayou, Ehlers, & Hobbs, 2000). Those who were followed up differed from drop-outs only in terms of higher initial injury scores (p = .035). Overall IES scores were not different at three years between the two groups but had shown a significant (p = .015) overall reduction. The findings on the Global Severity Index of the BSI showed no overall reduction at three years. However, an ANCOVA on three-year scores, controlling for initial score, showed those from the intervention to be significantly higher (p = .026) than the controls—that is, those who received treatment acknowledged greater distress.

In an enlightening internal analysis, the authors subdivided each condition on the basis of high or low initial (+23) IES scores. The ANCOVA on three-year scores showed a main effect of condition, the intervention group overall scored higher than the controls at three years, and very importantly, a significant initial IES score by treatment condition interaction (p = .043). For those with lower initial IES scores, average scores from both conditions had increased from about 8 to 12 by three years. Those in the control condition with high initial IES scores (X = 31.3) had decreased to 12 at three years (and in fact, were about 9 at the four-month follow-up). For those who received the brief intervention and who had high initial IES scores (X = 34.9), the decrease at four months was to about 33 and at three years was to 26. Obviously, this group with high initial intrusion and avoidance scores had not especially profited from the intervention. *Instead, the treatment may have delayed their recovery.*

It was also the case that at the three-year follow-up, when one compared the total group who received the intervention to the controls, the overall intervention group reported greater pain (p = .002) and more major chronic physical problems (20% versus 3.2%) than the controls. Even when initial hospital stay and initial injury severity were covaried out, these follow-up differences between groups remained. Initial IES score did not contribute to these differences.

Clinical Comment

It could be that the intervention group, by chance, had more severely injured survivors and that the lingering physical problems interacted with the initial psychological distress to prolong both. Alternatively, it could be that a brief early intervention was not only ineffective but also was possibly harmful (delayed natural recovery) to the natural psychological recovery process. This seemed to be the case with those who initially had high levels of intrusions and avoidance.

* * *

The second single-session early-intervention study (Conlon, Fahy, & Conroy, 1999) also was conducted in the United Kingdom. Forty MVA survivors (19 men, 32 women, ranging in age from 16 to 65) with relatively minor injuries (none were admitted to the hospital) who attended an emergency department were randomly assigned to a single-session intervention about one week after the MVA (n = 18) or to a measurement-only control condition (n = 22). Both groups were assessed approximately one week after the MVA (range 3 to 14 days) with the IES and CAPS (Clinical Administered PTSD Scale; Blake et al., 1990b) interview (one-week version). They were reassessed about three months later (mean of 99 days post-MVA, range 65–210 days) again with the IES and CAPS. (Only 32 were reinterviewed, and there was differential loss of participants from the intervention group 7/18 ([39%] versus 1/22 [5%] in the controls. Our calculations show this differential loss to be significant: $X^2[N = 40, df = 1] = 7.30, p = .007$).

The intervention lasted about 30 minutes and "encouraged expression of emotional and cognitive effects" of the MVA, and "provided education regarding posttraumatic stress symptoms and coping strategies" (p. 38). Treated participants were given an advice leaflet.

Although the two groups did not differ significantly on initial IES or CAPS scores, there was a noticeable difference on initial one-week CAPS (intervention: 37.8, control: 27.0). Thirty-one of 40 (77.5%) were labeled as "cases" based on initial IES scores of 12 or greater on either the intrusion or avoidance subscales. At three months, the level of caseness by IES was 35%, and 7 of 32 met CAPS criteria for PTSD ($n = 3$) or subsyndromal PTSD ($n = 4$).

There were no significant differences between the two conditions at the three-month follow-up on IES scores (intervention: 15.8, control: 16.1) or on CAPS scores (intervention: 11.2, control: 17.2). There had been a significant decrease over time for the two groups combined on IES ($p = .001$) and total CAPS ($p = .0002$) but no differential reduction. For the IES, the intervention group changed from 35.0 at pre- to 15.8 at post-, whereas the controls changed from 28.5 at pre- to 16.1 at post-. For the CAPS, the intervention group changed from 37.8 to 11.2, whereas the control group changed from 27.0 to 17.7, pre- to post-, respectively. (Unfortunately, the research team did not compare groups on post-scores with an ANCOVA covaring pre-scores. The arithmetic means point toward an effect of the intervention.)

Prediction analyses showed higher likelihood of "caseness" and poor outcome at three months in those with high initial IES scores or high initial CAPS scores, as well as those with older age. Although the categorical outcome data were not significantly different by condition, there were 3 out of 21 (14.3%) cases of diagnosed PTSD in the control group versus 0 out of 11 (0%) in the intervention group at three months.

The Conlon et al. (1999) study is a good complement to that of Hobbs et al. (1996) in that Conlon et al. used all outpatients who were not seriously enough injured to warrant admission, whereas Hobbs et al. recruited from an admitted (thus, more severely injured) population. Both show no short-term (three to four months post-MVA) effect; however, there are nonsignificant trends for Conlon et al.'s participants to improve more than controls, whereas the opposite is true in Hobbs et al. (But one must remember there was significantly greater loss of participants in the intervention condition.) Certainly, at this point one can find no reason to apply a brief (one session) early intervention to unselected MVA survivors who attend the ED.

EARLY INTERVENTION STUDIES: MULTIPLE SESSIONS

In the first controlled intervention study for survivors of MVAs in the Netherlands, Brom et al. (1993) studied the effectiveness of a psychological package designed to stimulate healthy coping following an MVA. They saw the reactions and needs of survivors as: (a) ranging from normal responses that do not require any assistance from professionals, (b) survivors helped by the support of trained victim assistants, and (c) counseling and crisis intervention for the serious life event.

The treatment package they developed included: (a) practical help and information (i.e., general information about reactions after a serious life event, symptom patterns one may experience, attempts to place reactions in the context of normal coping, and practical matters such as medical or financial matters); and (b) support (i.e., a safe and quiet environment to reassure the victim that the event is really over). Support is further meant as a structured experience whereby the victim can label his or her emotions and mobilize his or her own social network; (c) reality testing, where the intervention attempts to facilitate coping through confrontation and reality testing. Coping is thought of by Brom et al. as a process of forgetting and retrieving. Confrontation and reality testing regarding the symptoms the survivors are experiencing may help the symptoms become less frightening. Interventions were delivered over several sessions, occurring at least two to three months following the accident. The intervention was designed to aid in the early recognition of any psychological disorders and make appropriate referral to trained professionals.

Participants were drawn from a police registry of motor vehicle accident survivors. The initial sample was a list compiled over a one-year period of time. The accident was judged by five independent raters to be from moderately serious to serious, based on registration forms and then rating the severity of the accident. Inter-rater reliability of accident severity was somewhat poor, ranging from .51 to .71.

Within the first month after the MVA, the police informed the survivors about the project that was to be carried out. One group of participants received a letter asking them to participate in a research project and the other group received a written invitation to participate in a secondary prevention program. The selection to either group was random. The sample consisted of 83 participants (30 female, 53 male) in the monitoring group and 68 participants (32 female, 36 male) in the intervention group. Letters were mailed to 738 persons, with a response rate of 36% for the monitoring group and only 13% for the intervention group. Mean age was 39 and 36 years, respectively. At the time of follow-up, the drop-out percentage was 24% in the monitoring group and 16% in the intervention group. Outcome measures included the Impact of Event Scale (IES; Horowitz et al., 1979), using a Dutch translation; the Trauma Symptom Inventory, which is a selection of the SCL–90 (Arindell & Ettema, 1981), consisting of 29 items that are thought to reflect negative emotional experiences, tensions, sleep disturbances, and lack of interest in the external world; and the evaluation questionnaire, which was a short questionnaire asking the participants in the intervention group their degree of satisfaction with the elements of the treatment program. Treatment was carried out by two experienced therapists. Treatment consisted of three sessions that could be extended to six sessions.

The study found that one month after an MVA, about half of the survivors showed moderate to severe symptoms of intrusion and avoidance on the IES. By six months after the MVA, these symptoms had improved, although 8% were still rated as severe and another 10 to 17% showed moderate symptoms. About 90% of the intervention group indicated that they were content or very content with the intervention. Very importantly, there was no significant difference in the degree of improvement on the IES between the intervention group and the monitoring control group. Thus, Brom et al. (1993) were not able to prove the effectiveness of their intervention or that there intervention had more effectiveness than the passage of time.

A small-scale controlled trial in Israel by Gidron et al. (2001) changed the focus of early intervention research by focusing on MVA survivor cases attending the emergency department (ED) who were thought to be at high risk for developing PTSD (had heart rate of greater than 95 bpm at the ED, were likely to acknowledge peritraumatic dissociation, and had had psychological treatment before the MVA). Seventeen eligible MVA survivors (10 men, 7 women, of average age 38) were randomly assigned to two structured telephone conversations (interval between was not specified) with homework assignments (treatment) or to two telephone calls where the counselor provided supportive listening as the patient described the MVA.

In the structured condition, the therapist asks the patient to describe the MVA in a consistent temporal fashion while clarifying details. The therapist then "repeats the trauma narrative in an organized, labeled and logical manner" while describing implications to the patient. The patient is then asked to describe the MVA again in this structured fashion; the patient usually adds details. The patient is then asked, as homework, to practice telling friends and family the new, structured version of the narrative to enhance a reorganization of memory. At the second telephone call the patient is asked to practice the structured narrative with the therapist again and is told to seek out social support.

At a three- to four-month follow-up, the patients were assessed with Foa, Cashman, Jacoy, and Kevin's (1997) Posttraumatic Diagnostic Scale, as a structured interview, by someone blind to initial status. Five patients (29%) met criteria for PTSD: four of nine (44%) were controls versus one of eight (12.5%) from the treatment condition. Based on one-tailed tests, the treatment group reported significantly ($p < .05$) less frequent total PTSD symptoms (Tx-8.1, C-18.5), intrusion symptoms (Tx-1.6, C-5.8), and arousal symptoms (Tx-4.2, C-7.7). Thus, this "memory restructuring" therapy was effective with the high-risk population.

By far the strongest results from multiple-session, early-intervention studies are two from the Australian research team headed by Richard Bryant. In both studies, the populations have been individuals hospitalized because of trauma- (either MVAs or industrial accidents) related injuries who met criteria for Acute Stress Disorder (ASD). In the first study (Bryant, Harvey, Dang, Sackville, & Basten [1998]), 12 patients were randomized to a cognitive–behavioral therapy (CBT) condition (seven women, five men of average age 32.3 years) or to a supportive counseling condition (seven women, five men of average age 33.0 years). Participants were initially assessed about 10 days post-MVA. Those with traumatic brain injury, psychosis, or suicidal ideation were excluded.

The CBT condition was made up of five individually administered 90-minute sessions spread over about six weeks. The content included education about trauma reactions, progressive muscle relaxation, imaginal exposure to traumatic memories, cognitive restructuring, and graded in vivo exposure to avoided situations. A detailed treatment manual is available in Bryant and Harvey's book, *Acute Stress Disorder* (2000). The supportive counseling was made up of education about trauma and training in general problem-solving skills delivered in a supportive manner.

Assessments took place initially, at posttreatment and at a six-month follow-up, using both psychological tests and structured interviews for diagnosis of ASD or PTSD (posttreatment and follow-up). Mean IES scores changed differentially for the two groups: (CBT: 53.5 to 15.5 to 15.6; support: 53.7 to 40 to 37.3) as did Beck Depression Inventory (BDI; Beck et al., 1961) scores (CBT: 16.6 to 7.3 to 6.1; support: 17.2 to 13.7 to 13.5). In terms of categorical diagnoses, for the CBT condition 1 out of 12 (8.3%) met criteria for PTSD at post- and 2 out of 12 (16.7%) at the six-month follow-up. For the supportive counseling there were 10 of 12 (83.3%) with PTSD at post- and 8 of 12 (66.7%) at six months. The categorical differences were significant at both posttreatment and six-month follow-up.

It is interesting to note that the supportive counseling condition was not only ineffective, it might be slightly detrimental. In their naturalistic follow-up of MVA-related ASD (Harvey & Bryant, 1998b), seven of nine (77.8%) of those with initial ASD who were reassessed at six months met criteria for PTSD. Because of lost participants this value could range from 58.3% (7/12) to 83.3% (10/12). If the former value is correct, then the treatment has a slightly detrimental effect. In any event, it is clear that this systematic combination of cognitive and behavioral procedures, applied intensively over the first six to eight weeks postaccident, is effective in preventing the high-risk patient from converting to PTSD.

In the second study, Bryant, Sackville, Dang, Moulds, and Guthrie (1999) sought to learn what parts of their multicomponent CBT treatment were the most important. Participants were either MVA survivors or victims of nonsexual assault. They had not necessarily been hospitalized. Fifteen cases were excluded (current suicidal ideation, $n = 4$; psychosis or substance abuse, $n = 8$; traumatic brain injury, $n = 3$). Of the 66 who started treatment, there were 11 (16.7%) dropouts, evenly distributed across the three experimental conditions.

All three treatment conditions were conducted for five 90-minute sessions at about once per week. The primary experimental condition was described as prolonged exposure plus anxiety management. It had all of the components described previously for the CBT condition in Bryant et al. (1998b) and emphasized cognitive restructuring and correction after imaginal exposure and then graded in vivo exposure. The prolonged exposure-only condition did not include relaxation training and other anxiety management techniques but did include imaginal exposure and cognitive restructuring and correction. The supportive counseling condition is the same as described in Bryant et al. (1998b) and included trauma education and training in problem-solving skills.

Of the 45 who completed treatment, approximately half of those in each condition were female and half were MVA survivors. Average age was 33.9 years. On average they were 10.4 days posttrauma at the initial assessment. Thus, completing each condition were 15 in exposure plus anxiety management, 14 in prolonged exposure, and 16 in supportive counseling. Assessment took place at the pretreatment assessment, at posttreatment, and at a six-month follow-up.

In general, there was comparable noticeable improvement in both experimental treatment groups, which was significantly greater at posttreatment and follow-up than that seen for those in supportive counseling. For the IES, the scores were for exposure plus anxiety management (pre: 54.9, post: 23.5, follow-up: 18.8), exposure (pre: 54.1, post: 44.2, follow-up: 35.7). The CAPS was administered at posttreatment and follow-up. Scores for exposure plus anxiety management (post:25.7, follow-up: 29.6), for exposure (post: 21.2, follow-up: 27.5) and supportive counseling (post: 43.1, follow-up: 55.5) showed the same pattern as the IES.

In terms of categorical diagnoses, significantly fewer patients from the prolonged exposure plus anxiety management (3/15, 20%) and prolonged exposure (2/14, 14%) met criteria for PTSD at posttreatment than did those from supportive counseling (9/16, 56%). Each experimental condition was individually superior to supportive counseling; the two did not differ. At the six-month follow-up, 41 of 45 (91%) patients were reassessed. Again, fewer patients from prolonged exposure plus anxiety management (3/13, 23%) and prolonged exposure (2/13, 15%) met criteria for PTSD than from the supportive counseling condition (10/15, 67%). Each experimental condition was individually superior to the control condition. As in Bryant et al. (1998), the supportive counseling condition did no better than no treatment at the six-month point.

Although Bryant et al. (1999) label the condition as prolonged exposure, it clearly has an involved cognitive therapy component with the cognitive restructuring and correction an integral follow-up to the exposure. It does seem to be the case that the relaxation training and other anxiety management techniques add little to the exposure and cognitive restructuring. Across the two trials, the cognitive behavioral treatments have led to the prevention of PTSD in 31 of 38 (81.6%) patients. It seems clear that this intensive early intervention has a great deal to offer and points out the advantage to working with a high risk population such as those with initial ASD or sub-ASD.

Summary Comment

The studies reviewed thus far lead to three conclusions:

1. Single-session, early (first two weeks post-MVA) interventions, despite including apparently relevant elements, are ineffective at best and may be detrimental with those with high IES scores.
2. Multiple session cognitive–behavioral treatments administered early to high-risk MVA survivors seem to be effective in preventing later PTSD in a sizable portion of those studied.
3. Early education and supportive counseling over several sessions with high-risk MVA survivors does not appear to prevent short-term PTSD and may lead to a poorer outcome than doing nothing.

Longer Term Follow-Up

Much to their credit, the Australian team were able to follow-up many of the participants in their two controlled trials four years posttrauma

(Bryant, Moulds, & Nixon, 2003). They assessed 25 of 41 (62%) patients who received CBT and 16 of 24 (67%) of those who received supportive counseling. Five patients (original condition not specified) were excluded because of receiving additional treatment after the six-month point. Using the CAPS for diagnosis, they found 2 out of 25 (8%) from the CBT conditions met criteria for PTSD at four years versus 4 of 16 (25%) of those who had received supportive counseling, a nonsignificant difference. Average total CAPS scores for the two groups did show a significant advantage for CBT (17.8) over supportive counseling (30.5), with most of the difference being a result of the avoidance and numbing symptoms.

Given that their prospective two-year follow-up data show as many as 63 to 70% of those with ASD from MVAs meet criteria for PTSD at the follow-up, it seems clear that CBT treatment is very helpful over the long term, and that early supportive counseling has a beneficial long-term effect (less than half the rate of PTSD that one would expect with no treatment).

INTERVENTION WITH ESTABLISHED CASES

The first controlled treatment trial for MVA survivors with established PTSD was conducted in Canada by Fecteau and Nicki (1999). Twenty-four individuals with MVA-related PTSD of 3 to 95 months duration (mean elapsed time 19 months) were randomly assigned to either four individual, weekly, two-hour (range 1½ to 3 hours) treatment sessions or to an assessment-only control condition. Ten participants completed each condition (14 women, 6 men, of average age 41.3 years). One control participant had to be removed because of deterioration in clinical status; two treatment attenders dropped out and one never began treatment.

The treatment was structured and manualized. Session 1 included education about trauma reactions and relaxation training using diaphragmatic breathing. Home practice tapes of the relaxation were provided. Session 2 involved a detailed discussion of the MVA highlighting the cues that evoked anxiety. There followed some imaginal exposure to a therapist description of the accident; the latter description was audiotaped. Home practice of daily relaxation and daily reexposure to the trauma tape were initiated. Sessions 3 and 4 involved imaginal exposure to the trauma and gradually direct cognitive reappraisal of the trauma. Faulty cognitive assumptions were challenged. Graduated, self-directed in vivo exposure to feared travel stimulus situations was initiated to help overcome avoidance. The patient was also helped to develop a coherent narrative account of the trauma. All treatment was by a single experienced therapist.

Results showed significant ($p < .05$) posttest differences (by ANCOVA using pretest scores as the covariate) favoring the treatment group on total CAPS (treatment—70.9 to 37.5; control—77.3 to 74.6, pre- to post-, respectively) and on Cluster B and Cluster C symptoms, but not on Cluster D (arousal). Similar analyses showed significant effects on the IES and each subscale (total IES: treatment—46.1 to 15.5; control—51.3 to 48.8, pre- to post-, respectively). There was also a significant difference on Beck Anxiety Inventory (BAI) scores but not on the Beck Depression Inventory (BDI). At the categorical or diagnostic level, 4 of 10 (40%) of the treatment group had remitted fully whereas another had been reduced to subsyndromal PTSD. None of those in the control group reduced symptoms to less than PTSD.

At a three-month follow-up, on all 10 treated participants, by means of questionnaires only, the IES and BAI scores continued significantly reduced; at a similar six-month follow-up on eight participants, the BAI remained significantly improved, the IES showed a further reduction to 8.3, and the BDI scores showed significant improvement from the pretest (pre-: 26.3, post-: 20.1, six-month follow-up: 15.9).

Thus, this small-scale comparison of cognitive and behavioral procedures with patients with established PTSD to an assessment-only control clearly showed the advantage of CBT. The results were apparently maintained (and even improved) at follow-ups of three and six months.

Another group of Canadian investigators (Taylor et al., 2001) have reported on a large scale ($n = 50$), uncontrolled trial of a combination of cognitive and behavioral procedures, administered in a small-group format. Treatment was for 12 two-hour weekly sessions. Eleven groups comprised of four to six MVA survivors were conducted. Each group had two therapists, one of whom was from a set of three experienced CBT therapists.

Treatment was manualized and consisted of education about trauma and its consequences, cognitive restructuring, applied relaxation, graded imaginal exposure to the MVA and its aftermath, and graded in vivo exposure. Pleasant event scheduling was also used.

Fifty-eight MVA survivors met entry criteria; four never started treatment, and four dropped out in treatment, leaving 50 treatment completers. Forty-five provided four-month follow-up data. The sample was 68% female, of average age 35.6 years; 86% were Caucasian, 10% Asian. Forty-six (92%) met criteria for PTSD. The target MVA had occurred an average of 2.4 years earlier. Participants had experienced an average of 3.3 personal-injury MVAs over their lifetimes. Seventy-percent were involved in litigation.

Total CAPS scores for the sample for the three assessments (pre-, post-, three-month follow-up) were not presented; instead the authors claimed significant pre- to post- reductions on each of the four CAPS symptom clusters. There were no additional significant reductions from end of treatment to the three-month follow-up point. In terms of categorical changes, of the 50 (or 46) participants with PTSD at the start of treatment, 22 did not meet full criteria for PTSD at posttreatment. This translates into a success rate of 22 of 50 (44%). It could represent a success rate of 18 of 46 (39%). This success rate of 44% is approximately the same rate as reported by Fecteau and Nicki (1999). No information was reported on possible subsyndromal PTSD cases. Also, no results on possible changes in BDI scores was presented, nor was information on categorical diagnoses at three months presented.

Much of the paper was devoted to identifying variables associated with good versus poor outcome. Among those variables associated with poor outcome were presence of comorbid major depression, higher initial BDI scores, higher initial levels of pain severity, and lower Global Assessment Scale scores (GAS; Endicott et al., 1977). Overall, these results from Taylor et al. (2001) point to the difficulty of treating patients with chronic MVA-related PTSD who are continuing to be fairly impaired because of psychological and physical symptoms and also to be fairly depressed.

Ehlers (personal communication, May 9, 2002) has told us of preliminary results of another randomized, controlled trial of CBT with MVA survivors, conducted in the United Kingdom with David Clark and Richard Mayou. Using MVA survivors who were three to six months (mean 17 weeks) post-MVA and who met Structured Clinical Interview for DSM–III–R (SCID) diagnosis for PTSD, they randomly assigned 28 to CBT, 28 to a self-help booklet, and 29 to a wait-list with repeated assessments. The sample was 72% female, with an average age of 40. Using the Posttraumatic Stress Scale (PSS; Foa, Riggs, Dancu, & Rothbaum, 1993) as a measure of posttraumatic stress symptoms, they found those receiving CBT were significantly more improved at each reassessment point (three weeks; three, six, and nine months) than the self-help group or wait-list control who did not differ. The CBT group's Posttraumatic Diagnostic Scale (PDS; Foa et al., 1997) scores went from about 26 at the start of treatment to about 8 at three, six, and nine months. The self-help group went from about 28 to 20 at each of the follow-up points, whereas the wait-list went from 27 to 23 at three months and 20 at nine months. Almost 80% of those in the CBT condition were at "high end state functioning" at nine months compared to 30% in the wait-list and 5% of those receiving the self-help booklet. Categorical diagnostic data were not available. It seems clear that these results replicate ours, to be described in chapter 17, using a somewhat less chronic (3 to 6 months post-MVA) population than our sample (6 to 24 months post-MVA).

Beck and colleagues (personal communication, July 24, 2002; Shipherd, Beck, Hamblen, & Freeman, 2000) have described a group CBT treatment for MVA survivors with chronic PTSD and initial results from a group who suffered from both chronic PTSD and notable chronic pain (Shipherd, Beck, Hamblen, Lackner, & Freeman, in press). The treatment regimen is for 12 weekly sessions of approximately 90 minutes duration. It includes (and was modeled after) the CBT treatment described in Blanchard and Hickling (1997). Thus, components include education about PTSD, relaxation training, exposure to written descriptions of the MVA, graduated in vivo exposure to trauma cues, and various cognitive techniques. It also includes pleasant events scheduling and attention to anger and irritability. (The latest version of the group treatment [G. Beck, personal communication, September 5, 2002] has moved the exposure to written descriptions to much later in therapy, has moved the cognitive techniques to very early in treatment, and combines both imaginal and in vivo exposure.)

Results from six patients, all of whom met criteria for PTSD, revealed a reduction in CAPS score from 80.8 to 27.7 and a significant reduction in IES scores. Five of the six no longer met criteria for PTSD. Moreover, there was improvement in pain ratings for five of six patients.

In conclusion, although the results from the two Canadian trials are not overwhelming, they do indicate that MVA survivors with chronic PTSD do respond to systematic CBT. The new results from Ehlers (and from Shipherd et al.), combined with our own results—both those from the preliminary uncontrolled trials and those highlighted in chapter 17—the results of our randomized controlled trial, make the point that this more chronic population can be treated with good results (better than 75% success rate) with CBT.

16

THE EARLY, UNCONTROLLED ALBANY STUDIES OF THE TREATMENT OF MVA SURVIVORS

The assessment studies completed at Albany/Center for Stress and Anxiety Disorders led very naturally to an interest in trying to treat motor-vehicle-accident (MVA)-related posttraumatic stress disorder (PTSD). When this work began in September 1991, there were no published reports of controlled treatment trials for MVA-related PTSD. There was a limited case report literature (summarized in chapter 14). There was also guidance on how to approach the problem from the literature on treating Vietnam War veterans and rape victims. Two review papers were especially helpful as we entered the treatment arena, the first by Solomon, Gerrity, and Muff (1992) that reported 255 English language reports on the efficacy of various treatments for the psychological effects of exposure to traumatic events and the second by Meichenbaum (1994).

Our treatment of MVA survivors with PTSD was developed from both our clinical experience in the treatment of PTSD and the understanding gained in our MVA assessment study. As we studied the survivors with PTSD from MVAs, our understanding of the disorder and formulations on treatment have grown in several ways.

This chapter begins with a description of the thinking underlying our approach to treatment. The treatment is guided by these theoretical understandings. The description of our pilot studies are provided in detail, to illustrate and show the results that led to our current approach in treatment. Where it is useful, clinical examples and anecdotes are provided. The annotated treatment manuals are described in chapters 18 (cognitive–behavioral treatments) and 19 (supportive psychotherapy). The detailed description of the controlled study evaluating these two treatments, including long-term follow-up, is contained in chapter 17.

THE SOLOMON ET AL. REVIEW

As Solomon et al. (1992) pointed out, practically every form of psychotherapy has been tried on individuals suffering from PTSD. Although most uncontrolled case reports point out treatment efficacy, few have been subjected to systematic tests. In their review, Solomon et al. (1992) selected studies that treated PTSD while meeting the following criteria: (a) inclusion criteria of participants based on both exposure to a traumatic event and assessed according to *DSM–III* or *DSM–III–R* criteria (American Psychiatric Association, 1980, 1987), and (b) random assignment to the treatment of interest, and either an alternative treatment or a no-treatment (or wait-list) control group. Using these criteria, eleven studies met criteria for inclusion, including drug treatment studies.

Solomon et al. (1992) reported on six studies that used behavioral techniques and met their criteria. Behavioral interventions are designed to reduce the impact of the fear conditioning and the avoidant behavior. This is accomplished by either by having exposure to the feared situation (stimulus) repeated or prolonged or by imaginal or in vivo exposure. Techniques can use either systematic desensitization (i.e., gradually increasing the intensity of the feared stimulus) or flooding (i.e., extended exposure to high-intensity stimulus).

One of the most developed cognitive therapies for PTSD is Stress Inoculation Training (SIT; Veronen & Kilpatrick, 1983). SIT is actually a combination of therapies that include muscle relaxation, thought stopping, breathing control, communication skills, and guided self-dialogue consisting of cognitive restructuring (modifying the patient's thinking and underlying beliefs about self, world, and future) and stress inoculation (SI; discussing the patient's reaction to stressful situations, rehearsing coping skills, and testing the skills out under stressful conditions).

Foa et al. (1991) in an elegant study of different cognitive–behavioral procedures, compared Meichenbaum's SIT to Prolonged Exposure (PE), supportive counseling and a wait-list control condition for rape survivors with chronic PTSD (average time since assault was 6.2 years).

Foa et al. used a global outcome measure as well as symptom cluster-specific measures of PTSD. At posttreatment the SIT condition was superior to the supportive counseling and the wait list conditions overall and on the reduction of avoidance symptoms in particular. SIT was not statistically superior to the PE condition at posttreatment. At a 3½ month follow-up, the SIT and PE conditions were not statistically superior to the supportive counseling control group overall, or on any symptom cluster. However, although the PE participants showed continued improvements over the follow-up interval, those in the SIT condition showed a nonsignificant loss of treatment gains. In the PE condition, the patients intensely relived the trauma experience by repeatedly describing the event during therapy sessions, listening to an audiotape recording of the description of the trauma each day and through in-vivo exposure to feared and avoided situations.

As Solomon et al. (1992) pointed out, although still untested, behavioral techniques may prove to be more effective when combined with cognitive therapy. They describe the behavioral techniques as methods to activate fear and promote habituation, whereas cognitive therapies have been developed to reduce anxiety by providing the patient with skills to control the fear.

Psychodynamic Treatment and Hypnotherapy

Solomon et al. (1992) summarized the intent of psychodynamic therapies as helping the traumatized individual integrate the traumatic event into their understanding of the meaning of life, self-concept, and world image. The emotional reactions are thought to be the reaction of the traumatized person's dealing with discrepancies between internal and external information. The discrepancies serve to create motives for defense and control, as evidenced in PTSD by the symptom clusters of intrusion and avoidance. Similar to psychodynamic theory, the main goal of hypnotherapy is to allow the traumatized individual to release unconscious material and to integrate the traumatic event.

Solomon et al. (1992) reported that to date there has only been one controlled study of either psychodynamic or hypnotherapy approaches to the treatment of PTSD. This is the study by Brom et al. (1993), who compared patients receiving psychodynamic therapy, hypnotherapy, and systematic desensitization with a wait-list control group. All three treatment groups showed significantly greater improvements than a wait-list control group. The psychodynamic group was reported to show the greatest reduction in avoidance symptoms, with less change in intrusion symptoms. The hypnotherapy and desensitization groups showed the opposite trend, with a greater reduction in intrusion symptoms and less change shown in avoidance symptoms.

MEICHENBAUM'S REVIEW

The second important review was an encyclopedic effort by Meichenbaum (1994), who produced a clinical handbook/practical therapist manual for assessing and treating PTSD. Meichenbaum pointed out two characteristics of the treatment literature to date: (a) That clinicians have been extremely creative, as shown by the treatment literature to date, in using almost any type of intervention with PTSD survivors, and (b) that there is a remarkably limited good outcome data in the treatment literature reviewed. He cautioned that at the time of his review there was not sufficient evidence to suggest the superiority of any one form of treatment over any other, nor was there an appreciation of how various treatment components can be combined most effectively.

To illustrate the breadth of topics for treatments of PTSD, the following list is summarized by Meichenbaum (1994):

> Pharmacological interventions, crisis intervention, individual and group psychodynamic therapies, individual therapy, time limited dynamic therapies, time limited trauma therapy, individual behavior therapy, systematic desensitization and EMG biofeedback, eye movement desensitization and reprocessing therapy, guided imagery based intervention, individual and group cognitive-behavioral stress inoculation therapy, dialectical behavior therapy and problem solving, marathon therapy group, cognitive restructuring or cognitive processing therapy, inpatient treatment programs, eclectic inpatient program, multifaceted outpatient intervention, second generation inpatient program, readjustment counseling services, partial hospitalization and day treatment programs, outpatient group programs for women veterans, gestalt techniques, marital and family therapy, hypnosis and hypnotherapy, solution focused and strategic therapy, reauthoring therapy, transcendental meditation, abreactive treatments, post-traumatic therapy, reintegration therapy, general skills multimodal therapy, group psychotherapy, community-wide and school-based interventions, outpatient clinic, family based interventions, ritualistic approaches, art and movement therapies, relapse prevention programs, cross cultural counseling, integrative biopsychosocial approach, pastoral care and twelve step program, self-help audiotapes, outward bound programs, and more. (n.p.)

As one can see from Meichenbaum's list, the approaches to PTSD treatment have varied considerably. The treatments, according to Meichenbaum, have varied for several reasons, one because of the techniques being used, and two because of the population they are trying to reach.

ALBANY TREATMENT RATIONALE

DSM–III–R (American Psychiatric Association, 1987) and *DSM–IV* (American Psychiatric Association, 1994) criterion for PTSD, in addition to the experience of the traumatic event and initial subjective reaction to the trauma (Criterion A), describe three clusters of symptoms that make up PTSD: (a) reexperiencing of the traumatic event (Criterion B), (b) persistent avoidance of stimuli associated with the trauma or numbing or decrease in general responsiveness (Criterion C), and (c) persistent symptoms of increased arousal that was not present before to the trauma (Criterion D). However, because not all survivors of MVAs present identically (Blanchard et al., 1994a; Kuch et al., 1985), and because the need for treatment may vary across these survivors, we have come to believe that it might be more useful to conceptualize PTSD after an MVA as being made up of *four* interrelated sets of symptoms and clinical problems: (a) reexperiencing, (b) avoidance, (c) psychic numbing, and (d) hyperarousal. These symptom clusters as outlined below would appear to lead to distinct, well-defined treatment interventions, whose focus may need to shift considerably across different accident survivors. This is a critical component of our treatment rationale, in that each intervention has a defined purpose and rationale for its application to MVA survivors with PTSD.

It has been gratifying to find our clinical judgment implemented in 1996 (and published in Hickling and Blanchard, 1997) has been borne out by recent studies using confirmatory factor analysis. Both King, Leskin, King, and Weathers (1998) and Simms, Watson, and Doebbelling (2002) found a four-factor structure provided the best fit to data from veterans. The factors were intrusion, avoidance, numbing, and hyperarousal.

Reexperiencing

One of the hallmark symptoms of PTSD is the presence of intrusive thoughts, recollections, dreams, and so forth, of the crash, perhaps most graphically demonstrated by dissociative–flashback experiences or distress when exposed to situations that resemble the crash–trauma or some particular aspect of the MVA. MVA survivors in Western culture are likely to be faced with a multitude of driving situations, potentially leading to distress by exposure to driving experiences, when riding as a passenger in a car, watching the nightly news, or reading descriptions of local MVAs. One patient shared her experience of going home and seeing her very own accident graphically displayed on the 6:00 news!

We are in agreement with other research and clinical reports (e.g., Foa et al., 1989) that vicarious exposure and enforced reexperiencing of the trauma, coupled with some education and cognitive therapy designed to reinterpret the event and its outcome, is reasonable, and in our opinion indicated, given our current understanding of treatment effectiveness. This follows in part from the conceptualization of trauma memory and the reexperiencing of symptoms in terms of emotional processing (Foa et al., 1989). The trauma memory is then placed in the position of "reexperiencing with new understanding" and hopefully lessens anxiety, as the exposure without negative consequence should limit the potency of the stimulus with repeated pairings.

One focus of intervention with this symptom cluster is to try to help the patient understand that some reexperiencing symptoms are to be expected and are a "normal" part of the reaction to a significant trauma. Second, vicarious exposure can then occur, by either having the patient orally or in writing confront their personalized description of the MVA and their emotional reaction to the description. Again, because of the variety of MVA experiences (e.g., lying in a car trapped overnight, being extracted with the jaws of life, seeing a truck bearing down or sliding out of control on an icy road surface), it seems to us critical that the description for exposure be personalized. The focus is to try to help the patient access, and thereby confront, as many parts of the cognitive network of difficult memories as possible, making the memories conscious and salient, rather than allowing the patient to avoid them. This is done in a supportive therapeutic environment, with the negative consequences acknowledged but reinterpreted in as positive a fashion as possible.

Avoidance Symptoms

There has been considerable evidence that avoidance symptoms can be approached through education, graded exposure homework, applied relaxation (to assist in coping with the negative arousal that exposure will initially elicit), and cognitive techniques to aid in the reinterpretation of the experiences (e.g., Burstein, 1989; Foa & Kozak, 1986; Horne, 1993). Existing behavioral treatments for PTSD have used graded exposure (e.g., Munjack 1984), and cognitive therapy has been well-recognized as a therapy for phobic avoidance (e.g., Meichenbaum, 1977). Treatment may involve education to explain the development of a trauma reaction, using Mowrer's (1947) two factor theory, as Keane et al. (1985) did in their formulation of PTSD. This rationale helps in the repeated requests by the therapist to the patient for systematic exposure that is a part of graded in vivo exposure tasks or for in office, imaginal desensitization.

When a significant other or spouse is enlisted to help with in vivo exposure (or to at least minimally tolerate and understand the PTSD reaction that is occurring with their partner), the provision of a rationale and conceptualization of *why* the reaction has occurred is found to be of great benefit.

This has most often occurred in our experience when many MVA survivors describe feeling particularly uncomfortable, or even outright avoiding, riding in the car as a passenger. Instead, it is often the case that the MVA victim prefers to drive the vehicle ostensibly for the sense of control this provides. The perceived loss of control when riding in the car as a passenger, at some point in their psychological treatment, often requires an exposure-based treatment. Here the significant other can be of central importance in the completion of this assignment. His or her understanding and acceptance of the thinking behind the development of this symptom in the partner, and their own role in perpetuation and amelioration of the problem, at times can be critically important even with a largely individually based treatment model. Applied relaxation is also often used to assist the patient in dealing with the heightened overarousal that an exposure task may bring (e.g., Hickling, Sison, & Vanderploeg, 1986).

Psychic Numbing and Estrangement Symptoms

As Litz (1992) had noted, the symptoms of psychic numbing and estrangement are the least well-studied and understood cluster of symptoms that make up PTSD. Litz has proposed that the symptoms might represent a "selective emotional processing deficit," while Keane et al. (1985) conceptualized emotional numbing as an avoidance behavior representing an attempt to suppress all strong affect because it has become viewed as dangerous and a reminder of the trauma.

We have viewed the cluster of symptoms that make up psychic numbing (inability to recall an important aspect of the trauma, markedly diminished interest or participation in significant activities, feeling detached or estranged from others, restricted range of affect [e.g., unable to have loving feelings], and a sense of foreshortened future, as closely resembling depression [e.g., feels sad or empty, decreased concentration, irritability, markedly diminished interest or pleasure in all or almost all activities, feeling worthless, recurrent thoughts of death, and symptoms causing distress or impairment in social, occupational, or other important areas of functioning]). (See Table 16.1.)

When we began our work in the early 1990s it seemed to us that behavioral techniques such as pleasant events scheduling (Lewinsohn, Biglan, & Zeiss, 1973) appeared logically applicable. Pleasant event scheduling involves increased activity (within physical limitations of any sustained injuries) and an encouragement of increased interpersonal involvement with people whom the patient might have been close to before the MVA (but now feel estranged from). This appeared to be a reasonable and rationally based intervention in an area where there was little to guide current treatment efforts (e.g., van der Kolk, McFarlane, & Hart, 1996).

TABLE 16.1
Similar Symptoms of PTSD and Depression

PTSD	Depression
Psychic numbing (1) Markedly diminished interest or participation in significant activities	(1) Markedly diminished interest or pleasure in all, or almost all activities most of the day, nearly every day (as indicated by either subjective account or observation made by others)
(2) Restricted range of affect (e.g., unable to have loving feelings)	(2) Depressed mood most of the day, nearly every day, as indicated by either subjective report (e.g., feels sad or empty) or observation made by others (e.g., appears tearful)
(3) Difficulty concentrating	(3) Diminished ability to think or concentrate, or indecisiveness, nearly every day (either by subjective account or as observed by others)
(4) Difficulty falling or staying asleep	(4) Insomnia or hypersomnia nearly every day
(5) Sense of foreshortened future (e.g., does not expect to have a career, marriage, children or a normal life span)	(5) Recurrent thoughts of death (not just fear of dying); recurrent suicidal ideation without a specific plan, or a suicide attempt or a specific plan for committing suicide
(6) Irritability or outbursts of anger	(6) Psychomotor agitation or retardation nearly every day (observed by others, not merely subjective feelings of restlessness or being slowed down); *Note.* In children or adolescents, can be irritable mood
(7) Inability to recall important aspects of the trauma	(7) Diminished ability to think or concentrate, or indecisiveness, nearly every day (either by subjective account or as observed by others)
(8) Hypervigilance	(8) Psychomotor agitation or retardation nearly every day (observed by others, not merely subjective feelings of restlessness or being slowed down)

Subsequently, Jacobson et al. (1996), in an outstanding study, demonstrated that pleasant events scheduling, or as they termed it, *behavioral activation,* was an effective treatment for major depressive disorder. In fact, it was as effective as Beck's cognitive therapy that included it as a component.

In a reanalysis of assessment data from Cohort 1 we (Blanchard, Buckley, Hickling, & Taylor, 1998) demonstrated that PTSD and depression are separate but overlapping syndromes. Certainly, the symptom overlap is obvious in Table 16.1. Moreover, as noted in chapter 5, many MVA survivors with PTSD also meet the criteria for a major depressive episode.

The use of cognitive techniques with underlying depressive schema and with irrational beliefs (to be challenged as appropriate) was viewed as important. Our research and clinical observations found these negative cognitions to be occurring.

Hyperarousal

Patients with PTSD by definition present with hyperarousal symptoms, both in general and for specific situations reminiscent of their MVA. Relaxation has been shown to be an effective technique in helping to counter these symptoms in both a veteran (Hickling et al., 1986) and MVA population. For those individuals who require it, application of biofeedback techniques have also been used to facilitate the training of a reliable relaxation response.

In addition, monitoring of cognitions that occur during the exposure tasks is suggested to attend to any self-defeating or catastrophic thoughts that may be contributing to the elicitation or continuation of anxiety symptoms and subsequent avoidance. Foa et al. (1989) and Meichenbaum (1994) have noted the value of cognitive treatment techniques for trauma survivors.

An important behavioral–psychological sequelae of the MVA is the subsequent impact it can have on driving. In Western culture it is often difficult to live a full life without the use of motor vehicle transportation. As we have discussed, this reexposure to a stimulus that reminds the victim of his or her trauma is often experienced with discomfort or avoided as much as possible. Many people will endure requisite driving (e.g., to the store, work, etc.), but will avoid any pleasure or optional exposure to either driving or riding in a car. The *DSM–IV*, when strictly used, makes it difficult to accurately diagnose a specific phobia for driving, because (a) the anxiety can be accounted for by another mental disorder (i.e., PTSD), and (b) the anxiety may not invariably provoke an immediate anxiety response. There may also be occasions where the driving is not exposing the individual to the specific triggers necessary for elicitation of a phobic response. Finally, the response may not be seen so much as a *fear* but rather a situation that triggers uncomfortable memories, affect, and anxiety. Driving phobia has a solid research base for intervention, beginning with Wolpe (1973).

However, given the often central role the act of driving can play in MVA survivors, we have struggled with various descriptions of what we believe are often critically important aspects of the treatment effort. We currently use the term *driving phobia* as a rather narrow definition of describing a situation in which the individual avoids all driving or endures the driving (or riding) with a great deal of subjective discomfort. We initially used the term *driving reluctance* to describe a less powerful form of avoidance, where the individual avoids all or most discretionary driving (e.g., pleasure trips) or rides, avoids the site of the accident, or driving situations related to his or her own MVA (e.g., rainy or snowy weather, high speeds, etc.). We have come to term all of the latter part of *travel anxiety*, following Mayou and Bryant's (1994) lead.

Patients with MVA-related PTSD typically present with varying combinations of these four symptom clusters, with some elements from each of the four present to meet the diagnostic criteria. Treatment would then logically include procedures to help counter all four symptom clusters with relatively more emphasis on one versus the other, depending on the patient's idiosyncratic set of symptoms.

TREATMENT STUDY 1

As part of the research project funded by the National Institute of Mental Health (NIMH) investigating the psychological effects of MVAs, we obtained systematic data (described earlier in this book) on 158 motor vehicle accident survivors. As part of our ethical responsibilities in conducting this study, all MVA survivors who were found to have psychological problems were referred for treatment. A referral list of local providers willing and experienced in the treatment of trauma survivors had been developed before the initiation of the research project. Two of the providers were psychologists who also were involved in the NIMH study, one as a coprincipal investigator (second author) and one as an assessor of MVA survivors.

Providing treatment for MVA survivors by psychologists associated with the research study provided a unique opportunity to measure the change in symptoms across six-month periods of time by evaluators *independent* of the treating psychologist, yet allowed access to chart notes describing the interventions used within treatment. In addition, although the treatment had been individually tailored for each participant, the overall treatment rationale of the two treating psychologists was primarily cognitive–behavioral, allowing for comparison of treatment commonalities and differences across cases with similar primary diagnoses, but with great attention to the intricacies of individual case material. This group of treated MVA survivors became our first pilot investigation of the treatment of PTSD as part of the Albany MVA Project.

Participants

Participants were 2 males and 10 females, with a mean age of 31.9 years of age for the females and 33.0 years of age for the males, all of whom had been part of the Albany MVA research project (Cohort 1). Payment for psychological treatment was through no-fault insurance in New York state.

Procedures

As a participant in Cohort 1 of the MVA research project, each participant underwent a comprehensive psychological evaluation by one of the four experienced, doctoral-level psychologists, as described in chapter 4. A complete written report of all findings was made for each research participant at the conclusion of the initial assessment. At that time treatment recommendations and explicit referrals were made. A listing of local mental health practitioners who reportedly were familiar with PTSD and its treatment was then shared with the research participant.

Diagnosis of PTSD

PTSD was diagnosed using criteria outlined in the *DSM–III–R* (American Psychiatric Association, 1987) and based on the CAPS interview (see chapter 3). The diagnosis was reached independent of treatment, and was in fact the basis of recommending treatment following the initial interview as a participant in the MVA research project.

Results

A description of participants by age, sex, diagnosis, comorbid diagnosis, and treatment procedures can be found in Table 16.2.

Each of the participants was involved in a two-car MVA, with physical injury quotients (see chapter 9) at the time treatment began, ranging from .66 to 1.0. (See Table 16.3.)

Table 16.4 presents a breakdown of the main area of change within this initial treatment study, the change in CAPS scores across six-month periods of time. In addition to the total CAPS score, scores by symptom cluster for each case are also presented. As can be seen in this table, 10 patients improved on total CAPS scores and 2 patients essentially remained unchanged, or, in fact, showed a worsening of symptoms across treatment. The total number of treatment sessions that had taken place across that same period of time is also noted, as well as if psychological treatment was in progress during the evaluation period or whether treatment had been concluded.

Table 16.5 presents the changes that occurred in psychological test scores across the same six-month periods of time. As one can see, psychological test scores, as expected, parallel changes in CAPS scores and with treatment progress. The reported changes in Global Assessment Scale (GAS) scores for patients 205 and 277 is illustrative of a worsening clinical picture for both patients.

Table 16.6 presents reported change in psychosocial functioning. GAS scores, as one would predict, parallel changes in CAPS scores. The changes

TABLE 16.2
Research Participant Demographics and Diagnoses

Participant #	Age	Sex	Diagnosis 1	Diagnosis 2	Treatment procedures
102	43	F	PTSD		In vivo and imaginal exposure; EMG biofeedback
103	32	M	PTSD		Imaginal exposure; driving hierarchy and graded exposure
125	46	F	PTSD	Major depression, OCD, social phobia	Desensitization; driving; graded exposure
129	19	F	PTSD	Major depression	Imaginal exposure; desensitization
151	34	M	PTSD		Grief work; past trauma history; anger expression; social skills building; imaginal exposure
198	31	F	PTSD	Major depression	Anger management; social skills training; fear of death
200	24	F	PTSD		In vivo exposure; past trauma; assertiveness training; fear of death; couples treatment; grief work
203	24	F	Sub-PTSD		Anger management; past trauma; graded exposure
205	23	F	PTSD		In vivo exposure; fear of death; anger management
239	57	F	PTSD		Social skills training; assertiveness; anger management
277	22	F	PTSD		Imaginal and in vivo exposure; driving hierarchy
278	41	F	PTSD		Past traumatic losses; social skills training

Note. EMG = electomyograph; OCD = obsessive–compulsive disorder.

TABLE 16.3
Physical Injury Quotients (PIQ) for Study 1 Participants at Various
Assessment Points

Participant #	Initial PIQ	6-month PIQ	12-month PIQ
102	1.00	0.75	0.66
103	1.00	0.66	DO
125	0.83	0.50	0.33
129	0.66	0.00	0.00
151	0.88	0.44	0.66
198	1.00	0.66	0.50
200	0.66	0.66	0.83
203	0.88	0.88	0.88
205	1.00	0.75	0.83
239	1.00	0.66	0.66
277	0.92	0.50	0.83
278	1.00	0.66	0.75

Note. DO = Drop-out from assessment study.

in psychosocial functioning are consistent with reported improvement as psychological gains are realized.

Commonalities in Treatment

This first study of psychological treatment allowed us to look at what types of treatment interventions were used by experienced clinicians with cases of MVA-related PTSD and the frequency they were reportedly using for this limited population. It is of interest, but not surprising, that cognitive techniques were used as part of all 12-treatment cases. Although each psychologist operated independently in the treatment of any particular case, the overall orientation of both psychologists is eclectic and problem-focused. All 12 patients received some type of exposure-based treatment, either in office imaginal exposure or graded in vivo exposure. All of the treatment cases also received relaxation training. Treatment for driving-related reluctance or phobia secondary to the MVA was part of treatment in 11 of the 12 cases. Driving reluctance was defined as driving with significant reluctance, as shown by avoiding the accident area, restricting the driving speed, driving only on local roads, or being reluctant to be a passenger when others are driving.

Cognitive techniques of some kind were used in all of these treatment cases. Cognitive techniques included thought stopping, guided self-dialogue (with preparation for the event), confrontation with the feared situation and management of the event, coping with feelings of becoming over-whelmed, and reinforcement of the positive efforts and behaviors (Meichenbaum, 1977), cognitive restructuring (using an A–B–C–D paradigm for

TABLE 16.4

CAPS Scores and Symptom Clusters Across Six-Month Intervals for Treatment Study 1 Participants

Participant #	Total CAPS initial	Number of treatment sessions between initial & 6 months	Total CAPS 6 months	Number of treatment sessions between 6 months & 12 months	Total CAPS 12 months	Symptom cluster B			Symptom cluster C			Symptom cluster D		
						Initial	6 month	12 month	Initial	6 month	12 month	Initial	6 month	12 month
102	41	7	35	2	4	8	10	0	12	9	0	21	16	4
103	87	7	37	11	DO	20	10	DO	34	0	DO	33	27	DO
125	99	2	34	0	12	28	8	3	39	10	2	32	16	8
129	32	1	9	0	10	6	3	0	15	6	6	11	0	4
151	38	8	0	0	0	16	0	0	15	0	0	7	0	0
198	29	11	18	16	13	5	3	2	12	12	9	12	3	2
200	54	16	23	15	35	23	7	7	16	13	11	15	3	17
203	29	4	7	15	13	11	2	3	11	0	0	7	5	11
205	35	17	38	22	56	17	10	14	4	15	25	14	13	17
239	57	12	44	18	31	6	5	6	35	30	19	16	9	6
277	104	17	90	8	128	28	25	32	45	32	53	31	33	43
278	57	24	15	0	23	25	0	7	29	8	10	3	7	6
Mean	55.17	10.5	29.17	8.92	32.20	16.08	6.92	6.73	22.25	11.25	12.27	16.83	11.00	10.64

Note. DO = drop-out from assessment study.

TABLE 16.5
Psychological Test Scores Across Six-Month Time Intervals for Study 1 Participants

Participant #	Impact of Events Scale			Beck Depression Inventory			STAI–State			STAI–Trait			P–Inventory		
	Initial	6 months	12 months	Initial	6 months	12 months	Initial	6 months	12 months	Initial	6 months	12 months	Initial	6 months	12 months
102	3	28	*	8	18	*	44	94	*	38	68	*	0	14	*
103	58	45	DO	24	13	DO	86	65	DO	69	66	DO	33	30	DO
125	59	*	42	17	*	*	100*	*	57	44	*	62	*	*	4
129	29	*	7	7	*	20	73	*	62	66	*	61	14	*	18
151	27	7	7	8	8	2	73	52	59	58	52	48	1	3	0
198	7	18	7	17	15	26	43	73	53	63	62	74	12	20	16
200	47	41	32	12	21	25	38	72	98	31	84	86	9	19	23
203	39	9	16	6	1	4	57	47	42	45	45	43	0	2	5
205	29	42	43	10	8	13	64	61	55	45	59	69	9	14	13
239	37	*	28	22	*	20	95	*	96	80	*	80	23	*	20
277	51	59	70	33	39	50	85	79	91	77	83	105	30	39	44
278	8	38	20	13	11	16	45	58	45	66	62	62	25	16	22
Mean	32.8	31.9	22.4	12.3	14.9	15.8	66.9	66.7	63.0	56.8	64.5	65.0	14.2	17.4	13.4

Note. DO = Drop-out from assessment study.
* = Results not available.

TABLE 16.6
Changes in Psychosocial Functioning Across Six-Month Time Intervals

Participant #	GAS scores			Work/school			Family			Friends		
	Initial	6 months	12 months	Initial	6 months	12 months	Initial	6 months	12 months	Initial	6 months	12 months
102	61	75	85	2.5	0	0	1.00	2.00	1.33	1.0	1.0	2.0
103	45	65	DO	2.5	3	DO	2.83	2.00	DO	4.0	3.0	DO
125	41	60	61	2.5	2.0	1.0	3.00	1.00	1.00	5.0	1.0	1.0
129	60	70	71	1.0	1.0	1.0	1.50	1.67	1.67	2.0	1.0	1.0
151	50	91	95	0	1.0	1.0	1.00	1.00	1.00	1.0	1.0	1.0
198	60	51	50	2.0	3.0	4.0	1.50	2.50	2.50	3.0	2.0	2.0
200	51	55	61	1.0	2.0	2.0	2.20	2.00	2.00	2.0	3.0	3.0
203	55	50	75	0	0	0	1.00	1.50	1.00	1.0	1.0	1.0
205	60	55	40	1.5	3.0	2.0	1.00	2.40	2.00	1.0	2.0	4.0
239	50	59	50	1.5	2.0	1.0	3.00	2.50	3.25	1.0	3.0	3.0
277	40	40	40	2.5	0	4.0	2.00	2.00	2.50	1.0	3.0	2.0
278	41	60	50	1.0	2.0	3.0	1.00	1.00	2.00	1.0	2.0	4.0
Mean	51.6	61.0	69.7									

Note. DO = Drop-out from assessment study.

irrational thinking; Beck, Rush, Shaw, & Emery, 1979; Walen, DiGiuseppe, & Wessler, 1980), and modeling and role playing of the anxiety-provoking situations. Behavioral techniques to help manage the anxiety and subsequently to withstand any imagined or graded exposure were an integral part of the treatment provided.

Illustrative Cases

An illustration of one of the briefer courses of treatment (that actually took place in the hospital, because the individual was immobilized because of multiple fractures) began with the patient's being instructed in the normal course of PTSD symptoms and their development as per the two-factor theory. She was requested to describe the accident in detail, which was used for imaginal exposure in subsequent sessions, emphasizing the emotionally laden words and perceptions she provided. Cognitive techniques, including cessation of negative self-talk, substitution of statement mastery itself, as well as actual challenging of irrational catastrophic beliefs, were used to help her counter the negative affect brought on by her particular accident, which had her trapped in her car overnight, off the road, with beliefs that she certainly would bleed to death or die from shock before her discovery.

She was taught relaxation techniques, and these were used to counter any physiological discomfort brought on during imaginal desensitization and other moments of anxiety. Precipitants of anxiety were tied to negative cognitive schema and countered by the therapist with cognitive restructuring techniques challenging the irrational beliefs. The patient was asked to use this new technique for challenging the anxiety and the thoughts related to the onset of anxiety (e.g., "I'm going to be trapped and die in a car") between sessions. This thought was challenged as unlikely to happen, in fact had not happened before, and it was much more probable that she would become more cautious as a driver, have a safer car with air bags, and make as certain as one could it would not occur to her. Treatment was concluded before she could physically drive herself, but follow-up as part of the assessment study demonstrated that the later driving was performed without reported discomfort. One necessary component of this case was the attention to thoughts of mortality and the intense fear she had to endure until discovered by the highway patrol. In a recent paper (Blanchard et al., 1995), both the extent of physical injury *and* perception of one's life threat (fear of dying) were found to *independently* predict the onset of PTSD in a sample of 98 MVA survivors.

A second case involved a patient who was seen for only two visits before her extended vacation out of the country. Because of the very limited time before her scheduled departure, a modified, cued desensitization technique was developed. Details of the patient's MVA were presented, reviewed, and discussed to determine which images provoked the greatest distress. Both her subjective discomfort (SUDS) and pain perception were assessed at various points throughout the narration. She was instructed in diaphragmatic breathing and visualization techniques for relaxation, during which her SUDS and pain perception were assessed. A home desensitization procedure was introduced, with reported reduction in distress demonstrated by home practice and exposure as measured on rating sheets mailed over the time outside of treatment and by telephone contact.

Treatment Differences

The variety of MVAs, the subsequent physical and psychological problems that develop, often necessitate idiosyncratic responses to treatment. As can be seen in Table 16.1, a few of the cases required attention to past traumas in addition to the current MVA. Other cases dealt with anger management, and a few involved couples treatment.

Specific stimuli can also become uniquely tied to the particular MVA and cues associated with the memories and emotional responses. For instance, if an accident took place in a rainstorm, or during the autumn, these cues might provoke powerful emotional memories that would require specific attention to their importance.

Consider the case in which a patient had done well in treatment and called for another appointment because of resumption in her psychological distress. When she was asked what caused the relapse, it became apparent that seasonal cues (i.e., cooler temperature and barren trees in the Northeastern United States during late autumn) had contributed to a return of intrusive thoughts and feelings related to the MVA. Imaginal exposure to the stimuli of trees against an evening sky and images of winter scenes reminiscent of her MVA were presented in office imaginal exposure, paired with relaxation and cognitive restructuring of her response. Cognitive restructuring also occurred surrounding her heightened anxiety when thinking of her own mortality. An imaginal flooding strategy of staying with the scene of her death was used, and then paired with deep relaxation. This experience led to the patient's association of her loss of her mother. She then was able to realize she had "lived well" following her MVA. Anxiety was noted to drop significantly after that point in her treatment. In vivo exposure then followed, again using cognitive techniques of coping–mastery self-statements and decatastrophizing the memory with current events. Associated with the fear of another MVA occurring was a fear of her own death that appeared related to memories of her mother's death and the impact of that event happening to her, as noted earlier.

In an additional case, the impact of earlier trauma, including the loss of her home because of fire, and her attack and near rape as an adolescent had to be dealt with as a necessary component of treatment. The resultant fear was correlated with a worsening of physical pain and soft tissue damage in the shoulder and chest region as a result of the seatbelt that restrained her during her rear-end collision. The physical injury had limited her ability to draw and write. The injury, caused by a male driver, led her to the associated anger held toward her male assailants in her past, and the vulnerability she now perceived as a part of her current level of functioning. This was illustrated by the requisite physical examination of her shoulder injury and the proximity of the examination to her breast. This was associated by the patient with memories of sexual abuse. These memories were dealt with over the course of treatment, as well as memories of witnessing a suicide from a bridge similar to one in her MVA. These anxiety-provoking memories were addressed with coping strategies and methods to assertively deal with her own safety, which had in her perception been limited by the events of the MVA and the male driver who struck her car.

These cases illustrate how even similar themes (e.g., mortality) can be tied to individually salient cognitions and memories. If specific cues are ignored or not responded to (e.g., leafless trees in autumn/winter), powerful environmental stimuli can be missed and treatment rendered ineffective. Careful behavioral assessment and assessment of cognitive schema are essential if each individual is to have the optimal chance for improvement.

Thus, one is left with a picture that treatment can hold many commonalities that, in all likelihood, can be applied to almost every case. Yet one needs to be aware of the powerful impact of idiosyncratic responses from the recent trauma (and its associations with past traumas), and to be able to provide a flexible, yet theoretically driven, treatment intervention for each unique individual case.

Discussion

As we summarized the treatment outcome data, we began to believe that PTSD secondary to an MVA could be treated reasonably well. We thought that the cognitive–behavioral treatment model seemed to have a great deal of promise, particularly if flexibly applied. We believed that, although unintentional, the treatments did seem to hold a core group of consistent interventions, yet the model allowed the psychologist to attend to the needs of each unique presentation of difficulties. This, of course, is the model of private practice. Efficiency and rationally guided treatment was the model throughout the range of interventions.

Treatment length did vary considerably. This was not surprising given the myriad of possible factors thought to contribute to the onset and continuation of PTSD. The varied treatment length is also consistent with the work of Burstein (1986b), who showed that, although a significant number of MVA survivors improved in less than three months, a large number actually required prolonged treatment in excess of one year.

Finally, we were struck by how well the model of treatment led to a more systematic investigation of treatment of MVA-related PTSD. The methodology used in this initial study allowed for independent assessment of outcome while the treatment was conducted with the flexibility that practicing clinicians use in everyday treatment efforts. However, the rigor of the research-scheduled evaluations of symptom change allowed valid and reliable indexes of outcome. The CAPS provided a useful measure of chronicling change in PTSD overall, as well as allowing examination of the separate symptom clusters. In theory, we thought that if it was determined that one symptom cluster did not improve, the treatment could be reconsidered and newer interventions formulated and used.

The study set the stage for a more rigorous, manual-based intervention.

TREATMENT STUDY 2

Based on the success of the nonsystematic initial intervention, a more formal, manual-based intervention was designed. To prepare for a controlled investigation of MVA-related PTSD treatment, a treatment manual incorporating the knowledge gained from the first study was used as an initial outline. We next constructed a treatment manual (the most refined version is given in chapter 18 of this book), which designated session-by-session guidelines for a 10-session intervention (see Table 16.7). Although the outline was for 10 sessions, the treatment allowed flexibility for a range of 8 to 12 sessions, based on the symptoms presented and the judgment of the treating psychologist.

The second treatment study, completed as part of the Albany MVA Project, was a pilot study of the manual-based treatment and helped serve as a basis for a grant application for a controlled investigation of psychological treatment of PTSD secondary to MVA. A description of this study was published in 1997 by Hickling and Blanchard.

Participants

Recruitment of participants again used our physician referral network and advertisement in local newspapers. This resulted in approximately 110 telephone inquiries for possible treatment. Sixty-four MVA survivors were screened by telephone interview for possible PTSD or subsyndromal PTSD, using primarily the PTSD Checklist (PCL; Weathers et al., 1993). From the telephone interviews, 25 MVA survivors were invited for additional evaluation, with 21 keeping their appointment for in-depth assessment.

TABLE 16.7
Intensive Treatment Regimen for MVA–PTSD

Session #1: Introduction; Diagnostics by T; education = What is normal response to trauma; overview of treatment: different procedures to help with different symptom clusters; relaxation training—16 muscle group—instruction in home practice; verbal description of MVA and reactions by patient; Instruction to write it out in detail for next visit. *Patient expectancy questionnaire administered.*

Session #2: Read and elaborate description of MVA—instruction in home practice; relaxation training—16 muscle group, continued home practice; discussion of avoidance and idea of hierarchy of tasks; enlist significant other for next visit.

Session #3: Patient reads description of MVA and reaction, discuss negative self-talk, and begin substituting coping and mastery self-talk; avoidance-hierarchy—need for graduated approach behavior in vivo. Assign homework from hierarchy. Significant other to assist—explain symptoms and treatments to spouse, partner; relaxation (8 muscle group); continue all homework.

Session #4: Reading exposure to MVA and consequences—add coping outcomes; relaxation 4 muscle group; approach behavior homework; check on self-talk and introduce coping and mastery self-dialogue.

Session #5: Reading exposure to MVA—with coping; introduce relaxation-by-recall; approach behavior homework.

Session #6: Reading exposure to MVA— introduce cue-controlled relaxation as coping strategy; approach behavior homework; examination and correction of self-talk.

Session #7: Focus is on psychic numbing, depression, and existential issues; remind to continue all previous homework; how to ask for help (to counter mind reading); pleasurable activity scheduling; explore for depressive schema and faulty logics; continue approach behavior homework and correction of self-talk.

Session #8: Pleasurable activity scheduling; explore depressive schema and faulty logic—cognitive restructuring; other home practice.

Session #9: Same as Session #8.

Session #10: Final Visit—review procedures, remind to continue practice at home; cognitive schema restructuring; make assessment appointment and schedule follow-up visit.

Note. From Table 2, "The Private Practice Psychologist and Manual-Based Treatments: Post-Traumatic Stress Disorder Secondary to Motor Vehicle Accidents," by E. J. Hickling and E. B. Blanchard, 1997, *Behaviour Research and Therapy, 35*, pp. 1–13. Copyright 1997 Elsevier Science Ltd. Adapted with permission.

(The assessment was the same as described in chapter 4.) Fourteen MVA survivors were then found eligible for, and were offered, treatment based on the formal evaluation. Two of the participants declined the offer for treatment (one of these took a referral to a private practitioner) and 12 agreed to be treated with the manual-based intervention at no cost. Ten completed treatment and were then reassessed by independent evaluators at the completion of the treatment protocol. Two MVA survivors dropped out of treatment, one with the second author because of scheduling and transportation difficulties and one with the first author because of reinjuring her back, resulting in her becoming bedridden and thus unable to travel to attend treatment.

The participants for this pilot study of a manual-based treatment were 10 MVA survivors (nine female, one male) with a mean age of 45.6 (range 30–63 years). All participants met the following entry criteria: 18 years of age or older, had been in a motor vehicle accident six months or earlier than the time of his or her initial evaluation, and had sought medical attention for injuries related to the MVA within 72 hours of the MVA.

The rationale for treating survivors who continued to demonstrate symptoms after a six-month period of time was an attempt to account for the significant percentage of survivors who early on can show spontaneous improvement in PTSD symptoms over time without receiving treatment. The timetable for patient selection was determined from our studies of change in PTSD symptoms across time (Blanchard et al., 1995), where it was found that by six months after the initial assessment (mean of 69 days post-MVA) 50% of those who had originally met criteria for PTSD no longer met full criteria (see chapter 7). We thus reasoned that, if the victim was continuing to manifest noticeable, distressing symptoms after a six-month period of time, they were less likely to show improvement on their own and were on their way to becoming chronic. Subsequently, any change on criterion measures would be much more likely to reflect treatment effects rather than spontaneous improvement.

Demographic and descriptive information for the MVA survivors who completed treatment can be found in Table 16.8. A brief description of any continuing physical problems is also shown (when present), as well as any other comorbid Axis I diagnosis based on the *DSM–IV* (American Psychiatric Association, 1994).

Evaluation Methods

The initial diagnosis for PTSD was based on the CAPS (Blake et al., 1990a), described in detail earlier. All interviews were taped and reviewed (by the first author). MVA survivors were diagnosed using *DSM–IV* criteria (American Psychiatric Association, 1994).

All participants in the study also completed the following psychological tests: the Beck Depression Inventory (BDI; Beck et al., 1961), the State Trait Anxiety Inventory (Spielberger et al., 1970), the Impact of Event Scale (IES, Horowitz et al., 1979), and the PCL (Weathers et al., 1993) as a self-report measure of symptoms of PTSD.

The initial evaluation also used a locally constructed structured interview on the MVA and the survivor's reaction to the MVA (Appendix A). Evaluation of the pre-MVA and current psychosocial functioning of each

TABLE 16.8
Description of Treatment Sample

Participant #	Age	Sex	Weeks since MVA	Primary diagnosis	Comorbid diagnosis	Initial CAPS	Physical injuries
301	45	F	131	PTSD	MDE GAD	65	Continuing muscle pain in the cervical, upper and lower back region secondary to whiplash injury. Loss of range of movement in right arm with diminished grip strength. Continuing sharp pains in both her wrists and ankles. In addition, she was suffering from TMJ secondary to her MVA-related injuries.
302	36	F	36	PTSD	MDE	69	Continuing pain in her upper and lower back secondary to whiplash-type injury, which has also left her with continuing cervical pain. Parathesias in left hand and left foot. Lost grip strength in her left hand.
304	63	F	23	PTSD	Driving phobia MDE GAD	85	Continuing neck, shoulder, and lower back pain from whiplash-type injury. She also suffers from a noticeable headache problem since the accident.
306	63	F	18	PTSD	MDE GAD	86	Continuing neck and shoulder pain, in addition to chronic headaches.
310	30	F	16	Sub-PTSD	Driving phobia	37	No continuing physical problems secondary to the accident.
311	46	M	76	PTSD	GAD	46	Exacerbation of existing headache problem since the accident. Muscle pain and stiffness in cervical area. Traumatic arthritis in the right thumb joint results in unremitting pain. Loss of grip strength in the right hand. (May have done some cartilage damage.)

(continued)

TABLE 16.8 (Continued)

Participant #	Age	Sex	Weeks since MVA	Primary diagnosis	Comorbid diagnosis	Initial CAPS	Physical injuries
312	51	F	37	Sub-PTSD	MDE specific phobia	46	Loss of strength in right arm secondary to soft tissue damage. Continues to have chest pain secondary to a fractured sternum and headaches secondary to a concussion. (Did not suffer a blow to the head.)
313	36	F	16	PTSD	GAD	65	No physical problems currently related to the MVA.
316	54	F	85	PTSD	MDE	119	Two fractured vertebrate secondary to MVA (t-10, t-11) have left this participant with considerable loss of strength and unremitting pain on a daily basis. At the time of initial interview she had had one back surgery, which resulted in two supportive metal rods placed in her back to support her spine. Injuries were severe enough to keep her from returning to work.
324	32	F	82	PTSD	GAD	54	Continuing low back problems that result in significant pain and loss of ROM. Permanent deformity of her nose. Continuing dental restoration work. In addition, this participant is suffering from loss of range of movement and muscle strength in her right arm secondary to soft-tissue damage sustained during the accident. Combined with the back injuries, the injuries have been severe enough to keep this participant out of work.

Note. CAPS = Clinical Administered PTSD Scale; GAD = generalized anxiety disorder; MDE = major depressive episode; ROM = range of motion. From Table 1, "The Private Practice Psychologist and Manual-Based Treatments: Post-Traumatic Stress Disorder Secondary to Motor Vehicle Accidents," by E. J. Hickling and E. B. Blanchard, 1997, *Behaviour Research and Therapy, 35,* pp. 1–13. Copyright 1997 Elsevier Science Ltd. Adapted with permission.

victim was obtained through the use of the LIFE–Base (Keller et al., 1987). Four psychosocial functioning variables are obtained: (a) performance on major role function, either work (for those working 30 hours per week or more), school (for full-time students), or homemaking when the former categories did not apply; (b) quality of relationships with all first-degree relatives, including spouse or partner averaged across all family members who were rated; (c) quality of relationships with friends; and (d) participation and enjoyment of recreational activities. The variables are all rated on a 1 to 5 scale, where 1 represents no impairment and high functioning or very good relationship and 5 represents unsatisfactory performance or very poor relationship.

Follow-up evaluations at the conclusion of treatment and at a three-month posttreatment follow-up session, and were conducted by independent evaluators (advanced doctoral students in clinical psychology). Each student had been trained in the use of the structured interviews and administration of the psychological tests.

Treatment

Treatment was provided by both authors. Intervention was by a symptom-focused, psychological treatment designed to address PTSD and subsyndromal PTSD, found in MVA survivors. As outlined earlier, the treatment rationale was to attempt to intervene with the four interrelated symptom clusters we have conceptualized in PTSD: (a) reexperiencing, (b) avoidance symptoms, (c) psychic numbing, and (d) hyperarousal symptoms. The treatment manual (see chapter 18) was written to address each of the symptom clusters as well as other problems commonly found to be present in patients with PTSD following MVAs. The treatment methodology, although largely cognitive–behavioral in approach, tries to attend to the variability that can be found in the victim of traumatic events. Thus, attention to existential issues, mortality, anger, guilt, and so forth, was also provided using specified treatment interventions if necessary within the treatment manual.

Treatment Integrity

The pilot data were evaluated by graduate research assistants through the use of the Therapist's Behavior Checklist (TBC), a locally constructed measure of in-session activities. Average interrater reliability on the TBC categories was satisfactory (kappa = .71 , $p < .05$).

Treatment integrity and therapist adherence to the treatment protocol was determined by first calculating the percentage of the specific therapist behaviors and procedures for a particular session (based on the treatment manual) that actually occurred within the session. The overall average inclusion therapist adherence was 72%, with another 12% of specified therapist behaviors occurring at other points in the treatment. Second, the frequency of interventions *not specified* in the treatment manual occurring was calculated, with the overall average being 1%. Thus, we believe the treatment integrity was adequate.

Results of Treatment

Table 16.9 presents the pretreatment, posttreatment, and three-month follow-up CAPS scores for each participant, as well as any pretreatment and follow-up primary and comorbid Axis I diagnosis. Because each therapist had treated five of the cases, we analyzed the CAPS scores in a 2 (therapist) × 3 (assessments) repeated-measures ANOVA. It yielded a significant (p = .008) main effect of assessments but no main effect of therapist or interaction of therapist by assessment.

Follow-up analyses of the assessment main effect with correlated t-tests revealed a significant decrease in CAPS score from pretreatment to posttreatment (p = .001, effect size [Cohen's d] = 1.48) but no further significant improvement from posttreatment to follow-up. Analyses of each score of the four PTSD symptom clusters did show significant reduction on each symptom cluster (p = .003 or better).

Clinically, one would say all of the 10 patients had improved by the end of treatment. Five of the eight who started with full PTSD were at a non-PTSD level by the end of treatment. The other three MVA survivors had decreased symptoms sufficiently to be diagnosed as subsyndromal PTSD. By the time of the three-month follow-up, two of these three had, in fact, improved to non-PTSD. One of the two survivors who began with a diagnosis of subsyndromal PTSD was non-PTSD by the end of treatment. A summary of each survivor's change in diagnosis and CAPS scores can be found in Table 16.9.

Psychological Tests

Table 16.10 presents the group mean values for the five psychological tests administered at the three assessment periods. These data were analyzed using a one-way MANOVA, followed up with univariate ANOVAs and post-hoc tests.

The analyses of the psychological tests yielded a significant (p = .01) main effect for time. Univariate analyses revealed a significant decrease in symptoms on every measure used (p = .008 or better). All measures showed a significant decrease from pretreatment to posttreatment. The only measure

TABLE 16.9
Results From Pilot Trial of Treatment of MVA Survivors

Participant #	Primary diagnosis	Comorbid diagnosis (initial)	Initial CAPS	Post-CAPS	3 month follow-up CAPS	Primary diagnosis	Comorbid diagnoses (3 month follow-up)
301	PTSD	MDE GAD	65	25	28	Non-PTSD	MDE
302	PTSD	MDE	69	37	44	Non-PTSD	MDE
304	PTSD	Driving phobia MDE GAD		40	15	Non-PTSD	None
306	PTSD	MDE GAD	86	7	2	Non-PTSD	None
310	Sub-PTSD	Driving phobia	37	10	3	Non-PTSD	None
311	PTSD	GAD	46	29	15	Non-PTSD	None
312	Sub-PTSD	MDE Specific phobia	46	23	31	Sub-PTSD	Specific phobia
313	PTSD	GAD	65	31	33	Sub-PTSD	Specific phobia
316	PTSD	MDE	119	0	3	Non-PTSD	None
324	PTSD	GAD	54	14	13	Non-PTSD	None
Mean ratings			67.2	21.6	18.4		

Note. GAD = Generalized anxiety disorder; MDE = major depressive episode. From Table 3, "The Private Practice Psychologist and Manual-Based Treatments: Post-Traumatic Stress Disorder Secondary to Motor Vehicle Accidents," by E. J. Hickling and E. B. Blanchard, 1997, *Behaviour Research and Therapy, 35,* pp. 1–13. Copyright 1997 Elsevier Science Ltd. Adapted with permission.

TABLE 16.10
Summary of Psychological Distress Measures

Measure	Initial	Posttreatment	3 month follow-up	$F_{(29)}$	p
Beck Depression Inventory	16.9 (9.0)[a]	8.6 (5.6)[b]	5.9 (5.0)[b]	8.21	.004
State anxiety	70.2 (21.4)[a]	57.1 (13.8)[b]	48.5 (10.5)[c]	9.86	.001
Trait anxiety	67.3 (17.1)[a]	54.0 (13.9)[b]	47.9 (8.4)[b]	6.65	.008
Impact of Event Scale	41.9 (14.0)[a]	14.4 (13.3)[b]	10.2 (12.0)[b]	24.4	<.001
PTSD checklist	56.0 (12.0)[a]	34.4 (10.1)[b]	32.7 (11.5)[b]	17.3	<.001

Note. Means that share a superscript do not differ at .05 or greater. From Table 4, "The Private Practice Psychologist and Manual-Based Treatments: Post-Traumatic Stress Disorder Secondary to Motor Vehicle Accidents," by E. J. Hickling and E. B. Blanchard, 1997, *Behaviour Research and Therapy, 35*, pp. 1–13. Copyright 1997 Elsevier Science Ltd. Adapted with permission.

TABLE 16.11
Summary of Role Functioning Variables

Measure	Pre-MVA	Pretreatment	Posttreatment	3 month follow-up	F	p^*
Major role function work/school/homemaking	1.6 (0.5)[a]	2.9 (1.1)[b]	2.1 (1.1)[b]	2.2 (1.1)[b]	1.84	.257
Relationship with first-degree relatives & spouse/partner	2.0 (0.7)[a,b]	2.2 (0.7)[a]	1.9 (0.6)[b]	1.7 (0.7)[b]	5.24	.033
Relationships with friends	2.2 (0.8)[a]	2.7 (1.3)[a]	2.1 (1.1)[a]	1.6 (0.7)[b]	3.44	.093
Recreational activity	1.5 (0.7)[a]	3.4 (1.0)[b]	2.4 (1.2)[c]	2.4 (1.0)[c]	13.77	.003

Note. Means that share a superscript do not differ at .05 or higher. *Probability for *F* test is corrected by Pillias for sphericity. From Table 5, "The Private Practice Psychologist and Manual-Based Treatments: Post-Traumatic Stress Disorder Secondary to Motor Vehicle Accidents," by E. J. Hickling & E. B. Blanchard, 1997, *Behaviour Research and Therapy, 35*, pp. 1–13. Copyright 1997 Elsevier Science Ltd. Adapted with Permission.

that continued to show an improvement from posttreatment to the three-month evaluation period was on state anxiety.

Psychosocial Functioning

Ratings from the LIFE–Base and LIFE for psychosocial functioning were subjected to a repeated-measures MANOVA, followed by univariate ANOVAs, corrected for sphericity because of the four time points and post-hoc tests (see Table 16.11). A similar pattern of scores was found for each variable, where the survivor was functioning at a poorer level (higher numerical score) than before the MVA. The decline in functioning was significant for both major role function and participation in recreational activity. There was a significant improvement by the end of treatment for family relationships and participation in recreation and by three-month follow-up for relationships with friends.

Major role function did not improve significantly. We conjecture this could be because of continued physical limitations (see Table 16.8), which was present for most of the survivors and could very well be a function of patient selection from a pool of survivors who, to be eligible for treatment, needed to have sought care from a physician. It is of interest that the interpersonal relationship ratings show improvement beyond the pre-MVA level by follow-up.

Discussion

The changes in overall CAPS scores strongly suggest that this pilot investigation of a manualized-based treatment protocol was effective in reducing symptoms of PTSD in survivors of MVAs. It is also suggestive that the symptom improvement can be delivered in a relatively short period of time and that results last at least as long as three months. The results hold true for at least two psychologists who delivered the treatment and do not show differences in treatment outcome between therapists. Further, the scores found on psychological tests and LIFE–Base evaluations support the outcome of the pilot investigation.

The pilot study certainly contains many limiting factors. First, it is uncontrolled. However, data from a naturalistic follow-up of MVA survivors with PTSD found that from 6 months to 12 months only 5% of those who had PTSD at 6 months had fully remitted by 12 months and only another 5% showed some partial improvement spontaneously (Blanchard et al., 1996; see chapter 7). This pilot study would seem to suggest significantly greater improvement occurred than one would have expected without an effective treatment being in place. As earlier studies (chapter 7) have demonstrated, the high spontaneous recovery rate for a portion of survivors with

PTSD following MVAs, have made it difficult for interventions to demonstrate effectiveness within the first few months after the MVA. The rationale of providing a treatment at this later time period at least attempts to address that outcome concern.

STUDY 3

In our first attempt to obtain funding to conduct the controlled treatment trial, we were rebuffed by the NIMH Review Panel because of the lack of systematic data on the cognitive–behavioral treatment (CBT) program. In our second attempt we were again turned down because of the lack of systematic data on the supportive psychotherapy comparison condition. Under a grant from NIMH (R21-MH-55478), we completed the treatment manual for the supportive psychotherapy (SUPPORT; described in chapter 19) and Study 3. Results of this trial were published in Hickling and Blanchard (1999).

This study briefly summarizes the procedures used in SUPPORT, describes the sample and the assessment results for pretreatment, posttreatment, and three-month follow-up.

Participants

The eight participants were recruited from the same sources as those for Study 2 and were 4 to 34 months post-MVA (we relaxed our time criteria somewhat to recruit the sample promptly). There were no dropouts. There were three males and five females of average age 36.1 years. Descriptive information on the sample including psychiatric diagnoses and physical problems are presented in Table 16.12.

Assessment Procedures

All participants underwent our standard psychosocial assessment including MVA interview, CAPS, SCID, and several psychological tests including BDI, STAI, IES, and PCL. We did not complete a psychophysiological assessment on these participants. They were paid $25 for completing each assessment. The assessments were conducted by highly trained, advanced doctoral students in clinical psychology.

Treatment Procedures

As with Study 2 (CBT), treatment was scheduled for 10 sessions with a range of 8 to 12. Each of the two therapists (the two authors) treated four of the cases, following the manual.

TABLE 16.12
Description of Study 3 Treatment Sample

Participant #	Age	Sex	Weeks since MVA	Primary diagnosis	Comorbid diagnosis	Initial CAPS	Physical injuries
404	71	M	16	Sub-PTSD	None	20	Fractures to two neck vertebrate and one back vertebrate. Limited range of motion/chronic pain in back and neck. Blow to head and loss of consciousness for 3–4 hours. Posttraumatic headaches since MVA.
407	43	F	119	PTSD	Specific phobia GAD MD	79	Soft tissue injury to lumbar region. Ongoing problems with pain and lack of range of motion in lower back region.
408	26	M	131	PTSD	MD	58	Torn tendons/ligaments in neck. Rotator cuff tear on right shoulder. Experiences parathesias in both arms and hands since MVA. Very limited range of motion in right arm. Loss of range of motion in neck and weakness in both arms. Posttraumatic headache activity.
410	42	F	32	PTSD	Binge eating DO dysthymia	77	Soft tissue damage to neck and lower lumbar region. Restricted range of motion in right shoulder. Right shoulder easily fatigued with strenuous demands.
412	25	F	34	PTSD	MDD	43	Bruising to chest and legs. Friction burns from airbag at time of MVA. No continuing physical problems.
415	38	F	18	PTSD	Panic disorder with agoraphobia hypochondriasis	57	Continuing lumbar region back pain and restricted range of motion since the occurrence of the MVA.

(continued)

TABLE 16.12 (Continued)

Participant #	Age	Sex	Weeks since MVA	Primary diagnosis	Comorbid diagnosis	Initial CAPS	Physical injuries
417	25	F	25	PTSD	MDD GAD binge eating disorder	94	Exacerbation of pre-existing headache problem. Chronic pain problems in neck and shoulders subsequent to soft tissue injury (whiplash).
418	19	M	27	Sub-PTSD	None	30	Posttraumatic headaches on a near daily basis. Parasthesias through shoulders and thoracic region of back.

Note. GAD = generalized anxiety disorder; MDD = major depressive disorder. From Table 6, "The Psychological Treatment of Motor Vehicle Accident-Related Posttraumatic Stress Disorder: Conceptualization and Two Pilot Studies," by E. J. Hickling & E. B. Blanchard, 1999, *International Handbook of Road Traffic Accidents and Psychological Trauma*, pp. 321–329. Copyright 1999 Elsevier Science Ltd. Adapted with permission.

Session 1 was similar to the first session in the CBT condition. The symptoms of PTSD were described and those that the particular patient had were noted. All of these were described as the normal reactions to trauma. Thus, there was a strong attempt to "normalize" the patient's reactions. Then the rest of treatment was outlined.

Sessions 2 through 4 were devoted to taking a very detailed psychosocial history with particular emphasis on previous traumatic events and to previous interpersonal losses (deaths of grandparents, parents, other close people, divorces and breakups, moving, job losses, etc.). For each of these events there was questioning of how the person had dealt with these previous traumas and losses and reinforcement for any apparent successful coping in the past.

Sessions 5 to 10 then shifted to the present and how the patient was dealing with current difficulties in their lives. Problems involved marital and other intimate relationship difficulties, problems with in-laws and other family members, work difficulties, and so forth. In all instances the therapist listened actively, reflected affective content, and helped the patient sort out feelings and action plans, all in a supportive context.

Several things were explicitly avoided: There was no mention of relaxation training; there was no mention of exposure to driving situations (e.g., MVA site); there was no challenging of faulty or catastrophic thought about the MVA or its consequences. If the patient asked about driving-related matters, the response was that the patient should be guided by how he or she felt.

There was ample clinical material to occupy the sessions.

Results

The individual participant's CAPS scores from each assessment are summarized in Table 16.13. The scores were subjected to a one-way ANOVA that was highly significant ($p = .001$). Follow-up analyses on each symptom cluster were each significant ($p < .03$ or better). The primary change was from pretreatment to posttreatment. The additional average change from posttreatment to follow-up was not significant. As can be seen in the last column of the table, we were able to obtain one-year follow-up interviews on these participants.

Categorically, three of the six cases initially diagnosed with PTSD no longer met the criteria by the three-month point. One other PTSD case (#415) dropped to subsyndromal PTSD at posttreatment but again met full criteria for PTSD at the three-month follow-up. One of the two initial subsyndromal cases improved and the other did not.

The mean values from the psychological tests given at the three assessment points are summarized in Table 16.14.

TABLE 16.13
CAPS Results From Pilot Trial of Supportive Psychotherapy Treatment of MVA Victims

Participant #	Initial CAPS	Post-CAPS	3-month follow-up CAPS	1-year CAPS
404	20	19	18	16
407	79	75	61	59
408	58	13	0	0
410	77	37	2	7
412	73	13	14	10
415	57	35	39	27
417	94	41	36	32
418	30	15	16	25
	57.25	31.00	23.25	26.38

Note. CAPS = Clinical Administered PTSD Scale. From Table 7, "The Psychological Treatment of Motor Vehicle Accident-Related Posttraumatic Stress Disorder: Conceptualization and Two Pilot Studies," by E. J. Hickling & E. B. Blanchard, 1999, *International Handbook of Road Traffic Accidents and Psychological Trauma*, pp. 321–329. Copyright 1999 Elsevier Science Ltd. Adapted with permission.

TABLE 16.14
Summary of Psychological Distress Measures for Study 3 (Supportive Psychotherapy)

Measure	Initial	Posttreatment	3-month follow-up	F (2, 14)	p
Beck Depression Inventory	24.5 (13.0)	18.6 (12.3)	20.5 (16.6)	1.32	ns
State Anxiety	49.0 (15.2)	48.1 (15.0)	44.9 (18.9)	.371	ns
Trait Anxiety	54.9 (10.0)	48.1 (13.0)	49.5 (16.4)	2.23	ns
Impact of Event Scale	37.0 (19.1)	25.3 (17.1)	17.9 (21.2)	3.48	.06
PTSD Checklist	50.0 (19.5)	40.0 (15.9)	35.2 (15.9)	3.51	.06

Note. From Table 8, "The Psychological Treatment of Motor Vehicle Accident-Related Posttraumatic Stress Disorder: Conceptualization and Two Pilot Studies," by E. J. Hickling & E. B. Blanchard, 1999, *International Handbook of Road Traffic Accidents and Psychological Trauma*, pp. 321–329. Copyright 1999 Elsevier Science Ltd. Adapted with permission.

There was no appreciable change on depression as measured by the BDI or on state or trait anxiety. The two measures of posttraumatic stress symptoms, IES and PCL, each showed strong trends (p = .06) for there to be significant overall decreases from pretreatment to three-month follow-up.

Discussion

It seems clear that our SUPPORT condition is psychologically active. In fact, the results on PTSD-related measures are comparable to those found by Fecteau and Nicki (1999) described in chapter 15 (see Table 15.1). Thus, we have construed it as a comparison condition, not as an attention–placebo or inactive control.

In this condition we have tried to mimic what we believed might be "generic" psychotherapy in the mental health community. Thus, there is description of PTSD, normalization of the patient's experiences, a detailed exploration of the patient's past, and support for dealing with current problems. This is somewhat akin to Shear, Pilkonis, Cloitre, and Leon's (1994) comparison condition and in their evaluation of a cognitive–behavioral panic control treatment. Shear et al. (1994) found that a comparison condition that combined education about panic and several sessions of support was as effective as the primary CBT treatment for panic disorder.

Studies 2 and 3 set the stage for our randomized, controlled trial to be described in the next chapter. The combined results persuaded the NIMH to award us the funds for the project, which ultimately led to what we have called Cohort 2 in this book.

17

THE ALBANY TREATMENT STUDY: A RANDOMIZED, CONTROLLED COMPARISON OF COGNITIVE–BEHAVIORAL THERAPY AND SUPPORT IN THE TREATMENT OF CHRONIC PTSD SECONDARY TO MVAs

At long last, on the third try, we received an NIMH grant to conduct a randomized, controlled evaluation of our cognitive–behavioral therapy (CBT) treatment for chronic posttraumatic stress disorder (PTSD) resulting from personal injury motor vehicle accidents (MVAs). We began recruiting patients in November 1996, and completed our last two-year follow-up assessment in March 2003. As these dates will indicate, we had begun this study before all but one of the controlled trials described in chapter 15 were published. Brom et al. (1993) had described their early intervention trial with MVA survivors; however, the treatment was no more successful than the assessment-only control condition.

As we began this research, there were in existence two literatures on the treatment of PTSD in adults: one had focused on Vietnam veterans who were all male and who had suffered from PTSD and other problems for 10 to 30 years. A prototypical example of this literature was the study by Keane, Fairbank, Caddell, and Zimering (1989). The second literature had focused on rape victims who were all female and who had suffered from

PTSD for about six to eight years on average. A prototypical example of this literature was the study by Foa et al. (1991).

An advantage of focusing on MVA survivors with PTSD is that one can readily recruit both males and females and thus analyze for any gender differences in outcome. A second advantage of focusing on MVA survivors is that one has a population that is likely to have lingering physical problems, especially pain and reduced range of motion (ROM). (Reference to Tables 16.8 and 16.12 show the range of physical problems that patients with chronic PTSD from an MVA may have to live with.) We can thus examine the role that physical problems may play in hampering psychological recovery.

We made a decision to include both individuals who currently met *DSM–IV* (American Psychiatric Association, 1994) criteria for full PTSD and those with moderate to severe subsyndromal PTSD. Our reasons for including the latter were threefold: First, we had included such individuals in both of our pilot studies; second, and more important, these individuals were fairly symptomatic and distressed enough by their symptoms to seek treatment; they would have met criteria for anxiety disorder not otherwise specified. Third, as noted in chapter 8, almost one third of MVA survivors who initially met criteria for subsyndromal PTSD initially and who had not remitted by six months post-MVA deteriorated and developed a case of delayed-onset PTSD. We could have been purists and turned them away. Instead, we chose to include them.

The results of this trial have been published in a series of papers (Blanchard, Hickling, Devineni, et al., 2003; Blanchard, Hickling, Malta et al., in press; Blanchard, Hickling, Veazey, et al., 2002). In this chapter we summarize those results and add additional outcome data.

METHODS

Participants

As noted in chapter 4, we gathered initial assessment data on 161 individuals; 107 were eligible for treatment and 98 attended at least one treatment session. These 98 make up the sample to be described in this chapter. Seventy-eight completed treatment or the wait-list condition. The 20 dropouts came from the CBT condition ($n = 9$), the supportive psychotherapy (SUPPORT) condition ($n = 10$) or wait list ($n = 1$).

Demographic information on the treatment completers by condition (CBT: $n = 27$; SUPPORT, $n = 27$; wait list: $n = 24$) and on the dropouts ($n = 20$) is presented in Table 17.1. (The totals for the 98 are presented in chapter 4.)

TABLE 17.1
Demographic Information on Patient Completer Groups and Dropouts

Variable	Condition			
	CBT $n = 27$	SUPPORT $n = 27$	Wait list $n = 24$	Dropouts $n = 20$
Gender (M/F)	6/21	6/21	9/15	5/15
Age (mean)	40.6	40.6	42.1	35.6
SD	11.0	13.1	10.9	12.3
Ethnicity				
Caucasian/minority	26/1	25/2	21/3	16/4
Average years of education				
M	13.7	13.4	14.2	13.1
SD	2.3	2.2	2.3	2.5
Initial diagnosis				
PTSD	21	21	21	18
Subsyndromal PTSD	6	6	3	2
Initial CAPS score				
M	68.2	65.0	65.8	69.2
SD	22.7	25.9	26.6	15.1
Months since MVA				
M	11.5	14.6	15.1	9.8
SD	8.0	10.9	8.8	6.2
% with continuing				
physical problems	92.6	92.6	87.5	95.0
% involved in litigation	55.6	66.7	54.2	60.0

Note. CBT = cognitive–behavioral therapy. From Table 1, "A Controlled Evaluation of Cognitive Behavioral Therapy for Posttraumatic Stress in Motor Vehicle Accident Survivors," by E. B. Blanchard et al., 2003, Behaviour Research and Therapy, 41, pp. 79–96. Copyright 2003 Elsevier Science Ltd., Adapted with permission.

There were no significant differences among the three study groups on any of the tabulated variables. Although there were no significant differences between dropouts and completers, there were trends for the dropouts to be younger ($p = .07$), to have suffered the MVA more recently ($p = .08$), and to be more likely to be non-Caucasian ($p = .08$).

Thus, the study sample was 27% male, of average age 41.1 years, who were on average 13.7 months post-MVA. Ninety-one percent were suffering from lingering physical injuries and 59% were involved in litigation, despite New York's being a "no-fault" auto insurance state.

Therapists

To make the study as externally valid as possible, the three therapists were all community-based clinical psychologists in full-time private practice. They were paid on a per-session basis at a rate less than their standard fee but close to the local third-party reimbursement rate. Each had more than five years experience working with cases of PTSD in the local Veterans

next followed by a detailed review (for three sessions) of the patient's history with emphasis on past traumas and losses and how the patient dealt with them. The last six sessions were devoted to discussion of patient issues, other than the MVA, in a supportive and reflective framework.

Sessions were tape-recorded. Graduate students blind to treatment condition scored the tapes for the presence of certain therapist behaviors based on the treatment manuals. Of particular interest was the use of CBT techniques in the SUPPORT condition. We found 99% treatment fidelity in the CBT condition and 97% in SUPPORT. A reliability check on 20% of the tapes by a different doctoral student revealed a correlation of $r = .87, p < .001$ between the two scorings. A copy of the therapy-scoring sheet can be found in Appendix D.

RESULTS

Initial Outcome

Our primary analysis in this study was a comparison of CAPS scores for the three conditions from pretreatment to posttreatment. Those scores are in Table 17.2.

A repeated-measures ANOVA revealed a significant ($p < .001$) pre–post change and, it is important to note, a significant ($p < .001$) groups × pre–post interaction. A follow-up ANCOVA on posttest scores, using the pretest as the covariate, was significant ($p < .001$). Pairwise follow-up comparisons showed CBT superior to SUPPORT ($p = .002$) and to wait list ($p <$

TABLE 17.2
Pretreatment and Posttreatment CAPS Scores on All Groups

Group	Time	
	Pretreatment	Posttreatment
CBT ($n = 27$)		
M	68.2	23.7
SD	22.7	26.2
SUPPORT ($n = 27$)		
M	65.0	40.1
SD	25.9	25.7
Wait list ($n = 24$)		
M	65.8	54.0
SD	26.6	25.9

Note. CAPS = Clinical Administered PTSD Scale; CBT = cognitive–behavioral therapy. From Table 1, "A Controlled Evaluation of Cognitive Behavioral Therapy for Posttraumatic Stress in Motor Vehicle Accident Survivors," by E. B. Blanchard et al. 2003, *Behaviour Research and Therapy, 41*, pp. 79–96. Copyright 2003 by Elsevier Science Ltd., Adapted with permission.

.001). Very importantly, SUPPORT was superior to wait list ($p = .012$). Thus, it is clear that SUPPORT is an active comparison treatment, and the results established it as superior to wait list and repeated assessments. All three conditions (including wait list) individually showed significant pre–post changes.

When these analyses were repeated as a three-way ANOVA with the therapist as an additional independent variable, there were no main effects or interactions with the therapist variable. Thus, the therapists were equally effective.

Likewise, when we included patient gender as an additional independent variable and repeated the analyses as a three-way ANOVA, there was no main effect or interactions of gender. This is important because, as noted earlier, treatment of MVA survivors presents the opportunity to compare different genders on treatment response. To the best of our knowledge none of the studies summarized in chapter 15 (controlled trials of treatment of MVA survivors) have analyzed for possible effects because of gender of participant.

Reanalysis Including Dropouts

A reanalysis including data from dropouts revealed similar results, a significant ($p < .001$) main effect of pre–post, and a significant ($p < .001$) groups × pre–post interaction. The pairwise comparisons continue to show CBT superior to wait list ($p < .001$) and to SUPPORT ($p = .013$). SUPPORT was superior to wait list ($p = .052$). Thus, this intent to treat analysis yields essentially the same results as the primary analysis.

Analysis of PTSD Symptom Clusters

Table 17.3 presents CAPS scores for each of the four symptom clusters (reexperiencing, avoidance, numbing, hyperarousal) displayed by treatment condition and pre–post. The analysis of possible within-group change for each cluster is also presented.

Separate groups by pre–post repeated-measures ANOVAs were calculated on each symptom cluster, with follow-up comparisons. These analyses revealed that both those participants in CBT and those in SUPPORT showed significant ($p = .01$ or better) pre- to posttreatment changes in each of the four symptom clusters. Those in the wait list condition showed significant changes only for reexperiencing symptoms and avoidance symptoms. Examining the degree of differential change between conditions with ANCOVAs, for which pretreatment values were the covariate, we found that CBT changed more than wait list on all four clusters ($p = .003$ or better). When SUPPORT and wait list were compared, SUPPORT showed more change only for the hyperarousal symptoms ($p = .019$). In the

TABLE 17.3
Pretreatment and Posttreatment CAPS Symptom Cluster Scores for All
Three Conditions

Symptom cluster	Groups		
	CBT	SUPPORT	Wait list
Reexperiencing			
Pre-	18.9 (6.3)[a]	16.3 (9.7)[a]	16.2 (8.4)[a]
Post-	3.9 (6.7)[b]	8.6 (7.5)[b]	11.2 (8.0)[b]
Avoidance			
Pre-	12.3 (5.1)[a]	11.9 (5.9)[a]	12.3 (5.4)[a]
Post-	4.6 (5.2)[b]	7.0 (6.0)[b]	9.5 (5.9)[b]
Numbing			
Pre-	15.0 (9.7)[a]	16.2 (9.5)[a]	16.5 (7.9)[a]
Post-	6.1 (9.4)[b]	11.4 (9.6)[b]	14.5 (9.0)[a]
Hyperarousal			
Pre-	22.0 (7.8)[a]	20.6 (7.9)[a]	20.8 (9.3)[a]
Post-	9.2 (8.9)[b]	13.1 (8.4)[b]	18.8 (8.5)[a]

Note. Pairs of means within a column that share a superscript are not different at $p = .01$ level. Posttreatment means for cognitive–behavioral therapy are significantly ($p = .003$) lower than those for wait list for all four symptom clusters. Cognitive–behavioral therapy posttreatment means are significantly ($p < .05$) lower than those for SUPPORT for reexperiencing and numbing symptoms only. SUPPORT posttreatment mean for hyperarousal symptoms is significantly lower ($p = .019$) than that for wait list.

comparison of CBT to SUPPORT, CBT showed significantly ($p < .05$) more change for reexperiencing and numbing symptom clusters; the comparisons for avoidance and hyperarousal were not significant. Thus, it seems clear that the CBT treatment was highly effective with all four aspects of PTSD.

Categorical Analyses

A second way to consider the results is in terms of the categorical variable of whether participants changed diagnostic category (from full PTSD to subsyndromal PTSD or non-PTSD, or from subsyndromal PTSD to non-PTSD). This could be seen as a measure of clinically significant change. The categorical diagnostic data from before to after treatment are contained in Table 17.4.

These data were analyzed with a series of 2×2 chi squares comparing pairs of treatment groups on whether participants who initially met criteria for PTSD continued to meet it or had improved at posttreatment. The analyses revealed that CBT was superior to wait list ($p = .001$) and to SUPPORT ($p = .054$). SUPPORT was not superior to wait list ($p = .107$). In summary, for those with initial PTSD, 76.2% of those receiving CBT improved in terms of diagnostic status, as compared to 47.6% of those in SUPPORT and to 23.8% of those on the wait list who were assessed twice.

Our CBT outcome is comparable to that of Ehlers (personal communication, 2002) and superior to the results of Taylor et al. (2001; 44%) and

TABLE 17.4
Categorical Diagnostic Results for PTSD for All Groups Before
and After Treatment

Condition	Diagnoses at pretreatment	Diagnoses at posttreatment
CBT	PTSD (n = 21)	PTSD (n = 5) Sub-PTSD (n = 1) Non-PTSD (n = 15)
	Sub-PTSD (n = 6)	PTSD (n = 1) Sub-PTSD (n = 0) Non-PTSD (n = 5)
SUPPORT	PTSD (n = 21)	PTSD (n = 11) Sub-PTSD (n = 1) Non-PTSD (n = 9)
	Sub-PTSD (n = 6)	PTSD (n = 1) Sub-PTSD (n = 0) Non-PTSD (n = 5)
Wait list	PTSD (n = 21)	PTSD (n = 16) Sub-PTSD (n = 2) Non-PTSD (n = 3)
	Sub-PTSD (n = 3)	PTSD (n = 1) Sub-PTSD (n = 1) Non-PTSD (n = 1)

Note. CBT = cognitive–behavioral therapy. From Table 3, "A Controlled Evaluation of Cognitive Behavioral Therapy for Posttraumatic Stress in Motor Vehicle Accident Survivors," by E. B. Blanchard et al., 2003, *Behaviour Research and Therapy, 41*, pp. 79–96. Copyright 2003 Elsevier Science Ltd., Adapted with permission.

those of Fecteau and Nicki (1999; 50%). In fact, our results from the SUPPORT condition are comparable to those of Taylor et al. (2001) and Fecteau and Nicki (1999). The results from the wait list group are comparable to those we found in Cohort 1 between the 6-month and 12-month follow-ups.

For the patients with subsyndromal PTSD, both active treatments were equally effective (five of six improved, or 83.3%), and somewhat better than found for the wait list condition (one of three improved, or 33.3%). This difference approaches significance (p = .08). Clearly, patients with subsyndromal PTSD do well in treatment even after the patient has been symptomatic for a year.

Changes in Categorical Comorbidity

Although numerous reports on the treatment of PTSD, even PTSD secondary to MVAs, have reported on changes in symptoms of depression and anxiety as a result of CBT treatment (e.g., Ehlers, 2002; Fecteau &

TABLE 17.5
Categorical Changes in Comorbid Major Depressive Disorder and GAD

Condition	Diagnoses pretreatment		Diagnoses posttreatment	
Major depressive disorder				
CBT (n = 27)	MDD	11	MDD	2
			Non	9
	Non	16	MDD	0
			Non	16
SUPPORT (n = 27)	MDD	17	MDD	10
			Non	7
	Non	10	MDD	2
			Non	8
Wait list (n = 24)	MDD	10	MDD	7
			Non	3
	Non	14	MDD	2
			Non	12
GAD				
CBT	GAD	8	GAD	2
			Non	6
	Non	19	GAD	0
			Non	19
SUPPORT	GAD	11	GAD	9
			Non	2
	Non	16	GAD	1
			Non	15
Wait list	GAD	8	GAD	6
			Non	2
	Non	16	GAD	1
			Non	15

Note. CBT = cognitive–behavioral therapy; GAD = generalized anxiety disorder; MPD = major depressive disorder. From Table 4, "A Controlled Evaluation of Cognitive Behavioral Therapy for Posttraumatic Stress in Motor Vehicle Accident Survivors," by E. B. Blanchard et al., 2003, *Behaviour Research and Therapy,* 41, pp. 79–96. Copyright 2003 Elsevier Science Ltd. Adapted with permission.

Nicki, 1999), to the best of our knowledge, no one has performed the structured psychiatric interviews after treatment to see if patients change comorbid categorical diagnoses as a result of treatment.

Our assessments allowed us to fill this gap in knowledge about possible changes in comorbid Axis I conditions. (It should be remembered that these comorbid conditions were not explicitly targeted by the treatments.) Results from the two most common comorbid conditions, major depressive disorder, present in 38 of 78 (48.7%) of cases, and generalized anxiety disorder (GAD), present in 27 of 78 (34.6%) of cases, are presented in Table 17.5.

The data in Table 17.5 were analyzed by a similar series of 2×2 chi squares comparing treatment conditions on whether those initially positive for major depressive episode (or GAD) were still positive at the posttreatment assessment. For major depression, the analyses revealed that CBT led to significantly greater rate of recovery (82%) than SUPPORT (41%; $p = .005$) or wait list (30%; $p = .017$). The latter two conditions did not differ. Moreover, two cases in each of those conditions that had not met criteria for major depression at pretreatment did, in fact, deteriorate enough to meet the criteria at the posttreatment assessment. There was no such deterioration among those in the CBT condition.

For GAD, CBT led to significantly greater likelihood of remission (75%) than SUPPORT (18%) ($p = .013$), but not the wait list (25%; $p = .13$). Wait list and SUPPORT did not differ. Again, no participant who received CBT deteriorated, whereas one participant from each SUPPORT and wait list did deteriorate such that he or she met criteria for GAD at posttreatment when he or she had not met those criteria at pretreatment.

We find these collateral changes in the CBT condition very encouraging. These changes mean that the treatment does not need to be restricted to cases of pure MVA-related PTSD; instead, the typical individual who is likely to have comorbid major depression, and possibly comorbid GAD, experiences both an alleviation of PTSD and improvement in the other comorbid conditions.

It is important to note that the SUPPORT condition also helps the depression in a portion of those MVA survivors who are also suffering from major depressive disorder. We also note that there is little spontaneous remission of the comorbid psychiatric disorders with only assessment and passage of time.

Psychological Test Measures

The mean scores for each treatment condition at pretreatment and posttreatment on each of the psychological tests are presented in Table 17.6. These values were initially subjected to a MANOVA, which showed a significant groups by pre–post interaction. Follow-up univariate analyses on each measure revealed significant ($p = .001$ or better) groups by pre–post interactions on each measure.

Follow-up ANCOVAs with specific contrasts showed that the changes for the CBT condition were greater than those for SUPPORT or wait list ($p < .001$) on all six measures. The SUPPORT condition changed more ($p < .01$) than wait list on State Anxiety, GSI, and PCL.

There were significant ($p < .01$ or greater) within-group changes on all six measures for the CBT group. Those in SUPPORT showed significant ($p < .01$) changes on the PTSD specific measures, PCL and IES, and on the Global Severity Index and the measure of depressive symptoms, the BDI. The wait list group did not change on any measure.

TABLE 17.6
Psychological Test Results for All Groups at Pretreatment and Posttreatment

Measure	Time	Cognitive–behavior therapy	SUPPORT	Wait list
		Groups		
Global Severity	Pre-	70.1 (9.3)[a]	73.2 (6.4)[a]	72.1 (10.4)[a]
Index (GSI)	Post-	57.3 (12.6)[b]	67.6 (9.0)[b]	74.2 (6.3)[a]
BDI	Pre-	24.3 (10.8)[a]	26.2 (11.9)[a]	25.2 (11.9)[a]
	Post-	11.6 (12.3)[b]	19.7 (12.1)[b]	24.0 (12.1)[a]
State–Anxiety	Pre-	55.3 (14.1)[a]	56.3 (12.2)[a]	58.5 (10.9)[a]
	Post-	38.9 (14.0)[b]	50.7 (12.6)[a]	58.8 (12.3)[a]
Trait–Anxiety	Pre-	55.7 (14.0)[a]	56.7 (10.4)[a]	58.9 (10.1)[a]
	Post-	41.0 (16.5)[b]	52.4 (12.3)[a]	57.1 (9.9)[a]
PCL—Total	Pre-	54.4 (12.2)[a]	55.0 (14.7)[a]	55.9 (13.3)[a]
	Post-	31.3 (14.1)[b]	43.8 (14.6)[b]	53.9 (14.1)[a]
IES—Total	Pre-	40.4 (13.8)[a]	38.7 (20.9)[a]	40.2 (15.9)[a]
	Post-	12.1 (14.9)[b]	27.4 (19.1)[b]	36.6 (17.2)[a]

Note. BDI = Beck Depression Inventory; IES = Impact of Event Scale; PCL = PTSD Checklist. Means within a column that share a superscript do not differ at $p = .01$. From Table 5, "A Controlled Evaluation of Cognitive Behavioral Therapy for Posttraumatic Stress in Motor Vehicle Accident Survivors," by E. B. Blanchard et al., 2003, *Behaviour Research and Therapy, 41*, pp. 79–96. Copyright 2003 by Elsevier Science Ltd. Adapted with permission.

Changes in LIFE–Base Variables

Table 17.7 presents the results from the LIFE–Base variables for each group at pretreatment and posttreatment as well as the scores on the Global Assessment of Functioning (GAF, Axis V). These were subjected to an overall MANOVA with follow-up univariate ANOVAs. These variables reflect the Criterion F (of PTSD) caseness variables.

The groups by pre–post interaction term was significant ($p = .004$) for GAF scores and for scores on participation in recreation ($p = .038$). On GAF, follow-up analyses revealed the CBT group improved more ($p = .001$) than the other two conditions; the latter two did not differ. On recreation participation, CBT improved more than wait list ($p = .002$) but was not different from SUPPORT. SUPPORT and wait list did not differ.

All three groups had significant within-group changes on GAF from before treatment to after it. The CBT group showed significant within-group change on major role functioning, relations with friends, and participation in recreation, with the latter showing almost a whole step change. The SUPPORT group improved on major role functioning and relations with friends but not on recreation. Those in wait list showed no significant

TABLE 17.7
LIFE–Base Variables for Three Groups at Pretreatment and Posttreatment

Variable	Time	Conditions		
		CBT	SUPPORT	Wait list
Major role function	Pre	2.9[a] (1.7)	3.2[a] (1.4)	2.9[a] (1.4)
1 = no impairment, high level	Post	2.3[b] (1.4)	2.7[b] (1.4)	2.8[a] (1.4)
of functioning				
3 = mild impairment				
5 = severe impairment				
Relations with family	Pre	2.2[a] (0.7)	2.4[a] (0.9)	2.6[a] (0.9)
1 = very good	Post	1.9[a] (0.9)	2.2[a] (0.8)	2.3[a] (1.0)
3 = fair				
5 = very poor				
Relation with friends	Pre	2.6[a] (1.4)	2.9[a] (1.2)	2.7[a] (1.0)
1 = very good	Post	1.9[b] (1.1)	2.3[b] (1.2)	2.4[a] (1.2)
3 = fair				
5 = very poor				
Participation in recreation	Pre	3.2[a] (1.3)	3.1[a] (1.1)	3.5[a] (1.2)
1 = very good	Post	2.3[b] (1.3)	2.8[a] (1.1)	3.3[a] (1.2)
3 = fair				
5 = very poor				
Global assessment of	Pre	53.9[a] (11.4)	56.0[a] (9.7)	56.0[a] (13.1)
functioning (Axls V)	Post	75.8[b] (12.2)	64.3[b] (13.4)	60.4[b] (9.6)

Note. CBT = cognitive–behavioral therapy. Means within a column which share a superscript do not differ at *p* = .05. From Table 6, "A Controlled Evaluation of Cognitive Behavioral Therapy for Posttraumatic Stress in Motor Vehicle Accident Survivors," by E. B. Blanchard et al., 2003, *Behaviour Research and Therapy, 41*, pp. 79–96. Copyright 2003 by Elsevier Science Ltd. Adapted with permission.

within-group change. Participants receiving CBT and SUPPORT both improved about half a step on major role functioning, whereas wait list did not. No group improved on relations with family.

In summary, the initial results are very consistent: Those in the CBT condition improved more than those in the SUPPORT condition on the direct target of treatment (CAPS, PTSD diagnosis, PCL, IES) and than those on the wait list. They also improved more than these other two groups on categorical comorbid diagnoses and continuous measures of overall psychological distress (GSI), depression (BDI), anxiety (STAI), and overall functioning (GAF).

The SUPPORT condition, in turn, changed more than the WAIT LIST on CAPS, some PTSD measures, PCL, but not IES or categorical diagnoses. The SUPPORT condition also changed more than wait list on the GSI and State Anxiety scale, but not on comorbid diagnoses, BDI, or Trait Anxiety.

On all variables except the LIFE–Base variable of relations with family, those in CBT improved significantly. For those in SUPPORT, there was significant within-group improvement on all PTSD-related measures, CAPS, PCL, IES, reduced percentage of categorical diagnoses (48%), no change on anxiety (STAI, or diagnoses of GAD), and some improvement in depression (BDI and comorbid diagnoses of major depression).

The wait list group showed a significant decrease only on CAPS score, with 23.8% of initial PTSDs no longer meeting full criteria at retest.

Psychophysiological Testing

As mentioned earlier, we obtained psychophysiological testing data on all three groups before and after treatment. These data were reported in Blanchard, Hickling, Veazey, et al. (2002).

As has frequently been the case with our psychophysiological testing data, only heart rate (HR) yielded a significant ($p < .001$) groups × experimental phases interaction. Thus, we will focus entirely on the HR results. To simplify the analyses the HR data were reduced to reactivity scores by subtracting the preceding baseline from the HR value obtained with the stressor. This yields three values (mental arithmetic, Audio 1, Audio 2) per group at each pretreatment and posttreatment.

The next analysis was a repeated-measures ANOVA (groups × pre–post) on mental arithmetic reactivity scores, and a similar analysis on the combined HR reactivity scores for Audiotape 1 and Audiotape 2. The analysis on mental arithmetic reactivity yielded only a main effect of pre–post ($p = .005$). Average HR reactivity dropped from 9.5 bpm to 7.5 bpm.

For the idiosyncratic audiotaped descriptions of the accident, there was both a main effect of pre–post ($p < .001$) and the crucial interaction of groups × pre–post ($p = .01$). A follow-up ANCOVA on posttest scores, using the pretest as a covariate, was significant ($p = .004$). Pairwise comparisons of CBT to SUPPORT ($p = .001$) and CBT to wait list ($p = .001$) were significant, whereas SUPPORT and wait list did not differ. Thus, whereas the CBT treatment led to a 71% reduction in HR reactivity, the HR reactivity for SUPPORT was reduced by 23% and that for wait list was reduced by 28%. (See values in Table 17.8.)

Is the Change in HR Reactivity Related to Clinical Improvement?

Because the CBT condition was highly successful in reducing the symptoms of PTSD, we wondered whether the differential changes in HR reactivity merely reflected the clinical outcome. To address this issue, we combined the HR reactivity data from successfully treated patients in both CBT and SUPPORT ($n = 33$) and compared it to those of the treatment failures ($n = 18$) and to those in wait list. This reanalysis showed a significant effect of pre–post but no effect of groups or interaction of groups × pre–post.

TABLE 17.8
Combined Heart Reactivity Scores to Audiotapes for Each Treatment Group at Pretreatment and Posttreatment

	Treatment condition		
Time	Cognitive–behavioral therapy	SUPPORT	Wait list
Pretreatment	11.8 (9.6)	11.9 (9.7)	8.5 (6.1)
Posttreatment	3.4 (3.7)	9.2 (10.2)	6.1 (6.9)

Note. Table entries are means (and standard deviations) of heart-rate reactivity scores in beats per minute for the sum of two reactivity scores (value from audiotape minus preceding baseline) for idiosyncratic audio taped descriptions of participant's MVA. Cognitive–behavioral therapy showed greater change in heart-rate reactivity from pretreatment to posttreatment than SUPPORT or wait list. The latter two conditions did not differ. From Table 2, "Treatment-Related Changes in Cardiovascular Reactivity to Trauma Cues in Motor Vehicle Accident-Related PTSD," by E. B. Blanchard et al., 2002, *Behavior Therapy, 33*, pp. 417–426. Copyright 2002 by the Association for Advancement of Behavior Therapy. Adapted with permission.

Those in the "successfully" treated group showed a significant ($p < .001$) within-group reduction in HR reactivity, whereas the other two groups showed only trends. A similar "success" versus "failure" analysis, using only patients who met criteria for full PTSD, showed similar results: No groups × pre–post interaction and only the "successes" showed a significant within-group change. A second reanalysis using only patients who had received CBT (and thus had physiological reactivity directly targeted) also did not yield a significant groups × pre–post interaction. It thus seems that the psychophysiological results are not accounted for solely by clinical outcome.

We calculated correlations between change in CAPS scores and change in HR reactivity scores to see if there was a dose–response relation. The correlation ($r = .298, p = .010$) is significant but small. Likewise, the relation of change in HR reactivity to changes in symptoms of the CAPS (cues reminiscent of the stressor) was significant ($r = .295, p = .011$) but small.

Three-Month Follow-Up

Our initial follow-up assessment was completed three months after treatment. After the posttreatment assessment the therapist received a narrative summary for those in CBT or SUPPORT that he or she reviewed with the patient. At that point, the therapist made the judgment about whether to refer the patient immediately for additional treatment or to defer that decision until the three-month point. Referrals were made for eight cases.

Those patients who had completed the wait list condition were then offered treatment. Many declined. Only three completed the regular CBT treatment and were reassessed. Their data are contained in the one-year follow-up analyses. Others accepted some treatment but failed to complete

TABLE 17.9
Pretreatment, Posttreatment and Three-Month Follow-Up CAPS Scores on
Both Treated Groups

	Time		
Group	Pretreatment	Posttreatment	3-month follow-up
CBT (n = 27)			
M	68.2	23.7	22.1
SD	(22.7)	(26.2)	(24.8)
SUPPORT (n = 26)			
M	65.9	41.2	40.4
SD	(26.1)	(25.5)	(29.8)

Note. CBT = cognitive–behavioral therapy. From Table 2, "A Controlled Evaluation of Cognitive Behavioral Therapy for Posttraumatic Stress in Motor Vehicle Accident Survivors," by E. B. Blanchard et al., 2003, *Behaviour Research and Therapy, 41*, pp. 79–96. Copyright 2003 by Elsevier Science Ltd. Adapted with permission.

a course comparable to the experimental conditions. They were not reassessed after this nonprotocol treatment.

We were able to retain 53 of the 54 patients who initially completed either CBT or SUPPORT (98.2% retention). One participant dropped out of SUPPORT.

Table 17.9 contains the CAPS scores of these 53 patients at pretreatment, posttreatment, and three-month follow-ups. They were subjected to a groups × time repeated-measures MANOVA that had a significant effect of time ($p < .001$) and a significant interaction of groups × time ($p = .048$). A follow-up ANCOVA on the follow-up scores with pretest as the covariate was significant ($p = .003$), again showing the short-term advantage of CBT over SUPPORT. The changes in CAPS scores from posttreatment to three-months were not significant.

Categorical Analysis

At the three-month point, 4 of 21 (19%) participants with initial PTSD in the CBT condition still met criteria for PTSD, compared to 12 of 21 (57%) comparable participants in the SUPPORT condition ($p = .034$). One participant from CBT had improved further, whereas one participant from SUPPORT deteriorated.

Psychological Test Measures

The three-month psychological test scores are shown in Table 17.10. Scores from those in CBT showed slight (nonsignificant) deterioration, whereas scores of those receiving SUPPORT showed slight (nonsignificant) improvement. Between-group comparisons on these follow-up scores were

TABLE 17.10
Psychological Test Results for Treated Groups at Three-Month Follow-Up

Measure	Cognitive–behavioral therapy	SUPPORT
Global Severity Index (GSI)	58.4 (14.3)[a]	65.3 (13.1)[b]
BDI	12.6 (13.5)[a]	17.8 (13.0)[a]
State–Anxiety	42.6 (15.4)[a]	49.1 (14.5)[b]
Trait–Anxiety	40.6 (15.3)[a]	52.3 (12.6)[b]
PCL–Total	31.1 (14.2)[a]	40.8 (14.4)[b]
IES–Total	12.2 (13.6)[a]	24.0 (20.1)[b]

Note. Means within a row that share a superscript do not differ at $p = .05$. BDI = Beck Depression Inventory; IES = Impact of Event Scale; PCL = PTSD Checklist.

significant ($p = .05$) (with the CBT group lower) on all measures except the BDI for which there was a trend ($p = .08$).

LIFE–Base Measures

The posttreatment and three-month scores on the psychosocial functioning ratings from the LIFE are summarized in Table 17.11. There was no significant within-group change for either set of patients. Comparisons of the three-month follow-up ratings by ANCOVA using the pretreatment score as the covariate yielded significant differences (with CBT showing superior functioning) for participation in recreation ($p = .042$) and GAF scores ($p = .044$), with a trend ($p = .056$) for relations with friends. Major role functioning and relations with family were not different.

We had expected that the psychosocial variables might show improvement, especially among those treated with CBT, by the follow-up point. We had reasoned that those in CBT would have seen a noticeable decrease

TABLE 17.11
Three-Month Follow-Up Scores on LIFE–Base Variables for Cognitive–Behavioral Therapy and SUPPORT

Variable	Assessment time	CBT	SUPPORT
Major role functioning	Post 3 months	2.6 (1.6)	2.8 (1.2)
		2.5 (1.5)	2.5 (1.3)
Relations with family	Post 3 months	1.8 (0.7)	2.1 (0.7)
		1.9 (1.0)	2.2 (0.9)
Relations with friends	Post 3 months	1.9 (1.1)	2.3 (1.2)
		1.8 (1.1)	2.5 (1.2)
Participation in recreation	Post 3 months	2.3 (1.3)	2.8 (1.1)
		2.4 (1.3)	3.0 (1.3)
Global Assessment Scale	Post 3 months	76.2 (13.3)	64.3 (15.8)
		73.7 (14.1)	63.4 (15.7)

Note. From Table 6, "A Controlled Evaluation of Cognitive Behavioral Therapy for Posttraumatic Stress in Motor Vehicle Accident Survivors," by E. B. Blanchard et al., 2003, *Behaviour Research and Therapy, 41*, pp. 79–96. Copyright 2003 by Elsevier Science Ltd. Adapted with permission.

in PTSD symptoms by the end of treatment and that psychosocial functioning would begin to improve noticeably once the symptoms no longer interfered. Such was not the case, however.

One-Year Follow-Up

One year after completing treatment, we attempted to reassess all treated participants. We successfully reassessed 28 of 30 (93%) who had received CBT (includes three wait list crossovers) and 24 of 27 (89%) who had received SUPPORT, for an overall follow-up rate of 91%. The five dropouts were compared to completers. The only significant difference was that dropouts were significantly (p = .009) less educated (10.8 years versus 13.9 years) than completers. The dropouts were also more likely to be female (100% versus 75%) and younger (38.6 years versus 41.4) and more likely to be non-PTSD (80% versus 63.5%) at end of treatment. None of these differences were significant.

CAPS

The complete set of CAPS scores (pre-, post-, three-month follow-up, one-year follow-up) are contained in Table 17.12. (We present the compete history because the scores in Table 17.12 are from a slightly different sample than the pre–post analyses.)

Because we have already described the superiority of CBT over SUPPORT at posttreatment and the three-month follow-up, we used only the three-month and one-year data in a groups × time (3 months follow-up to 12 months follow-up) repeated-measures ANOVA. There was no main effect of pre–post, indicating no significant overall decrease in CAPS scores nor an interaction of groups × time. There was, however, a significant main effect of groups (p = .036). The usual ANCOVA on one-year follow-up scores with pretest scores as the covariate was significant (p = .01), indicating the continued superiority of CBT over SUPPORT.

TABLE 17.12
CAPS Scores for Two Treatment Conditions Across All Phases of
Treatment and One-Year Follow-Up

	Condition	
Time of assessment	Cognitive–behavioral therapy	SUPPORT
Pretreatment	64.4 (24.0)	66.3 (26.9)
Posttreatment	23.2 (26.1)	40.9 (25.9)
3-month follow-up	21.9 (24.9)	40.0 (30.3)
12-month follow-up	21.3 (28.4)	35.5 (27.5)

TABLE 17.13
Categorical Diagnoses for Two Treatment Conditions Across All Phases of
Treatment and One-Year Follow-Up

Condition	Diagnosis at pretreatment	Diagnosis at posttreatment	Diagnosis at 3-month follow-up	Diagnosis at 12-month follow-up
CBT	PTSD-21	PTSD 5 Sub 1 Non 15	PTSD 5 Sub 2 Non 14	PTSD 3 Sub 4 Non 14
	Sub PTSD 7	PTSD 1 Sub 0 Non 6	PTSD 1 Sub 0 Non 6	PTSD 1 Sub 0 Non 6
SUPPORT	PTSD-18	PTSD 10 Sub 1 Non 7	PTSD 11 Sub 0 Non 7	PTSD 9 Sub 0 Non 9
	Sub-PTSD-6	PTSD 1 Sub 0 Non 5	PTSD 1 Sub 0 Non 5	PTSD 1 Sub 1 Non 4

Note. CBT = cognitive–behavioral therapy.

Categorical Diagnoses

Table 17.13 contains the categorical diagnoses of participants in the two conditions at posttreatment, three-month follow-up, and one-year follow-up, as a function of pretreatment diagnosis (full PTSD or subsyndromal PTSD). Comparisons of the fraction of the samples at one-year who meet full PTSD versus less than that were significant ($p = .026$), favoring the CBT condition. From three-months to one-year, two of those who had received CBT improved from full PTSD to subsyndromal PTSD; likewise, two of those who received SUPPORT improved from full PTSD to non-PTSD.

Psychological Tests

Table 17.14 presents one-year values for the psychological tests as well as all of the preceding scores. Comparing these values to those from the three-month follow-up point revealed no significant effect of time nor interaction of groups × time. The main effect of groups approached significance ($p = .094$). Follow-up univariate analyses revealed main effects of groups (lower scores for those receiving CBT) for STAI–State, STAI–Trait, IES, and GSI of the Brief Symptom Inventory (BSI; Derogatis, 1993); PCL and BDI scores were not significantly different.

Examining the scores, one sees that for those in CBT, there was a noticeable drop (less distress) at the end of treatment and then either relative

TABLE 17.14
Psychological Test Results for MVA Survivors From Two Treatment
Conditions Across All Phases of Treatment and One-Year Follow-Up

Measure	Treatment condition	Time of assessment			
		Pre-treatment	Post-treatment	3-month follow-up	12-month follow-up
Global Severity	CBT	69.7 (9.1)	57.7 (12.5)	59.5 (13.9)	58.8 (15.1)[a]
Index of BSI	SUPPORT	74.3 (6.0)	68.0 (9.0)	66.2 (13.1)	65.3 (10.8)[b]
Beck Depression	CBT	22.8 (11.4)	11.8 (12.3)	12.6 (12.8)	13.8 (14.2)[a]
Inventory	SUPPORT	27.0 (11.8)	20.4 (12.3)	18.8 (13.4)	18.8 (11.9)[a]
STAI–State	CBT	53.9 (14.0)	39.5 (13.1)	42.9 (14.8)	38.0 (12.3)[a]
	SUPPORT	57.8 (11.9)	51.3 (12.4)	50.9 (14.6)	50.0 (12.7)[b]
STAI–Trait	CBT	53.8 (13.7)	41.4 (15.3)	41.6 (14.7)	42.2 (15.8)[a]
	SUPPORT	56.4 (10.1)	52.3 (11.6)	49.1 (10.9)	49.4 (12.9)[b]
PTSD Checklist	CBT	52.1 (12.3)	31.8 (14.0)	33.1 (13.1)	35.0 (17.5)[a]
	SUPPORT	56.3 (14.4)	44.2 (13.9)	41.6 (14.3)	39.2 (14.9)[a]
Impact of	CBT	38.1 (13.7)	13.1 (15.3)	12.6 (13.5)	14.2 (17.5)[a]
Event Scale	SUPPORT	40.5 (20.4)	27.1 (18.9)	24.3 (19.6)	19.2 (17.5)[b]

Note. CBT = cognitive–behavioral therapy. Twelve-month follow-up means that share a superscript were not significantly different at $p = .05$.

stability (STAI–State, GSI) or slight, progressive deterioration (BDI, STAI–Trait, PCL, IES). For those who received SUPPORT, there is gradual improvement over time for all six measures.

Comorbid Psychiatric Diagnoses

Table 17.15 presents the frequencies with which participants in CBT or SUPPORT met criteria for either major depressive disorder or GAD across the four assessment points.

Whereas there had been a clear advantage in relief from major depression for those receiving CBT over SUPPORT at end of treatment, the

TABLE 17.15
Frequency of Comorbid Diagnoses for Two Treatment Conditions Across
All Phases of Treatment and One-Year Follow-Up

Comorbid diagnoses	Treatment condition	Time of assessment			
		Pre-treatment	Post-treatment	3-month follow-up	12 month follow-up
Major depressive	CBT	11/28	2/28	3/28	5/28
disorder	SUPPORT	16/24	13/24	11/24	9/24
Generalized anxiety	CBT	8/28	2/28	3/28	3/28
disorder	SUPPORT	10/24	9/24	7/24	10/24

Note. CBT = cognitive–behavioral therapy.

differences between the two groups was not statistically significant at one year (CBT: 18%, SUPPORT: 38%). Three of those in CBT had deteriorated over the year, whereas there was steady improvement over the year for those who had received SUPPORT (from 54% to 38%). These categorical changes are probably reflected in the BDI scores.

For comorbid GAD, those who had received CBT continued to show a significant ($p = .01$) advantage (11%) in not meeting criteria for GAD over those who had received SUPPORT (42%).

LIFE–Base Variables

Table 17.16 presents the means for the four LIFE–Base variables and GAF for all four assessments for those who received CBT or SUPPORT.

We analyzed these data by comparing 3-month and 12-month ratings in groups × time ANOVAs. There were no significant effects except for GAF. The CBT group was higher than the SUPPORT group ($p = .016$) across time. There was no significant within-group change on any variable from 3 months to 12 months.

TABLE 17.16
One-Year Follow-Up Scores on LIFE–Base Variables for
Cognitive–Behavioral Therapy and SUPPORT

Variable	Assessment time	Cognitive–behavioral therapy	SUPPORT
Major role functioning	Pre-	2.6 (1.6)	3.1 (1.4)
	Post-	2.3 (1.5)	2.9 (1.4)
	3 months	2.4 (1.4)	2.7 (1.3)
	12 months	2.1 (1.3)	2.6 (1.1)
Relations with family	Pre-	2.2 (0.7)	2.4 (0.9)
	Post-	1.8 (0.7)	2.2 (0.9)
	3 months	1.9 (0.9)	2.2 (0.9)
	12 months	2.0 (0.8)	2.2 (0.9)
Relations with friends	Pre-	2.6 (1.4)	2.9 (1.2)
	Post-	2.0 (1.1)	2.3 (1.2)
	3 months	1.9 (1.2)	2.5 (1.2)
	12 months	1.9 (1.2)	2.3 (1.2)
Participation in recreation	Pre-	3.1 (1.3)	3.1 (1.2)
	Post-	2.1 (1.2)	2.7 (1.1)
	3 months	2.2 (1.2)	3.0 (1.3)
	12 months	2.3 (1.2)	2.7 (1.2)
Global assessment of functioning	Pre-	60.3 (11.0)	55.5 (9.9)
	Post-	76.4 (12.1)	64.5 (13.6)
	3 months	74.3 (13.5)	64.2 (15.6)
	12 months	73.5 (15.6)	63.8 (13.7)

Moderating Variables

We examined several factors that we believed might influence long-term follow-up. The first of these was whether individuals from either condition experienced new MVAs or other new traumas, because new traumas could lead to loss of therapeutic gains or deterioration. The second factor was whether individuals received additional treatment after the completion of the original treatment.

There was no difference in the experiencing of new MVAs. However, for the experience of other new trauma, those who had been in SUPPORT (29%) were significantly ($p = .036$) more likely to have these events happen than those who received CBT (7%). There was no apparent effect of new trauma on CAPS scores at three months or one year. There was also no effect of experiencing new traumas on any of the six psychological tests.

Effects of Additional Treatment

Those who initially received SUPPORT (42%) were also significantly ($p = .01$) more likely to have received additional mental health treatment than those who received CBT (11%). It should be remembered that any additional mental health treatment was provided by someone other than the three therapists involved in the study (to avoid any apparent conflict of interest), and thus its content is not available to us.

We compared those 13 individuals who received additional treatment to the 39 who did not on the CAPS and all of the other psychological tests. These 13 showed a trend ($p = .09$) to be more likely to have shown no improvement or to have worsened (54%) than the 39 who did not seek additional treatment (28%). Those who received additional treatment had higher CAPS scores at the end of treatment and at follow-ups than those who did not. Analyses of the psychological tests yielded similar results, with the group receiving additional treatment significantly ($p = .02$ or better) higher at three months and one year on the BDI, State–Anxiety, PCL, and the Global Severity Index of the BSI. It is possible the higher level of symptoms led the treatment seekers to find additional treatment. In summary, it seems clear that the effects of CBT treatment for MVA-related PTSD persisted for the first year following treatment, with no instances of relapse to PTSD. There was an increase in the rate of meeting criteria for major depression over the year in this group. The psychological test scores remained fairly stable over the follow-up, indicating no major relapses but also no noticeable additional improvement.

For SUPPORT, there was continued gradual improvement on the psychological test measures over time and a slight decrease in categorical diagnoses of full PTSD. These participants were also significantly more likely to seek and obtain additional mental health services during the follow-up.

We can feel reasonably confident in these one-year follow-up data because more than 90% were retained. This is much better than the usual naturalistic follow-up study (see chapter 7).

Two-Year Follow-Up

Although we had excellent retention for the one-year follow-up, this was not the case with the two-year follow-up. We were able to reassess 32 of 52 (61.5%) treated MVA survivors who provided one-year follow-up data. Those who completed the follow-up did not differ from the dropouts on any demographic, pretreatment, or posttreatment variables. There were 10 dropouts from CBT and 10 from SUPPORT. A description of completers and dropouts is detailed in Table 17.17.

CAPS and Psychological Tests

Despite arithmetic differences in two-year CAPS scores favoring the CBT condition (19.6) over the SUPPORT condition (27.6), there was no significant difference between the two groups. Table 17.18 presents the values for the CAPS, GAF, and the six psychological tests at pretreatment, posttreatment, one-year and two-year follow-ups for those 32 patients who completed the latter follow-up.

We conducted two-way ANOVAs with repeated measures on the one-year and two-year values, to determine if there had been any significant change over the second year of follow-up and whether the means at the two-year follow-up were different. There were no main effects of time for any variable, despite a general trend for arithmetically lower scores at two years than at one year (except for those in the SUPPORT condition whose scores for the IES and PCL were slightly higher).

On three measures, IES, PCL, and STAI–State, the scores from those in the CBT condition were significantly ($p < .05$) lower than those who had received SUPPORT.

Categorical Diagnoses

Table 17.19 presents the categorical PTSD diagnostic data for those who had received the two conditions as a function of Year 1 diagnostic status. Of those who had received CBT, the only change was the deterioration of one participant, who met subsyndromal PTSD at Year 1 to full PTSD at Year 2. For those who had received SUPPORT initially, two of those with full PTSD at Year 1 had improved enough to drop to subsyndromal PTSD. One the other hand, one who had been subsyndromal PTSD at Year 1 deteriorated to full PTSD, as did two participants who had been non-PTSD at Year 1. There was thus a net increase of one (to a total of 5 of 13) in

TABLE 17.17
Demographic and Clinical Data on Treated MVA Survivors Who Completed or Did Not Complete Two-Year Follow-Up

Variable	Cognitive–behavioral therapy	SUPPORT	Dropouts
Gender (male/female)	6/13	3/10	6/14
Age (at initial assessment)	43.3 (10.5)	39.5 (16.4)	40.9 (10.6)
Ethnicity (Caucasian/minority)	18/1	11/2	20/0
Marital status (married, cohabitating/single, divorced, widowed)	12/7	5/8	10/10
Education (years completed)	14.5 (2.4)	13.2 (1.7)	13.8 (2.0)
Working outside of home (full-time, part-time/not working)	10/9	8/5	11/9
Initial diagnosis			
PTSD	14	10	15
Sub-PTSD	5	3	2
Non-PTSD	0	0	3
Major depression (yes/no)	10/9	8/5	9/11
GAD (yes/no)	5/14	6/7	7/13
Initial CAPS	68.9 (23.7)	68.4 (25.1)	59.9 (26.7)
Posttreatment diagnosis			
PTSD	4	7	6
Sub-PTSD	1	0	1
Non-PTSD	14	6	13
Major depression (yes/no)	3/16	8/5	5/15
GAD (yes/no)	2/17	6/7	2/18
Posttreatment CAPS	24.3 (27.4)	39.5 (25.0)	32.9 (28.0)
Additional trauma (including MVA) posttreatment to 1 year follow-up (yes/no)	1/18	4/9	6/14
1-year follow-up to 2-year follow-up (yes/no)	0/19	4/9	—
Additional treatment posttreatment to 1 year follow-up (yes/no)	2/17	5/8	6/14
1-year follow-up to 2-year follow-up (yes/no)	5/14	3/10	—

Note. CAPS = Clinical Administered PTSD Scale; GAD = generalized anxiety disorder.

those from SUPPORT who met full PTSD at two years. The two conditions did not differ significantly (17.6% for CBT versus 38.5% for SUPPORT).

Table 17.20 presents similar categorical diagnostic data for major depressive disorder and GAD. One of those from CBT improved and no longer met criteria for major depression; for those who had received SUPPORT,

TABLE 17.18
CAPS Scores and Other Psychological Test Scores From Two Treatment Conditions Across All Phases of Treatment and Two-Year Follow-Up (For Those Who Completed Two-Year Follow-Up)

Psychological test	Treatment condition	Time of assessment			
		Pre-treatment	Post-treatment	1 year follow-up	2 year follow-up
CAPS	CBT	68.9 (23.7)	24.3 (27.4)	22.5 (31.6)	21.7 (26.5)
	SUPPORT	68.4 (25.1)	39.5 (25.0)	30.9 (21.8)	27.6 (21.5)
Beck Depression	CBT	23.4 (12.1)	12.9 (13.6)	15.2 (16.0)	12.3 (15.1)
Inventory	SUPPORT	25.5 (14.3)	22.4 (15.0)	18.5 (14.1)	19.0 (15.4)
STAI–State	CBT	55.2 (15.2)	39.5 (14.6)	37.3 (13.1)	37.5 (15.2)
	SUPPORT	56.4 (13.8)	51.9 (15.4)	49.2 (14.6)	46.7 (17.8)
STAI–Trait	CBT	53.3 (15.7)	41.1 (17.7)	41.4 (18.5)	38.4 (16.4)
	SUPPORT	57.0 (12.3)	54.0 (14.6)	47.5 (16.4)	47.0 (18.3)
PTSD Checklist	CBT	53.2 (12.2)	31.4 (15.0)	35.6 (19.8)	31.0 (15.2)
	SUPPORT	56.5 (16.6)	44.6 (17.8)	39.7 (15.7)	41.6 (14.3)
Impact of Event	CBT	39.5 (11.0)	13.9 (16.9)	15.5 (19.0)	10.1 (13.0)
Scale	SUPPORT	39.8 (25.1)	26.7 (20.5)	17.5 (19.4)	22.2 (20.3)
Global Severity	CBT	69.0 (10.5)	56.3 (14.1)	56.7 (15.8)	55.9 (15.4)
Index of BSI	SUPPORT	73.8 (6.8)	68.9 (11.2)	64.0 (13.2)	62.2 (13.6)
Global Assessment	CBT	57.8 (11.0)	76.2 (13.3)	72.7 (17.6)	72.2 (17.5)
of Scale	SUPPORT	53.8 (10.7)	64.2 (15.8)	58.3 (22.1)	64.8 (14.0)

Note. CAPS = Clinical Administered PTSD Scale; CBT = cognitive–behavioral therapy.

three improved and two deteriorated, leaving 5 of 13 (38.5%) from the SUPPORT condition still meeting full major depression criteria.

For GAD, one from CBT improved but two deteriorated, leaving 1 of 17 meeting criteria (5.9%). For those from the SUPPORT condition, one improved and none deteriorated, leaving 30.8% meeting GAD criteria.

Although all of the categorical diagnostic data favor CBT over SUPPORT arithmetically, none of the arrays are statistically significant.

Psychosocial Variables

Table 17.21 presents the mean ratings for the four LIFE–Base variables at the one-year and two-year follow-up points. Two-way ANOVAs on each variable revealed no significant within-groups change on any variable from one year to two years posttreatment. In fact, the only significant difference between the two conditions was by ANCOVA, with pretreatment as the covariate, on participation in recreation; CBT was significantly ($p = .042$) more engaged in recreational activities than SUPPORT.

TABLE 17.19
Categorical Diagnoses for Two Treatment Conditions at One-Year and
Two-Year Follow-Ups

Condition	Diagnoses at one-year follow-up	Diagnoses at two-year follow-up
Cognitive–behavioral therapy	PTSD - 3	PTSD - 2
		Sub = 0
		Non = 1
	Sub-PTSD - 4	PTSD - 1
		Sub = 3
		Non = 0
	Non-PTSD - 12	PTSD - 0
		Sub = 0
		Non = 12
SUPPORT	PTSD - 4	PTSD - 2
		Sub = 2
		Non = 0
	Sub-PTSD - 1	PTSD - 1
		Sub = 0
		Non = 0
	Non-PTSD - 8	PTSD - 2
		Sub = 0
		Non = 6

TABLE 17.20
Categorical Diagnoses for Two Treatment Conditions at One-Year and
Two-Year Follow-Ups

Condition	Diagnoses at one-year follow-up	Diagnoses at two-year follow-up
Cognitive–behavioral therapy	MDD - 4	MDD = 3
		Non = 1
	Non-MDD - 15	MDD = 0
		Non = 15
	GAD - 2	GAD = 1
		Non = 1
	Non-GAD - 17	GAD = 2
		Non = 15
SUPPORT	MDD - 6	MDD - 3
		Non = 3
	Non-MDD - 7	MDD - 2
		Non = 5
	GAD - 5	GAD = 4
		Non = 1
	Non-GAD - 8	GAD = 0
		Non = 8

Note. GAD = generalized anxiety disorder; MDD = major depressive disorder.

TABLE 17.21
Two-Year Follow-Up Scores on LIFE Base Variables for
Cognitive–Behavioral Therapy and SUPPORT

Variable	Assessment time	Cognitive–behavioral therapy	SUPPORT
Major role functioning	Pre-	2.8 (1.8)	3.2 (1.1)
	Post-	2.6 (1.6)	2.8 (1.2)
	1 year	2.4 (1.5)	2.5 (1.1)
	2 years	2.5 (1.4)	2.7 (1.4)
Relations with family	Pre-	2.1 (0.8)	2.4 (0.9)
	Post-	1.8 (0.7)	2.1 (0.7)
	1 year	2.0 (0.9)	2.1 (0.8)
	2 years	1.9 (0.8)	2.1 (1.2)
Relations with friends	Pre-	2.7 (1.6)	2.8 (1.0)
	Post-	2.0 (1.3)	2.3 (1.3)
	1 year	1.8 (1.2)	2.4 (1.2)
	2 years	2.1 (1.3)	2.6 (1.5)
Participation in recreation	Pre-	3.4 (1.4)	3.2 (1.1)
	Post-	2.3 (1.4)	2.8 (1.3)
	1 year	2.3 (1.4)	2.6 (1.0)
	2 year	2.2 (1.3)	3.0 (1.4)
Global assessment scale	Pre-	57.8 (11.0)	53.8 (10.7)
	Post-	76.2 (13.3)	64.2 (15.8)
	1 year	72.7 (17.6)	64.2 (13.9)
	2 years	72.2 (17.6)	64.5 (13.4)

SUMMARY OF FOLLOW-UP RESULTS

One can draw several conclusions from the follow-up data.

1. Over the first year of follow-up, those who had received CBT were significantly better than those who had SUPPORT on variables related to PTSD (CAPS, diagnostic status, PCL, IES) and generally better on the other psychological status measures. These differences remained despite those in SUPPORT being more likely to have received additional treatment. On the psychosocial variables from the LIFE–Base, only GAF scores were different. One can feel reasonably confident about these conclusions because more than 90% of participants were reassessed during the first year.

2. By the second year follow-up, despite a continued arithmetic advantage for those who had received CBT over those who received SUPPORT, on only three psychological tests—PCL, IES, and STAI–State—were the differences statistically different. This is probably attributable, at least in part, to a loss of

more than one third of the sample, and the subsequent loss of statistical power to detect differences.

3. There was very little within-group change on any measure over the two years of follow-up for those who received CBT initially. Time did not seem to lead to appreciable further change.

4. By way of contrast, those who initially received SUPPORT showed gradual but steady improvement over the two years, with many two-year scores being noticeably better than at posttreatment. This could be a result of (a) consolidation of treatment gains over time, (b) being more likely to receive additional treatment in follow-up, and (c) a statistical regression to the mean.

PREDICTION OF INITIAL BENEFIT

The last issue we addressed in the Albany project was determining if we could predict who would benefit from each of the treatments over the short term. Thus, we addressed four prediction questions from the results for CBT and four similar questions for those in SUPPORT.

We sought to predict at posttreatment: (a) the CAPS score as an indication of overall level of posttraumatic stress symptoms and (b) whether the patient had improved categorically or not—that is, had those with initial PTSD improved to subsyndromal PTSD or non-PTSD and had those with initial subsyndromal PTSD improved to non-PTSD? At the three-month follow-up point, we sought to predict (a) three-month follow-up CAPS and (b) who had maintained improved status or had gained improved status over the follow-up interval versus who was unchanged.

For the prediction of posttreatment status we used variables available at the pretreatment assessment. For the prediction of three-month follow-up status, we used the pretreatment predictors plus variables available at posttreatment.

We followed our previous plan of first calculating the zero-order association between predictor and outcome for a wide array of variables. Those individual correlations that were significant at the .05 level for either condition were retained for the multivariate analyses.

Table 17.22 presents the variables that survived this screen for the posttreatment prediction situations. Table 17.23 presents the variables that survived the screen for the three-month follow-up predictions. (The potential pool was larger in the latter table because we included variables available at pretreatment and at posttreatment; however, only posttreatment variables entered.)

TABLE 17.22
Univariate Predictors for Posttreatment CAPS and Improvement Status for Patients Receiving Cognitive–Behavioral Therapy or SUPPORT

Predictor	Posttreatment CAPS		Posttreatment improved status 1 = improved, 2 = not improved	
	CBT	SUPPORT	CBT	SUPPORT
Years of education	−.234	.402*	−.350	.361
Number of months post-MVA	.178	.464*	.356*	.338
Subjective probability of dying in MVA	.389*	.396*	.233	.375*
Fatality in MVA (1 = yes, 2 = no)	−.532**	a	−.369*	a
Attribution of blame to other driver	−.136	.157	−.416*	.328
Days of work missed	.520**	.331	.347	.369
Pretreatment CAPS	.494**	.705***	.143	.578**
Pretreatment CAPS avoidance	.340	.537**	.340	.398*
Pretreatment CAPS numbing	.054	.632***	.054	.538**
Pretreatment CAPS arousal	−.013	.641***	−.013	.409*
Pretreatment BDI	.380*	.370	.043	.457*
Pretreatment GAF rating	−.202	−.490**	.110	−.362
1 month post-MVA GAS	.195	−.485*	.110	−.421*
Pretreatment major role functioning	.388*	.490*	.199	.409*
Pretreatment relations with family	.205	.289	.016	.433*
Pretreatment major depression (1 = yes, 2 = no)	.053	.648***	−.290	.577**
Pretreatment mood disorder (1 = yes, 2 = no)	.015	.648***	−.358	.577**
Pretreatment GAD (1 = yes, 2 = no)	−.002	.254	−.056	.497**
Pretreatment any Axis I disorder (1 = yes, 2 = no)	.015	.556**	−.358*	.445*
Pretreatment HR reactivity (Audio 1 + Audio 2)	−.217	.487*	−.193	.207
Headaches as results of MVA (1 = yes, 2 = no)	−.104	−.354	.005	−.511**
Pretreatment whiplash (1 = yes, 2 = no)	−.073	−.297	.066	−.485*
Litigation underway (1 = yes, 2 = no)	−.244	−.315	−.042	−.419*

Note. BDI = Beck Depression Inventory; CAPS = Clinical Administered PTSD Scale; CBT = cognitive–behavioral therapy; GAD = generalized anxiety disorder; GAS = Global Assessment Scale; HR = heart rate.
[a]There were no fatalities in MVAs for SUPPORT participants.
*p < .05. **p < .01. ***p < .001.

Examining the correlations in Table 17.22, it is clear that no single variable is a significant predictor across the two treatments for both posttreatment CAPS and clinical status. By way of contrast, when one looks at the variables that have significant zero-order correlations in predicting three-month follow-up variables, several posttreatment variables correlate significantly in all four instances, including posttreatment CAPS, posttreatment BDI, Trait Anxiety and Global Severity Index, and posttreatment clinical status as improved or not.

TABLE 17.23
Univariate Predictors for Three-Month Follow-Up CAPS and Improvement
Status for Patients Receiving Cognitive–Behavioral Therapy or SUPPORT

Predictor	3-month CAPS		3 months posttreatment improved status 1 = improved, 2 = not improved	
	CBT	SUPPORT	CBT	SUPPORT
Posttreatment CAPS	.882***	.935***	.786***	.695***
Posttreatment improved (1 = yes, 2 = no)	.546**	.710***	.548***	.617***
Posttreatment BDI	.785***	.629***	.687***	.732***
Posttreatment trait anxiety	.585***	.410*	.522**	.621***
Posttreatment GSI	.698***	.494*	.546**	.555**
Posttreatment Global Injury Score	.422*	.473*	.336	.168
Posttreatment severity of injuries	.535**	.468*	.393*	.365
Posttreatment GAD (1 = yes, 2 = no)	.061	.297	−.018	.360
Posttreatment mood disorder (1 = yes, 2 = no)	.578***	.464*	.443*	.463*
Posttreatment any Axis I disorder (1 = yes, 2 = no)	.366*	−.161	.308	−.120
Additional psychological treatment (1 = yes, 2 = no)	−.470**	.116	−.443*	−.064
Posttreatment HR reactivity (Audio 1 + Audio 2)	.132	.419*	.159	.549**

Note. BDI = Beck Depression Inventory; CAPS = Clinical Administered PTSD Scale; CBT = cognitive–behavioral therapy; GAD = generalized anxiety disorder; GSI = Global Severity Index; HR = heart rate.
* $p < .05$. ** $p < .01$. *** $p < .001$.

Prediction of Posttreatment and Three-Month Follow-Up CAPS Scores

Table 17.24 presents the final prediction equations, including the values of R^2 for posttreatment CAPS scores for CBT and SUPPORT. To conserve space, the final prediction equations for the three-month follow-up CAPS scores are also presented.

Examining these results, we find that pretreatment CAPS is a significant predictor of posttreatment CAPS for both CBT and SUPPORT. For predicting three-months CAPS, the only predictor to load in both instances is posttreatment CAPS score. In fact, these correlations (CBT, $r = .882$; SUPPORT, $r = .933$) are like test–retest reliability coefficients.

In predicting the immediate posttreatment CAPS score, an indication of injury severity, days of work missed, is a predictor for those receiving CBT. For those receiving SUPPORT, comorbid major depression and the subjective fear of dying in the MVA were predictors. All three of these variables initially predict who is likely to develop PTSD from an MVA (see chapter 6).

TABLE 17.24
Prediction (Multiple Regression) of Posttreatment and Three-Month Follow-Up CAPS Scores for CBT and SUPPORT Completers

Variable	Multiple R	R^2	ΔR^2	Significance of ΔR^2	Zero order r	Partial r	Beta	Significance
			CBT—posttreatment					
Days of work missed	.516	.266	.266	.003	.518	.493	.437	.007
Pretreatment CAPS	.654	.427	.161	.010	.494	.468	.409	.010
			SUPPORT—posttreatment					
Pretreatment CAPS	.705	.497	.497	<.001	.705	.591	.470	.002
Pretreatment diagnosis of major depression	.783	.613	.116	.013	.648	.522	.389	.007
Subjective probability of death in MVA	.835	.697	.083	.019	.388	.465	.292	.019
			CBT—3-month follow-up					
Posttreatment CAPS	.882	.777	.777	<.001	.882	.882	.882	<.001
			SUPPORT—3-month follow-up					
Posttreatment CAPS	.933	.871	.871	<.001	.933	.933	.933	<.001

Note. CAPS = Clinical Administered PTSD Scale; CBT = cognitive–behavioral therapy.

TABLE 17.25
Prediction (Logistical Regression) of Posttreatment and Three-Month Follow-Up Clinical Improvement Status for Cognitive–Behavioral Therapy and SUPPORT Completers

Predictor variable	Zero-order Correlation	B	Wald	Significance	% correct prediction			Significance of change
					Improved	Unimproved	Total	
Cognitive–Behavioral Therapy—posttreatment								
Baseline case (call everyone improved)					100	0	77.8	
Months post-MVA	.356	.145	4.083	.043				.019
% blame to other driver	-.416	-.036	3.400	.065				.032
Constant	—	-.710	.191	.658	95.2	50.0	85.2	
SUPPORT—posttreatment								
Baseline case (call everyone unimproved)					0	100	50	
Pretreatment major depression	.577	10.23	.011	.918				.001
Pretreatment GAD	.497	15.06	.014	.907				<.001
Headaches as result of MVA	-.511	-20.54	.010	.920				.002
Constant	—	-24.68	.005	.943	76.9	100	88.5	
Cognitive–Behavioral Therapy—3-month follow-up								
Baseline case (call everyone improved)					100	0	73.3	
Posttreatment CAPS Intrusion	.548	1.098	4.854	.028				
Constant	—	-4.194	6.852	.009	95.5	87.5	93.3	<.001
SUPPORT—3-month follow-up								
Baseline case (call everyone unimproved)					0	100	50	
Posttreatment diagnosis (1 = PTSD, 2 = sub–, 3 = non)	.732	-23.54	.000	.997				<.001
Posttreatment BDI		1.957	.000	.997				.002
Posttreatment HR Reactivity (Audio 1 + Audio 2)	.549	3.066	.000	.996				<.001
Constant	—	15.200	.000	.999	100	100	100	

Note. BDI = Beck Depression Inventory; GAD = generalized ansiety disorder; HR = heart rate.

Prediction of Posttreatment and Three-Month Follow-Up Clinical Status

Table 17.25 presents the final logistical regression equations to predict posttreatment clinical status for CBT and SUPPORT. Also included are the equations for three-month follow-up clinical status.

In all instances we are able to improve on the base rate case of calling everyone improved (for CBT) or everyone unimproved (for SUPPORT). For SUPPORT the predictor variables are all related to comorbidity at the initial assessment, major depression, GAD, or posttraumatic headaches.

In predicting follow-up clinical status, only posttreatment variables load significantly. Posttreatment CAPS does not enter the logistical regression equations despite very high zero-order correlations. Instead for CBT only the posttreatment intrusion symptom score enters and improves prediction from the base rate of 73.3% to 93.3%. For the three-month SUPPORT prediction, three variables, posttreatment BDI score, posttreatment HR reactivity to the audiotapes, and immediate posttreatment diagnostic status, lead to 100% correct classification.

Overall, the results show that prediction is a complex business for which many classes of variables can play a significant role. Of course, these results are in need of replication given our relatively small samples.

OVERALL CONCLUSIONS FROM THE STUDY

We have provided interim summaries of the results of our study throughout this chapter. Here we want to draw some general conclusions. It seems clear to us that the CBT treatment is effective for MVA survivors with chronic PTSD and comorbid depression and generalized anxiety. The benefits hold up well in the intermediate and long-term. Simply put, we believe this treatment works. It is described in step-by-step detail in the next chapter (chapter 18).

It also seems clear that brief supportive psychotherapy (SUPPORT) is effective for these MVA survivors with chronic PTSD. The benefits, although not as great as those from CBT, are greater than going through detailed assessments and the passage of time (wait list) and they hold up over the intermediate and long-term. In fact, those who received SUPPORT show gradual continued improvement over follow-up. This treatment is also described in step-by-step detail in chapter 19.

Following both our theoretical and conceptual biases, and our own data, we would recommend CBT over SUPPORT for the MVA survivor with chronic PTSD. But clearly SUPPORT is superior to doing nothing and leads to substantial clinical benefit.

18

THE TREATMENT MANUAL:
AN IN-DEPTH LOOK AT THE
ALBANY MVA PROJECT'S
COGNITIVE–BEHAVIORAL THERAPY

As one looks at the Albany motor vehicle accident (MVA) treatment projects, it becomes obvious that much more is taking place than is summarized in generalized statements and group data. The purpose of this chapter is to expand and elaborate on what is occurring in the cognitive–behavioral therapy (CBT) treatment intervention. This will be done by following two concurrent paths: First, we will describe the components of the treatment manual used within the Albany MVA treatment study. Second, we will use case vignettes and examples to illustrate points drawn from research studies and from clinical practice to highlight what we believe are the most important aspects of intervention.

SESSION 1

Review Symptoms and Diagnoses

The initial session involved a review of the evaluation results with each patient. This included a review of their MVA description, their reaction to the MVA, and their specific symptoms of posttraumatic stress disorder (PTSD; and other Axis I diagnoses if applicable). We used the symptom summary sheet from the CAPS to guide this portion of the review. This was a logical and important step in the intervention studies for the following reasons: First, because someone other than the treating psychologist generally did the evaluation, this allowed the psychologist and patient to "get on the same page." Second, by sharing the evaluation results, a sense of understanding of the problem was communicated. Third, rapport building was begun, emphasizing that "the patient had been heard" during this feedback and that any subsequent changes that had occurred since the initial feedback during the evaluation phase of the treatment study was shared at this time.

In traditional practice, this same process occurs when a diagnosis is shared and the psychologist begins to outline a treatment plan based on a summation of the patient's presenting problems. Subsequently, we had used this step as a rapid way of building the therapeutic alliance. In practice this alliance-building begins in a much more traditional fashion from the referral process and any communication made by referring physicians or other health providers regarding the need for psychological treatment. The treating psychologist would use this information as the basis for an assessment of the problem the patient is experiencing followed by an outline of the psychological treatment.

Discuss Normal Reaction to Trauma and Information on PTSD

A second goal of the first session was to provide a discussion of a "normal reaction to trauma." By this we mean giving the patient a rationale that explains how trauma is experienced in a behavioral, cognitive, and emotional context. This is intended to reassure the patient that he or she is not "going crazy" or "losing his or her mind." The latter is often expressed by the patient as one of his or her greatest fears. Instead the patient is reassured that what is being experienced is not unexpected or infrequent reaction to an abnormal situation. This is done in the following way:

> It is normal to have some increased anxiety or apprehension when you are back in a situation that had led to trauma and it is also normal to have some fear or anxiety when confronted with situations in which there is a potential for harm or even threat of death. Thus, although your initial reaction was normal in that almost everyone would have similar feelings and reactions, we believe the symptoms you are experiencing are of sufficient severity and are continuing for a sufficient period of time that they are causing problems in your daily living. The symptoms you are having are consistent with a disorder called posttraumatic stress disorder.

As you can see, any discussion of a normal reaction to trauma and the symptoms that individuals are experiencing will lead to a discussion of PTSD. We then explain that our understanding of PTSD and the symptom clusters that occur can be addressed by specific psychological treatments. This is done with a sample dialogue such as the one that follows:

> We see PTSD as having four main clusters of symptoms. These symptom clusters include (a) *intrusive reexperiencing* of the trauma; (b) *avoidance* of either thoughts, situations, or feelings related to the trauma and *avoidance* of situations and behaviors that remind one of the trauma, and an inability to remember some parts of the trauma; (c) *psychic numbing* or depression (feeling cut off, less engaged in the world than one used to be), loss of interest in previously enjoyed activities; and (c) *hyperarousal* where physiologically the body is now much more aroused or pumped up and one is prone to startle, to have increased heart rate, difficulty concentrating, be more irritable, and have more sleep difficulties than before the trauma.
>
> Treatment will include the systematic application of psychological techniques to modify or deal with each of these four symptom clusters. People with these particular clusters of symptoms, as we've said earlier, are believed to be suffering from posttraumatic stress disorder (PTSD). You may have heard or read about PTSD in connection with Vietnam War veterans or with rape or assault victims or even survivors of natural disasters. In our work we have found that as many as 40% of MVA victims who are injured and seek medical attention will have PTSD or a mild form of it following their trauma.
>
> If you remember, you have had symptoms (recall the list of symptoms that was reviewed earlier) _____. What we are going to do in our treatment is to target our intervention around helping each of those symptoms of PTSD. To do that, let me first explain what we believe leads to PTSD.

In the initial session we discussed the diagnosis of PTSD, and what that means, as well as other populations of survivors with PTSD that they may be more familiar with. As you see, we also let them know that based on our earlier work, as many as 40% of the MVA survivors who had sought medical treatment for their MVA will either have PTSD or a milder form of it shortly after the trauma. This is meant to reassure and to put the symptoms into context of what is normal in an abnormal situation.

The next major focus in the first session is to provide a psychological understanding of PTSD. We have tended to use Mowrer's (1947) and Keane et al.'s (1985) two-factor theory of PTSD. Although there are a number of other models that could be used, we have found these explanations easy to explain, and they lend themselves to a ready explanation of the treatments that we use to help the survivors. The model also normalizes why their avoidance is understandable. It also gives a rationale about why the exposure treatment that they will be asked to engage in will theoretically address the symptoms in that particular avoidance cluster that are disruptive to their functioning. Again, a dialogue made be something such as this:

As stated earlier, the reexperiencing symptoms are a normal reaction to trauma. It is important to understand that what you are going through is what a lot of people go through. Subsequently, this does not mean that you are "going crazy" or that you are losing control and entering into a psychotic process or doing anything that is necessarily out of the ordinary. Almost everyone who has been in a traumatic accident will experience some of these symptoms. This quite understandably can lead to a fearful response. Subsequently, fear can be thought of, in this instance, as a conditioned or learned response to driving or traveling, or other memories and reactions to the accident. The first factor was a scary, terrifying accident. The fear reactions to this real threat can then generalize to additional stimuli that are reminiscent of the trauma and driving, such as thoughts, symbols on TV, sounds, and so forth; these things can then produce the same or similar responses. These anxiety and fear responses are conditioned or associated or connected to a large array of stimuli through an automatic conditioning or learning process so that one can have a very significant reaction seemingly almost out of the blue.

The second factor in this model is that the avoidance response will further the learning. By this we mean that because there is such a strong reaction to the stimuli, people learn to escape or decrease that reaction by avoiding the situations that will produce it. People, therefore, learn to escape the negative feelings or behaviors that would have occurred had they come face-to-face with things that provoke these anxiety feelings. Once people learn to avoid or escape these situations, the avoidance behavior will continue to be supported by the reduction of the fear or anxiety. You get a brief period where the anxiety is lessened, and this feels so positive and is understandable, that more of it will happen. It makes sense, who would want to stay in a situation that makes you feel awful or anxious? (Most people try to avoid fear arousing or threatening situations except for some that are acceptable, such as horror movies, bungee jumping, scary rides, etc.)

Subsequently, what you have been doing is normal in that you are trying to avoid painful feelings that most others would also try to avoid. However, to get better, much of the treatment will be teaching you methods so you can master these anxiety and fear responses and thereby face the situations with greater control and less symptomatic response.

For each of the symptom clusters there will be an intervention or part of the treatment designed to help you master those particular symptoms. This may include a number of behaviors that you are currently not engaging in for a variety of reasons. We will be getting to these later.

Relaxation Training

The last goal of the first session is the provision of relaxation training. We have used a 16 muscle group relaxation during the first session that is easy to learn and easy to demonstrate. The procedures we used are consistent with those described in Bernstein and Borkovec's *Progressive Relaxation Training Manual* (1973). The relaxation training is explained as a skill that will take some time to learn. Therefore, we want to get started as soon as possible. A description of the 16-muscle groups relaxation can be found in Appendix C. Again, this part of the session is introduced in the following way:

Relaxation training is a very old, well-studied method of treating anxiety and fear. What we mean by relaxation is different from what most people generally refer to as relaxation. We refer to relaxation as a specific, physiological adaptation that is a learned skill. Relaxation training consists of teaching that skill by first systematically tensing and then relaxing the major muscle groups of the body. After going through a series of tension-release exercises, and paying careful attention to those sensations, most people are able to learn to feel a subjective sense of deep relaxation. With practice you will be able to learn to become deeply relaxed very quickly. The goal, in fact, will be to teach you to relax deeply and quickly throughout the course of treatment. Once you learn how to deeply relax we will be able to have you apply this relaxation skill to those anxiety-provoking and feared situations and tolerate them much more easily. Physiologically, it is difficult to have significant anxiety when one is in a relaxed state.

It is important to remember that learning relaxation is like learning to ride a bicycle. It is a motor skill. It is essential that you practice this regularly. As you practice, you will begin to recognize how tension develops in your body early on, so you will be more readily able to lower that subjective sense of tension and have ways to cope with it when it arises. We will be asking you to practice the relaxation twice per day. Remember that this is what we have found to be optimal for learning the skill. The exercises take about 15 to 20 minutes each time. They get progressively shorter as you gain skill. If you cannot practice twice a day, once per day is acceptable but is not as beneficial as the twice-per-day routine. In general, like any skill, the more you practice the more benefit the training will have for you.

We then demonstrate the muscle groups used in the exercise for the patient. If applicable, we show the patient how to adapt the tense–release step for possible physical injuries. It is explained what they should be doing (and thinking) during the exercise and, that if there are physical injuries, to use flexibility and adaptation in using the skill. We try to focus on the contrast between tension and subjective relaxation after the muscle is released. Patients are told, "You don't need to strain or aggravate a muscle to get benefit. It is the contrast and focus we are after during this first exercise." We remind patients to pay attention because they will be keeping their eyes closed initially during the training session so they can better attend to the internal changes as they occur. See Appendix C for a description of the 16-muscle group exercise used during the session.

The sequence of muscle tension used for the 16-muscle group exercise is hand and lower arm (right, left, then both together); upper arm (right, left, then both together); lower leg and foot (right, left, then both together); thighs and hips (both simultaneously); abdomen (drawn in); chest and breathing; shoulders, upper neck, back of neck, lips, eyes, lower forehead, and upper forehead. Have the patient remove glasses and loosen any tight clothing. Demonstrate the tension–release cycle with the right arm. Inform the patient that he or she needs to pay attention to the sensations when they are first tensing and relaxing various muscle groups, again focusing on the contrast between the two sensations. Caution them not to tense too hard and because that could possibly cause more pain to any physical injury. Rather, they should tense enough to create tension so that they will demonstrate to themselves a clear difference and be able to remember the difference between muscle tension and relaxation.

Following the relaxation training the therapist rates the patient on the Behavioral Relaxation Rating Scale (BRRS; Poppen, 1988). After the therapist rates the patient's level of relaxation, gradually alert the patient to end the relaxation exercise. Then have the patient use a 10-point scale (0 = not relaxed, 10 = extremely relaxed). Give the patient an audio-taped copy of the exercise. This can either be made as the therapist is instructing the patient in the technique or it can be prepared ahead of time.

Written Description of the MVA Assignment

We conclude the first session by requesting the patient to provide, by the next session, a written description of his or her MVAs. We stress that what we are asking is different from a "police report" of the facts; rather, "It is a full description of the event as you remember it. The description should include what happened, where it happened, how or why it occurred, as well as any memories, images, sights, sounds, smells, or anything else that stands out in your recollection, even if it seems insignificant to you at this point. All memories may serve as a bridge back to the MVA memories."

We emphasize that this is not an "English assignment," but rather a critical aspect of gathering the details to aid the treatment of their anxiety and intrusive thoughts. We tell the patient not to worry about the sentence structure or the grammar. They can do this task chronologically if it is best for them, or in fragments as they remember the details. We reassure them that this may be, in fact, a very hard assignment for them because thinking about the MVA and remembering it are things that they may currently be avoiding. We remind them, however, that the price of avoidance, as per the two-factor theory of PTSD, is a subsequent increase and maintenance of those symptoms. This part of treatment, therefore, is seen as a beginning step in taking charge of the symptoms, organizing them, and confronting the memories that perpetuate their discomfort. This part of treatment is introduced as follows:

> The next aspect of treatment will use exposure to your memories of the motor vehicle trauma. What we are asking at this point is for you to provide a written description, in your own words, of what happened. This will not be just the facts of what happened, where it happened or how or why it occurred, but is as full description of the event as you can recall it. We are asking for your memories, images, sights, sounds, smells, any part of the MVA that stands out. It is much like a snapshot that is taken at a moment where small details might be focused on just because of the part of the accident you are attending to, or any other aspect of the trauma, even though to you it may be insignificant. Subsequently, pay as much attention as you can to those events and details, to write a personalized description of what you went through and your reactions. This should include not only what you were thinking and feeling as well as what you did; it should include everything that was going on. Be sure to include what led up to the accident, what occurred during the accident in detail and any subsequent details. Please write it out in as much detail as you can and bring it with you on our next visit. Typically, one to three pages of text is recommended.
>
> It is not important that this be a prize-winning essay. You do not even have to write complete sentences; in fact, short phrases will do if that is your style. Please remember your unique details. This description of the accident will become a very important part of treatment. We will be using this to elaborate those aspects that might be contributing to any ongoing anxiety and provide intervention for those thoughts or memories. We will also be using it to build a behavioral program as well as to formulate possible cognitive ways to help you with what you are thinking about the accident. These interventions will be based on the details that are gathered in this first exercise as well as on our ongoing efforts related to driving and the accident.
>
> It is important that we both realize that this request may be hard for you to complete. In fact, what you are being asked to do is to

confront something that may be much easier to avoid. As we discussed today, avoidance has carried the price of continuing the symptoms and not letting you get better. So, if this takes several attempts before it is finished, that is understandable. You may need to start with one effort and go back to it again and perhaps, again. We are not looking so much for a polished, finished work but a work that has as much detail as you can provide.

Some patients will complain that they do not write very well. If this occurs, repeat the material above—that "it does not have to be a prize winning essay—and does not have to be in complete or polished sentences, but it does need to be done."

Treatment Parameters and Focus of Intervention

Treatment session concludes with any limits or boundaries that are placed in treatment being reviewed and agreed to by both the patient and therapist. For example, if the treatment will not address that the patient is dealing with the chronic pain problem, a marital problem, or an ongoing problem that is also adding to the stress of the patient, this needs to be specified and explained. We explicitly tell patients with continuing pain and reduced mobility or range of motion that the treatment, in fact, is not designed to help their pain or relieve their physical injuries. We do tell them, however, that if treatment is successful, it *may* enable them to cope with the pain problem better. A sample dialogue might be something like:

> Before we end there is one other point we should cover. The focus of the treatment will be primarily on the psychological reactions to the MVA that you are experiencing. I realize that you are also in significant pain–discomfort, but I am not pursuing a treatment designed to help with that. Although some of the skills such as the relaxation may help a bit with pain-related muscle tension; also improvement in mood has also been shown to help some people dealing with pain. These areas of pain, of necessity, will have to be dealt with outside of our meetings, with your doctor or physical therapist. Is that clear and agreeable? Good! Now we have a lot to do. I'll see you next week.

The parameters of treatment in private practice, in fact, probably will allow the patient to receive medication from a treatment physician–psychiatrist or to attend group treatment or couples therapy elsewhere. Obviously, these were not allowed in our treatment studies. As summarized in chapter 17, we believe the CBT treatment is an effective intervention. The exigencies of real life and providing care for a complicated disorder will require flexibility and creativity in treatment. The structure of this chapter should be seen more as a guideline than anything else. In managed care settings this approach might involve a behavioral contract around symptom reduction, and then delineate any limitations that might be done in the treatment planning at this time (e.g. "We will meet for 8 to 10 sessions and evaluate the progress at that time. If things need to continue at that point, we will proceed. If things are not proceeding as anticipated, we will re-evaluate your treatment needs then").

Homework

The patient is encouraged to practice the assigned homework– relaxation training twice daily (an audiotape is provided for home practice of the relaxation exercise that may be made either at the time that they are instructed or ahead of time if that is the therapist's inclination) and to write out a thorough description of their MVA.

To encourage the completion of these tasks, a homework diary is given to each patient. Patients are asked to record whether they practiced the relaxation once or twice each day, and to record on a 0–10 scale how relaxed they were by the end of the exercise (0 = not relaxed, 10 = extremely relaxed). The additional tasks on the homework sheet are briefly mentioned as tasks they will be doing when they are ready, but for now they are to disregard those sections of the worksheet. A separate sheet with the instructions for writing out the MVA description is also provided at the end of the session. (See Figure 18.1.)

Each patient is questioned about the availability of a tape recorder for using the relaxation tape, and if there are any possible obstacles, such a place to practice, child care, and so forth. These are problem-solved before the end of the session. Patients are encouraged to call if there is any need, even clarifying instructions, and a return appointment is set for the next week. (See Exhibit 18.1 for a checklist of first-session tasks.)

EXHIBIT 18.1
Checklist for Session 1

_____ 1. Review MVA description
_____ 2. Review PTSD rationale and treatment rationale
_____ 3. Introduce 16-muscle group relaxation
_____ 4. Provide patient with tape of 16-muscle group relaxation
_____ 5. Rating scale of patient response to relaxation completed (BRRS)
_____ 6. Patient rating of relaxation completed
_____ 7. Homework assigned to: (a) write out MVA description, (b) practice and rate relaxation.
_____ 8. Give homework sheet to patient and explain it.

Note. BRRS = Behavioral Relaxation Rating Scale.

Subject name: _____

Homework Diary

	Day						
	Mon.	Tues.	Wed.	Thurs.	Fri.	Sat.	Sun.
ACTIVITY Date							
Relaxation practice Number of times completed							
How relaxed? (0–10)							
Number of times completed							
How relaxed? (0–10)							
Read MVA description aloud How many times?							
Travel behavior Attempted							
SUDS							
Attempted							
SUDS							
Pleasurable activity Attempted							

Figure 18.1. Homework diary. Relaxation rating: 0 = not relaxed; 10 = extremely relaxed. SUDS rating (Subjective Units of Discomfort): 0 = not at all distressed, 10 = extremely distressed, panic.

SESSION 2

Reading and Elaboration of MVA Description

The second session begins with the patient reading and elaborating on his or her written description of the MVA. The therapist, as necessary, can ask questions or make comments to elicit as thorough a response as the survivor can produce. The patient reads the description aloud, and the therapist looks to round out the scene. It is important to include details of the injuries, pain, long-term consequences, loss of vehicle, continued physical problems, as well as thoughts and fears, and so forth, as the description is read. It is also important to note and be able to point out to the patient his or her reaction to the scene, particularly where he or she exhibits discomfort. Remind the patient that it is normal to want to avoid certain aspects of the scene that can lead to discomfort, but that it is good he or she can approach it. Tell the patient that this procedure of reading and remembering the accident will be of considerable importance to full recovery. If there are omissions, mistakes, or errors, these should be acknowledged, as should positive aspects of the outcome and experiences. An illustration of this process is as follows.

Clinical Hint

Occasionally a patient will claim to have "forgotten" the writing assignment. Our recommended response to this situation is to forcefully, but gently, emphasize that the written description is a very important part of treatment, and that the patient *must* do it for the next session.

> That was a very good description. Thank you. What I would like to do, however, is to spend some time going back and reviewing some of the particular details of the accident. You wrote about a page and many of the details from start to finish are very vague. What I would like you to do is go back now, go through the description with me out aloud, elaborating for me how you were feeling, some of the thoughts you were having, and some of the particulars about what happened. For instance, as you were sitting in the car waiting for the emergency people to get you out, I remember your saying at the first session that you were very scared at that time and thought you might die. That is exactly the kind of thing that needs to be put into your description. Are there other thoughts that come to mind as we think back to that particular time? . . . I also would like you to elaborate on some of the feelings you had as you were riding in the ambulance on the way to the hospital. Those details were left out here and I remember that those were very powerful for you. The time you were lying on the gurney in the emergency room was also very provoking for you. How could you put that into the story?"

We find it helps to ask, and to acknowledge, that writing the description was very hard. We again remind each patient that the memory of the MVA is something that he or she carries in a personal way. We remind patients that it is important to think about or remember those aspects of the accident that they may have been avoiding.

The patient is then asked, as part of homework, to read the description *aloud* several times per day to themselves (three times each day at least). They are instructed to add any new memories that occur as they review the accident and to elaborate the written descriptions as the new memories occur. (We believe that reading the MVA description aloud engages more attention and focuses attention on the specific memories.)

One variation of this is to have patients record their MVA description on an audiotape. Foa's group has used this approach with rape victims, and we have occasionally used this same method more recently with MVA accident survivors. We also know from our work with physiological assessments that auditory stimuli tend to be a strong provocation for physiological and subjective distress. Therefore, the use of these types of stimuli is particularly useful for a daily exposure that the patient can control and use in his or her home.

One clear advantage of the written method is it provides a record that can be copied and stored in a chart. The record then is available each session and does not rely on the patient to bring the tape or description with him or her. Reading aloud also allows easy modification of details as the story is told and retold. Audiotapes can be made during the session and then provided for the patient to listen to at home. Tapes can be forgotten by the patient if they need to bring them to the next session for review. Although it is possible to have a high-speed recorder available, one can see the possible inconvenience the tape versus the written method necessitates. We believe also it is harder for the patient to avoid the material if he or she reads it aloud. It also seems to allow for an incorporation of the material into shorter and better-managed pieces that is consistent with our cognitive approach to treatment.

Discussion of Avoidance

A discussion of avoidance and its place in the development and continuation of PTSD is then provided. It is emphasized again how this avoidance is normal, that it does not signify weakness but rather is a normal effort at adaptation. Unfortunately, the avoidance has the undesirable effect, as explained at the first session, of ultimately worsening, rather than improving, the PTSD symptoms. An example of this might be as follows:

> As we explained during the first session, we believe that the nature of posttraumatic stress disorder symptoms naturally leads to avoiding the accident site and any other reminders that would contribute to negative feelings and anxiety. However, the most recognized intervention to overcome these fears and anxieties and any subsequent avoidances is by systematically facing a feared situation through exposure. Although some of this will be done during our sessions through verbal description, treatment will again focus either on in vivo, or real life, exposure or on imaginal exposure using those descriptions with just your words and images. This gradual exposure will help you access the cognitive networks of cues and thoughts that relate to anxiety and its arousal. We will be talking about that more in the next few weeks.

Again, each patient is reminded how avoidance develops, how it is normal, and that, to overcome it, he or she will be asked to face these situations both as a driver and as a passenger. The therapist acknowledges how difficult this may be but insists that this needs to be done. We reassure each patient that this will be done gradually in small manageable steps and that he or she will be prepared to succeed. It is important that each patient understand that he or she will have to rely on his or her own fortitude to persevere and confront difficult aspects of PTSD symptoms during anxious times and places driving.

Including the Significant Other

The patients are encouraged to bring their partners in during the next (third) session. The rationale is that the symptoms the patients are exhibiting and the treatments we will be using to help them may also affect their partners. We reassure patients that partners are only told what is agreed on to share regarding their particular symptoms. The partners are given a general education about anxiety and how avoidance symptoms develop. Ideally, this will then lead to a nonjudgmental method of helping the partner help the patient with his or her ongoing homework. Exposure homework will be discussed in detail as it relates to driving or facing fearful situations. Patients need to be reminded that they should only be doing this exposure, however, once they have learned relaxation. Again, remind them how relaxation is an important skill, their regular and ongoing practice of the relaxation will give them this critical skill.

Relaxation Training

Relaxation training is repeated within the session. Once patients have learned the exercise, it is important to help them understand that, in a relaxed state, they can now begin to think about those situations that ordinarily provoke them. But they will feel less arousal when using relaxation. If they have not begun to learn the skills (through regular home practice), we will need to be certain that they do so before we can proceed with the next phase of treatment. We begin the relaxation early so that they will have the time to acquire sufficient skill to allow us to begin an exposure-based treatment. They need to practice regularly so they can gain that ability. Regular home practice cannot be stressed too much. The goal is to have each patient relax quicker and deeper as they gain in skill. They are told that this will be accomplished by progressively using shorter relaxation inductions in subsequent sessions. If the patient is having trouble acquiring relaxation skills, as indicated by not reporting relatively deep relaxation within session, this is investigated immediately. If patients are not practicing regularly, discuss why and stress the need for regular practice.

Homework Sheets

The homework sheet is reviewed again, and now patients are requested to complete the number of times they read the MVA description on a daily basis in addition to continuing to record the number of times they practiced the relaxation and to rate their level of subjective relaxation at the end of each effort. Make sure they are completing the homework sheet, because this adds to the compliance with the exercise. (See Exhibit 18.2.)

EXHIBIT 18.2
Checklist for Session 2

_____ 1. Complete/elaborate MVA description (keeping copy for chart)
_____ 2. Discuss role of avoidance in PTSD
_____ 3. Ask that significant other come to next session
_____ 4. Repeat 16-muscle relaxation
_____ 5. Patient rating of relaxation completed
_____ 6. Therapist rating of patient's relaxation completed (BRRS)
_____ 7. Give additional homework sheets

Note. BRRS = Behavioral Relaxation Rating Scale.

SESSION 3

Every session begins with a review of the homework that the patient had been asked to complete us to this point. This session begins with (a) patient reading his or her description of the MVA and reviewing the patient's reactions. The patients are to elaborate or note any changes as they read and react to their reading. (b) Any reactions, especially negative reactions within the MVA, or related descriptions are discussed. This material is used as a lead into the self-talk treatment rationale introduced during this session.

It is in the third session that patients are introduced to coping self-statements and how to replace negative thoughts and feelings that contribute to the anxiety and avoidance with more positive thoughts. As per Meichenbaum's (1985) Stress Inoculation Training (SIT), the patients are instructed in ways they can use coping self-statements. These methods are (a) to help prepare for situations that they are able to predict will be potentially stressful (e.g., when they are to return to the scene of the MVA, or ride in a car, or go to their lawyer's office for a deposition); (b) during a stressful situation as a way to talk their way through it (e.g., as they are driving, watching a movie, seeing a friend who had been injured in the crash); and (c) after the stressful situation is over, as a way of rewarding themselves or improving how they coped with the situation. An example of how this is introduced is as follows:

By now it should have become obvious that there are thoughts and feelings that are experienced before, during, and after stressful situations. As you are also more and more aware, many of these thoughts and feelings are negative. The purpose of part of our session today is to teach you about coping self-statements and to try to replace the negative thoughts and feelings, which contribute to anxiety and avoidance, with more positive thoughts.

This may feel somewhat artificial at first, because you are deliberately (rather than spontaneously) altering your thoughts and internal dialogue. But bear with me; as you will see, it will work.

There are three ways that one can use coping self-statement. (a) You may use positive thoughts or statements to help prepare yourself for potentially stressful situations whenever you are able to predict ahead of time that a situation will be hard or stressful. There will be times when you know you will be driving in a difficult spot, or perhaps meeting with a lawyer or facing a situation that has been anxiety provoking in the past. (b) You can use the coping statements during a stressful situation as a way to talk yourself through it. (c) Finally, you can use coping self-statements when the stressful situation is over by rewarding yourself for the way in which you coped with the situation.

Many times it will be possible to predict ahead of time when an anxiety-provoking situation is going to occur. In fact, in a moment we are going to develop a list of some situations that you are currently avoiding or that set the stage for fear and anxiety for you. We will also have you rank those. During those situations you will be able to begin to apply some of the coping statements to get through them. These may occur either while driving or riding in a car, when you are seeing something that reminds you of the accident, having nightmares, or whenever or wherever these moments happen.

Fortunately, we are able to predict some things that will be occurring even before the time, but unfortunately, we may spend a great deal of time worrying beforehand, anticipating with catastrophic thoughts, things that begin with "what ifs." Rather than worry, we are going to have you begin to spend some of the time thinking more positively about the event, focusing your attention on the skills you already have to deal with the demands of that situation. Some examples of self-statements that can be used before a situation include, "What is it I have to do? What kind of plan can I develop to handle this? The situation is not impossible, I can handle this and get through it"; "Stop worrying, worrying isn't going to help anyway"; "I have a great number of resources that I can use to deal with this."

In particular, you need to remind yourself that you are a good driver (if the patient was) and a careful and safe driver. (If the MVA occurred because of a driver's carelessness or risk-taking, this can be reframed as "You know what went wrong in the MVA and you can avoid that in the future.")

"Secondly, there isn't time to deal with the stressful situation before it occurs. Things happen we couldn't plan for. Then it's important to remember that you don't need to panic and think about all of the bad things that can happen; rather you can focus your attention on what you need to do and what is happening at the moment." This is done one step at a time. Here are some examples of self-statements to use during a stressful situation that you couldn't plan for ahead of time. "I can deal with this situation if I just do one step at a time." " I've gotten through these situations before; they are not going to overwhelm me; it just feels that way at times." "I can see this situation as a challenge or opportunity to improve rather than viewing it negatively as an impending disaster." "These are the things I need to do to get through the situation (then list the steps)."

Finally, there are times where the situation is over and one can review the progress one has made. This is suggested in the following way:

When the stressful situation is over, you should not dwell on it but rather you should try to evaluate it and learn from the experience. Whatever worked, pay attention to that. If something did not work, how might it have been done differently? Remember, it is important not to punish yourself for being less than perfect, but instead to recognize your effort and the small or large improvements that are taking place. Remember to reward yourself for what was done right, the ways you improved by using these positive self-statements. Some examples of these self-statements might be: "I made a good effort." "I'm learning how to deal with the situation more effectively, it takes time." "I knew I could handle this but it does take more time than one would like." "This task was hard for me but I did it." "I did some of this very well, but there are still some parts of it I need to improve on."

The therapist should note at times that patients have a tendency to denigrate their own efforts by saying things such as, "Anyone could have done that." The therapist at these times can intervene by saying, "You are not just anyone, what you did was hard for you and you need to give yourself appropriate credit." "I know it was hard and I applaud you for that, and you need to learn how to applaud yourself at these times as well."

Finally, this session is concluded by saying something such as, "In order to learn coping self-statements effectively, you will need to practice. Using the coping self-statements is a skill like any other skill we are trying to teach you. The more you practice, the more automatic it will become. Become familiar with how you can do this and how you don't do this. It is also important to understand the situation that is causing those negative thoughts. But first we need to have you develop a better understanding of what you are avoiding and what situations are causing the most problems."

A sample of coping statements specific for MVA survivors can be found in Figure 18.2.

Instructions: Below you will find some sample statements that you can say to yourself in place of negative "automatic" thoughts that may occur in stressful situations. You can print out this page and keep it with you as a reminder or you can put a copy in a prominent place until you become familiar with the technique. If you don't find these stress-coping statements helpful, there is space on the sheet to add your own. Feel free to try different statements in different situations until you find some that work.

1. *In preparation for stressful situations that you can predict will occur, try the following:*

   (a) "What is the specific thing I have to do?"
   (b) "What plan can I develop for dealing with this?"
   (c) "This situation is not impossible—I can handle this."
   (d) "Don't worry—Worrying isn't going to help anyway."
   (e) "I have a great many resources—I can put them to use in this situation."
   (f) "What am I scared of?"
   (g) "I have a lot of support from people who deal with this problem a lot."

2. *During the course of a stressful situation, try the following (confrontation and coping):*

   (a) "I can manage this situation, if I just do one step at a time."
   (b) "I've gotten through tougher situations that this before—This will not overwhelm me—it just feels that way at times."
   (c) "I can see this situation as a challenge or as an opportunity to improve rather than as an annoyance or burden."
   (d) "These are the specific things I need to do to get through the situation" (then list the steps)."
   (e) "Relax, calm down—I'm in control of this—take a slow, deep breath."
   (f) "Let's keep focused on the present—What do I have to do?"
   (g) "The feelings are a signal to use the coping skills I'm learning—I can expect the fear to rise, but it will not stop or overwhelm me—Think—this feeling will pass, it always has."

3. *After the situation is over, try the following:*

   (a) "Whatever worked, pay attention to it."
   (b) "Don't be so hard on myself, rather recognize the good effort and any improvement, large or small."
   (c) "All things considered, I did a good job."
   (d) "I'm learning how to deal with that situation more effectively—the next time, I'll be even better."
   (e) "I knew I could handle this—it just takes some time, patience, and effort."
   (f) "I am making progress."

Figure 18.2. Positive coping self-statements.

An example of the use of coping self-statements would be as follows: A patient expressed difficulty returning to the scene of her MVA. She knew she had to pass the scene of the MVA because of a return visit home for the holidays. The MVA had occurred when visiting her parents over the Thanksgiving weekend. To help prepare for the trip, the patient tried to predict what the scene would be like. She knew it would be a fast highway, because her parents lived on Long Island. She reminded herself that she had, in fact, grown up in that same region of the country, and for many years had driven the highways. She developed a plan (similar to how she learned to drive the highways around her home), of staying in a particular lane, reminding herself of how long it was between exits, and using coping statements (such as those found in Figure 18.2), that this was something she could handle. She told herself, "This is a difficult, but not impossible, situation. There is no need to worry about the event before it has actually even occurred."

To talk her way through the situation, she broke the necessary tasks into manageable steps. She reminded herself that, when she feels she is about to be overwhelmed, in fact, she has managed high levels of anxiety before and now holds even more newly developed skills (e.g., relaxation and coping self-statements) to talk her way through the time on the highway.

Last, she was reminded that whatever happens, it will help her improvement overall. If all goes well, she will gain in confidence. The exposure *will*, in all likelihood, create some anxiety, which is exactly what she is trying to do. This will allow her to learn how to manage it better. The last reminder was to tell herself that this takes time, and that by making this effort she is furthering her overall improvement. At this point the avoidance hierarchy is introduced.

Avoidance Hierarchy

The patient is instructed in how to develop a graduated list of travel tasks for in vivo exposure. The patient, with the therapist, negotiates the first steps to the hierarchy to be used as homework. It is important to introduce to the patient the Subjective Units of Discomfort Scale (SUDS) and how to record them for situations over the next week. We have tended to use a 0–100 SUDS scale, where 0 = no discomfort and 100 = great, almost overwhelming discomfort. It is often helpful to begin this assignment using examples generated from the patient in earlier meetings or at this time during this session. Generally we have the patient describe three to five situations. The patient is then instructed over the next week to continue developing the list until they have 10 to 15 scenes or situations in total. Each situation is to be rated on the SUDS scale. It is important that the

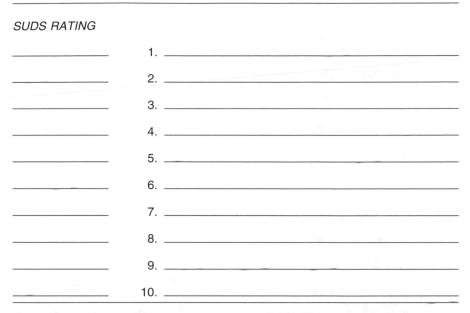

SUDS RATING

_____	1.	_____
_____	2.	_____
_____	3.	_____
_____	4.	_____
_____	5.	_____
_____	6.	_____
_____	7.	_____
_____	8.	_____
_____	9.	_____
_____	10.	_____

Figure 18.3. Avoidance hierarchy. 0 = no discomfort; 100 = great discomfort.

therapist continues until it is clear that the patient is able to rate and find situations that are both on the lower end of the scale, in the middle of the scale, and at the upper end of the scale. An example of an avoidance hierarchy can be found in Figure 18.3.

We have had a number of common situations that are frequently avoided. These can be found in Figure 18.4. This list can be provided to the patients as a prompt, which may or may not be appropriate for them to look over and maybe add some examples to their personal list.

Meeting With Significant Other

During the third session, we try to formally meet with the significant other. In clinical practice, it is also important to meet with the significant other as part of the evaluation before treatment. This meeting with the significant other allows one to gain a fuller sense of the impact of the MVA on the patient's behavior and home life and to understand what resources exist or not, to aid in treatment. Some spouses may, in fact, be taking over a great number of the roles, which include shopping, driving children to activities, dropping spouses off to work that may have been part of the MVA survivor's usual role before the MVA. This help may have started

1. Driving past the scene of the accident.

2. Riding as a passenger in a car.

3. Seeing an MVA on TV or in the movies.

4. Seeing a photo of an accident in the newspaper.

5. Hearing an accident described on television.

6. Having acquaintances ask about the MVA or how you're doing since the accident.

7. Going through a deposition related to the MVA.

8. Driving on highways.

9. Driving in congested areas.

10. Driving in bad weather (snow, dark, rain, etc.).

11. Riding in the back seat of a car.

Figure 18.4. List of typically avoided situations for MVA survivors.

because the patient was physically hurt and it was a supportive gesture to make. Unfortunately, this seemingly helpful act may, in fact, be perpetuating the problem by being overly helpful and allowing the MVA survivor to avoid potentially anxiety-provoking situations. It is also important to corroborate the symptoms that the patient is exhibiting, first for accuracy and also for potential distortions in perception that would be helpful in setting up a cognitive–behavioral intervention.

As we discussed in an earlier chapter (see chapter 13), the meeting may be extremely valuable for forensic use if one will be called on to testify as an expert in the case. It is often the case that even if one is providing clinical treatment the treating psychologist or therapist will be called as an expert witness in a personal injury lawsuit because the therapist has gained a great amount of knowledge about the patient. The better one can substantiate the information one has gained, how it was gained, and how that led to one's intervention, can all be critical in personal injury cases.

The major goals, however, of bringing the significant other to treatment is to gain an ally, or in the very worst case scenario to help a spouse not become an inadvertent obstacle, in the treatment of the patient with PTSD. The first portion of the joint session is providing information about PTSD, what it is, how often it occurs, and how it is treated. This information is given in a general fashion, again being sensitive to the limit of confidentiality agreed to by the patient. It is easy at this point, however, to share the symptoms that the significant other has described and relate them back to the definition of PTSD and the psychological treatment.

The goals of meeting the significant other, therefore, include first learning the spouse's perception of the MVA's impact on the patient and the family. This can range from discussions of drastic changes in sleep, driving, mood, change in libido (all of which can drastically impact even strong marriages), to the significant other being surprised that his or her partner entered treatment at all. We, in fact, have seen patients who covered up from significant others, until they were asked to bring them into a session, the fact that they were even in psychological treatment. In these latter situations, the significant other is of course surprised that the patient met the criteria for any type of psychiatric disorder. Thus, the importance of the meeting cannot be overemphasized. This part of the session obviously reflects a pattern of interaction between significant others and how sharing between partners may or may not occur. This can often help the therapist better know how to proceed within treatment.

Second, and with the patient's willingness to divulge information, the symptoms and overview of treatment can be provided more specifically. The goal is to try to enlist the significant others' support and understanding. Significant others are given an explanation of what PTSD is and the role conditioning, learning, and avoidance plays in its presentation and continuation. It is at this time that we begin to discuss how the significant other–spouse–friend will be asked to be a "potential partner" in treatment. By this we mean that, because their partners (the patients) will be deliberately exposed to feared–anxiety provoking situations, it is useful for the person closest to them to be aware of why and how these situations will be mastered. Even if they are only aware of this taking place, one hopes the significant others would be better prepared to allow the patients access to cars, child care, and other support as a way of helping provide more effective treatment. There will be times when the partner with PTSD will need privacy for relaxation and some support and encouragement to do things that are difficult.

Ideally, the significant other will also be used as a driver at times for the partner in specified ways, because many MVA victims are often afraid and fearful when riding in the passenger seat. In fact, giving up the control as a driver is often one of the feared situations that are a necessary part of any exposure-based intervention. Obviously, the better prepared and supportive the partner can be in this situation, the more successful treatment will become. It is important that they do not become "junior therapists" as part of helping the patient. We emphasize that the MVA victim stays in charge of what is needed, how to best deliver this information, and to use the therapist in any way possible to facilitate these steps when and if they become needed. We clearly state we want the significant others to be the best partners they can for each other at this time. Our goal is for the partner to understand the disorder, how the patient is trying to get better, how difficult that can be, and how to use the relationship as partners to support that process.

A plan is then formulated as to how the partners may need to interact differently (i.e., to be encouraging and positive at best; to be neutral or not an obstacle at worst), when the patient is requested as part of his or her treatment to seek out difficult or avoided situations. Partners can play a potentially large and often central role in a survivor's life. As stated earlier this can lead to the partner's "helpful behavior" such as driving the patient everywhere, or doing the "extra driving errands," which will inadvertently limit the patient's potential exposure. This situation can arise by doing nothing more than trying to be a helpful and understanding partner. At worst, partners can be negative and hostile toward the behaviors that have occurred since the MVA. Because they do not understand why their significant others (the patients) are acting the way they are, and think they should be over it by now, partners at times can be quite denigrating and harsh in their appraisal of what has changed in their partners and wonder what is wrong with them. They see their partners as acting "crazy" and that there is no good reason why they are not back doing what they used to do.

Clinical Hint

Although we do not have any empirical evidence on the usefulness of bringing the partner into treatment, clinically we believe that the involvement of the spouse can be potentially critical. For example, if a patient is becoming discouraged and his or her PTSD or depression is worsening, the spouse's understanding, watchfulness, and support at those times can be essential. Significant others often will tell the therapist about changes in driving reactions, sleep, and appetite changes, interactions with friends and family members, that patients do not bring up, even when asked. Again, although psychologists need to be aware of the possible distortions from both participants in the session, when the couple is interviewed jointly you often see a reasonable corroboration of details quickly reached. When the situation is viewed quite differently between the partners, the subsequent dialogue has often seemed to be of great help in strengthening and clarifying the overall relationship. There are several instances clinically where this clarification of the relationship, in fact, has been one of the greatest benefits the patient eventually states was realized in treatment.

Relaxation Training

At this point in the third session, the spouse is asked to leave and the patient is introduced to a shortened version of progressive muscle relaxation, eight-muscle relaxation. A copy of this can be found in Appendix C. Eight-muscle relaxation is introduced in the following way:

> As you become more skilled in using the 16-muscle groups relaxation, you should find that relaxation is occurring more quickly and more deeply. It is important, however, to be able to relax more quickly and easily in a variety of situations. In fact, as you are becoming aware, we will be having you in situations that can evoke a great deal of anxiety. Rather than having you leave the situation for 15 to 20 minutes to tense and relax 16 muscle groups and then return, you will need to learn how to relax quickly and deeply. The next step in learning how to do this is to decrease the number of muscle groups that you will tense and relax. Today we will be reducing that number to eight. The muscle groups we will be using are both arms together, both legs together, including the hips, abdomen, chest using deep breathing, shoulders, back of neck, eyes and forehead.

An audiotape of this exercise is provided, and homework is encouraged between sessions. The patient's response to the relaxation can be rated on the BRRS scale, and the patient at the conclusion of the exercise is asked to rate his or her subjective level of relaxation, using the same 0–10 scale he or she has been using as part of homework. Any questions or problems are addressed before ending the session.

Homework again is given, and includes reading the MVA description aloud, relaxation practice, use of coping self-statements, and development of an avoidance hierarchy.

Patients are reminded that the goal of treatment is the application of these techniques as they have been learned. By this we mean that they may be driving in a car trying to master those situations that are now provoking them. Often as a bridge, patients are provided a brief imaginal situation drawn from their hierarchy, and the eight-muscle relaxation exercise is used as a method to counter anxiety as it is provoked. This helps reinforce the cognitive stimulus (of the imagined scene) as the provocation, and is a way to show that they hold tools (coping self-statements and relaxation) that can be applied to counter the anxiety as it is provoked. The imaginal exposure is gently introduced at this time to illustrate the method. MVA victims are given the suggestion to try this method as they gain sufficient skill to reduce any anxiety that occurs. This can serve as a bridge and complement to in vivo exposure as that is introduced in the next session. (See Exhibit 18.3.)

EXHIBIT 18.3
Checklist for Session 3

_____ 1. Collect last session homework
_____ 2. Review MVA description
_____ 3. Introduce self-coping statements
_____ 4. Give handouts for:
     (a) Self-coping statements (Figure 18.2)
     (b) Avoidance Hierarchy (Figure 18.3)
     (c) Frequently avoided situations (Figure 18.4)
_____ 5. Meet with significant other
_____ 6. Introduce 8-muscle group relaxation
_____ 7. Have patient rate relaxation
_____ 8. Therapist rates patient's relaxation
_____ 9. Give audiotape for 8-muscle group relaxation exercise
_____10. Give homework sheet to patient

SESSION 4

As with each session, this fourth session begins with a review of how the homework assignments went. The homework list has been growing. Up to this point the homework will include relaxation training, reading of the MVA description, use of coping self-statements in travel situations, and developing the avoidance hierarchy. Each of these needs to be reviewed and any problems discussed and clarified.

As the MVA description is read, it is now possible to use the coping statements before, during, and after the oral rendition. The same is true of the avoidance hierarchy, which will now include the aspects of the exposure exercise that elicits a range of SUDS ratings when the patient confronts the listed events.

It is crucial that attention is paid to progress of the homework up to this point. It is necessary to clear up any misconceptions that could lead to inadvertent heightened anxiety or subsequent escape. Encouragement of steps to this point are critical, and is important to make sure the patient is cooperative and in agreement with the treatment up to this point.

Introduction of Cognitive Reappraisal

The next major treatment intervention is the introduction of cognitive reappraisal. This is introduced as the patient is building on the coping statements learned earlier, as a way of addressing how one thinks about a situation. As they are becoming more and more aware of their thoughts, how they think about a situation can have a significant effect on what they experience and what they subsequently do. The interpretation of a situation and automatic thoughts are then explained as patterns of appraisal that are *learned* (sometimes rapidly as in the case of a traumatic event), and subsequently can be *unlearned*.

We have used the A–B–C–D model of Ellis (1962) and cognitive reappraisal techniques and distortions in thinking such as those described by Aaron Beck (Beck et al., 1979). These distortions can include premature conclusions, reality testing, all or nothing, thinking, overgeneralizations, and so forth. A handout of examples is then provided to each patient. (See Figure 18.5 for an example of such a handout.)

Cognitive reappraisal is introduced as follows:

> As we talked about last time, it is possible to recognize situations that cause problems in the thoughts and feelings and reactions you have in those situations. By trying to use the coping self-statements, it shows how we think about the situation and can determine if it is going to provoke the problem. Therefore, the way that we perceive or deal with situations can change our understanding or interpretation of events. For example, two people can drive on the same stretch of road. One person will have no difficulty at all. The other person can see the amount of traffic or the speed of the traffic as potentially dangerous and, therefore, something that will produce threat. The situation is identical, the perception is different, and as a result the reaction is also different for the two individuals.
>
> We all tend to have characteristic ways of thinking or making inter- pretations of events. Many of us tend to see situations in certain ways. Unfortunately, many of these ways of seeing can be self-defeating, causing us to distort a situation or see it as potentially more harmful or dangerous than it really is. These thinking patterns, however, are sometimes so automatic that we do not even realize that we are doing it. By paying attention to the situations that produce anxiety and our reactions to those situations, we can learn about the self-statements and thoughts that are best viewed as maladaptive ways of thinking and thereby learn to evaluate and change those ways of thinking.

This is a difficult concept for many people to grasp. We spend a great deal of time making sure that people understand how thoughts affect their reactions and draw on past examples from the patient to make this clearer.

An example of this in session is as follows:

Therapist: M, you have talked about how, when you leave the safety of your neighborhood, you find the busy highway that you need to travel to work as very threatening and dangerous. In fact, you had never been in an accident up until the accident that brought you into treatment. You, therefore, were able to make that trip many times without anything negative happening. Now, when you get on the highway, you see the speed and amount of traffic, especially during

Instructions: Below you will find two items that will help remind you how to use the cognitive reappraisal technique. First, the A–B–C–D model depicts what the sequence of events are when you are trying to change an overly negative interpretation about a situation. The Activating Event (A) is what actually happened during the stressful situation: the Belief (B) you have about the situation is how you went about interpreting it; the Consequence (C) are the feelings you had and how you acted in the situation; finally, how you Dispute (D) or reevaluate your "automatic" negative appraisal with the goal of replacing those maladaptive beliefs and perceptions with more realistic and accurate ones is the active part of cognitive reappraisal.

Here is an outline of the cognitive reappraisal model:

A = Activating event (What happened?)
B = Belief (What were you thinking when it happened?)
C = Consequence (How did you feel and what did you do in the situation?)
D = Dispute (How might you challenge the overly negative beliefs?)

We know it takes some time to learn about our thoughts and how they can affect our feelings and behaviors. It is important, however, that you begin to understand how you think about something can have a dramatic effect on how you will feel and what you will be able to do. We often misattribute the difficulty to an external event (the scene of the accident, riding as a passenger, hearing a screech of brakes) as the reason we become anxious or upset. The A–B–C–D model begins the process of showing how it is our thoughts ("I can't stand seeing where the accident occurred. You shouldn't drive that way; it's awful to not have control when in a car. See, another accident almost happened! I told you it's not safe on the road.") lead to the feelings of anxiety, fear, tension, etc., not the event. Some of the fallacies of thinking or distortions can be summarized as a tendency to catastrophize an event, and think of the "what if's" that go along with a situation that could spell out disaster. It doesn't matter that the disaster didn't occur, the fact that it might becomes the focus of your reaction. This tendency to overemphasize danger and minimize safety following a car crash is common, and illustrates how a thought can lead to an undesirable reaction. The same is true that a squeal proves how unsafe it is on the roads (it could be a noisy brake pad, or someone stopping in plenty of time, just overreacting), or now seeing the driver of a car as unsafe because you're not driving, even when the facts are the driver has a very safe record of driving. The thoughts lead to the reaction. Over the next few weeks try to see if you can see where your thoughts might be similar to one of the situations above, or listed on our list of common problem areas. Then see if you can *dispute* the thought, by asking yourself where the proof is for the thought or if there might be other ways, more realistic ways to see the same events. Where is the proof that people should drive the way you think they should? It's true it might be better if they drove slower, less close, etc., but your saying it should be one way won't change the reality of how people will and do drive on the road.

(Practice by using handout on common cognitive distortions and commonly avoided situations).

Figure 18.5. Cognitive reappraisal.

rush hour, as very dangerous. Is it possible that you might be magnifying or overemphasizing the amount of danger that you are actually in?

M: It's possible, but again, if I'm going to have an accident, it is more likely that people are going to mess up at exactly this time!

Therapist: M, is that true? Are you certain that most accidents occur on highways or, in fact, that more accidents occur at slower speeds for a variety of other reasons?

M: I don't really know, it seems that way to me.

Therapist: So at least it is possible that what you have thought about the situation that may, in fact, not be the case.

M: It's possible.

Therapist: In fact, we can look back on your life and say you've driven this road thousands and thousands of times and never had a mishap or that you had seen very few accidents. Is that true, M?

M: Yes, that's true.

Therapist: So, again, if we can help you address the distortions here in your thinking, I think we will be able to help you find ways of helping to modify the amount of anxiety.

We then go on to explain the following ways:

Therapist: There are several maladaptive ways of thinking; some may be more characteristic or true of you than others. Subsequently, we are going to have you pay close attention and learn patterns of how your thinking affects your life. How we would like to do this is by using a very straightforward model developed by Albert Ellis, the A, B, C, D model of how to understand and address our thoughts.

A handout (see Figure 18.6) is then given to the patient, and this model of cognitive intervention is explained.

Examples of activating events are numerous. *Activating events* can include internal physiological states, emotions, and thoughts about the event, news stories, comments from friends and family, and meetings with attorneys, and so forth. Each of these scenes–stimuli are pointed out to the patients by the consequence of the act as it occurs (i.e., how it makes them feel). Most patients can easily identify what happened to make them feel scared, anxious, angry, and so forth. The very process of analyzing the events in this cause–effect manner helps as the therapist explores with patients that the events are not random or without prediction. Some patients will initially

A = Activating event (What happened?)
B = Belief (What were you thinking)
C = Consequence (What emotional and behavioral reaction did you experience?)
D = Dispute (How to challenge your B's)

Distortions in Thinking (Examples)

1. Premature conclusions/jumping to conclusions.
2. Reality testing (i.e., not assuming things to be true, when in fact, they may not be true).
3. All or none/black or white thinking
4. Sweeping generalization.
5. Predicts the future.
6. Mind reading.
7. Overestimating/underestimating.
8. _____

Figure 18.6. Cognitive reappraisal.

argue that there is no clear antecedent stimulus, but they can be brought around. It is certainly true *at times* that the stimuli that set off reactions may not be obvious or definitive. But the process of looking, and the belief and direction the process provides can be extremely important for the patient's regaining control of his or her own emotional and behavioral responses.

Perhaps the most difficult process is helping the patient discern what types of beliefs or images drive his or her own emotional and behavioral reactions. Patients will express ideas such as: "I've escaped being killed *during my first accident*, I won't be as lucky *a second time!*" "I'll never get better, I'm going to feel like this for the rest of my life!" "I can't stand feeling like this, and if anything bad happens again, I'll lose my mind." "If I'm not totally better, I can't function at all." "It's unfair that this happened to me, *it should have happened to other people.*" I'll never get over hating the man that did this to me!" "I just know that something bad will happen again." "I should have been able somehow to make a difference, even leaving a few minutes earlier, or turned the wheel a moment before, it might have saved me all this pain and upset." "I'll never be safe again when I'm behind the wheel or riding in a car. *Safety is just an illusion.* You never know what can happen." "I know what people are thinking, and they hold me responsible for what happened to. . . ."

Each of these beliefs can be challenged by the therapist in a fashion determined by the context of the therapeutic relationship. As Beck et al. (1979) have pointed out, the cognitive therapist must first be a good psychotherapist, realizing the importance of the therapeutic alliance. This certainly is true in working with this accident survivor population. Subse-

1. Overprediction of your own fear when in a car.
2. Overprediction of danger when in a car.
3. Heightened attention to potential threats while driving.
4. Decreased attention to factors related to your safety while in a car.
5. Not acknowledging your own driving skills.
6. Not acknowledging the competency of other driver's skills.
7. Castastrophizing outcome of future MVA (if it happened).
8. Not acknowledging your own ability to cope and deal with future MVA or injury.

Figure 18.7. Common cognitive distortions following an MVA.

quently, an appreciation of the relationship determines how directly or indirectly the faulty pattern of thinking is addressed. We have found that Beck's notion of cognitive distortions give an efficient educational avenue for teaching the patient about the type of errors in thinking that may lead to powerful emotional consequences. The use of cognitive reappraisal is introduced, primarily using an educational approach at first around the negative emotional or behavioral consequences. The therapist then points out the potential impact of the faulty belief system on the patient's subsequent emotional and behavioral responses. This is accomplished by use of the patient's examples and posing questions that challenge the beliefs that the patient holds. A handout of cognitive reappraisals is provided (see Figure 18.5). A handout of common cognitive distortions that follow MVAs is also given to the patient (Figure 18.7).

Often, we will add the examples used in the session at the bottom of the sheet to help the patient remember the process of challenging the pattern of thinking that took place during the session. To go back to some of the examples in the prior paragraph such as, "I know I'll never get better, I'm going to feel like this the rest of my life." The therapist challenges the patients' beliefs by asking them how they know. They have to come to the conclusion that this is not a definite fact but rather an opinion based on a typically emotional or frustrating time. In fact, they do not know how they are going to feel the rest of their lives and, in fact, there are many people who have been worse and even they have been able to regain a great deal of function. The different kinds of distortions are presented to them as per Beck et al.'s understanding. All are nonthinking, overgeneralizations, use of reality testing, jumping to premature conclusions, and so forth, and all given as examples for how one's pattern of thinking can effect their subsequent reactions.

Consistent with Beck et al.'s (1979) concern with the therapist's qualities and therapeutic relationship, we believe that a great deal more than just the *cognitive* technique is taking place within the treatment sessions.

There is a powerful element of human concern and empathy that is conveyed when an individual shares with the therapist the horror of a trauma that he or she went through and how that horror continues to haunt him or her to this day. This type of powerful emotion is as prevalent in MVA traumas as other with other types of trauma (i.e., rape, physical injury, natural disasters, or war). The importance of providing hope and a sense of how past experiences, perhaps other traumas, have helped prepare individuals to arrive at this moment, and to move on, is an important therapeutic message.

Discussion of Driving Hierarchy and Driving Anxiety

One area of impact almost universally experienced among MVA survivors in our research and clinical experience has been the negative impact on driving. Some survivors will, as a result of fear and anxiety, experience anxiety only at the site of the MVA. Other drivers, however, will have ceased all driving since the MVA. Some individuals will have made one or two efforts at driving, and then became fearful, anxious, or even experienced a panic attack, resulting in a significant curtailing of driving (and riding) activities. The range of impact can vary dramatically. As a result, the intervention for this problem area may also vary considerably.

Let us take the example of a patient who has stopped all driving. This patient stops because each time he gets into the vehicle he becomes anxious or when he tries to drive, even locally on uncrowded streets, he feels considerable anxiety and fear. If necessary, one could begin the driving hierarchy for exposure-based intervention where the patient initially starts just by sitting in an automobile and starting the engine. There is no intent or plan to drive the vehicle at that point. The patient is instructed to stay and use his relaxation and coping self-statements until he is completely relaxed within the vehicle.

The next step in the hierarchy would be to apply these techniques to backing the car out of the driveway and entering into a comfortable neighborhood where the patient is familiar and at ease. This can be done initially on a Sunday or Saturday morning when traffic is likely to be much reduced. Systematically, driving can be increased up the driving hierarchy as the patient can tolerate and demonstrate success. It is important that the patient does not proceed too fast, that he has mastered each step in the hierarchy. Regular review of the hierarchy of driving behavior is crucial. If possible there should be daily driving. Opportunities such as changes in weather, perhaps use of friends to increase proximity of other vehicles, and speed of traffic surrounding the vehicle can be attempted.

It is also useful if the driving serves some type of functional, legitimate purpose. For example, we have had patients complete errands, see friends that provide positive reinforcement as well as a purposeful activity that gives some sense of accomplishment. If certain driving (e.g., busy streets or highways, especially at rush hour) is avoided, it may be possible to tie-in a reinforcing event (lunch with a friend or picking up a husband from an airport) at the completion of the driving assignment.

Just as there can be considerable variability of the impact of an MVA on driving, the length of treatment for this particular problem may vary as well. It is not uncommon to need several weeks of sessions to adequately attend to each aspect of the travel hierarchy. Longer time may even be required.

If the patient seems stuck and making little progress with an item from the driving hierarchy, imaginal desensitization can also be used before in vivo exposure. In fact, we would recommend that an imaginal element of exposure be used before attempting in vivo experiences.

It may be helpful at times for the therapist to accompany the patient in the vehicle while he or she is attempting particularly fearful driving situations. In some situations or circumstances significant others can assume the role of "coaching" or support under the direction of the treating therapist. During driving tasks it is important to be reassuring, positive, and provide modeling of cognitive statements or reappraisal techniques as it is thought beneficial.

In all likelihood undertaking items on the driving hierarchy will provide a great deal of clinical material about the way that negative self-talk and catastrophic thinking occurs. Having the patient make notes on particular tasks and difficulties and paying close attention to their subjective reactions is one way of bringing the thoughts more actively and accurately into the therapy sessions. Magnification by the patient of danger, and minimizing his or her own skills and record of safety, are quite common and often are one of the first areas of intervention.

Self-talk may include the acknowledgment that, although it is true that one cannot control the behavior of other drivers, one can keep "good control" of one's own vehicle and operate in a safe, prudent fashion. As a driver patients are under no obligation to operate their vehicles at a speed they consider unsafe for the road conditions or when it is not safe, in response to other vehicles crowding or blowing their horns impatiently. Some patients need to repeat these cognitions to themselves ("I'm a good and safe driver") as they drive in a somewhat "mantra like" fashion.

For behaviors that occur infrequently, such as being cut off at high speeds or having an unsafe driver make a rapid unsignaled lane change, resulting in other accidents, imaginal exposure is often critical. Here, the practice can occur with provision of behavioral techniques (e.g., relaxation), cognitive techniques (e.g., coping self-statements and cognitive reappraisal), until the anxiety–hyperarousal response is minimized or eliminated. The cognitive practice seems to help the confidence of the patient–driver as well as provide the new manner by which he or she can imagine and rehearse how he or she would react and deal with the situation.

For example, one patient was extremely concerned that, when she drove, another vehicle would cut her off and force her off the road. This fear was particularly true while driving on highways, even though she had never had an accident on the highway and her accident occurred at a stoplight close to her home. She was instructed to imagine that a car was about to cut her off the road and she needed to apply emergency driving techniques such as slamming on her brakes, changing lanes, or pulling off to the side of the road as necessary to avoid impact. In these situations she could see herself doing that in an effective, safe manner, dealing with the situation as best as she could.

It was also important to include the catastrophic thoughts and the worst-case scenarios (including death as a provoker of fear) and let them be addressed as fully as possible. Here, the thought of the car crashing into her car was explicitly experienced imaginably. She could imagine the sound and the feel of the car being forced into the guardrail and the impact as she is being spun around and subsequently injured. She was instructed that this again was her thinking about the event and to use her relaxation and cognitive techniques to talk her way through imaginal reaction. That is, she was to imagine that this was just a fearful thought and that she, in fact, was very safe in the room while she "tried the thoughts on." Although the thoughts may be very scary, they, in fact, were not happening and she had good control over herself and the reactions that she was going to experience. As she practiced using relaxation to calm her physiological arousal and talking to herself about how the thoughts could not harm her but that the fear of the thoughts was what was driving the behavior, she was able to resume greater and greater control.

Clinically, patients will become concerned about what they perceive as highly dangerous situations. The use of imaginal exposure using both mastery of the situation and then the worst-case scenario of the situation is one technique that we have found effective in helping people minimize the anxiety of the experience and to deal more positively with the situations, when and if they do occur.

Addressing the fear is as important as addressing the mastery behaviors. This scene is again repeated as often as necessary until a sense of "boredom" typically follows. This may take several sessions of exposure to occur, but just as with the repeated scene of his or her own MVA, the repeated imaginal exposure of the feared situation will often lead to a decline in anxiety and the provocation of emotional reaction can be extinguished.

Relaxation Training

During the fourth session a briefer four-muscle relaxation exercise is introduced. The tape of the exercise is provided for home practice. The introduction to briefer relaxation uses a dialogue as follows:

> In keeping with our notion of shorter, more easily applied relaxation training, it is time once again to teach you a briefer relaxation exercise. We would like to emphasize that the goal for relaxation is to apply the relaxation to any situation where anxiety and fear will occur during the exposure homework you are being asked to do. You are to utilize relaxation to counter that uncomfortable physiological change. Today we will be shortening the exercise again, this time to include just four-muscle groups, which will be as follows: both arms together, chest and stomach using a deep breath, neck and shoulders, and face and eyes.

At the conclusion of the exercise, the therapist again rates the patient's response with the BRRS, and then asks the patient to rate his or her relaxation. It is important to discuss any difficulties they may have had with briefer relaxation. Patients are provided a four-muscle relaxation tape and instructed to practice this by either alternating the exercises they have learned with this new exercise or just using the four-muscle relaxation exercise if they feel they have as good a result. If there is difficulty in transitioning to the briefer relaxation technique, they should return to the eight-muscle relaxation exercise, and use the four-muscle exercise following the longer exercise, or to try the four-muscle relaxation exercise and only use the eight-muscle relaxation exercise if they believe it would deepen the response. A copy of the four-muscle relaxation exercise can be found in Appendix C. (See Exhibit 18.4.)

EXHIBIT 18.4
Checklist for Session 4

_____ 1. Review MVA description
_____ 2. Review exposure hierarchy and assign greater exposure as ready
_____ 3. Introduce cognitive reappraisal
_____ 4. Give A–B–C–D handout
_____ 5. 4-muscle group relaxation
_____ 6. Rate 4-muscle group relaxation (BRRS & patient)
_____ 7. Give audiotape

Note. BRRS = Behavioral Relaxation Rating Scale.

of the exercise the patients are then told that they are going to do the exercise again, but this time just by memory. We would like them just to recall the sense or feelings of being relaxed. Before starting, I would like you to signal by raising your right forefinger if you cannot relax any of these particular muscle groups. Once the four-muscle groups have been reviewed try to focus on a particular muscle group and identify any feelings or sensations of tension or tightness that may be present. Once we have completed the four-muscle relaxation we want you to recall what is was like for the muscles to be completely relaxed and passively to imagine that muscle group with all the tension gone and letting the muscle relax.

See Exhibit 18.5 for a checklist of this session.

EXHIBIT 18.5
Checklist for Session 5

_____ 1. Review MVA description
_____ 2. Collect homework, review avoidance hierarchy, discuss problems, and apply cognitive–behavioral techniques
_____ 3. Apply imaginal desensitization as warranted
_____ 4. Introduce relaxation by recall
_____ 5. Rate relaxation
_____ 6. Give relaxation by recall tape

SESSION 6

Following review of all homework assignments and the patient's reading of the MVA description, cognitive techniques to deal with any reactions and experiences triggered by tasks on the driving hierarchy are applied or discussed. By this time many patients are often not exhibiting the same amount of distress when they read the MVA description as they did initially. Some patients are, in fact, beginning to be quite bored by the assignment. If this seems to be occurring, the reading exposure can be reduced to one time per day or less, based on the judgment of the therapist. It is important not to stop this part of the treatment prematurely but it is also important to attend to the patient's willingness to comply with a portion of the treatment that no longer seems to be meeting any agreed on need.

The driving hierarchy continues to be the focus for most patients, and cognitive–behavioral intervention is primarily the treatment provided. Some supportive counseling and encouragement may also be helpful in aiding the patient's confidence as they challenge the more difficult tasks from their personal hierarchy of feared travel situations. Here, the experience of the therapist is important in guiding the pace and the direction of treatment.

By this point some patients have understood the basic ideas of graduated in vivo exposure and correcting their negative self-talk and even spotting and correcting cognitive fallacies. These patients need more of the same with support and occasional guidance of the therapist. Primarily, the therapist needs to continue to supply gentle but firm pressure to continue up the hierarchy. These can be critical steps, such as for one patient whose car had gone off the road and tumbled down a hillside. For this woman, it was revisiting the accident site, getting out of her car and looking down to the place where she had been trapped for more than two hours, suffering from cracked vertebrae and other serious injuries. It was as if visiting the site removed a cloud from her brain and her emotions.

Other patients will take longer, in part because they have difficulty with the correction of self-talk or even understanding logical fallacies. It is also possible that they are able to progress up the hierarchy only at a slow pace.

The important part of the session is the discussion of driving hierarchy tasks and the cognitions the approach behavior elicits. These discussions also provide opportunity for the therapist to reinforce the patient for successful progress.

Cue-Controlled Relaxation

Cue-controlled relaxation is introduced, by repeating the relaxation-by-recall method introduced during the previous session. *If this has been going well*, cueing is explained to the patient as a method to relax quickly and efficiently in all of the situations that may arise. Cueing is explained to the patients as a method to help them relax quickly and efficiently in a wide variety of situations they may encounter.

Cue-controlled relaxation is taught by first having patients take a deep breath, pairing exhalation with subvocalizing the word "relax." This is done both with the patient's eyes open and closed. The use of imagery may also be encouraged. By this we have them think of some relaxation situations that have been tied to images or memories of being deeply relaxed. The notion of cueing as an automatic process is introduced; the automaticity is taught by having the patient perform the cue-controlled relaxation as many times per day as possible until it becomes automatic. They are given the homework task of using cue-controlled relaxation a minimum of 12 times per day. Ways to help the response become automatic are suggested such as to have the relaxation used whenever they come to a traffic light, hanging up the telephone, or engaged in any other frequently occurring events during their day.

Cue-controlled relaxation is introduced with a dialogue such as follows:

We would like you to now begin a new type of relaxation. Just as you learned how to relax by remembering how the muscle felt following the tensing and relaxing in relaxation-by-recall, we are now going to tie that relaxation to situations and events. First, please take a nice deep diaphragmatic breath, and as you exhale repeat to yourself the word "relax." Try this first with your eyes closed and then with your eyes open. If you like, you can use imagery to help you become more relaxed and gently going through your body from head to toe, remembering what the relaxation felt like. We would then like you to become very automatic in this process. Cue-controlled relaxation is a type of relaxation that can be tied to activities such that the cue of the situation will lead you to become increasingly relaxed. Some of this will be easy because each time you start the car, stop at a traffic light, at a stop sign, or in traffic, we would like you to take a breath, exhale, relax, and think the word "relax." It may also be done whenever you are hanging up the telephone at work or at home or during some other tasks that you frequently find yourself engaged in. This may be drinking from a cup or performing any activity such as closing a document on a computer. This only takes a few seconds and there are many ways you can fit this into your life. If you can do this you will then be able to have this type of response for lowering the anxiety and arousal through the day. Also, you will have this ability to relax available to you when you need it in anxiety-provoking situations.

Clinically, individuals will often enjoy the process of cued relaxation. One individual in treatment expressed how much she enjoyed actually going to traffic lights or stop signs and that these were going to be her "pauses that refresh." She looked forward to this and had clearly countered the initial anxiety that had been present when she feared that each stop sign or stop light became a place where she might be rear-ended, similar to the accident she had been involved in. Again, this should be individually tailored to each individual's particular ways of viewing and dealing with the world around them. (See Exhibit 18.6.)

EXHIBIT 18.6
Checklist for Session 6

_____ 1. Collect homework; reduce reading of MVA description as indicated
_____ 2. Review avoidance hierarchy; discuss cognitive strategies used; assist in application of cognitive–behavioral strategies as necessary
_____ 3. Introduce cue-controlled relaxation

SESSIONS 7 THROUGH 9

In our treatment study the review of all relevant homework continues during every session. As the patient continues to make progress some tasks may diminish greatly in importance (e.g., driving or reading of the MVA description). These adaptations should be tailored under the therapist's direction to the frequency and type of continuation that is desired.

The later treatment sessions are used to address the varied combination of other symptom clusters that arise for this population. These major themes and symptom clusters often fall into the following classifications: (a) psychic numbing; (b) existential issues; (c) estrangement, social isolation, and depression; and (d) anger. This transition is begun by reminding the patient of the symptom clusters or concerns that they presented with during their initial treatment session when the first evaluation had been reviewed.

Psychic Numbing

For those patients who experience psychic numbing, we begin by describing that psychic numbing and estrangement are viewed by us as a symptom complex that can be thought of as a selective emotional processing deficit (Litz, 1992). Numbing is then viewed as an avoidance behavior, and in this instance it is an effort to avoid the strong affect that the symptoms held in check because those feelings are viewed as dangerous and a reminder of the trauma. Feelings related to this numbing are discussed, beginning with session 7, as are any possible signs of current depression.

Over the course of treatment patients often come to express how overwhelmed they have been by the enormity of the event and the changes it has had on their lives. They do not know how to label this event but feel cut off or somehow different. The trauma uses up all of their energy. It absorbs their thoughts, their dreams, and cuts them off from those parts of their lives that used to be held in such importance.

A woman in treatment shared how initially following her MVA she was euphoric. To have survived her MVA was, in fact, exhilarating. Her van had gone off a bridge and was then sent off an embankment, rolling over two to three times, until settling with this woman trapped upside down inside her vehicle. Rescue workers were able to extricate her within 30 to 40 minutes following the crash. She had been alert during all that time and uncertain as to whether she would ever be safely removed from a vehicle as badly damaged as hers. She was taken to a local medical center and released with injuries to her back and neck. She was told several times that even though her airbag and seat belt had been used, she was lucky to be alive.

The next day she went to see her vehicle. She had been driving a minivan. When she saw the crushed vehicle she began to shake all over. All she could think of was, "Oh, my God, they're right the way the van crumpled around me, I should have died."

Another MVA victim had crashed a car into a telephone pole when a drunk driver forced her off the road. Although she escaped relatively unharmed, she thought that as the pole approached she was close to being dead. She remembers thinking "my daughter only works a block from here and I'll never see her again. She may drive by my car on the way home and this is the way she is going to last see me." She wondered what would happen to her husband and mother. She began to seek treatment when such thoughts would not remit.

In both instances the individuals became cut off from a strong feeling that had been a large part of their lives. They felt hollow inside or numb. They could not rally the feelings that it took to engage in relationships in the way that they had in the past. In these instances, the numbness was viewed as a way of trying to deal with the enormity of the events they survived. It was viewed as a way that their mind needed to interact with their bodies, to use resources to reconstruct this point in time of their lives and then reengage as appropriate to the world around them.

Patients are encouraged to take several small steps to reengage in activities that used to involve pleasure and a sense of joy or positive feelings within their life. The use of pleasant event scheduling is important for this type of intervention (see section on estrangement in this chapter).

Many times the discussion of death and one's mortality will involve issues of spirituality and religion. As psychologists, we have made it clear that we hold no answers in these areas. However, we do not avoid these areas and use these themes as important with regard to determining the meaning of these ideas and issues for the patient and how it has affected their lives. The effect of their lives on others, what remains to be done, why and how they survived, are often topics that survivors need and wish to bring up. When an injury such as persistent pain reminds them of the MVA or limitations of areas of interest that they used to be able to engage in eagerly, such as a hobby or ability to exercise, individuals look for a reason why this has occurred to them. They need to find a way to draw meaning from the event and place it into the context of their lives. To help with this, one must know the patient by the history he or she has told, the accident survived, and the way he or she now lives. We believe that this therapeutic relationship is one of the main reasons that therapists need more than just a cognitive–behavioral approach; as we pointed out earlier, the therapist has to be well-trained in general.

Existential Issues

One predominant theme frequently found in MVA survivors, *in our research and practice*, has been a fear of death and graphic reminders of one's mortality that *are slow to leave*. Rather than solely treat this as a cognition that generates anxiety, we have found it helpful to explore with patients questions regarding *their* mortality and their underlying beliefs and fears. Inquiry into the meaning and possible internal cognitive dialogues are explored, but without any clear perception of a "correct answer." We have found it helpful to place their ideas in the context of a therapeutic relationship, allowing these areas to be explored in a safe and supportive atmosphere.

For instance, one survivor spoke about how she knew that there was no way she should have survived her accident. She, in fact, had had friends who had died in an accident that was much less severe than the one she was in. However, she had walked away relatively unscathed physically. She had thought that before the MVA she was an atheist, but her mother's speaking of a "guardian angel" and how there are forces that move in our lives that one cannot perceive caused her to rethink her position on religion and whether or not there might be a greater purpose in her life. Clearly, these are powerful ideas that can drive a person's behavior in positive directions. We have used these dialogues to help individuals find meaning and structure concerning why and how they are going to engage in daily activities and perhaps have goals that will help move them in desired directions.

Clinically, patients have expressed the fear that the near death experience has generated and the impression that they had been but an instant from losing their sense of self. Some patients express their beliefs that there is no afterlife, and subsequently they focus on the fragility of their lives and how instantaneously the life can end. This has been expressed by patients who have stated that had their car been just 10 feet farther down the road, they would have gone over an embankment into a frozen river and clearly no one would have been able to find them, let alone rescued them. Although they view this as purely "just dumb luck" they, at this time, realized that there is no moment in life that they wish to "give away." They want to try to seize every moment they can and make it as meaningful as possible.

Others will discuss the unfinished goals and plans they held and how these have become more focused. One individual had always talked about taking a trip through Europe but had always been too busy. He had married, had children, and found that there was no way that he could accomplish this goal. Following his accident he discovered there had to be a time and way to do this and it became a goal that he did ultimately pursue. Following his trip he realized that this was perhaps one of the most important and memorable times in his life, not just for him but his family as well.

In addition, many individuals may express thoughts about how, had they died, this would have affected others. It seemed important to discuss the relationships that are or are not in a place and why perhaps this accident gives them a chance to alter this. Individuals who have marital problems or who are having issues with family have a chance now to approach them with perhaps a new sense of importance, urgency, or patience in terms of how they choose to deal with others. Individuals are often aware of how they may not have a say if an accident occurs, especially if they did not view themselves at fault for the MVA. However, they are quickly able to articulate how they hold themselves responsible for their behavior each day. Given this shift in perspective, they can readily find a motivation or impetus to act on beliefs that had not been a priority before their MVAs.

Finally, belief in an afterlife and God are often tested, and how these beliefs are held may also be offered to the therapist as important areas that the patient will want to discuss. If the therapist is uncomfortable dealing with issues of spirituality and religion, the therapist may need to have resources within the community, such as priests or clergy, that they can comfortably refer the patient to.

Estrangement and Social Isolation

Estrangement can be conceptualized as being manifested through the acts of social isolation and a lack of positive events. These behaviors are described to the patient as *adding to the* sense of isolation (and possibly depression). For patients who have become socially isolated and have been avoiding friends, family, and previously pleasurable events, a formal program of reaching out to those social contacts is described and planned. This can include how to ask for help or contact, as well as problem solving around these issues.

Patients will often give an excuse or explanation for why they have given up activities (e.g., that they do not feel up to it or that they are willing to wait until they feel better, then they will do those things again). We counter this kind of thinking with, *"It is important to do the things now that might give you pleasure and then you will feel better rather than waiting to feel better spontaneously on your own before you do things you used to enjoy."* As a result we want them to do homework assignments, to try designated behaviors (e.g., call designated people without waiting for the impulse to do so to occur), or see specific people without waiting for the change in feelings to occur. We also give a positive expectation to the outcome that if they will do these things, that this action is one of the things that will make them feel better. We describe how it has worked in other groups (i.e., depressed patients, and PTSD patients). Although many patients state they certainly do not feel like undertaking such activities, we assure them they have an improved chance of feeling better if they do the assignment than if they just waited for things to improve on their own. Here we might cite the data about spontaneous improvement cited in earlier studies.

Patients' typical response to reengagement in previously enjoyed behaviors or to recontacting a friend is one of pleasure and surprise. As this occurs, we try to build on these positive reinforcements. Patients are asked for previously enjoyed but now (possibly) avoided or limited activities. If they are unable to generate such a list themselves, they are assisted in this task. This is the provision of pleasant events scheduling (PES) as described by Lewinsohn and Libet (1972), several decades before, and how it can be used as a treatment for depression (Lewinsohn, Biglen, & Zeiss, 1976). Assigning pleasant events is used as a method of intervening within this psychic numbing symptom cluster.

Clinically, dealing with the numbing symptoms patients who have been in an MVA are approached similarly to depressed patients. By this we mean that it is pointed out that many of the events that once gave them pleasure may no longer accomplish this end. It is important to ascertain whether this emotional distance is because of physical limits (e.g., "I can't engage in sports because of my bad back") or for psychological reasons (e.g., "The things might be available but it is hard for me to find the energy to go and do it"). Patients are encouraged to generate a list of events that once held pleasure for them, or at least sounded as if they might be pleasurable. As shown earlier in this text (chapter 17), the symptom cluster for Criterion C showed significant improvement from the time of initial evaluation following treatment. The data from treatment does not allow us to discern what aspect of the treatment package may have been most helpful, but our impression is that the increased activity and social contact was an important element of that overall improvement.

Anger Management

Cognitions related to fear *and discomfort of affective* expression are also explored and addressed with cognitive techniques introduced earlier in treatment. Related to this is often a common theme of anger management. Many patients show increased hostility and irritability. The difficulty in managing anger is consistent with difficulty in the management of any strong affect, but rather than suppress the emotion, leading to numbing, difficulty in modulating the expression of anger may occur. The anger may be directed at the other driver, "the system" of insurance companies, lawyers, and litigation doctors that may be treating them or providing mandated independent evaluations. Survivors often feel as if they are "on trial" while they perceive themselves as the injured party. Cognitive techniques can be tried to deal with assumptions of justice–fairness, control, and so forth, as well as behavioral techniques of relaxation to try to moderate the emotional reactivity as per earlier methods. There have been a number of articles and books providing approaches to deal with anger (e.g., DiGiuseppe, Tafrate, & Eckhardt, 1994; Fein, 1993).

Anger often comes in the aftermath of MVA trauma. A patient will angrily describe how "I didn't do anything wrong! I wasn't driving out of control! I did nothing to increase my risk while waiting at a stop sign! I don't even know who to feel most angry at, the other driver, the weather, or God."

It is of interest that in our study, and in practice, we did not often evaluate the drunk driver, the driver "clearly in the wrong," or the driver perceived as responsible for the MVA. We did see drivers who "contributed" to the accident by going too fast or not using caution when it may have helped. Survivors included drivers in cars where the passenger had suffered head injuries or may have died. But again, they were often able to find reasons, in addition to themselves, as to why they should be angry at somebody or something else.

Our interventions with anger have followed the cognitive model of much of our treatment. One of the earliest interventions by Novaco (1975) appears based on the notion that individuals who are angry have a deficit in verbal mediation of behavior. Ellis (1977) proposed the model of irrational beliefs that leads to anger.

DiGiuseppe et al. (1994) proposed a multiple component treatment that assesses for the patient's presence or absence of verbal mediating self-statements; presence of negative, positive, or vengeful automatic thoughts and irrational beliefs; as well as the patient's social skills for problem solving. They use exposure to anger-provoking situations and thoughts as a critical component of the intervention, coupled with cognitive coping statements and interventions for the automatic thoughts believed to drive the anger.

Clinically, we found that with the use of cognitive coping statements such as, "Don't assume the worst." "You can react in ways other than anger." "How else might I react here?" can help in anger-provoking scenes. Identifying underlying beliefs using the A–B–C–D model of Ellis (1962) can help clarify cognitions related to the anger, such as "I'm being treated unfairly, and I can't stand it." Cognitions related to how they believe they have been treated, their stamina and endurance, and the fairness of life can be challenged and restructured within the therapeutic intervention. The cognitions can be disputed, challenging the idea that they can stand it and that, "Where is it written anywhere that they, in fact, should be treated fairly? Who said the world is fair anyway?"

Behaviorally, relaxation skills are also used. Brief relaxation can be suggested as a response to rising anger, followed by the use of the cognitive techniques. The guidelines of Deffenbacher (1995) point out that many angry individuals seem to hold the following cognitive biases and errors: overestimation and underestimation (i.e., overestimate the probability of a negative event and underestimate the personal or other coping resources), misattribution and single explanation (i.e., jump to highly, personalized conclusions; acting as if these conclusions are true); polarized conceptualization (i.e., good/bad, right/wrong, etc.); overgeneralization (i.e., broad sweeping conclusions such as everyone is *dumb, worthless, always this way*, etc.); inflammatory thinking (i.e., labeling events or people in highly negative ways such as *creep, bitch*, etc.), catastrophizing (i.e. casting events in highly negative extreme ways such as *awful, terrible, can't stand it*, etc.), and demanding and commanding (i.e., where they elevate their preferences and desires to moral edicts and commandments such as things *ought to be, have to be, should be*, etc.). When these distortions are present, anger responses become more likely. We have seen similar errors in thinking in our clinical experience. Some individuals will benefit from role playing or assertiveness training to better manage situations that provoke the anger and related behavior. Exposure to anger-provoking situations and phrases might also be used and then managed within the treatment setting by developing a reaction other than a rapid response and escalation to angry feelings.

By this point in treatment we allowed the interventions to become more individualized. However, if the patient had not returned to the site of the MVA, and it was possible to do so, we tried to have it stated as a behavioral goal. We would again review the initial symptoms of each patient and try to address what remained for areas of improvement. This also allowed us to adjust whether treatment would conclude at 9, 10, or up to 12 sessions. This was agreed to with each patient, ensuring understanding of treatment goals and planned termination. (See Exhibit 18.7 for a checklist that pertains to Session 7.)

EXHIBIT 18.7
Checklist for Session 7

_____ 1. Review homework and collect; reading of MVA description can be discontinued at this time if there is no physiological arousal or reaction reported
_____ 2. Broaden focus of treatment to potentially include:
   (a) psychic numbing
   (b) "existential issues"
   (c) estrangement, social isolation, and depression
   (d) anger
_____ 3. Introduce pleasant events scheduling
_____ 4. Provide handout on PES

Note. PES = Pleasant Events Schedule (Lewinsohn & Libet, 1972).

Overview for Sessions 8 and 9

Check driving and behavioral avoidance hierarchy work. Check homework for a list of pleasant events scheduling and possible utilization. Check on social contact and whether social activity involvement was pursued. If it was, discuss reactions. If it was not, explore reasons and encourage more vigorously.

If present, begin to explore possible cognitive schema related to depression, faulty logic, and apply cognitive restructuring. Explore possible avoidance of strong affect and if possible develop methods outside or within-treatment session to increase therapeutic exposure to those affects. Review and encourage continued home practice. Reading of MVA description can be discontinued. Suggest return to full 16-muscle relaxation tape at least twice per week, especially if there is report of muscle tension. Continue with themes identified in Session 7 (anger, mortality, estrangement, etc.) relevant to the particular individual. (See Exhibit 18.8 for a checklist for Sessions 8 and 9.)

EXHIBIT 18.8
Checklist for Sessions 8–9

_____ 1. Collect PES and review application
_____ 2. Review cognitive restructuring as appropriate
_____ 3. Continue with exposure/imaginal treatment as warranted
_____ 4. Continue with treatment of individual themes as identified

Note. PES = Pleasant Events Schedule.

CONCLUDING TREATMENT: SESSION 10 OR FINAL SESSION

Over the remaining sessions all the active ingredients of treatment are used and adjusted as necessary. Patients may continue with driving and behavioral avoidance hierarchy work. Social contact and pleasant event scheduling may be a necessary shift in focus, or it may have minimal utility. If depression is present, intervention for it is necessary. Any method of treatment consistent with the needs of the patient may be provided. It is in these latter sessions that the individualistic needs of the patient are addressed in the manualized treatment. In clinical practice, flexibility should be used, and treatment length adjusted accordingly.

In actual clinical practice, the format provided can be easily modified to suit each patient's needs. The length of treatment may also vary considerably. Burstein (1986b) has commented in his work on the considerable variability

EXHIBIT 18.9
Checklist for Session 10 (Final Session)

_____ 1. Review all treatment procedures
_____ 2. Review approach/avoidance behavior
_____ 3. Review relaxation techniques learned
_____ 4. Review coping self-statements
_____ 5. Review cognitive restructuring techniques
_____ 6. Review pleasant events scheduling and social interaction
_____ 7. Review other important interventions/themes in treatment (e.g., anger management, fear of dying, prior losses, etc.).
_____ 8. Provide posttreatment assessment and review (e.g., PCL, IES, BDI, STAI)

Note. BDI = Beck Depression Inventory; IES = Impact of Event Scale; PCL = PTSD Checklist; STAI = State–Trait Anxiety Inventory.

that exists in treatment. Treatment length of greater than a year is not uncommon. (See Exhibit 18.9 for a checklist to be used in the final session.)

CLOSING COMMENTS

This chapter provides a detailed description of the multifaceted, CBT treatment approach developed to treat MVA survivors with PTSD. Although many of the interventions described are cognitive–behavioral in their theoretical base, the treatment acknowledges and plans for the provision of other diverse, related treatment areas and methods. Issues of one's mortality, dealing with past losses, and earlier traumas can often arise as a part of treatment.

Although the treatment manual was time-limited, for many individuals additional treatment appears warranted. Again, we are encouraged that the outcome data from our focused, targeted treatment indicates that the treatment is a clinically useful method to guide the practicing clinician. One variable that we believe contributes to the persistence of PTSD may be a chronic physical problem that does not improve (see chapter 9). We believe that continued pain or altered lifestyle following an MVA can adversely interact with the subsequent emotional adjustment of the MVA survivor. This is not to say that patients with permanent physical injury cannot improve emotionally; our work clearly suggests they can. (See chapter 16, study 2 and study 3, for a description of persistent physical problems.) However, the interaction between physical and emotional factors can be powerful. This may, in fact, turn out to be one of the potentiating variables for the more chronic PTSD that shows a slower rate of improvement. Our data are suggestive but not definitive on this point. Even if this turns out to be true, the chronic physical problems are believed to be *only one* of the potentially contributing variables, *not* the only one.

Earlier trauma has also shown itself as a variable adding to the occurrence of PTSD following MVA. Treatment may need to deal with these issues as well, and with the expression this vulnerability or related issues manifest in psychological distress. This was noted in case examples in chapter 15 and in one of the earliest reports of MVA PTSD (McCaffrey & Fairbank, 1985).

Medications, although not the focus of this book, also can have a role in the treatment of PTSD from MVAs. Whether to help with the comorbid depressions that are often present, the chronic pain, sleep disturbance, symptoms of anxiety, a combined psychological and pharmacological intervention may, at times, be the treatment of choice. The decision to provide medications would, at this time, appear more based on clinical judgment than any objective guideline.

19

SUPPORTIVE PSYCHOTHERAPY MANUAL

As reviewed in chapter 17, the Albany Motor Vehicle Accident (MVA) Treatment Project included three conditions: a cognitive–behavioral therapy (CBT) treatment (described in the previous chapter), a supportive psychotherapy treatment condition (SUPPORT), and a wait-list control condition. As part of our initial preparation for the controlled evaluation of the CBT treatment it was necessary to provide a reasonable non-CBT alternative (see chapter 16). Subsequently, we developed a supportive psychotherapy condition that could be given in a similar fashion by multiple therapists, using a manualized format. This chapter will describe that supportive psychotherapy condition. This review is particularly important because the supportive psychotherapy condition turned out to be an effective intervention for MVA-related psychological disorders. Although not as effective an intervention as the CBT, SUPPORT was more effective than the wait-list condition. Moreover, in comparison to treatments described in other studies (e.g., Taylor et al., 2001), it was equally powerful for MVA survivors as some of the CBT interventions reported in the literature. The purpose of this chapter is to describe the supportive psychotherapy treatment provided at the Albany MVA Treatment Project.

INITIAL STUDIES

As described earlier, a supportive psychotherapy condition was developed as a second treatment to allow comparison between active treatments in the controlled investigation. The supportive psychotherapy condition was conceptualized as essentially anything but what was specifically offered in the CBT condition. By this we mean we wanted to be supportive and encourage individuals over time but needed to clearly avoid implementing any of the specific cognitive–behavioral procedures described in chapter 18. It was essential that there be minimal and clearly specified overlap or confusion about the type of intervention given to the different groups of patients. The treatment needed to last an average of 10 sessions to be comparable to the CBT intervention in length and to control for time of therapist contact. The supportive condition also needed some flexibility to meet the needs of each individual treated. Finally, the therapy also needed to be given by equally experienced clinicians to account for that variable which potentially affected care.

The initial focus for the supportive psychotherapy sessions was to spend a great deal of time gathering the patient's history (with particular attention to past traumas and losses, as well as current stresses the individual may be going through, and also a general developmental history) and to explore how the individual had dealt with these losses and events historically. Sessions were supportive, not just for traumatic events but for any life event the individual wished to discuss. In the supportive psychotherapy condition a wide variety of topics were encouraged for exploration and discussion. Supportive psychotherapy was an effort to provide a similar amount of content within the therapeutic situation and to provide an interesting and caring professional to listen to and respond to the individual seeking help. It is critical, however, that these activities would not be construed as either behavioral, directive, or cognitive in form. There was subsequently no suggestion made by the therapist for exposure to avoid situations or activities, there was no relaxation training, and there was no attempt to correct any perceived fallacies of logic.

DESCRIPTION OF SUPPORTIVE PSYCHOTHERAPY INTERVENTION

As stated, the supportive psychotherapy condition was manualized and conceptualized as an educative and supportive psychotherapy condition. There were three major tasks the therapist was hoping to accomplish over 10 therapy sessions: (a) education of the patient about the nature of posttraumatic stress disorder (PTSD) and explanation of what a normal reaction to severe trauma is. This process was designed to (i) help the patient put a professional label on his or her subjective reactions and behaviors following the MVA, and (ii) to "normalize" the experience for the patient. It was expected that an understanding of the nature of his or her symptoms and learning that many accident victims and other victims of traumatic events experience all or part of syndrome would help the patient feel better about him- or herself and thus feel less troubled by the symptoms they were experiencing. The data reviewed earlier in chapter 15, however, have not supported that this reassurance or knowledge has any lasting positive effect; in fact, there may be deleterious effects if one recalls the follow-up data of Mayou et al. (2000). (b) Provide psychological support to the patient as he or she explores the personal meaning of the symptoms and his or her own idiosyncratic developmental history of traumatic events, losses, and past coping responses. This means that the therapist was engaged in active listening and reflection in the context of a warm, nonjudgmental, and empathic therapeutic relationship. (c) Probably the most difficult task was to refrain from using routine cognitive–behavioral procedures and inquiry that were part of the CBT treatment condition.

Although the assumption for this work was that the therapist had, in fact, a general cognitive–behavioral orientation to treatment, there were several interventions that the therapist in the supportive psychotherapy condition was not allowed to perform. It is important to remember that the same therapists were trained in both conditions and provided treatment during the controlled treatment intervention in both the CBT condition and the SUPPORT condition. This feature of the research controlled for therapist gender, experience, and other nonspecific interpersonal qualities. There were internal validation checks performed throughout the study to make sure there was no therapeutic drift from one type of intervention to the other that would jeopardize the integrity of the treatment interventions provided (see chapter 17).

This need for therapeutic consistency led to the development of a list of "shall nots" that was included as part of the treatment manual. These were as follows:

1. *There should be no formal teaching of relaxation skills or suggestions on how to apply such skills to travel or other anxiety arousing situations.* If the patient routinely (i.e., before coming to treatment) practices some form of meditation or relaxation, this should be noted within the treatment notes but ignored as an active part of therapy. Direct questions from the patient about the application of relaxation skills or calming techniques were met with a very noncommittal *"If it part of your routine, you should probably stay with it." "It is up to you to decide what is best for you"* as opposed to providing any support or direction in the continuation or necessity of this part of intervention. If the patient did not have any formal training in meditation or relaxation skills, at no time during the intervention were

these skills to be introduced or suggested as potentially beneficial if gained elsewhere.

2. *There should be no formal or informal suggestion of reengaging in feared or avoided travel behaviors (driving, riding, etc.,) or travel or MVA-related thoughts.* The therapist, as stated previously, was to refrain from any exposure-based interventions or cognitive reappraisal. If the patient were to ask directly about beginning to drive again or returning to the MVA scene, and so forth, he or she was to be told something such as *"You're the best judge of what's best for you; listen to your body and go with your feelings; try not to let others force you into situations that might frighten you. When you are ready to (resume activities), you will know it."*

If the patient were to ask about thoughts about the MVA such as intrusions or flashback-like experiences, again, it was emphasized that the patient is the best judge of whether or not to talk about the MVA with others or to think about the MVA. They were reminded that these experiences were part of the normal reaction to trauma. The patient was instructed to listen to his or her body and to go with those feelings and perceptions as to what was the best path at this time for their improvement.

3. *There should be no "formal or informal" correction of self-defeating self-talk.* Again, no attempt to directly or subtlety influence cognitive distortions was to be part of this intervention. When examples of potential cognitive distortions arose (e.g., "I don't think I'll ever get over my memories"), the therapist was instructed to give a supportive response. These might include statements such as, *"I hear that this is still hard for you despite the passage of _____ months. If you remember what you were told earlier, people are different in how long it takes to get over the trauma. We would expect you to gradually get over this as memories fade. You have taken the first step by acknowledging that the problem is present."* If the patient were to say something such as, "I find myself afraid that another accident will happen and I doubt my driving skills," the therapist is expected to reply, *"I understand you are having some self-doubts and are worried. These are natural reactions to an accident like yours. We would expect you to gradually get over this as the memories fade."*

4. *There should be no formal or informal correction of logical fallacies.* When possible fallacies arose, such as "I am very unlucky in everything I do, I'm always screwing up or getting in trouble," the patient was to be acknowledged as far as the feeling con-

tent, such as "*You continue to feel bad about the accident and its consequences, these are normal reactions to an event like yours.*"

The therapist was instructed to focus primarily on how events, thoughts, other's reactions, make the patient *feel* and an acknowledgment and legitimatization of those feelings. Time was spent on what the patient was saying rather than trying to correct or alter those feelings or perceptions. Time was also spent during the session about how the patient dealt with day-to-day problems. As with many individuals, it is easy to spend a great deal of time being caught up with the day-to-day struggles of physical problems, returning to work, dealing with family members, which often became the focus of therapeutic intervention.

Direct questions, especially those seeking advice on how to deal with the MVA and PTSD-related symptoms and issues, however, were to be dealt with by saying something such as, "*What I think is not important, it is what you* feel *that is important. You (the patient) need to learn to listen to your body and feelings and be guided by those. Everyone is different and has their own idiosyncratic (individual) path to recovery and way of reacting and feeling about events. You're the best judge of what is right for you.*"

Exhibit 19.1 presents an outline of supportive psychotherapy treatment, which summarizes this discussion.

EDUCATIONAL AND SUPPORTIVE TREATMENT FOR MVA-PTSD: TREATMENT SESSION 1

This session begins as the CBT treatment began by reviewing the initial assessment report with the patient. This typically included a description of the MVA, the patients' reaction to the MVA, any symptoms of PTSD, and other disorders that were identified. Again, the rationale behind this review was to ensure that the clinician and patient share an understanding of how the patient feels, what has occurred thus far, and to list what the patient's needs are in treatment as well as to facilitate rapport building.

In clinical practice, again, a typical assessment of the problem would have taken place and treatment would begin with the summation of the patient's problems and the symptoms he or she is seeking help with.

The second major point to be made was what we considered to be a normal response to trauma. Again, it was explained to the patient that

EXHIBIT 19.1
Outline of Supportive Psychotherapy Treatment

Outline of Treatment

Session 1

Review MVA and patient's symptoms, both physical and psychological. Explain what PTSD is and review all 17 symptoms. Emphasize that it is the natural response to trauma.

Session 2

Explore developmental history for previous trauma and major losses as well as how the patient coped in the past.

Session 3

Continue developmental history review.

Session 4

Continue development history review.

Session 5

Announce a shift in focus from historical material to how the patient is dealing with current issues and problems.

Sessions 6, 7, 8, 9

Continue to focus on how patient is dealing with current issues and problems.

Session 10

Wrap up and review. Schedule reassessment and follow-up visit with therapist.

almost anyone going through a trauma might experience a significant impact behaviorally, cognitively, and emotionally. The rationale for beginning with this information was an effort to reassure the patient that he or she is "not crazy" or "losing his or her mind," but rather to put responses in the context of the reaction to a traumatic event. This was to reassure the patient that he or she is experiencing an understandable human response to trauma, and the information provided was meant to convey this understanding. Suggested dialogue might be something such as,

> It is normal to have some increased anxiety or apprehension when you are back in a situation that had led to trauma. It is also normal to have some fear and anxiety when confronted with situations in which there is a potential for harm or even threat of death. Thus, although your initial reaction was normal and almost everyone would have some of those feelings and reactions, we believe the symptoms you are now experiencing are of sufficient severity and have continued for a sufficient period of time that they are causing problems in your daily life.

These symptoms fall into four main clusters or groups.

We then explain the detailed symptoms and symptom clusters (with attention to the particular patient's pattern of idiosyncratic response) and describe each of the 17 symptoms of PTSD as they fit into these symptom clusters.

We believe the four symptom clusters include: (a) intrusive reexperiencing of the trauma; (b) avoidance of either thoughts, situations, or feelings related to the trauma and avoidance of situations or behaviors that remind one of the trauma and the ability to remember some parts of the trauma; (c) psychic numbing or depression (feeling cut off from others, less engaged in the world than one used to be), loss of interest in previous enjoyed activities; and (d) hyperarousal where physiologically the body is more responsive and prone to startle, and the individual has increased heart rate, difficulty concentrating, becomes more irritable, and has more sleep difficulties than in the past.

We go on to diagnose the condition and to agree on the diagnosis using a dialogue such as:

> People with the particular cluster symptoms that you are having are said to suffer from posttraumatic stress disorder (PTSD). You may have heard or read about PTSD in conjunction with veterans of foreign wars or with rape or assault victims or survivors of natural disasters. In our work we have found as many as 40% of MVA victims who are injured and seek medical attention will have PTSD or a milder version of it early on. As you remember you have had symptoms such as (remind them of the symptom patterns that they are having). As stated earlier these reexperiencing symptoms are normal reactions to trauma. It is important to understand that what you are going through is what the majority of people go through. Subsequently, this does not mean that you are going crazy or that you are loosing control by entering into "psychotic process" or doing something that is even out of the ordinary. Almost everyone will experience some of these symptoms.

At that time the patient is then provided an overview of how the sessions will be conducted. What we hope that they will do in each session is to discuss some of their history because it is important to know who they are and how in the context of their life they are dealing with this particular trauma. We will then spend time discussing the problems that the MVA has caused and help them sort through their feelings and ideas about how to best proceed at this time.

SESSIONS 2, 3, AND 4

The focus of therapy now shifts to the patient's developmental history, with special attention to earlier trauma, losses, and how the patient dealt with these events. Many people find this a natural process to undertake, particularly when going to visit a psychologist. The dialogue may go something such as:

> I know that during the initial assessment some background information on you was initially gathered. Today, I want to return to that information and go into greater detail about your earlier history so I can better understand who you are and what your life was like before the accident. We know that everyone is always the product of all of our previous experiences. So, I want to understand your particular history and how you dealt with life crises in the past, so that together we can gain a better understanding of how you developed into who you are today and how you are dealing with the problems that you are now faced with. Let's begin with where you were born and your early years. I see from you earlier history that you were born _____; tell me more about that. What was that like? How much do you remember?

The first session provides the groundwork so that the second session will very naturally lead to greater interest in the developmental history of the patients. This interest in the patients' feelings and interpretations of their history and important historical events and losses is then explored through Sessions 3 and 4. We also routinely explore in some detail how they coped with the previous traumas and previous losses.

SESSIONS 5 THROUGH 9

During Session 5 there is a potential shift to a more current focus in problem-solving and discussion than there has been up to this point. Again, there is much flexibility around the timing of this shift, and this was left to the experienced therapist when these shifts would take place. The therapy was again primarily directed by the patient's needs and by the therapist's guiding the sessions by focusing on the material the patient discussed and engaging them in conversation around these themes. Often the material would shift to more present-day material around this time in treatment. If not, this shift, was presented with statements such as, "I think I have a better understanding of who you are and of your history now. I appreciate all that you have been sharing." (We would then comment on the significant earlier events, losses and traumas and how the patient dealt with them.)

> Everything you have told me about your past indicates that you have been a strong and resilient person in the past (if that's true—or modify to address their particular adaptation as appropriate). I expect that you will continue to be much like that in the future. Research tells us that the best predictors of how a person will behave and cope in the future is how you behaved and coped in the past. Starting today I would like to shift the focus more to the present and how you are dealing with

the current events, situations and problems in your life. So, let's begin there. How do you feel you're doing overall?

From here the focus was to provide support to the patient as he or she deals with current issues (including symptoms of PTSD). The therapist needs to continually review mentally the "Thou shalt nots" and the focus continued in this vein *on the present* through Session 9.

SESSION 10

As with any type of intervention, psychotherapy has a termination session. During Session 10, this would include summarization of the work done up to this point, reassurance of the potential gains that the patient can continue to make, and follow-up visits and evaluations were scheduled.

SUMMARY

The supportive psychotherapy condition and the positive results that were gained from providing it are important for several reasons. (a) They question our basic understanding of the active ingredients that are necessary to intervene and successfully treat PTSD. The majority of our literature to date has been based on cognitive–behavioral theories and interventions for our understanding of the processes that contribute and maintain PTSD symptoms in individuals. It has long been presumed that, if there is not sufficient exposure attempted to change the cognitive processes, then individuals would continue to suffer because of these principles of how and why symptoms develop and are maintained. The fact that supportive psychotherapy by design did not try to affect the symptoms in ways that would readily challenge this presumption. (b) Supportive psychotherapy is often a treatment that is neglected in the literature. Nevertheless, it is often a large component of many interventions and has sound tradition within both psychological and psychiatric treatments. Our studies have shown consistently that there is empirical support for supportive psychotherapy and its application to a PTSD population. Individuals who suffer from unremitting problems such as ongoing pain, change in life style, often even with the best of cognitive–behavioral and psychological interventions, will continue to need ongoing supportive services to maintain as high a functioning level as possible. The type of intervention, initially created by Rogers (1951) and emulated in our treatment intervention, would suggest that this continues to be a potent therapeutic effort.

(c) There is a considerable body of literature that suggests that nonspecific variables in treatment are, in fact, responsible for much of the change that we measure. These nonspecific variables may include therapist variables, changes in environment, and changes in therapeutic milieu that are hard to be certain of or to express. This intervention would certainly support the fact that elements of supportive therapy are a viable part of ongoing treatment.

The therapists involved in the research were all experienced therapists who had at least 10 years postdoctoral experience working with patients. They were comfortable and familiar with working with the PTSD population as well. Contributing to the nonspecific variables that could well have contributed to the benefits gained in therapy was the fact that the participants had sought help for PTSD at a center labeled as a specialty clinic for this problem. They were motivated to change.

Potential confounding variables thought to lend themselves to an understanding of the treatment results are also important. Recall from chapter 4 that each individual engaged in our treatment studies underwent a great deal of psychological assessment. The assessment process alone often took between four to six hours initially and one to three hours during subsequent follow-ups. Each therapist then took the report generated from that assessment and reviewed it again with each patient. If for no other reason, the amount of exposure to the feared situation, the structure of how the MVA was thought of and applied to a professional report, certainly lends itself to an indirect exposure and cognitive restructuring format. Some of the brief interventions, in fact, have used a restructuring of one's disorganized perception of the MVA with good results (see chapter 15 and Gidron et al., 2001).

Although not intended as a part of the study, these variables described earlier may very well be a contributing factor to the potency of the supportive psychotherapy intervention. However, the exposure from assessment alone should have had greater impact than on the wait-list condition if the exposure involved in the assessment techniques alone was sufficient for making the change in psychological test measures and structured interviews. Again, one needs to look to the process of how change was directed via psychological intervention.

As chapter 17 documents, the SUPPORT condition with its emphasis on education about PTSD and a review of past problems and how the patient dealt with them is clearly psychologically active and leads to substantial improvement that is well-maintained over time.

20

CLOSING REMARKS

This book provides a comprehensive review of what we presently know about the psychological effects of motor vehicle accidents (MVAs) on the survivor of the crash. We have shared the considerable work that has taken place since the first edition of the book in 1997 until the fall of 2002. Our knowledge has grown considerably. The summaries of this information are the main body of the book, and we will not rehash them. Rather, we would like to use this final chapter as a place to share our thoughts on the work to date and other work that needs to be done in the future. It is not meant to be exhaustive.

Since the publication of the first edition in 1997, there have been several well-controlled investigations into the psychological treatment of posttraumatic stress disorder (PTSD) following MVAs. Overall, we can say with great confidence that this disorder can be treated with a good degree of success. We still do not know what treatments work best and the best timing of interventions. Survivors who are refractory to treatment have not received attention to date. Even with 70 to 80% effectiveness in treatment, we are still failing with a number of individuals.

Briefer, more effective interventions are needed. Interventions designed to prevent high-risk individuals from developing subsequent PTSD would be helpful. The treatment literature on acute stress disorder (ASD) has demonstrated that effective treatments exist. Additional brief, crisis-focused interventions might be developed to intervene with high-risk individuals. Results to date have failed to support the effectiveness of single-session education or debriefing alone. Brief, theoretically derived treatments may be developed. If they are, the timing, targeted patients, and clinicians to provide the interventions will become the focus of additional research.

Better interventions will continue to require good assessments. Effective screening tools, possibly using biological or physiological indexes, might also be established. Ongoing debates (e.g., Harvey & Bryant, 2002) about whether to continue with the diagnostic category of ASD or to use provisional PTSD with less emphasis on dissociation may also help in continuing the evolution of the diagnostic formulation. In the case of MVA-related trauma, this would be extremely beneficial.

Historically, we admitted patients into our studies that closely resembled patients that might be found in most clinical settings. Patients often had multiple diagnoses, medical complications, and issues of lost employment and disability. Although the protocol used in our treatment studies was not designed to treat multiple conditions, it did show a strong effect for improving comorbid conditions.

We again raise the concern that results can be viewed from many perspectives. Both categorical change and reduction in symptoms of PTSD were the primary measures that we used; both showed improvements in our treatment studies. However, as effective as the treatments were, they did not eradicate the entire list of symptoms. Patients continued to have symptoms that might have been problematic, even if they had remitted to a point that they no longer met diagnosis of PTSD. One could argue that even one symptom (e.g., sleep disturbance, nightmares, avoidance of an important part of one's past life) would be sufficient cause to continue treatment. Allowance of the patients' perspective about the timing of termination would be critical if placed in the context of how decisions ideally are made in clinical practice. There was no doubt in our minds that on several occasions, longer treatment would have produced continued improvement. Future studies need to be conducted to test empirically if these gains can be demonstrated.

Malatesta (1995) has argued that manual-based treatment creates an illusion whereby simple treatment can be effective for extremely complex problems. Although she was writing about another diagnostic group, the statement certainly holds some truth for this population and our use of manualized intervention. The concerns of survivors of trauma with PTSD are many. The fact that treatments are showing such positive outcome is encouraging. We must never forget, however, that in clinical practice success needs to be measured on a case-by-case basis.

FINAL THOUGHTS

Although not the focus of this book, the treatment approaches, assessments, and application we have described for the MVA survivor may well be found to serve trauma survivors of other populations. In our experience, the approaches, modified for special needs of the individual case, have been effective with survivors of physical injuries, railroad accidents, boating accidents, airplane crashes, rape, and assault. Although sensitive to the particular needs of each subpopulation of trauma survivors, the same core interventions have seemingly been equally effective.

This then leads one to discuss the paradigm of the MVA survivor as a model for PTSD research and trauma. The population holds several advantages. First, it is the most common trauma in the United States. This affords access to people to study as well as ensuring usefulness in applying the findings to a large population of interest. One does not need to wait for war or natural disaster to study the effects of trauma. The trauma of everyday life has been shown to produce significant distress. The distress is also obviously different than that of traumas such as war, which has received perhaps the most study to date. However, PTSD as a result of MVA affects both men and women, young and old, and allows for intervention closely following the trauma up to several years later.

We do know that ideally, some MVA victims require immediate attention for services shortly after their MVA. They need to return to a life free from anxiety and depression, including while they drive and travel. Although many improve spontaneously, many will not. The survivors of MVAs have been articulate and desirous of sharing their experience and interested in working on their treatment. We firmly believe that the people seen in our research setting closely approximate individuals in the "real world."

Millions of people each year are involved in MVAs, many of which result in personal injury. These individuals often also experience considerable psychological distress. Although a great deal has been learned, much remains to be discovered to better help and understand these survivors. We hope that this book has helped to meet that considerable need.

APPENDIX A
MVA Interview

Name _____

Subject No. _____

Date _____

I will now be asking you a number of different questions related to the accident.

1. Can you tell me the date of the accident? _____

2. Were you the driver or a passenger in the car?
   (1 = Driver) (2 = Passenger) (3 = Pedestrian)

3. Can you describe for me what happened? _____
   _____
   _____

4. _____ one vehicle _____ number of vehicles _____ pedestrians

5. Did you suffer any physical injuries from the accident?
   (1 = Yes, 2 = No)

6. If yes, please describe _____
   _____
   _____

7. Were other people injured in the accident?
   (1 = Yes, 2 = No)

8. If yes, please describe. _____
   _____
   _____

9. Was anyone killed or seriously injured?
   (1 = Yes, 2 = No). If yes, describe _____
   _____
   _____

10. Did you miss any work/school because of the accident?
    (1 = Yes, 2 = No)

11. If yes, (a) how much? _____ (days/weeks).
    (b) Are you still out of work/school?
    (1 = Yes, 2 = No).

12. Was there much damage to your vehicle? (1 = Yes, 2 = No)
   _____ dollars or total loss.

13. If there was another vehicle, how much damage did it sustain?
   _____ dollars or total loss.

14. When did you first see a physician about your accident?
   Date: _____ / _____
         Mo.   Yr.

15. What doctors have you seen? (List specialty) _____
   _____
   _____

16. Were you hospitalized? (1 = Yes, 2 = No)
   If yes, for what and for how long? _____

   Number of days _____

17. What have your physical symptoms been like since the accident
   occurred? _____
   _____
   _____

18. Are you continuing to have any pain or discomfort from the
   accident? _____

   Describe: _____
   _____

19. Are you taking any medication for the pain?
   (1 = Yes, 2 = No)

20. What medicines have you been placed on? _____
   _____
   _____

21. Did you suffer any blow to your head? (1 = Yes, 2 = No)

22. Did you suffer any loss of consciousness during the accident?
   (1 = Yes, 2 = No)
   How long? _____

23. Have you noticed any drop in concentration? (1 = Yes, 2 = No)
   How bad? _____
   (0 = Not at all to 10 = Totally unable to concentrate).

24. Do you have headaches as a result of/or since the accident?
   _____ If yes, give Headache Questionnaire after interview.

25. What is your estimate of present functioning?
    (0 = Not functioning, 100 = Preaccident functioning) _____

26. What do you think your probability of returning to your preaccident functioning? (0%–100%) _____

27. Are you driving at the present time? (1 = Yes, 2 = No).
    If no, why not? _____
    _____

28. If you are, how has your driving/riding been affected by the accident?
    _____

29. In reference to your present travel, <u>answer Yes or No:</u>
    Restricted to local driving _____, Avoidance of certain
    roads _____, Avoid highway driving _____, Avoid accident
    area only _____, Reluctant to ride in a car _____ Restrict
    speed _____, Avoid pleasure trips, drive to work only _____,
    Not drive at all _____, Other (describe) _____

NOTE

At this point, switch to CAPS Interview, Form 1, Current and Lifetime.

Introduce by saying "Now I want to ask you a series of questions about your ACCIDENT and your reactions to it, especially over the <u>past month.</u>

During, or immediately after the accident, were you fearful or afraid?
    YES   NO

How fearful or afraid were you? (Rate: 0 = None, 100 = Intensely afraid or terrified)
    Rating: _____

Did you have any feelings of helplessness during or immediately after the accident?
    YES   NO

How helpless did you feel? (Rate: 0 = No helplessness, 100 = Extreme helplessness).
    Rating: _____

Note: Continue with these MVA-related questions after the CAPS.

30. During the accident, how much danger did you feel that you were in?
    Rate: 0 = None, 100 = Extreme, life-threatening. _____

31. Did you feel as if you might die?
    (Rate: 0 = No, 100 = Certain I would die) _____

32. Have you ever had such feelings in the past? (1 = Yes, 2 = No)
    If yes, describe _____
    _____
    _____

33. Have you ever had any auto accidents in the past?
    (1 = Yes, 2 = No) _____

34. If yes, please describe, giving dates, severity, and circumstances. _____
    _____
    _____

35. How vulnerable do you feel now when you drive or are a passenger in
    a car? (Rate: 0 = None, 100 = Extremely) _____

36. How much control did you feel during the accident?
    (0 = None, 100 = Complete) _____

37. If it was a two-car accident, how culpable do you feel the other driver
    was? (Rate: 0 = None, 100 = Totally) _____

38. Did you feel responsible for the accident? If yes, rate:
    (0 = Not at all, 100 = Completely) _____

38A. How much responsibility for the accident would you put on road
    conditions, weather, or condition of your car?
    (Rate: 0 = None, 100 = Totally) _____

39. Were there drugs or alcohol associated with the accident?
    (1 = Yes, 2 = No). If yes, list: _____
    _____
    _____

40. Had you been drinking or using any drug(s) prior to the accident?
    (1 = Yes, 2 = No). If yes, were you at all impaired in performance by
    alcohol or drugs? _____

41. If others were involved, were any of the others drinking or using drugs?
    (1 = Yes, 2 = No).

42. Were any traffic tickets issued? 1 = Yes, 2 = No.
    If yes, to whom _____
    _____

43. Aside from accident related issues, are there any other stressors effecting
    your life? (1 = Yes, 2 = No)
    Describe: _____
    _____
    _____

44. Is there any litigation expected or underway as a result of this car accident? _____

_____

_____

45. If yes, please describe: _____

_____

_____

46. Lawyers' names and addresses: _____

_____

_____

_____

_____

47. Now that we have talked about the accident in a variety of ways, are there any last-minute memories, or memories that seem more vivid, such as things you saw, heard, felt, or smelled? _____

_____

_____

_____

_____

_____

_____

_____

Note: Go next to psychosocial database.

PREVIOUS MEDICAL HISTORY

Have you had any previous serious illnesses?

Describe: _____

_____

_____

_____

_____

_____

How would you rate your health before the accident?
(100 = "Super Healthy," 0 = Chronic, interfering health problems)

_____

How do you rate your health since the accident?
(Rate, 100 = "Super Healthy," 0 = Chronic, interfering problems)

_____

How have you coped with earlier illnesses/injuries (if applicable)?

_____

_____

_____

Any previous psychiatric history? _____

_____

_____

Any family history of panic or anxiety? _____
Any family history of note, either medical or other pain and accident-related histories? _____

_____

_____

APPENDIX B
Longitudinal Course Scoring Form

This interview is designed to cover the patient's psychiatric course during the past 26 weeks. Recovery from previous episodes–conditions or the development of new episodes–conditions and their course are also to be determined. This information is to be recorded on the Longitudinal Picture of Psychiatric Status. The scales for these ratings are given in Keller et al. (1987).

Before conducting the interview the interviewer should review previous follow-ups, giving special attention to the most recent one.

It may be helpful to fill in various items related to the patient's status at the time of the previous interview *on the pages of this form* (such as the kind of physical injuries, name of lawyers, etc.). In particular, *note on your interview forms* which PTSD symptoms were positive at the last interview, as well as which other psychiatric diagnoses were positive.

It will help if you fill in the ratings for all PTSD symptoms and all psychiatric disorders for the first week of the follow-up with the values you obtained at your last interview.

On conducting the interview the interviewer may use clinical judgment as to the best way to elicit information regarding course. The following guidelines are offered to assist in this process.

GUIDELINES

1. Begin the interview by obtaining an overview of what has happened to the patient since the time of the last interview. This overview serves as a time to both reacquaint (or acquaint) the patient and interviewer while providing information on whether the patient has recovered, relapsed, or developed new conditions.
2. The interviewer should then return to questions about the patient's condition 26 weeks previously. For example, the interviewer might begin by saying:

   The last time we spoke together you were (descriptions of patient's condition at that time, e.g., "You were feeling very depressed and had trouble sleeping," "You were feeling well"). How have things been since then?

   When did you begin to feel better? Worse?

417

3. The interviewer is to then trace the Psychiatric Status Ratings (PSR) for these episodes–conditions forward to the present, probing until the best level of recovery is determined. Although these ratings are made on a week-by-week basis, the patient does not have to be asked about how he or she was feeling during each week. Instead, *change points* that correspond to PSR ratings should be determined and the interviewer should make the weekly ratings based on these change points. To help the participant date these change points, the interviewer should ask such questions as "Was that in November?" "Did that happen before or after Christmas?" etc.

4. If the occurrence of a new episode–condition is established, the interviewer should return to the probes to determine the development of other episodes of the same or different type.

ACCIDENT-RELATED ISSUES

When we last spoke it was about one month (or whatever is the appropriate interval) since your accident.

PHYSICAL INJURY

(If Previous Physical Injury)

At that time you were recovering from (fill in injuries)

1. _____

2. _____

3. _____

4. _____

How has that been? Would you say you have fully recovered from 1.?

(yes, no) _____

(If "yes") At what point would you say you had fully recovered?

_____

(Use LIFE methodology to try to pinpoint week of recovery and note on Rating Sheet #1.)

(If "no") Have you improved at all? (yes, no) What are your problems

with 1. now?_____

At what point did you notice improvement? _____

(Use LIFE methodology to try to pinpoint time of noticeable improvement and note on Rating Sheet #1.)

Now, would you say you have fully recovered from 2.?
(yes, no) _____

(If "yes") At what point would you say you had fully recovered?
_____

(Use LIFE methodology to try to pinpoint week of recovery and note on Rating Sheet #1.)

(If "no") Have you improved at all? (yes, no) What are your problems with 2. now? _____

At what point did you notice improvement? _____

(Use LIFE methodology to try to pinpoint time of noticeable improvement and note on Rating Sheet #1.)

3. (yes, no)

Fully recovered _____

Noticeable improvement _____

4. (yes, no)

Fully recovered _____

Noticeable improvement _____

(If *no* previous physical injury noted at initial interview.)

Did you have any delayed physical consequences of accident? _____
_____
_____

(Obtain details and date physical symptoms began, current status, and when they ended.)

LEGAL ISSUES

Were any traffic citations or arrests made as a result of the accident?
(yes, no)

Details _____
_____
_____

Has any legal action occurred over the accident? (yes, no)

Details _____

_____

_____

When did this first occur? _____

_____

_____

(Use LIFE methodology to try to pinpoint time of first legal action related to MVA.)

(If patient had seen a lawyer by first interview.)

When we last spoke, you mentioned that you had contacted (name of lawyer).

_____

Are you filing any kind of civil suit related to the accident?
(yes, no, maybe)

What is the status? _____

(Try to get date suit was filed and any other chronology.)

Has someone else filed a civil suit against you as a result of the accident?
(yes, no)

When did you first learn of it? _____

(Use LIFE methodology to pinpoint date.)

What is its status? _____

INSURANCE ISSUES

Have you had any dealings with your insurance company over the accident? (yes, no)

Details _____

Has there been any difficulty? (yes, no)

Details and chronology _____

DRIVING STATUS

Now when we last spoke, you told me (driving status—particular impairment or discomfort).

_____

_____

Are you driving now? (yes, no)

(If this is a *change* from last interview obtain details.) _____

_____

   When did the change occur? _____

(Use LIFE methodology to pinpoint time of change.)

If patient was "driving reluctant" or "driving phobic" obtain details of current status, pinpoint when patient returned to:

(a) driving to work _____

(b) driving alone _____

(c) driving for pleasure _____

(e) traveling on road where accident occurred _____

(f) or traveling at time of day of accident _____

Were any of these endured with moderate to severe discomfort? _____

(Use LIFE methodology to pinpoint changes in driving status.)

_____

_____

   Have you had any additional auto accidents since we last talked? (yes, no)

   (If "yes") Details, date, new symptoms.

   _____

   Has anyone in your immediate family been involved in an auto accident since we last spoke? (yes, no)

   (If "yes") Details, date

   _____

   Have you been involved in any other traumatic events since we last spoke? (yes, no)

   Details, dates (Use LIFE Methodology.)

   _____

   Has anyone in your family been involved in a traumatic event? (yes, no)

   Details, dates:

   _____

Date of last interview: _____

DRIVING STATUS FOLLOW-UP

Code	1	2	3	4	5	6	7	8	9	10	11	12	13	14	15	16	17	18	19	20	21	22	23	24	25	26
Treatment Session:																										
Driving Status:																										
Driving at night																										
*Endured with anxiety																										
Driving in snow																										
*Endured with anxiety																										
Driving in rain																										
*Endured with anxiety																										
Driving on the highway																										
*Endured with anxiety																										
Driving around area of MVA																										
*Endured with anxiety																										
Restricts speed																										
Avoids pleasure trips																										
*Endured with anxiety																										
Avoids being a passenger																										
*Endured with anxiety																										

Avoids heavy traffic situations									
*Endured with anxiety									
Drives to work only									
*Endured with anxiety									

Note. For Week 1, use ratings from previous interview for driving status.

Avoidance

4 = Not applicable
3 = Completely avoids activity/always restricts speed
2 = Avoids activity unless absolutely necessary
1 = Avoids activity in some situations/sometimes restricts speed
0 = No effect of MVA on activity/never restricts speed

*Anxiety

3 = Not applicable
2 = Performs activity with noticeable anxiety
1 = Performs activity with some anxiety
0 = No anxiety noted

Date of last interview: _____

FOLLOW-UP #1

Code	1	2	3	4	5	6	7	8	9	10	11	12	13	14	15	16	17	18	19	20	21	22	23	24	25	26
Physical injury																										
1.																										
2.																										
3.																										
4.																										
5.																										
New physical problems																										
1.																										
2.																										
3.																										
Legal issues*																										
1st legal action*																										
Initiated suit*																										
Learning of being sued*																										
New MVA*																										
Family MVA																										

New trauma*														
Family trauma*														

Note. For Week 1, use ratings from previous interview for physical injury and driving status.

Physical Injury
3 = noticeable impact on ADL from injury
2 = symptoms still present, but improved
1 = symptoms are barely noticeable
0 = symptom is absent

*Mark the week in which this occurred with an asterisk.

Date of last interview: _____

PSYCHIATRIC STATUS RATING

Code	1	2	3	4	5	6	7	8	9	10	11	12	13	14	15	16	17	18	19	20	21	22	23	24	25	26
1) Panic disorder																										
a. w/Agoraphobia																										
2) Agoraphobia w/o panic																										
3) Social phobia																										
4) Specific phobia																										
5) Generalized anxiety disorder																										
6) Obsessive—compulsive disorder																										
7) Anxiety disorder—Not otherwise specified																										
8) Adjustment disorder																										
9) Major depressive disorder																										
10) Dysthymia																										
11) Cyclothymic disorder																										
12) Depression—Not otherwise specified																										
13) Bipolar I																										
14) Bipolar II																										

15) Somatization disorder										
16) Pain disorder										
17) Hypochondriasis disorder										
18) Anorexia nervosa										
19) Bulimia nervosa										
20) Binge eating disorder										
21) Body dysmorphic										
22) Alcohol abuse										

Note. For Week 1, use ratings from previous interview. 5 = Currently meets subsyndromal *DSM–IV* criteria; 4 = Previously met subsyndromal *DSM–IV* criteria, but there is now little or no evidence for disorder; 3 = Currently meets full *DSM–IV* criteria; 2 = Previously met full *DSM–IV* criteria, but now has symptoms for less than full criteria; 1 = Previously met full *DSM–IV* criteria, but now there is little or no evidence for disorder; 0 = Ratings when participant has not previously met criteria for disorder.

PSYCHIATRIC STATUS RATING

Code	1	2	3	4	5	6	7	8	9	10	11	12	13	14	15	16	17	18	19	20	21	22	23	24	25	26
23) Alcohol dependence																										
24) Psychological substance abuse																										
a.																										
b.																										
c.																										
25) Psychological substance dep.																										
a.																										
b.																										
c.																										
Treatment status																										

Note. PSR reliability: 1 = very good; 2 = good; 3 = fair; 4 = poor; 5 = very poor.

Date of last interview: _____

PTSD SYMPTOM FOLLOW-UP

SYMPTOM	Pre-CAPS	1	2	3	4	5	6	7	8	9	10	11	12	13	14	15	16	17	18	19	20	21	22	23	24
CAPS #1																									
CAPS #2																									
CAPS #3																									
CAPS #4																									
CAPS #5																									
CAPS #6																									
CAPS #7																									
CAPS #8																									
CAPS #9																									
CAPS #10																									
CAPS #11																									
CAPS #12																									
CAPS #13																									
CAPS #14																									
CAPS #15																									
CAPS #16																									
CAPS #17																									

Note. For Pre-CAPS, use the sum of frequency and intensity from previous CAPS. For Week 1, if conducting posttreatment interview, apply Grid Rating Scale to Pre-CAPS scores. If conducting a three-month or one-year follow-up interview, transfer Grid Rating Scale scores from last follow-up grid.
Grid rating scale: 0 = symptom was absent at last interview; 1 = symptom was previously present and is now absent; 2 = symptom present at a subclinical level; 3 = symptom abated but still present at a clinical level; 4 = symptom present at a clinical level, no abatement; 5 = symptom has become worse since the last interview.

APPENDIX C
Transcript of the Home Practice Relaxation Tape

This is the tape to assist you with your home practice of relaxation. You will be going through the same exercises we practiced in the clinic. You should be comfortably seated in a recliner or upholstered chair or lying on a bed. Be sure to remove your glasses if you wear them. Also, loosen any tight or restrictive clothing that you have on.

Now begin to let yourself relax, close your eyes, and we will go through the relaxation exercises. . . .

I want you to begin by tensing the muscles in your right lower arm and right hand. Study the tensions in the back of your hand and your right, lower arm. . . . Study those tensions and now relax the muscles. . . , Study the difference between the tension and the relaxation. . . . Just let yourself become more and more relaxed. If you feel yourself becoming drowsy, that will be fine too. As you think of relaxation and of letting go of your muscles they will become more loose and heavy and relaxed. . . . Just let your muscles go as you become more and more deeply relaxed.

Next, I want you to tense the muscles in your left hand and left lower arm. Tense those muscles and study the tensions in the back of your left hand and in your left lower arm. . . . Study those tensions and now relax the muscles. . . . Study the difference between the tension and the relaxation. . . .

This time I want you to tense both hands and both lower arms by making fists, tensing the muscles in both hands and both lower arms. Study those tensions . . . and now relax them. . . . Study the difference between the tension and the relaxation. You are becoming more and more relaxed. Drowsy and relaxed. . . . As you become more relaxed you feel yourself settling deep into the chair. All your muscles are becoming more and more comfortably relaxed. Loose and heavy and relaxed.

This time I want you to tense the muscles in your right upper arm by bringing your right hand up toward your shoulder and tensing the biceps muscle. Study the tensions there in your right upper arm . . . study those tensions . . . and now relax your arm. . . . Study the difference between the tension and the relaxation.

This time I want you to tense the muscles in your left upper arm by bringing your left hand up to your shoulder, tensing the muscle in your left biceps area. Study those tensions in your left biceps . . . study those tensions . . . and now relax the arm. . . . Study the difference between the tension and the relaxation. . . . The relaxation in going deeper and still deeper. You are relaxed, drowsy and relaxed. Your breathing is regular and relaxed. . . . With each breath you take in, your relaxation increases. Each time you exhale, you spread the relaxation throughout your body.

This time I want you to tense both upper arms together by bringing both hands up to your shoulders, tense the muscles in both upper arms, both biceps areas. Study those tensions . . . and now relax the muscles. . . . Study the difference between the tension and the relaxation. . . . Just continue to let your muscles relax. . . .

Next, I want you to tense the muscles in your right lower leg. Tense the muscles in your right lower leg, particularly in your calf and study the tensions there in your right lower leg. Study those tensions . . . and now relax the muscles. . . . Study the difference between the tension and the relaxation. Note the pleasant feelings of warmth and heaviness that are coming into your body as your muscles relax completely. . . . You will always be clearly aware of what you are doing and what I am saying as you become more deeply relaxed.

Next, I want you to tense the muscles in your left lower leg, in the left calf area. Study the tensions in your left lower leg. Study those tensions . . . now relax the muscles. . . . Study the difference between the tension and the relaxation. . . . Just continue to let your leg relax.

Now, this time I want you to tense both lower legs together. Tense the muscles in both lower legs, both calf muscles. Study those tensions . . . and now relax your legs. . . . Study the difference between the tension and the relaxation. . . . Just continue to let those muscles relax. Let them relax. . . .

Now the very deep state of relaxation is moving through all the areas of your body. You are becoming more and more comfortably relaxed . . . drowsy and relaxed. You can feel the comfortable sensations of relaxation as you go into a deeper . . . and deeper state of relaxation.

Next, I want you to tense the muscles in your thighs by pressing your legs together from the knees upward. Press your upper legs against each other and study the tensions throughout your thighs. Study those tensions . . . now relax the muscles. . . . Study the difference between the tension and the relaxation. . . . Just let those muscles continue to relax.

This time I want you to tense the muscles in the abdominal area by drawing your abdominal muscles in tightly. Draw them in tightly and study the tensions across the entire abdominal region. . . . Study those tensions . . . and now relax the muscles. . . . Just let them relax and study the difference between the tension and the relaxation. Just let yourself become more and more relaxed. . . . As you think of relaxation, and of letting go of your muscles, they will become more loose and heavy and relaxed. . . . Just let your muscles go as you become more and more deeply relaxed.

This time I want you to tense the muscles in your chest by taking a deep breath and holding it. Hold it, hold it . . . and now relax. . . . Study the difference between the tension and the relaxation. . . . The relaxation is growing deeper and still deeper. You are relaxed, your breathing is regular and relaxed. . . . With each breath you take in your relaxation increases. Each time you exhale, you spread the relaxation throughout your body.

This time, I want you to tense the muscles in your shoulders and upper back by hunching your shoulders and drawing your shoulders upward toward your ears. . . . Study those tensions across your upper back . . . study those tensions . . . and now relax your muscles. . . . Study the difference between the tension and the relaxation. . . . Note the pleasant feelings of warmth and heaviness that are coming into your body as your muscles relax completely. . . . You will always be clearly aware of what you are doing and of what I am saying as you become more deeply relaxed.

Next, I want you to tense the muscles in the back of your neck by pressing your head backward against the rest or against the bed. Study the tensions in the back of your neck, across your shoulders, and the base of your scalp. . . . Study those tensions . . . and now relax the muscles. . . . Study the difference between the tension and the relaxation.

Next, I want you to tense the muscles in the region around your mouth by pressing your lips together tightly. Press your lips together tightly without biting down and study the tensions in the region around your mouth. . . . Study those tensions . . . and now relax the muscles. . . . Study the difference between the tension and the relaxation. . . . You are becoming more and more relaxed. . . . Drowsy and relaxed. . . . As you become more relaxed, feel yourself settling deep into the chair. All your muscles are becoming more and more comfortably relaxed. . . . Loose and heavy and relaxed.

This time I want you to tense the muscles in the region around your eyes by closing your eyes tightly. Just close your eyes tightly and study the tensions all around your eyes and upper face. . . . Study those tensions . . . and now relax the muscles. . . . Just continue to let them relax and study the difference between the tension and the relaxation. . . . The very deep state of relaxation is moving through all of the areas of your body. . . . You are becoming more and more comfortably relaxed. Drowsy and relaxed. . . . You can feel the comfortable sensations of relaxation as you go into a deeper and deeper state of relaxation.

Next I want you to tense the muscles in your lower forehead by frowning and lowering your eyebrows downward. . . . Study the tensions there in your lower forehead and the region between your eyes. Study those tensions . . . and now relax the muscles. . . . Study the difference between the tension and the relaxation.

This time I want you to tense the muscles in your upper forehead by raising your eyebrows upward and wrinkling your forehead. . . . Raise them up and wrinkle your forehead. . . . Study the tension in the upper part of your forehead. Study those tensions . . . now relax the muscles. . . . Study the difference between the tension and the relaxation. . . .

Now I want you to relax all the muscles of your body. . . . Just let them become more and more relaxed. I am going to help you to achieve a deeper state of relaxation by counting from 1 to 5 . . . and as I count you feel yourself becoming more and more deeply relaxed, farther and farther down into a deep restful state of deep relaxation. 1 . . . You are going to become more deeply relaxed. 2 . . . Down, down into a very relaxed state. 3 . . . 4 . . . More and more relaxed. 5 . . . Deeply relaxed. . . .

Now I want you to remain in your very relaxed state. I want you to begin to attend just to your breathing. Breath through your nose. Notice the cool air as you breath in, and the warm moist air as you exhale. Just continue to attend to your breathing. Each time you exhale mentally repeat the word *relax*. Inhale . . . exhale . . . relax. Inhale . . . exhale . . . relax.

Now I am going to help you to return to your normal state of alertfulness. In a little while I shall begin counting backward from 5 to 1. You will gradually become alert. When I reach 2, I want you to open your eyes. When I get to 1, you will be entirely aroused up in your normal state of alertfulness.

Ready? 5 . . . 4 . . . You are becoming more and more alert, you feel very refreshed. 3 . . . 2 . . . Now your eyes are open and you are beginning to feel very alert, returning to your normal state of alertfulness. 1 . . . This is the end of your relaxation tape.

APPENDIX D
Therapist Activity Checklist

Patient # ___ Therapist ___ Session Date ___ Rater ___ Date Rated ___

Instructions: *Listen to the audiotape of the therapy session. Check each of the therapist behaviors that occurred in the session. Note any other therapist behavior or topics of special emphasis.*

_____ Describe symptoms of PTSD
_____ Explain that PTSD symptoms are normal response to trauma
_____ Describe treatments approaches for different PTSD symptom clusters
_____ Describe treatment as help in understanding one's history and how one coped with previous losses, trauma, etc.
_____ Discuss *original* MVA and reaction
_____ Reinterpreted aspects of *original* MVA
_____ Review patient-generated MVA description

RELAXATION TRAINING

_____ Number of muscle groups
_____ Relaxation-by-recall
_____ Cue-controlled relaxation
_____ Check on homework
_____ Explain rationale for:
    _____ Approach behaviors
    _____ Relaxation
_____ Self-dialogue model
_____ Discuss catastrophic cognitions
_____ Cognitive distortions and logical fallacies
_____ Discuss reactions to homework
    _____ Reading MVA description
    _____ Approach behavior—MVA and travel related
        _____ Other people
        _____ Pleasurable events
_____ Imaginal exposure
_____ Elicit self-dialogue
Successful _____ Unsuccessful _____
_____ Reinforce self-dialogue
_____ Correct self-dialogue
_____ Provide self-talk

_____ Challenge faulty assumptions
_____ Provide empathy and support

ASSIGN HOMEWORK

_____ Relaxation
_____ Read/write MVA description
_____ Approach behaviors:
    _____ Hierarchy list
    _____ MVA and traveling-related
    _____ Other people
    _____ Pleasurable activities
_____ Use of cognitive techniques/altered coping statements
_____ Discuss anger management
_____ Discuss time management
_____ Discuss physical status and limitations
_____ Discuss legal or insurance issues
_____ Review patient's history of:
    _____ Early development
    _____ Separations and developmental milestones
    _____ Previous trauma and losses
_____ Inquire about patient's feelings related to historical events
_____ Inquire about how patient coped with previous difficulties
_____ Elicit description of current problems
_____ Discuss how patient is coping with current problems
_____ Inquire about patient's feelings related to current problems
_____ Other person brought into session
_____ Review treatment
    Tape unscorable _____ Tape incomplete _____
Other _____
_____
_____
_____

REFERENCES

Allodi, F. A. (1974). Accident neurosis: Whatever happened to male hysteria? *Canadian Psychiatric Association Journal, 19,* 291–296.

American Association for Automotive Medicine. (1985, Revision). *The Abbreviated Injury Scale.* Des Plaines, IL: American Association for Automotive Medicine.

American Psychiatric Association. (1980). *Diagnostic and statistical manual of mental disorders* (3rd ed.). Washington, DC: American Psychiatric Association.

American Psychiatric Association. (1987). *Diagnostic and statistical manual of mental disorders* (3rd, Rev.). Washington, DC: American Psychiatric Association.

American Psychiatric Association. (1994). *Diagnostic and statistical manual of mental disorders* (4th ed.). Washington, DC: American Psychiatric Association.

Andersson, A-L., Bunketorp, O., & Allebeck, P. (1997). High rates of psychosocial complications after road traffic injuries. *Injury, 28,* 539–543.

Andersson, A-L., Dahlback, L-O., & Allebeck, P. (1994). Psychosocial consequences of traffic accidents: A two year follow-up. *Scandinavian Journal of Social Medicine, 22,* 299–302.

Arindell, W. A., & Ettema, H. (1981). Dimensionele structuur, betrouwbaarheid en validiteit van de Nederlandse bewerking van de Symptom Checklist (SCL-90). *Nederlands Tijdschrift Voor de Psychologie, 36,* 77–108.

Barton, K. A., Blanchard, E. B., & Hickling, E. J. (1996). Antecedents and consequences of acute stress disorder among motor vehicle accident victims. *Behaviour Research and Therapy, 34,* 805–813.

Beck, A. T., Rush, A. J., Shaw, B. F., & Emery, G. (1979). *Cognitive therapy of depression.* New York: Guilford Press.

Beck, A. T., Steer, R. A., & Garbin, N. G. (1988). Psychometric properties of the Beck Depression Inventory: Twenty-five years of evaluation. *Clinical Psychology Review, 8,* 77–100.

Beck, A. T., Ward, C. H., Mendelson, M., Mock, J., & Erbaugh, J. (1961). An inventory for measuring depression. *Archives of General Psychiatry, 5,* 561–571.

Bernstein, D. A., & Borkovec, T. D. (1973). *Progressive relaxation training: A manual for the helping professions.* Champaign, IL: Research Press.

Best, C. L., & Ribbe, D. P. (1995). Accidental injury: Approaches to assessment and treatment. In J. R. Freedy & S. E. Hobfoil (Eds.), *Traumatic stress: From theory to practice* (pp. 315–337). New York: Plenum Press.

Blake, D. D., Weathers, F. W., Nagy, L. M., Kaloupek, D. G., Charney, D. S., et al. (1995). *Clinician-Administered PTSD Scale for DSM–IV (CAPS–DX).* Boston: National Center for Posttraumatic Stress Disorder, Behavioral Science Division, Boston VA Medical Center.

Blake, D. D., Weathers, F. W., Nagy, L. M., Kaloupek, D. G., Gusman, D. G., et al. (1995). The development of a Clinician-Administered PTSD Scale. *Journal of Traumatic Stress, 8*, 75–90.

Blake, D., Weathers, F., Nagy, L., Kaloupek, D., Klauminzer, G., et al. (1990a). *Clinician-Administered PTSD Scale (CAPS)*. Boston: National Center for Post-Traumatic Stress Disorder, Behavioral Science Division–Boston VA.

Blake, D., Weathers, F., Nagy, L., Kaloupek, D., Klauminzer, G., Chaney, D., et al. (1990b). *Clincian Administered PTSD Scale (CAPS), Form 2—One Week Symptom Status Version*. Boston: National Center for Post-Traumatic Stress Disorder, Behavioral Science Division–Boston VA.

Blanchard, E. B. (1990). Elevated basal levels of cardiovascular responses in Vietnam veterans with PTSD: A health problem in the making? *Journal of Anxiety Disorders, 4*, 233–237.

Blanchard, E. B., & Buckley, T. C. (1999). Psychophysiological assessment and PTSD. In P. Saigh & D. Bremner (Eds.), *Post-traumatic stress disorder: A comprehensive approach to research* (pp. 248–266). Needham, MA: Allyn & Bacon.

Blanchard, E. B., Buckley, T. C., Hickling, E. J., & Taylor, A. E. (1998). Post-traumatic stress disorder and co-morbid major depression: Is the correlation an illusion? *Journal of Anxiety Disorders, 11*, 354–355.

Blanchard, E. B., & Hickling, E. J. (1997). *After the crash: Assessment and treatment of motor vehicle accident survivors*. Washington, DC: American Psychological Association.

Blanchard, E. B., Hickling, E. J., Barton, K. A., Taylor, A. E., Loose, W. R., et al. (1996). One-year prospective follow-up of motor vehicle accident victims. *Behaviour Research and Therapy, 34*, 775–786.

Blanchard, E. B., Hickling, E. J., Buckley, T. C., Taylor, A. E., Vollmer, A., et al. (1996). The psychophysiology of motor vehicle accident related post-traumatic stress disorder: Replication and extension. *Journal of Consulting and Clinical Psychology, 64*, 742–751.

Blanchard, E. B., Hickling, E. J., Devineni, T., Veazey, C. H., Galovski, T. E., et al. (2003). A controlled evaluation of cognitive behavioral therapy for posttraumatic stress in motor vehicle accident survivors. *Behaviour Research and Therapy, 43*, 417–426.

Blanchard, E. B., Hickling, E. J., Forneris, C. A., Taylor, A. E., Buckley, T. C., et al. (1997). Prediction of remission of acute post-traumatic stress disorder in motor vehicle accident victims. *Journal of Traumatic Stress, 10*, 215–234.

Blanchard, E. B., Hickling, E. J., Galovski, T., & Veazey, C. (2002). Emergency room vital signs and PTSD in a treatment seeking sample of motor vehicle accident survivors. *Journal of Traumatic Stress, 15*, 199–204.

Blanchard, E. B., Hickling, E. J., Malta, L. S., Freidenberg, B. M., Canna, M. A., et al. (in press). One and two year prospective follow-up of cognitive–behavior therapy or supportive psychotherapy. *Behaviour Research and Therapy*.

Blanchard, E. B., Hickling, E. J., Malta, L. S., Jacquard, J., Devineni, T., et al. (in press). Prediction of response to psychological treatment among motor vehicle accident survivors with PTSD. *Behavior Therapy*.

Blanchard, E. B., Hickling, E. J., Mitnick, N., Taylor, A. E., Loos, W. R., et al. (1995). The impact of severity of physical injury and perception of life threat in the development of post-traumatic stress disorder in motor vehicle accident victims. *Behaviour Research and Therapy, 33*, 529–534.

Blanchard, E. B., Hickling, E. J., & Taylor, A. E. (1991). The psychophysiology of motor vehicle accident related post-traumatic stress disorder. *Biofeedback and Self-Regulation, 16*, 449–458.

Blanchard, E. B., Hickling, E. J., Taylor, A. E., Buckley, T. C., Loos, W. R., et al. (1998). Effects of litigation settlements on posttraumatic stress symptoms in motor vehicle accident victims. *Journal of Traumatic Stress, 11*, 337–354.

Blanchard, E. B., Hickling, E. J., Taylor, A. E., Loos, W. R., & Gerardi, R. J. (1994a). Psychological morbidity associated with motor vehicle accidents. *Behaviour Research and Therapy, 32*, 283–290.

Blanchard, E. B., Hickling, E. J., Taylor, A. E., Loos, W. R., & Gerardi, R. J. (1994b). The psychophysiology of motor vehicle accident related post-traumatic stress disorder. *Behavior Therapy, 25*, 453–467.

Blanchard, E. B., Hickling, E. J., Taylor, A. E., & Loos, W. R. (1995). Psychiatric morbidity associated with motor vehicle accidents. *Journal of Nervous and Mental Disease, 183*, 495–504.

Blanchard, E. B., Hickling, E. J., Taylor, A. E., Forneris, C. A., Loos, W. R., et al. (1995). Effects of varying scoring rules of the Clinician-Administered PTSD Scale (CAPS) for the diagnosis of post-traumatic stress disorder in motor vehicle accident victims. *Behaviour Research and Therapy, 33*, 471–475.

Blanchard, E. B., Hickling, E. J., Taylor, A. E., Loos, W. R., & Forneris, C. A. (1996). Who develops PTSD from motor vehicle accidents? *Behaviour Research and Therapy, 34*, 1–10.

Blanchard, E. B., Hickling, E. J., Veazey, C. H., Buckley, T. C., Freidenberg, B., et al. (2002). Treatment-related changes in cardiovascular reactivity to trauma cues in PTSD. *Behavior Therapy, 33*, 417–426.

Blanchard, E. B., Hickling, E. J., Vollmer, A. J., Loos, W. R., Buckley, T. C., et al. (1995). Short-term follow-up of post-traumatic stress symptoms in motor vehicle accident victims. *Behaviour Research and Therapy, 33*, 369–377.

Blanchard, E. B., Jones-Alexander, J., Buckley, T. C., & Forneris, C. A. (1996). Psychometric properties of the PTSD Checklist (PCL). *Behaviour Research and Therapy, 34*, 669–673.

Blanchard, E. B., Kolb, L. C., Pallmeyer, T. P., & Gerardi, R. J. (1982). A psychophysiological assessment procedure for post-traumatic stress disorder in Vietnam veterans. *Psychiatric Quarterly, 54*, 220–229.

Blonstein, C. H. (1988). Treatment of automobile driving phobia through imaginal and in vivo exposure plus response prevention. *Behavior Therapist, 11*, 70–86.

Boudewyns, P. A., & Hyer, L. (1990). Physiological responses to combat memories and preliminary treatment outcome in Vietnam veteran PTSD patients treated with direct therapeutic exposure. *Behavior Therapy, 21,* 63–87.

Breslau, N., Davis, G. C., & Andreski, P. (1995). Risk factors for PTSD-related traumatic events: A prospective analysis. *American Journal of Psychiatry, 152,* 529–535.

Breslau, N., Davis, G. C., Andreski, P., & Peterson, E. (1991). Traumatic events and post-traumatic stress disorder in an urban population of young adults. *Archives of General Psychiatry, 48,* 216–222.

Briggs, A. C. (1993). A case of delayed post-traumatic stress disorder with "organic memories" accompanying therapy. *British Journal of Psychiatry, 163,* 828–830.

Brom, D., Kleber, R. J., & DeFares, P. B. (1989). Brief psychotherapy for post-traumatic stress disorder. *Journal of Consulting and Clinical Psychology, 57,* 607–612.

Brom, D., Kleber, R. J., & Hofman, M. C. (1993). Victims of traffic accidents: Incidence and prevention of post-traumatic stress disorder. *Journal of Clinical Psychology, 49,* 131–140.

Bryant, B., Mayou, R., & Lloyd-Bostock, S. (1997). Compensation claims following road accidents: A six-year follow-up study. *Medical Science and Law, 37,* 326–336.

Bryant, R. A. (1996). Posttraumatic stress disorder, flashbacks, and pseudomemories in closed head injury. *Journal of Traumatic Stress, 9,* 621–629.

Bryant, R. A., & Harvey, A. G. (1995a). Acute stress response: A comparison of head injured and non-head injured patients. *Psychological Medicine, 25,* 869–873.

Bryant, R. A., & Harvey, A. G. (1995b). Avoidant coping style and post-traumatic stress following motor vehicle accidents. *Behaviour Research and Therapy, 33,* 631–635.

Bryant, R. A., & Harvey, A. G. (1995c). Psychological impairment following motor vehicle accidents. *Australian Journal of Public Health, 19,* 185–188.

Bryant, R. A., & Harvey, A. G. (1996). Initial posttraumatic stress responses following motor vehicle accidents. *Journal of Traumatic Stress, 9,* 223–234.

Bryant, R. A., & Harvey, A. G. (2000). *Acute stress disorder: A handbook of theory, assessment, & treatment.* Washington, DC: American Psychological Association.

Bryant, R. A., & Harvey, A. G. (2002). Delayed-onset posttraumatic stress disorder: A prospective evaluation. *Australian and New Zealand Journal of Psychiatry, 36,* 205–209.

Bryant, R. A., & Harvey, A. G. (2003). The influence of litigation on maintenance of posttraumatic stress disorder. *Journal of Nervous and Mental Disease, 191,* 191–193.

Bryant, R. A., Harvey, A. G., Dang, S. T., & Sackville, T. (1998). Assessing acute stress disorder: Psychometric properties of a structured clinical interview. *Psychological Assessment, 10,* 215–220.

Bryant, R. A., Harvey, A. G., Dang, S. T., Sackville, T., & Basten, C. (1998). Treatment of acute stress disorder: A comparison of cognitive–behavioral therapy and supportive counseling. *Journal of Consulting and Clinical Psychology*, 66, 862–866.

Bryant, R. A., Harvey, A. G., Gordon, E., & Barry, R. J. (1995). Eye movement and electrodermal responses to threat stimuli in post-traumatic stress disorder. *International Journal of Psychophysiology*, 20, 209–213.

Bryant, R. A., Harvey, A. G., Guthrie, R. M., & Moulds, M. L. (2000). A prospective study of psychophysiological arousal, acute stress disorder and posttraumatic stress disorder. *Journal of Abnormal Psychology*, 109(2), 341–344.

Bryant, R. A., Marasszeky, J. E., Crooks, J., & Gurka, J. A. (2000). Posttraumatic stress disorder after severe traumatic brain injury. *American Journal of Psychiatry*, 157, 629–631.

Bryant, R. A., Moulds, M. L., & Guthrie, R. M. (2000). Acute Stress Disorder Scale: A self-report measure of acute stress disorder. *Psychological Assessment*, 12, 61–68.

Bryant, R. A., Moulds, M. L., & Nixon, R. (2003). Cognitive behavior therapy of acute stress disorder: A four-year follow-up. *Behaviour Research and Therapy*, 41, 489–494.

Bryant, R. A., & Panasetis, P. (2001). Panic symptoms during trauma and acute stress disorder. *Behaviour Research and Therapy*, 39, 961–966.

Bryant, R. A., Sackville, T., Dang, S. T., Moulds, M., & Guthrie, R. (1999). Treating acute stress disorder: An evaluation of cognitive behavior therapy and supportive counseling techniques. *American Journal of Psychiatry*, 156, 1780–1786.

Buckley, T. C., Blanchard, E. B., & Hickling, E. J. (1996). A prospective examination of delayed onset PTSD secondary to motor vehicle accidents. *Journal of Abnormal Psychology*, 105, 617–625.

Burstein, A. (1986a). Can monetary compensation influence the course of a disorder? *American Journal of Psychiatry*, 143, 112.

Burstein, A. (1986b). Treatment length in post-traumatic stress disorder. *Psychosomatics*, 27, 632–637.

Burstein, A. (1989). Post-traumatic stress disorder in victims of motor vehicle accidents. *Hospital and Community Psychiatry*, 40, 295–297.

Burstein, A., Ciccone, P. E., Greenstein, R. A., Daniels, N., Olsen, K., et al. (1988). Chronic Vietnam PTSD and acute civilian PTSD: A comparison of treatment experiences. *General Hospital Psychiatry*, 10, 245–249.

Cardena, E., Koopman, C., Classen, C., Waelde, L. C., & Spiegel, D. (2000). Psychometric properties of the Stanford Acute Stress Reaction Questionnaire (SASRQ): A valid and reliable measure of acute stress. *Journal of Traumatic Stress*, 13(4), 719–734.

Conlon, L., Fahy, T., & Conroy, R. (1999). PTSD in ambulant RTA victims: A randomized controlled trial of debriefing. *Journal of Psychosomatic Research*, 46, 37–44.

Cooper, N. A., & Clum, G. A. (1989). Imaginal flooding as a supplementary treatment of PTSD in combat veterans: A controlled study. *Behavior Therapy, 20*, 381–391.

Dalal, B., & Harrison, G. (1993). Psychiatric consequences of road traffic accidents. *British Medical Journal, 307*, 1282.

Deffenbacher, J. L. (1995). Ideal treatment package for adults with anger disorders. In H. Kassinove (Ed.), *Anger disorders: Definition, diagnosis, and treatment* (pp. 151–171). Washington, DC: Taylor & Francis.

Delahanty, D. L., Herberman, H. B., Craig, K. J., Hayward, M. C., Fullerton, C. S., et al. (1997). Acute and chronic distress and posttraumatic stress disorder as a function of responsibility for serious motor vehicle accidents. *Journal of Consulting and Clinical Psychology, 65*, 560–567.

Derogatis, L. R. (1983). SCL–90–R. *Administration, scoring and procedures manual.* Towson, MD: Clinical Psychometric Research.

Derogatis, L. R. (1993). *Brief Symptom Inventory (BSI). Administration, Scoring, and Procedures Manual.* Minneapolis, MN: National Computer Systems.

DiGiuseppe, R., Tafrate, R., & Eckhardt, C. (1994). Critical issues in the treatment of anger. *Cognitive and Behavioral Practice, 1*, 111–132.

Dougall, A. L., Ursano, R. J., Posluszny, D. M., Fullerton, C. S., & Baum, A. (2001). Predictors of posttraumatic stress among victims of motor vehicle accidents. *Psychosomatic Medicine, 63*, 402–411.

Ehlers, A., Hofmann, S. G., Herda, C. A., & Roth, W. T. (1994). Clinical characteristics of driving phobia. *Journal of Anxiety Disorders, 8*, 323–339.

Ehlers, A., Mayou, R. A., & Bryant, B. (1998). Psychological predictors of chronic posttraumatic stress disorder after motor vehicle accidents. *Journal of Abnormal Psychology, 107*, 508–519.

Ellis, A. (1962). *Reason and emotion in psychotherapy.* New York: Lyle Stuart.

Ellis A. (1977). *How to live with and without anger.* New York: Readers' Digest Press.

Endicott, J., Spitzer, R. L., Fleiss, J. L., & Cohen, J. (1977). The Global Assessment Scale: A procedure for measuring overall severity of psychiatric disturbance. *Archives of General Psychiatry, 33*, 766–771.

Epstein, R. S. (1993). Avoidant symptoms cloaking the diagnosis of PTSD in patients with severe accidental injury. *Journal of Traumatic Stress, 6*, 451–458.

Fairbank, J. A., DeGood, D. E., & Jenkins, C. W. (1981). Behavioral treatment of a persistent post-traumatic startle response. *Journal of Behavior Therapy and Experimental Psychiatry, 12*, 321–324.

Fecteau, G., & Nicki, R. (1999). Cognitive behavioural treatment of post traumatic stress disorder after motor vehicle accident. *Behavioural and Cognitive Psychotherapy, 27*, 201–214.

Federoff, I. C., Taylor, S., Asmundson, G. J., & Koch, W. J. (2000). Cognitive factors in traumatic stress reactions: Predicting PTSD symptoms from anxiety sensitivity and beliefs about harmful events. *Behavioural and Cognitive Psychotherapy, 28*, 5–15.

Fein, M. (1993). *"A common sense guide to coping with anger": Integrated anger management.* Westport, CT: Praeger.

Feinstein, A., & Dolan, R. (1991). Predictors of post-traumatic stress disorder following physical trauma: An examination of the stressor criterion. *Psychological Medicine, 21,* 85–91.

First, M. B., Spitzer, R. L., Gibbon, M., & Williams, J. B. W. (1996). *Structured Clinical Interview for DSM–IV Axis I Disorders (SCID–I Version 2.0).* New York: Biometrics Research Department, New York State Psychiatric Institute.

First, M. B., Spitzer, R. L., Gibbon, M., Williams, J. B. W., & Benjamin, L. (1996). *Structured Clinical Interview for DSM–IV Axis II Personality Disorders (SCID–II Version 2.0).* New York: Biometrics Research Department, New York State Psychiatric Institute.

Foa, E. B., Cashman, L., Jacos, L., & Kevin, P. (1997). The validation of a self-report measure of posttraumatic stress disorder: The Posttraumatic Diagnostic Scale. *Psychological Assessment, 9,* 445–451.

Foa, E. B., & Kozak, N. J. (1986). Emotional processing of fear: Exposure to corrective information. *Psychological Bulletin, 99,* 20–35.

Foa, E. B., Riggs, D. S., Dancu, C. V., & Rothbaum, B. O. (1993). Reliability and validity of a brief instrument for assessing post-traumatic stress disorder. *Journal of Traumatic Stress, 6,* 459–473.

Foa, E. B., Rothbaum, B. O., Riggs, D. S., & Murdock, T. B. (1991). Treatment of post-traumatic stress disorder in rape victims: A comparison between cognitive–behavioral procedures and counseling. *Journal of Consulting and Clinical Psychology, 59,* 715–723.

Foa, E. B., Steketee, G., & Rothbaum, B. O. (1989). Behavioral/cognitive conceptualizations of post-traumatic stress disorder. *Behavior Therapy, 20,* 155–176.

Foeckler, M. M., Gerrard, F. H., Williams, C. C., Thomas, A. M., & Jones, T. J. (1978). Vehicle drivers and fatal accidents. *Suicide and Life-Threatening Behavior, 8,* 174–182.

Forneris, C. A., Blanchard, E. B., & Jonay, T. Y. (1996, March). Psychophysiological sequelae of sexual assault. *Proceedings of 27th meeting of Association for Applied Psychophysiology and Biofeedback* (pp. 38–39). Wheat Ridge, CO: Association for Applied Psychophysiology and Biofeedback.

Frederick, C. J. (1985). Selected foci in the spectrum of posttraumatic stress disorders. In J. Laube & S. A. Murphy (Eds.), *Perspectives on disaster recovery.* East Norwalk, CT: Appleton-Century-Crofts.

Freedman, S. A., Brandes, D., Peri, T., & Shalev, A. Y. (1999). Predictors of chronic post-traumatic stress disorder. *British Journal of Psychiatry, 174,* 353–359.

Frommberger, U. H., Stieglitz, R-D., Nyberg, E., Schlickewei, W., Kuner, E., et al. (1998). Prediction of posttraumatic stress disorder by immediate reactions to trauma: A prospective study in road traffic accident victims. *European Archives of Psychiatry and Clinical Neuroscience, 248,* 316–321.

Fuglsang, A. K. (2001, Spring). *The assessment of ASD and PTSD in a sample of traffic accident victims*. Paper presented at the annual meeting of International Society of Traumatic Stress Studies, New Orleans.

Gidron, Y., Gal, R., Freedman, S., Twiser, I., Lauden, A., et al. (2001). Translating research findings to PTSD prevention: Results of a randomized-controlled pilot study. *Journal of Traumatic Stress, 14*, 773–779.

Gilliam, G., & Chesser, B. R. (1991). *Fatal moments: The tragedy of the accidental/ killer*. Lexington Books. Lexington, MA: D. C. Heath.

Goldberg, D. P. (1972). The detection of psychiatric illness by questionnaire. *Institute of Psychiatry Maudsley Monographs. No. 21*. London: Oxford University Press.

Goldberg, D. P., Cooper, B., Eastwood, M. R., Kedward, H. B., & Shepherd, M. (1970). A standardized psychiatric interview for use in community surveys. *British Journal of Preventive and Social Medicine, 24*, 18–23.

Goldberg, L., & Gara, M. A. (1990). A typology of psychiatric reactions to motor vehicle accidents. *Psychopathology, 23*, 15–20.

Gray, M. J., Wang, J., Litz, B., & Lombardo, T. (2001, December). *Evaulation of the Life Events Checklist Psychometric Properties*. Paper presented at the 17th annual meeting of the International Society for Traumatic Stress Studies, New Orleans, LA.

Green, M. M., McFarlane, A. C., Hunter, C. E., & Griggs, W. M. (1993). Undiagnosed post-traumatic stress disorder following motor vehicle accidents. *Medical Journal of Australia, 159*, 529–534.

Green, R. L. (1991). *The MMPI-2/MMPI: An interpretive manual*. Boston: Allyn & Bacon.

Greenberg, S. A., & Shuman, D. W. (1997). Irreconcilable conflict between therapeutic and forensic roles. *Professional Psychology: Research and Practice, 28*, 50–57.

Guilford, J. P. (1965). *Fundamental statistics in psychology and education*. New York: McGraw Hill.

Harber, K. D., & Pennebaker, J. W. (1992). Overcoming traumatic memories. In S. A. Christianson (Ed.), *The handbook of emotion and memory: Research and therapy* (pp. 359–387). Hillsdale, NJ: Erlbaum.

Harvey, A. G., & Bryant, R. A. (1996, August). *Incidence and diagnostic issues in acute stress disorder*. Paper presented at American Psychological Association, Toronto, Canada.

Harvey, A. G., & Bryant, R. A. (1998a). Acute stress disorder after mild traumatic brain injury. *Journal of Nervous and Mental Disease, 186*, 333–337.

Harvey, A. G., & Bryant, A. G. (1998b). The relationship between acute stress disorder and posttraumatic stress disorder: A prospective evaluation of motor vehicle accident survivors. *Journal of Consulting and Clinical Psychology, 66*, 507–512.

Harvey, A. G., & Bryant, R. A. (1999a). Acute stress disorder across trauma populations. *Journal of Nervous and Mental Disease, 187*, 443–446.

Harvey, A. G., & Bryant, R. A. (1999b). Predictors of acute stress following motor vehicle accidents. *Journal of Traumatic Stress, 12*, 519–525.

Harvey, A. G., & Bryant, R. A. (1999c). The relationship between acute stress disorder and posttraumatic stress disorder: A 2-year prospective evaluation. *Journal of Consulting and Clinical Psychology, 67*, 985–988.

Harvey, A. G., & Bryant, R. A. (2000a). Memory for acute stress disorder symptoms: A two-year prospective study. *Journal of Nervous and Mental Disease, 188*, 602–607.

Harvey, A. G., & Bryant, R. A. (2000b). Two-year prospective evaluation of the relationship between acute stress disorder and posttraumatic stress disorder following mild traumatic brain injury. *American Journal of Psychiatry, 157*, 626–628.

Harvey, A. G., & Bryant, R. A. (2002). Acute stress disorder: A synthesis and critique. *Psychological Bulletin, 128*, 886–902.

Helzer, J. E., Robins, L. N., & McEvoy, L. (1987). Post-traumatic stress disorder in the general population: Findings of the Epidemiologic Catchment Area Survey. *New England Journal of Medicine, 317*, 1630–1634.

Hickling, E. J., & Blanchard, E. B. (1992). Post-traumatic stress disorder and motor vehicle accidents. *Journal of Anxiety Disorders, 6*, 283–304.

Hickling, E. J., & Blanchard, E. B. (1997). The private practice psychologist and manual-based treatments: A case study in the treatment of post-traumatic stress disorder secondary to motor vehicle accidents. *Behaviour Research and Therapy, 35*, 191–203.

Hickling, E. J., & Blanchard, E. B. (1999). The psychological treatment of motor vehicle accident-related posttraumatic stress disorder: Conceptualization and two pilot studies. In E. J. Hickling & E. B. Blanchard (Eds.), *The international handbook of road traffic accidents: Psychological trauma, treatment and law* (pp. 321–339). London: Elsevier Science.

Hickling, E. J., & Blanchard, E. B. (unpublished manuscript). *Motor vehicle accident treatment manual.*

Hickling, E. J., Blanchard, E. B., Buckley, T. C., & Taylor, A. E. (1999). Effects of attribution of responsibility for motor vehicle accidents on severity of PTSD symptoms. *Journal of Traumatic Stress, 12*(2), 345–353.

Hickling, E. J., Blanchard, E. B., Mundy, E., & Galovski, T. E. (2002). Detection of malingered MVA related posttraumatic stress disorder: An investigation of the ability to detect professional actors by experienced clinicians, psychological tests and psychophysiological assessment. *Journal of Forensic Psychology Practice, 2*, 33–53.

Hickling, E. J., Blanchard, E. B., Schwarz, S. P., & Silverman, D. J. (1992). Headaches and motor vehicle accidents: Results of psychological treatment of post-traumatic headache. *Headache Quarterly, 3*, 285–289.

Hickling, E. J., Blanchard, E. B., Silverman, D. J., & Schwarz, S. P. (1992). Motor vehicle accidents, headaches, and post-traumatic stress disorder: Assessment findings in a consecutive series. *Headache, 32*, 147–151.

Hickling, E. J., Loos, W. R., Blanchard, E. B., & Taylor, A. E. (1997). Treatment of post-traumatic stress disorder (PTSD) after road accidents. In M. Mitchell (Ed.), *The aftermath of road accidents*. London: Routledge.

Hickling, E. J., Sison, G. F. P., & Vanderploeg, K. D. (1986). The treatment of post-traumatic stress disorder with biofeedback and relaxation training. *Biofeedback and Self-Regulation, 11*, 125–134.

Hickling, E. J., Taylor, A. E., Blanchard, E. B., & Devineni, T. (1999). Simulation of motor vehicle accident-related PTSD: Effects of coaching with DSM–IV criteria. In E. J. Hickling & E. B. Blanchard (Eds.), *International handbook of road traffic accidents: Psychological trauma, treatment and law* (pp. 305–320). London: Elsevier Science.

Hobbs, M., Mayou, R., Harrison, B., & Worlock, P. (1996). A randomized controlled trial of psychological debriefing for victims of road traffic accidents. *British Medical Journal, 313*, 1438–1439.

Hoffman, B. F. (1986). How to write a psychiatric report from litigation following a personal injury. *American Journal of Psychiatry, 143*, 164–169.

Holen, A. (1993). The North Sea oil rig disaster. In J. P. Wilson & B. Raphael (Eds.), *International handbook of traumatic stress syndromes*. New York: Plenum Press.

Horne, D. J. (1993). Traumatic stress reactions to motor vehicle accidents. In J. P. Wilson & B. Raphael (Eds.), *International handbook of traumatic stress syndromes* (pp. 499–506). New York: Plenum Press.

Horowitz, M. J., Wilmer, N., & Alvarez, N. (1979). Impact of Events Scale: A measure of subjective stress. *Psychosomatic Medicine, 41*, 209–218.

Horton, A. M. (1993). Post-traumatic stress disorder and mild head trauma: Follow-up of a case study. *Perceptual and Motor Skills, 76*, 243–246.

Jacobson, N. S., Dobson, K. S., Truax, P. A., Addis, M. E., Koerner, K., et al. (1996). A component analysis of cognitive–behavioral treatment for depression. *Journal of Consulting and Clinical Psychology, 64*, 295–304.

Jeavons, S. (2000). Predicting who suffers psychological trauma in the first year after a road accident. *Behaviour Research and Therapy, 38*, 499–508.

Jones, I. H., & Riley, W. T. (1987). A post-accident syndrome: Variations in the clinical picture. *Australian and New Zealand Journal of Psychiatry, 21*, 560–567.

Keane, T. M., Caddell, J. M., & Taylor, K. L. (1988). Mississippi Scale for Combat-Related Stress Disorder: Three studies in reliability and validity. *Journal of Consulting and Clinical Psychology, 56*, 85–90.

Keane, T. M., Fairbank, J. A., Caddell, J. M., & Zimering, R. T. (1989). Implosive (flooding) therapy reduces symptoms of PTSD in Vietnam combat veterans. *Behavior Therapy, 20*, 245–260.

Keane, T. M., Kaloupek, D. G., Blanchard, E. B., Hsieh, F. Y., Kolb, L. C., et al. (1998). Utility of psychophysiological measurement in the diagnosis of posttraumatic stress disorder: Results from a Department of Veterans Affairs Cooperative Study. *Journal of Consulting and Clinical Psychology, 66,* 914–923.

Keane, T. M., Kaufman, M. L., & Kimble, M. O. (2000). Peritraumatic dissociative symptoms, acute stress disorder, and the development of posttraumatic stress disorder: Causation, correlation or epiphenomenon? In L. Sanches-Planell & C. Diez-Quevedo (Eds.), *Dissociative stages* (pp. 21–43). Barcelona: Springer-Verlag.

Keane, T. M., Malloy, P. F., & Fairbank, J. A. (1984). Empirical development of an MMPI sub-scale for the assessment of combat-related post-traumatic stress disorder. *Journal of Consulting and Clinical Psychology, 52,* 888–889.

Keane, T. M., Zimering, R. T., & Caddell, J. M. (1985). A behavioral formulation of post-traumatic stress disorder. *Behavior Therapist, 8,* 9–12.

Keller, M. B., Lavori, P. W., Friedman, B., Nielsen, E., Endicott, J., et al. (1987). A longitudinal interval follow-up evaluation: A comprehensive method for assessing outcome and prospective longitudinal studies. *Archives of General Psychiatry, 44,* 540–548.

Kelly, R., & Smith, B. (1981). Post-traumatic syndrome: Another myth discredited. *Journal of the Royal Society of Medicine, 74,* 275–277.

Kessler, R. C., McGonagle, K. A., Zhao, S., Nelson, C. B., Hughes, M., et al. (1994). Lifetime and 12-month prevalence of DSM–III–R psychiatric disorders in the United States. *Archives of General Psychiatry, 51,* 8–19.

Kessler, R. C., Sonnega, A., Bromet, E., Hughes, M., & Nelson, C. B. (1995). Post-traumatic stress disorder in the national Comorbidity Survey. *Archives of General Psychiatry, 52,* 1048–1060.

Kilpatrick, D. G., Saunders, B. E., Amick-McMullan, A., Best, C. L., Veronen, L. J., et al. (1989). Victim and crime factors associated with the development of crime-related post-traumatic stress disorder. *Behavior Therapy, 20,* 199–214.

King, E. W., Leskin, G. A., King, L. A., & Weathers, F. W. (1998). Confirmatory factor analysis of the clinician-administered PTSD scale: Evidence for the dimensionality of posttraumatic stress disorder. *Psychological Assessment, 10,* 90–96.

Koch, W. J., & Taylor, S. (1995). Assessment and treatment of victims of motor vehicle accidents. *Cognitive and Behavioral Practice, 3,* 327–342.

Kolb, L. C., & Keane, T. (1988). *Cooperative Studies Program No. 334, "Physiology study of chronic post-traumatic stress disorder."* Washington, DC: Veterans Administration.

Koren, D., Arnon, I., & Klein, E. (1999). Acute stress response and posttraumatic stress disorder in traffic accident victims: A one-year prospective, follow-up study. *American Journal of Psychiatry, 156,* 367–373.

Koren, D., Arnon, I., & Klein, E. (2001). Long term course of chronic posttraumatic stress disorder in traffic accident victims: A three-year prospective follow-up study. *Behaviour Research and Therapy, 39,* 1449–1458.

Kraft, T., & Al-Issa, I. (1965). The application of learning theory to the treatment of traffic phobia. *British Journal of Psychiatry, 111,* 277–279.

Kuch, K. (1987). Treatment of PTSD following automobile accidents. *Behavior Therapist, 10,* 224–242.

Kuch, K. (1989). Treatment of post-traumatic phobias and PTSD after car accidents. In P. A. Keller & S. R. Hayman (Eds.), *Innovations in clinical practice A source book* (pp. 263–271). Sarasota FL: Professional Resource Exchange.

Kuch, K., Cox, B. J., Evans, R. J., & Shulan, I. (1994). Phobias, panic and pain in 55 survivors of road accidents. *Journal of Anxiety Disorders, 8,* 181–187.

Kuch, K., Evans, R. J., Watson, P. C., Bubela, C., & Cox, B. J. (1991). Road vehicle accidents and phobias in 60 patients with fibromyalgia. *Journal of Anxiety Disorders, 5,* 273–280.

Kuch, K., Swinson, R. P., & Kirby, M. (1985). Post-traumatic stress disorder after car accidents. *Canadian Journal of Psychiatry, 30,* 426–427.

Kulka, R. A., Schlenger, W. E., Fairbank, J. A., Hough, R. L., Jordan, B. K., et al. (1988). *National Vietnam Veterans Readjustment Study Advanced Data Report: Preliminary findings from the National Survey of the Vietnam generation. Executive Summary.* Washington, DC: Veterans Administration.

Kulka, R., Schlenger, W., Fairbank, J., Hough, R., Jordan, B., et al. (1990). *Trauma in the Vietnam War generation.* New York: Brunner/Mazel.

Levine, B. A., & Wolpe, J. (1980). In vivo desensitization of a severe driving phobia through radio contact. *Journal of Behavior Therapy and Experiment Psychiatry, 11,* 281–282.

Lewinsohn, P. M., Biglan, A., & Zeiss, A. M. (1976). Behavioral treatment of depression. In P. O. Davidson (Ed.), *The behavioral management of anxiety, depression and pain.* New York: Brunner/Mazel.

Lewinsohn, P. M., & Libet, J. (1972). Pleasant Events Activity Schedule and Depression. *Journal of Abnormal Psychology, 79,* 291–295.

Litz, B. T. (1992). Emotional numbing in combat-related post-traumatic stress disorder: A clinical review and reformulation. *Clinical Psychology Review, 12,* 417–432.

Lyons, J. A., & Scotti, J. R. (1995). Behavioral treatment of a motor vehicle accident survivor: An illustrative case of direct therapist exposure. *Cognitive and Behavioral Practice, 2,* 343–364.

Malatesta, V. J. (1995, May). Technological behavior therapy for obsessive compulsive disorder: The need for adequate case formulation. *Behavior Therapist,* 88–89.

Malloy, P. F., Fairbank, J. A., & Keane, T. M. (1983). Validation of a multimethod assessment of post-traumatic stress disorders in Vietnam veterans. *Journal of Consulting and Clinical Psychology, 51,* 488–494.

Malt, U. (1988). The long-term psychiatric consequences of accidental injury: A longitudinal study of 107 adults. *British Journal of Psychiatry, 153,* 810–818.

Malt, U. F., Blikra, G., & Hoivik, B. (1989). The three-year biopsychosocial outcome of 551 hospitalized accidentally injured adults. *Acta Psychiatrica Scandanavia, 80,* 84–93.

Malt, U. F., Hoivik, B., & Blikra, G. (1993). Psychosocial consequences of road accidents. *Eur Psychiatry 8,* 227–228.

Malta, L. S., Blanchard, E. B., Taylor, A. E., Hickling, E. J., & Freidenberg, B. M. (2002). Personality disorders and posttraumatic stress disorder in motor vehicle accident survivors. *Journal of Nervous and Mental Disease, 100,* 767–774.

March, J. S. (1993). What constitutes a stressor? The "Criterion A" issue. In J. R. T. Davidson & E. B. Foa (Eds.), *Post-traumatic stress disorder: DSM–IV and beyond* (pp. 37–54). Washington, DC: American Psychiatric Association.

Marmar, C. R., Weiss, D S., Schlenger, W. E., Fairbank, J. A., Jordan, B. K., et al. (1994). Peritraumatic dissociation and posttraumatic stress in male Vietnam theater veterans. *American Journal of Psychiatry, 151,* 902–907.

Mayou, R. (1995). Medico-legal aspects of road traffic accidents. *Journal of Psychosomatic Research, 39,* 789–798.

Mayou, R. A. (2002). Psychiatric consequences of motor vehicle accidents. *Psychiatric Clinics of North America, 25,* 27–41.

Mayou, R. A., & Bryant, B. M. (1994). Effects of road traffic accidents on travel. *International Journal of the Care of the Injured, 25,* 457–460.

Mayou, R., & Bryant, B. (1996). Outcome of "whiplash" neck injury. *Injury, 27,* 617–623.

Mayou, R., & Bryant, B. (2001). Outcome in consecutive emergency department attenders following a road traffic accident. *British Journal of Psychiatry, 179,* 528–534.

Mayou, R., & Bryant, B. (2002). Psychiatry of whiplash neck injury. *British Journal of Psychiatry, 100,* 1–8.

Mayou, R., Bryant, B., & Duthie, R. (1993). Psychiatric consequences of road traffic accidents. *British Medical Journal, 307,* 647–651.

Mayou, R., Bryant, B., & Ehlers, A. (2001). Prediction of psychological outcomes one year after a motor vehicle accident. *American Journal of Psychiatry, 158,* 1231–1238.

Mayou, R. A., Ehlers, A., & Bryant, B. (2002). Posttraumatic stress disorder after motor vehicle accidents: 3-year follow-up of a prospective longitudinal study. *Behaviour Research and Therapy, 40,* 665–675.

Mayou, R. A., Ehlers, A., & Hobbs, M. (2000). Psychological debriefing for road traffic accident victims: Three-year follow-up of a randomized controlled trial. *British Journal of Psychiatry, 176,* 589–593.

Mayou, R., Tyndel, S., & Bryant, B. (1997). Long-term outcome of motor vehicle accident injury. *Psychosomatic Medicine, 59,* 578–584.

McCaffrey, R. J., & Fairbank, J. A. (1985). Behavioral assessment and treatment of accident-related post-traumatic stress disorder: Two case studies. *Behavior Therapy, 16,* 406–416.

McFarlane, A. C. (1988). The longitudinal course of posttraumatic morbidity: The range of outcomes and their predictors. *Journal of Nervous and Mental Disease*, *176*, 30–39.

McFarlane, A. C., Atchison, M., & Yehuda, R. (1997). The acute stress response following motor vehicle accidents and its relation to PTSD. *Annals of the New York Academy of Sciences*, *821*, 437–441.

McMillan, T. M. (1991). Post-traumatic stress disorder and severe head injury. *British Journal of Psychiatry*, *159*, 431–433.

Meichenbaum, D. (1974). *Cognitive behavior modification*. Morristown, NJ: General Learning Press.

Meichenbaum, D. (1977). *Cognitive behavior modification: An integrative approach*. New York: Plenum Press.

Meichenbaum, D. (1985). *Stress inoculation training*. New York: Pergamon Press.

Meichenbaum, D. (1994). *A clinical handbook/practical therapist manual: For assessing and treating adults with post-traumatic stress disorder (PTSD)*. Waterloo, Canada: Institute Press.

Mendelson, G. (1981). Persistent work disability following settlement of compensation claims. *Law Institute Journal*, *55*, 342–345.

Middleboe, T., Anderson, H. S., Birket-Smith, M., & Friis, M. L. (1992). Minor head injury: Impact on general health after 1 year. A prospective follow-up study. *Acta Neurologica Scandinavia*, *85*, 5–9.

Miller, H. (1961). Accident neurosis. *British Medical Journal*, *1*, 919–925; 992–998.

Modlin, H. C. (1967). The post-accident anxiety syndrome: Psychosocial aspects. *American Journal of Psychiatry*, *123*, 1008–1012.

Mowrer, O. H. (1947). On the dual nature of learning: The reinterpretation of "conditioning" and "problem solving." *Harvard Educational Review*, *17*, 102–148.

Munjack, D. J. (1984). The onset of driving phobias. *Behavior Therapy and Experimental Psychiatry*, *15*, 305–308.

Murray, J., Ehlers, A., & Mayou, R. A. (2002). Dissociation and post-traumatic stress disorder: Two prospective studies of road traffic accident survivors. *British Journal of Psychiatry*, *180*, 363–368.

Muse, M. (1986). Stress-related post-traumatic chronic pain syndrome: Behavioral approach to treatment. *Pain*, *25*, 389–394.

Napier, M. (1991). The medical and legal trauma of disasters. *Medico-Legal Journal*, *59*, 157–179.

Nigl, A. (1984). *Biofeedback and behavioral strategies in pain treatment*. New York: SP Medical and Scientific Books.

Nixon, R., & Bryant, R. A. (in press). Peritraumatic and persistent panic attacks in acute stress disorder. *Behaviour Research and Therapy*.

Norris, F. H. (1992). Epidemiology of trauma: Frequency and impact of different potentially traumatic events on different demographic groups. *Journal of Consulting and Clinical Psychology*, *60*, 409–418.

North, C. S., Smith, E. M., & Spitznagel, E. L. (1994). Posttraumatic stress disorder in survivors of a mass shooting. *American Journal of Psychiatry, 151*, 82–88.

Novaco, R. W. (1975). *Anger control.* Lexington, MA: Lexington.

Ochberg, F. M. (1991). Post-traumatic therapy. *Psychotherapy, 28*, 5–15.

Parker, N. (1977). Accident litigants with neurotic symptoms. *Medical Journal of Australia, 2*, 318–322.

Peniston, E. G. (1986). EMG biofeedback-assisted desensitization treatment for Vietnam combat veterans post-traumatic stress disorder. *Clinical Biofeedback and Health, 9*, 35–41.

Peters, L., Andrews, G., Cottler, L. B., Chatterji, S., Janca, A., et al. (1996). The composite international diagnostic interview post-traumatic stress disorder module: Preliminary data. *International Journal of Methods in Psychiatric Research, 6*, 167–174.

Pitman, R. K., Altman, B., Greenwald, E., Longpre, R. E., Macklin M. L., et al. (1991). Psychiatric complications during flooding therapy for post-traumatic stress disorder. *Journal of Clinical Psychiatry, 52*, 17–20.

Pitman, R. K., Orr, S. P., Forgue, D. F., deJong, J. B., & Claiborn, J. M. (1987). Psychophysiologic assessment of post-traumatic stress disorder imagery in Vietnam combat veterans. *Archives of General Psychiatry, 44*, 970–975.

Pitman, R. K., Sanders, K. M., Zusman, R. M., Healy, A. R., Cheema, F., et al. (2002). Pilot study of secondary prevention of posttraumatic stress disorder with propranolol. *Biological Psychiatry, 51*, 189–192.

Pitman, R. K., Sparr, L. F., Saunders, L. S., & McFarlane, A. C. (1996). In B. A. van der Kolk, A. C. McFarlane, & L. Weisaeth (Eds.), *Traumatic stress: The effects of overwhelming experience on mind, body, and society* (pp. 378–397). New York: Guilford Press.

Platt, J. J., & Husband, S. D. (1986). Posttraumatic stress disorder and the motor vehicle accident victim. *American Journal of Forensic Psychology, 5*, 39–42.

Polter-Efron, R., & Polter-Efron, P. (1995). *Letting go of anger: The 10 most common anger styles and what to do about them.* Oakland, CA: New Harbinger.

Poppen, R. (1988). *Behavioral relaxation training and assessment.* Elmsford, NY: Pergamon Press.

Quirk, D. A. (1985). Motor vehicle accidents and post-traumatic anxiety conditioning. *Ontario Psychologist, 17*, 11–18.

Regier, D. A., Myers, J. K., Kramer, M., Robins, L. N., Blazer, D. G., et al. (1984). The NIMH Epidemiologic Catchment Area Program. *Archives of General Psychiatry, 41*, 934–941.

Resnick, P. J. (1997). Malingering of posttraumatic disorders. In R. Rogers (Ed.), *Clinical assessment of malingering and deception* (pp. 130–152). New York: Guilford Press.

Robins, L. N., Helzer, J. E., Croughan, J., & Ratcliff, K. (1981). National Institutes of Mental Health Diagnostic Interview Schedule: Its history, characteristics, and validity. *Archives of General Psychiatry, 38*, 381–389.

Robins, L. N., Helzer, J. E., Croughan, J. L., Williams, J. B. W., & Spitzer, R. I. (1981). *NIMH Diagnostic Interview Schedule. Version III*. Rockville, MD: NIMH, Public Health Service (Publication #ADM-T-42-3; 5-81, 8-81)

Rogers, C. R. (1951). *Client-centered therapy*. Boston: Houghton Mifflin.

Rogers, R., (Ed.). (1997a). *Clinical assessment of malingering and deception*. New York: Guilford Press.

Rogers, R. (1997b). Researching dissimulation. In R. Rogers (Ed.). *Clinical assessment of malingering and deception* (pp. 398–326). New York: Guilford Press.

Rothbaum, B. O., & Foa, E. B. (1993). Subtypes of post-traumatic stress disorder and duration of symptoms. In J. R. T. Davidson & E. B. Foa (Eds.), *Post-traumatic stress disorder: DSM–IV and beyond* (pp. 23–35). Washington, DC: American Psychiatric Press.

Rothbaum, B. O., Foa, E. B., Riggs, D. S., Murdock, T., & Walsh, W. (1992). A prospective examination of post-traumatic stress disorder in rape victims. *Journal of Traumatic Stress, 5*, 455–475.

Rovetto, F. M. (1983). In vivo desensitization of a severe driving phobia through radio contact with telemonitoring of neurophysiological reactors. *Journal of Behavior Therapy and Experimental Psychiatry, 14*, 49–54.

Schnyder, U., Moergeli, H., Klaghofer, R., & Buddeberg, C. (2001). Incidence and prediction of posttraumatic stress disorder symptoms in severely injured accident victims. *American Journal of Psychiatry, 158*, 594–599.

Scotti, J. R., Wilhelm, K. L., Northrop, L. M. E., Price, G., Vittimberga, G. L., et al. (1992, November). *An investigation of post-traumatic stress disorder in vehicular accident survivors*. Paper presented at the 26th Annual Meeting of the Association for Advancement of Behavior Therapy, Boston.

Shalev, A. Y., Freedman, S., Peri, T., Brandes, D., & Sahar, T. (1997). Predicting PTSD in trauma survivors: Prospective evaluation of self-report and clinician-administered instruments. *British Journal of Psychiatry, 170*, 538–544.

Shalev, A. Y., Freedman, S., Peri, T., Brandes, D., Sahar, T., et al. (1998). Prospective study of posttraumatic stress disorder and depression following trauma. *American Journal of Psychiatry, 155*, 630–637.

Shalev, A. Y., Orr, S. P., & Pitman, R. K. (1993). Psychophysiologic assessment of traumatic imagery in Israeli civilian patients with post-traumatic stress disorders. *American Journal of Psychiatry, 150*, 620–624.

Shalev, A. Y., Peri, T., Canetti, L., & Schreiber, S. (1996). Predictors of PTSD in injured trauma survivors: A prospective study. *American Journal of Psychiatry, 153*, 219–225.

Shalev, A. Y., Sahar, T., Freedman, S., Peri, T., Glick, N., et al. (1998). A prospective study of heart rate response following trauma and the subsequent development of posttraumatic stress disorder. *Archives of General Psychiatry, 55*, 553–559.

Sharp, T. J., & Harvey, A. G. (2001). Chronic pain and posttraumatic stress disorder: Mutual maintenance? *Clinical Psychology Review, 24*, 857–877.

Shear, M. K., Pilkonis, P. A., Cloitre, M., & Leon, A. C. (1994). Cognitive–behavioral treatment compared with nonprescriptive treatment of panic disorder. *Archives of General Psychiatry, 51,* 395–401.

Shipherd, J. C., Beck, J. G., Hamblen, J. L., & Freeman, J. B. (2000). Assessment and treatment of PTSD in motor vehicle accident survivors. In L. VandeCreek & T. L. Jackson (Eds.), *Clinical practice: Innovations in clinical practice— A sourcebook* (pp. 135–152). Sarasota, FL: Professional Resource Press/ Professional Resource Exchange.

Shipherd, J. C., Beck, J. G., Hamblen, J. L., Lackner, J. M., & Freeman, J. B. (in press). A preliminary examination treatment for posttraumatic stress disorder in chronic pain patients: A case study. *Journal of Traumatic Stress.*

Simms, L. J., Watson, D., & Doebbelling, B. N. (2002). Confirmatory factor analyses of posttraumatic stress symptoms in deployed and nondeployed veterans of the Gulf War. *Journal of Abnormal Psychology, 111,* 637–647.

Smith, M. J. (1998). *Post-traumatic stress disorder following road traffic accidents: A prospective longitudinal one-year follow-up study of PTSD in RTA victims differentiated on severity of event by admission to hospital, one group admitted, one group not admitted.* Doctoral Thesis, University of London.

Solomon, S. D., Gerrity, E. T., & Muff, A. M. (1992). Efficacy of treatment for posttraumatic stress disorder. *Journal of American Medical Association, 268,* 633–638.

Spiegel, D., & Cardena, E. (1991). Disintegrated experience: The dissociative disorders revisited. *Journal of Abnormal Psychology, 100,* 366–378.

Spielberger, C. D., Gorsuch, R. L., & Lushene, R. E. (1970). *STAI Manual for the State-Trait Anxiety Inventory.* Palo Alto, CA: Consulting Psychologists Press.

Spitzer, R. L., Williams, J. B. W., Gibbon, M., & First, M. B. (1990a). *Structured Clinical Interview for DSM–III–R, non-patient edition. (SCID–NP) (Version 1.0).* Washington, DC: American Psychiatric Association.

Spitzer, R. L., Williams, J. B. W., Gibbon, M., & First, M. D. (1990b). *Structured Clinical Interview for DSM–III–R Personality Disorders (SCID-II) (Version 1.0).* Washington, DC: American Psychiatric Association

Tarsh, M. J., & Royston, C. (1985). A follow-up study of accident neuroses. *British Journal of Psychiatry, 146,* 18–25.

Taylor, S., Fedoroff, I., & Koch, W. J. (1999). Posttraumatic stress disorder due to motor vehicle accidents: Patterns and predictors of response to cognitive-behavior therapy. In E. J. Hickling & E. B. Blanchard (Eds.), *The international handbook of road traffic accidents: Psychological trauma, treatment and law* (pp. 353–375). Oxford: Elsevier Science.

Taylor, S., & Koch, W. T. (1995). Anxiety disorders due to motor vehicle accidents: Nature and treatment. *Clinical Psychology Review, 15,* 721–738.

Taylor, S., Koch, W. J., Fecteau, G., Fedoroff, I. C., Thordarson, D. S., et al. (2001). Posttraumatic stress disorder arising after road traffic collisions: Patterns of response to cognitive–behavior therapy. *Journal of Consulting and Clinical Psychology, 69,* 541–551.

Thompson, G. N. (1965). Post-traumatic psychoneurosis: A statistical survey. *American Journal of Psychiatry, 121*, 1043–1048.

Traffic Safety Facts 1994: A Compilation of Motor Vehicle Crash Data From the Fatal Accident Reporting System and General Estimates Systems. (1995, August). Washington, DC: National Highway Traffic Safety Administration, U.S. Department of Transportation. (Supplemented with 1995 data).

Ursano, R. J., Fullerton, C. S., Epstein, R. S., Crowley, B., Kao, T., et al. (1999a). Acute and chronic posttraumatic stress disorder in motor vehicle accident victims. *American Journal of Psychiatry, 156*(4), 589–595.

Ursano, R. J., Fullerton, C. S., Epstein, R. S., Crowley, B., Vance, K., et al. (1999b). Peritraumatic dissociation and posttraumatic stress disorder following motor vehicle accidents. *American Journal of Psychiatry, 156*(11), 1808–1810.

Van der Kolk, B. A., McFarlane, A. C., & Hart, O. V. (1996). A general approach to treatment of post-traumatic stress disorder. In B. Van der Kolk, A. C. McFarlane, & L. Weisaeth (Eds.), *Traumatic stress: The effects of overwhelming experience on mind, body, and society* (pp. 417–440). New York: Guilford Press.

Veazey, C. H., Blanchard, E. B., Hickling, E. J., & Buckley, T. C. (in press). Physiological responsiveness of motor vehicle accident survivors with chronic posttraumatic stress disorder. *Applied Psychophysiology and Biofeedback.*

Veronen, L. J., & Kilpatrick, D. G. (1983). Stress management for rape victims. In D. Meichenbaum & M. E. Jaremko (Eds.), *Stress reduction and prevention.* New York: Plenum Press.

Vingilis, E., Larkin, E., Stoduto, G., Parkinson-Heyes, A., & McLellan, B. (1996). Psychosocial sequelae of motor vehicle collisions: A follow-up study. *Accident Analysis and Prevention, 28*, 637–645.

Walen, S. R., DiGiuseppe, R., & Wessler, R. L. (1980). *A practitioner's guide to rational–emotive therapy.* New York: Oxford University Press.

Watson, C. G., Juba, M. P., Manifold, V., Kucala, T., & Anderson, P. (1991). The PTSD interview: Rationale, description, reliability, and concurrent validity of a DSM–III–R based technique. *Journal of Clinical Psychology, 47*, 179–188.

Weathers, F. W., Blake, D. D., Krinsley, K. E., Haddad, W., Huska, J. A., et al. (1992, November). *The Clinician-Administered PTSD Scale: Reliability and construct validity.* Paper presented at the 26th annual meeting Association of Advancement of Behavior Therapy, Boston.

Weathers, F. W., Keane, T. M., & Davidson, J. R. T. (2001). Clinician-Administered PTSD Scale: A review of the first ten years of research. *Depression and Anxiety, 13*, 132–156.

Weathers, F. W., & Litz, B. T. (1994). Psychometric properties of the Clinician-Administered PTSD Scale, CAPS–I. *PTSD Research Quarterly, 5*, 2–6.

Weathers, F. W., Litz, B. T., Herman, D. S., Huska, J. A., & Keane, T. M. (1993, October). *The PTSD checklist: Reliability, validity & diagnostic utility.* Paper presented at the annual meeting of the International Society for Traumatic Stress Studies, San Antonio, TX.

Weathers, F., Litz, B., Huska, J. A., & Keane, T. M. (1994). *PCL–C for DSM–IV (PTSD Checklist)*. Boston: National Center for PTSD, Behavioral Science Division, Boston VA.

Weighill, V. E. (1983). Compensation neurosis: A review of the literature. *Journal of Psychosomatic Research, 27*, 97–104.

Wing, J. K., Cooper, J. E., & Sartorious, N. (1974). *Measurement and classification of psychiatric symptoms*. Cambridge: Cambridge University Press.

Wolpe, J. (1962). Isolation of a conditioning procedure as the crucial psychotherapeutic factor: A case study. *Journal of Nervous and Mental Disease, 134*, 316–329.

Wolpe, J. (1973). *The practice of behavior therapy* (2nd ed.; pp. 250–257). New York: Pergamon Press.

Youngjohn, J. R. (1995). Confirmed attorney coaching prior to neuropsychological evaluation. *Assessment, 2*, 279–283.

AUTHOR INDEX

ABOUT THE AUTHORS

Edward B. Blanchard received his PhD in clinical psychology from Stanford University in 1969. After holding faculty positions at the University of Georgia, University of Mississippi Medical Center, and University of Tennessee Center for Health Sciences, he came to the University at Albany, State University of New York in 1977 and has remained there since. In 1990 he was named Distinguished Professor of Psychology. He is currently director of the Center for Stress and Anxiety Disorders at the University at Albany.

He began work on posttraumatic stress disorder in collaboration with Dr. Larry Kolb at the Albany Veterans Administration in 1981, focusing primarily on assessment research with Vietnam War veterans. In 1990 he began collaborative research on motor vehicle accident survivors with Dr. Hickling.

Edward J. Hickling received his PsyD in clinical psychology from the University of Denver, School of Professional Psychology, in 1982. He worked as the director of training and as a consultation liaison psychologist at the Veterans Administration Medical Center in Albany, New York, until 1987, when he left to enter full-time private practice. In addition to his practice in clinical psychology, he is on the faculty at the Sage Colleges and Albany Medical College. His earlier research in posttraumatic stress disorder included the assessment and treatment of Vietnam War veterans. He has collaborated with Dr. Blanchard since 1990 on psychological assessment and treatment of motor vehicle accident survivors.